FATHER GABRIEL OF ST. MARY MAGDALEN, O.C.D.

DIVINE INTIMACY

Volume II

Ash Wednesday through Pentecost

IGNATIUS PRESS SAN FRANCISCO

This enlarged and revised edition was
previously published by Dimension Books, Inc.
Translated from the Sixteenth Italian Edition
Carmelite Monastery of Pittsford, N.Y.

With ecclesiastical approval

Reprinted with permission of Dimension Books, 1987
ISBN 0-89870-143-0
Library of Congress catalogue number 86-83132
Printed in the United States of America

LENTEN SEASON

EASTER SEASON

107 — ASH WEDNESDAY

Be merciful, O Lord, for we have sinned *(Resp Ps)*

1. "You are dust and to dust you shall return" (Gen 3:19). These words were spoken for the first time by God to Adam as a consequence of his sin, and are repeated by the Church to every Christian to remind him of three fundamental truths: his nothingness, his status as sinner, and the reality of death.

Dust, the ashes which the priest puts on our foreheads today, has no substance; the lightest breath will disperse it. It is a good representation of man's nothingness: "Lord . . . my lifetime is as nothing in your sight" (Ps 39:5), exclaims the psalmist. Our pride needs to be broken before this truth! In ourselves, we are not only nothing, we are also sinners, who make use of the very gifts of God to offend him. Today the Church calls upon us, her children, to bow our heads to receive the ashes as a sign of humility, imploring pardon for our sins; at the same time she reminds us that as punishment for our offenses, we must one day return to dust.

Sin and death are the bitter and inseparable fruits of man's rebellion against God. "God did not make death" (Wis 1:13); it came into the world through sin; and the sad "wages of sin is death" (Rom 6:23). Created by God for life, joy, and holiness, we bear in ourselves an eternal seed (GS 18); therefore we cannot but suffer in the face of sin and death which threaten to impede us in the attainment of our goal, and hence, in the full realization of our being. Yet the Church's invitation to reflect upon these painful truths is not intended to dishearten us by a pessimistic view of life, but rather to open our hearts to repentance and hope. If Adam's disobedience introduced sin and death into the world, Christ's obedience brought their remedy. Lent prepares us to celebrate the paschal mystery which is precisely the mystery through which Christ saves us from sin and from eternal death, while it converts physical death into the way to true life, to beatific and never-ending communion with God. Sin and death are conquered by Christ's death and resurrection; we shall share in his victory in proportion as we share in his death and resurrection.

2. "Thus says the Lord: 'Return to me with all your heart, with fasting, with weeping, and with mourning; and rend your hearts and not your garments' " (Joel 2:12-13). The essential element in conversion is really heartfelt contrition: a heart broken and mortified in its repentance for sin. Sincere repentance, in fact, includes the desire to amend one's life, and leads in practice to such an attainment. No one is exempt from this obligation: all of us, even the most virtuous, always need conversion; that is, we need to turn to God more completely and more fervently, and to overcome the weaknesses and frailties which lessen our total orientation toward him.

Lent is the traditional time for this spiritual renewal: "Now is the acceptable time . . . now is the day of salvation" (2 Cor 6:2), notes St. Paul; each of us should make it a decisive moment in the history of our own personal salvation. "We beseech you on behalf of Christ, be reconciled to God," he insists, and adds: "we entreat you not to accept the grace of God in vain" (ib. 5:20; 6:1). It is not only the soul in mortal sin that needs to be reconciled with the Lord; every lack of generosity or of faithfulness to grace hinders intimate friendship with God, chills our relations with him, and is a rejection of his love; all of this requires penance, conversion and reconciliation.

In the Gospel (Mt 6:1, 6-18), Jesus himself points out the chief means of sustaining the work of conversion: almsgiving, prayer, fasting; and he insists on the part our interior dispositions play in making these effective. "Almsgiving atones for sins" (Sir 3:30), but only when done with a sincere desire to please God and to relieve some one in need—not from a desire for praise. Prayer unites man with God and implores his grace when it pours forth from the depths of the heart, but not when reduced to vain ostentation or empty words. Fasting is a sacrifice which pleases God and atones for our faults, provided this mortification of our body is accompanied by the much more important mortification of self-love. Only then, Jesus concludes by saying, "your Father who sees in secret will reward you" (Mt 6:4, 6:18), that is, he will forgive your sins and grant you ever increasing grace.

You are merciful to all, O Lord, and hate nothing you have created. You overlook the sins of men to bring them to repentance. You are the Lord, our God. (Entrance Ant.)

O God, bless the sinner who asks for your forgiveness, bless all those who receive these ashes. Grant that they may keep this Lenten season in such a way that, fully renewed in spirit, they may celebrate with joy the paschal mystery of Christ.

Roman Missal (Blessing of Ashes)

O Jesus, how long is the life of man, even though it is said to be short! It is short, my God, for gaining through it a life that cannot end; but it is very long for the soul that desires to come into the presence of its God.

Then, my soul, you will enter into your rest when you become intimate with this supreme Good, understand what he understands, love what he loves, and rejoice in what gives him joy. Now, you will find you have lost your changeable will; now, there shall be no more change! . . . You shall always want to enjoy him together with his love. Blessed are those who are written in the book of this life. But you, my soul, if you are written there, why are you sad and why do you disturb me? Hope in God, for even now I will confess to him my sins and his mercies . . . O Lord, I want to live and die in striving and hoping for eternal life more than for the possession of all creatures and all their goods; for these will come to an end. Do not abandon me, Lord, because I hope that in you my hope will not be confounded.

If we are sorry for having offended him our faults and evils will not be remembered. Oh, compassion so measureless! What more do we desire? Is there by chance anyone who is not ashamed to ask for so much? Now is the time to take what this compassionate Lord and God of ours gives us. Since he desires our friendship, who will deny it to one who did not refuse to shed all his blood and lose his life for us?

St. Teresa of Jesus, *Soliloquies* 15:1, 17:5-6; 14:3

108 — THEREFORE CHOOSE LIFE

Blessed is the man whose delight is in the law of the Lord (Ps 1:1-2)

1. When Moses was exhorting the people of Israel to be faithful to God, he proposed a far-reaching choice to them: either love the Lord, obey his commandments, and thus obtain his blessings, or turn your back on him, follow other gods, and, as a result, proceed in the face of divine curses. "I have set before you life and death, blessing and curse; therefore choose life, that you may live" (Deut 30:19). God alone is the "one who is living", the source of life; only one who chooses him and his word, chooses life, and through this choice will live. It is not enough to make this choice once for all, it must be renewed and lived day by day, in important situations and in the most humble; everything must be seen, weighed and chosen in the light of faith, as fixed by God and in harmony with his word.

Human weakness on the one hand and the cares of daily life on the other often distract us from this fundamental duty; so, during Lent, the Church invites us all to deeper recollection, to more frequent listening to the word of God, and to more ardent prayer (SC 109), so that each of us may examine our conduct and seek to make it more conformable to the law of the Lord and to his will. Lent should be a period of real spiritual exercises directed toward revising and reforming our lives in order to prepare us to celebrate with greater purity and fervor the mystery of Easter in which the work of salvation culminates and is accomplished.

It would be futile to deceive ourselves: "No one can serve two masters" (Mt 6:24). Christianity does not admit compromise: one cannot choose God and at the same time follow the world, give in to passions, embrace selfishness, favor greed or ambition. Whoever wavers and does not put himself completely on the side of God, of the gospel and of Christ, clearly shows that he is not wholly convinced that God is the one only Lord who deserves to be loved and served with all our heart. Hence we need to meditate again on the words of Scripture: "Therefore choose life, that you may live . . . loving the Lord your God, obeying his voice, and cleaving to him; for that means life to you . . ." (Deut 30:20).

2. Jesus had hardly finished foretelling his passion, when he added: "If any man would come after me, let him deny himself and take up his cross daily and follow me" (Lk 9:23). Concerning himself he said: "the Son of man must suffer many things and be rejected . . . be killed and on the third day be raised" (ib. 22). Here, for the first time, our Lord revealed the paschal mystery, his passing from suffering and death to the resurrection, to eternal glory. This is an obligatory step for all who follow him: each must take up his own cross and follow Christ until death with him, and thereby rise again with him and in him. This is the only way to celebrate the Easter mystery if we are to be participants in a personal way, and not just spectators. The cross, and the tribulations which are always part of man's life, serve to remind us Christians of the only road to salvation, and therefore to true life. "For whoever would save his life will lose it; and whoever loses his life for my sake, he will save it" (ib. 24). If we reject the cross, refuse mortifications, give way to our passions and wish at all costs to assure ourselves of a comfortable, pleasurable life, we risk sin and, for that reason, spiritual death also. On the other hand, if we are prepared to deny ourselves even to sacrificing our lives by expending them with generosity in the service of God and our fellow man, even to losing our temporal life in the process, we shall be saved for all eternity. "For what does it profit a man if he gains the whole world and loses or forfeits himself?" (ib. 25).

To choose life is to follow Jesus, by denying ourselves and carrying our cross. The actual mortification and renunciation of self are not as important as the fact that we are embracing these for the sake of our Lord, that is, for love of him, because of our desire to conform ourselves to his passion, death, and hence to his resurrection as well. This is not only for the sake of our own eternal salvation, but more exactly because of that intimate need of love which impels us toward sharing everything in the life of our Beloved. Just as Jesus suffered, died, and rose again to save all men, so we, as Christians, desire to participate in his mystery and to cooperate with him in the salvation of our brethren.

O Lord, I was stupid and ignorant; I was like a beast toward you. Nevertheless I am continually with you; you hold my right hand. You guide me with your counsel, and afterward you will receive me in glory.

Whom have I in heaven but you? And there is nothing on earth that I desire besides you . . . you are my portion for ever. Those who are far from you shall perish . . . But for me it is good to be near you, my God.

Psalm 73:22-28.

I choose you, my God; I choose to love you, to walk in your ways, to keep your commandments and your statutes and your ordinances, that I may live and that you may bless me. Do not let my heart turn away, nor be drawn away to worship other gods and serve them. I choose to love you, O Lord my God, and to obey your voice and to cleave to you, for you are my life.

cf. Deuteronomy 30:16-20.

O Word, Lamb who bled and hung forsaken on the cross . . . you said: "I am the way, the truth, and the life" and that no one can go to the Father except through you. Open the eyes of our intellect to see . . . and our ears to hear the teaching you give us . . .

Your teaching is this: voluntary poverty, patience before insults, doing good to those who do us harm, and being little, humble, trampled upon and abandoned in the world; . . . with tribulations and persecutions from the world and the devil, both visibly and invisibly, and by our own flesh, which, rebellious as it is, is always ready to revolt against its Creator and to fight against the spirit. This then is your teaching: to bear all with patience, and to fight with the arms of hatred for evil and of love for the good.

O sweet and gentle doctrine! You are that treasure which Christ chose for himself and left to his disciples. Greater riches than this he could not leave . . . May I be clothed in you, O Christ-man—clothed in your hardships and disgrace; in no other way may I be happy.

St. Catherine of Siena, *Letters 226,* v.3

109 — FASTING PLEASING TO THE LORD

The sacrifice acceptable to you, O God, is a broken spirit; a broken and contrite heart, O God, you will not despise

(Ps 51:19)

1. "Why have we fasted and you see it not? Why have we humbled ourselves, and you take no knowledge of it?" (Is 58:3) Here we have the people of Israel, who were scrupulously observing their legal fast, raising their voice to God, almost as if claiming rights because of their penitential practices, which had lacked any real spirit of piety. God answered them: "Yes, your fast ends in quarreling and fighting . . . Is this the manner of fasting I wish?" (ib. 4-5).

By means of Scripture, the Church instructs her children in the true meaning of Lenten penance for, as St. Leo the Great comments: "it is useless to deny food to the body if the soul does not reject sin" (St. Leo the Great, 4th Ser. of Lent). If mortification does not lead to an interior effort to eliminate sin and practice virtue, it cannot be pleasing to God, who wants us to serve him with a heart that is humble, pure and sincere. Selfishness and the tendency to assert our ego too often lead us to put ourselves at the center of the universe; we trample on the rights of others and in doing so evade the fundamental law of brotherly love. That is why those Jews who fasted, wore sackcloth and slept on ashes, but did not cease oppressing their neighbors, were severely rebuked by

God, and their acts of penance were rejected. It is of little or no use to impose physical privations on ourselves if we are unable to renounce our own interests in order to respect and promote those of our neighbor; if we will not give up our views in favor of some one else's; if we do not try to get along with everyone and bear wrongs patiently.

Sacred Scripture makes it very definite that what makes penitential practices acceptable to God lies in the area of charity. Fasting that is pleasing to the Lord, "is it not to share your bread with the hungry and bring the homeless poor into your house; when you see the naked to cover him? . . . Then shall your light break forth like the dawn, and your healing shall spring up speedily" (Is 58:7-8). Then the "light" of a good conscience will shine before God and men, and the "wound" of sin will be healed by real love for God and for neighbor.

2. The disciples of the Baptist were surprised that Jesus' followers did not observe the fast as they did, and asked the Master about it one day. Jesus answered: "Can the wedding guests mourn as long as the bridegroom is with them?" (Mt 9:15) For the Jews, fasting was a sign of sorrow and of penance to be practiced particularly in times of calamity to beseech God's mercy, or to signify repentance for sin. But while the Son of God is on earth to celebrate his marriage to mankind, fasting seems out of place; joy is more fitting than tears for Christ's disciples. He had come to free them from sin, so that their salvation is not so much a matter of corporal mortification as of opening their hearts completely to the word and grace of the Savior. Certainly, Jesus had no intention of doing away with fasting; in fact, he taught with what purity of intention it was to be practiced, shunning every kind of ostentation that was aimed at attracting the praise of others. "When you fast, anoint your head and wash your face . . . that your fasting may not be seen by men but by your Father who is in secret; and your Father . . . will reward you" (Mt 6:17-18). The Lord tells the disciples of the Baptist: "The days will come when the bridegroom is taken away from them, and then they will fast" (Mt 9:15). The wedding feast, of which Jesus spoke, comparing himself to the groom, and his disciples to the wedding guests, will not last very long; a violent death will carry off the bridegroom, and then the guests, having gone into mourning, will fast.

Nevertheless, our Christian fast is not simply a sign of grief that the Lord is so far away; it is also a sign of faith and hope in him who remains invisibly among his friends in the Church, in the sacraments, in his word; one day he will return in a form that is both visible and glorious. The Christian fast is a mark of vigil, but of a joyful vigil, "awaiting our blessed hope, the appearing of the glory of our great God and Savior Jesus Christ" (Tit 2:13). Fasting like any other form of corporal mortification, has as its purpose the attainment of a greater detachment from worldly pleasures, so as to make our hearts freer and more capable of tasting the joys of God, and hence the joy of the Lord's Easter.

Let us give thanks always and everywhere to you, Lord, blessed Father, omnipotent and eternal God, through Christ our Lord. Through his example and his grace the faith of those who fast is nourished, hope revived, charity strengthened, since he is truly the living bread which sustains us to life eternal, and the food which builds up the strength of our souls.

Your Word, through whom all things were created, is indeed the food not only of men, but of angels as well. Your servant Moses was nourished by such food when he was about to receive the law, and he fasted forty days and forty nights from all material food, to make himself better prepared to taste your ineffable sweetness. He reached the point of not even feeling physical hunger and forgot to eat, because the strength of your glory enlightened him and he found nourishment in the fruitful word of the divine Spirit.

Oh! let me never lack this bread, for which we should always hunger, which is Jesus Christ, our Lord.

Gregorian Sacramentary

O Lord, when I fast, sustain my mind and stir up in me a salutary remembrance of all that you mercifully did for me by fasting and praying . . . O Creator of heaven, what mercy could be greater than that which made you come down from heaven, so that you might endure hunger, that in your person satiety might suffer thirst, strength experience weakness, perfect health be wounded, and life itself taste death . . . What mercy could be greater than for the Creator to become a creature and the Lord a servant? . . . the redeemer to be sold, the one that is exalted be humiliated, and the one who is to rise be slain?

Among the works of charity to be done, you bid me feed the hungry, but you—to give me food when I was starving—first offered yourself to the executioners. You bid me welcome travelers, but for my sake, you entered your own house and your own did not receive you.

How my soul praises you for showing yourself so ready to reconcile all my wrongdoing, for you heal all my wounds, snatch my lie from depravity and satisfy my heart with your good things.

Grant that, while I fast, I may humble my soul, seeing how you, O teacher of humility, humbled yourself, being made obedient even to death on the cross.

St. Augustine, *Sermon* 207:1-2

110 — CALLED TO PENANCE

For you, O Lord, are good and forgiving, abounding in steadfast love to all who call on you (Ps 86:5)

1. Jesus "saw a tax collector named Levi sitting at the tax office; and he said to him: 'Follow me!' " (Lk 5:27). Jesus is truly the Lord, who calls whom he wills; his call was so strong that it drew a tax collector from his trade, which was perhaps not always an

honest one, and made a disciple of him, even an apostle, one of the twelve: Matthew. Once he was conscious of having been called, he did not hesitate for a moment, but "left everything and rose and followed him" (ib. 28). Because of their greed for money and the heavy assessments they imposed on the people, the tax collectors were considered public sinners and were therefore shunned by everyone. But Jesus acted differently: he was the Savior and thus he went in search of any who needed salvation and offered it to him; here he even offered a privileged vocation to a publican. To those who were scandalized at seeing him at table in Matthew's house in the company of many other tax collectors, our Lord said: "I have not come to call the righteous, but sinners to repentance" (ib. 32).

One could say that the essential condition for being called by Jesus is to be a sinner. And in truth, since Adam's fall, all men are such; but only those who have the humility to acknowledge this and who feel the need for salvation are fitted to respond, like Matthew, to the Lord's call. Indeed, he calls us with a definite purpose: to do penance and be converted. Whoever thinks himself just, as the Pharisees did, and does not admit his need of conversion, by that very fact closes his heart to the grace of salvation. This sin of spiritual pride, the most insidious of all sins, can sometimes take root even in "devout persons". But the man who is sincerely humble and knows that he belongs in the ranks of the sick and sinners, can be sure he will not be shunned by Christ; in fact Christ seeks out such to heal and convert and free from sin. It was just for this that he came. The doctor is not concerned about those who are well, but with the sick; and our Savior is not concerned over the just—yet who is just in God's sight?—but with sinners.

2. The call to penance produced great results in Matthew whose radical conversion transformed a publican into an apostle. Always, but especially during Lent, the Church, like Jesus, continues to call upon men to do penance (SC 9:109). The answer each one of us makes should be like Levi's: not to hesitate when faced with the necessity of changing our mentality and our behavior; not to fear leaving possessions, habits, persons who are dear to us, or interests that are profitable, when any of these stand in the way of our conversion or hinder us in fully answering God's call. "It is only by putting to death what is old"—says the Council—"that we are able to come to newness of life" (AG 8).

Penance, essentially, always requires a change of life: from sin to virtue, lukewarmness to fervor, fervor to sanctity. This interior change cannot be effected without divine help, but the Lord is not stingy in this regard, and even as he is calling a man to penitence, he is offering the grace necessary for this conversion.

For the Christian, to heed the call to do penance and to open his heart to the grace of conversion, means living his baptism, the sacrament through which "men are plunged into the paschal mystery of Christ; they die with him, are buried with him, and rise with him" (SC 6). It is for just this reason that during Lent the Liturgy often dwells on baptismal themes. Death and resurrection in Christ, which are operative from baptism, are not a static fact which happened once for all, but a vital dynamic fact which should involve the Christian in the Lord's death and resurrection every day. "For you have died" says St. Paul (Col 3:3): it is the death of a profound renunciation of selfishness, pride, greed, sensuality; in a word, it is death to self in order to live fully the new life of a creature completely raised up in him who died and rose again for the salvation of all mankind. This is the real meaning of penance, of conversion, and therefore of the renunciation which they require. The Christian does not deny himself nor renounce himself for the pleasure of renouncing or of dying, but for the joy of living in Christ, of fulfilling himself completely by participating in the resurrection of his Lord.

Incline your ear, O Lord, and answer me, for I am poor and needy. Preserve my life, for I am godly; save your servant who trusts in you.

Be gracious to me, O Lord, for to you do I cry all the day. Gladden the soul of your servant, for to you, O Lord, do I lift up my soul. For you, O Lord, are good and forgiving, abounding in steadfast love to all who call on you. Give ear, O Lord to my prayer.

Psalm 86:1-6.

O Lord of my soul and my good! When a soul is determined to love you by doing what it can to leave all and occupy itself better in this divine love, why don't you desire that it enjoy soon the ascent to the possession of perfect love? I have poorly expressed myself. I should have mentioned and complained that we ourselves do not desire this. The whole fault is ours if we don't soon reach the enjoyment of a dignity so great, for the perfect attainment of this true love of God brings with it every blessing. We are so miserly and so slow in giving ourselves entirely to God that ... we do not fully prepare ourselves ... Since we do not succeed in giving up everything at once, this treasure as a result is not given to us all at once ...

Indeed a great mercy does he bestow on anyone to whom he gives the grace and courage to resolve to strive for this good with every ounce of energy. For God does not deny himself to anyone who perseveres. Little by little he will measure out the courage sufficient to attain this victory ... If the beginner with the assistance of God struggles to reach the summit of perfection, I believe he will never go to heaven alone; he will always lead many people along after him. Like a good captain he will give whoever marches in his company to God ... But for me a great deal of courage is necessary in order not to turn back—and a great deal of assistance from God.

St. Teresa of Jesus, *Life* 11:1-4.

111—FIRST SUNDAY OF LENT

YEAR A

You shall worship the Lord your God and him only shall you serve.
(Mt 4:10)

On the first Sunday of Lent the Liturgy sets before us the poles between which the history of salvation develops: man's sin and Christ's redemption. Man had just been created by God (1st Reading: Gen 2:7-9; 3:1-7), and came from his hands pure and entire, made to his image and likeness; he was living in innocence and joy and friendship with his Creator. But the evil One, envious of man's well-being, was lying in wait and struck him with a triple temptation in regard to God's command: "Of the tree of the knowledge of good and evil you shall not eat, for in the day that you eat of it you shall die" (Gen 2:17). The temptation not to believe the word of God: "you will not die" (Gen 3:4); the temptation of pride: "you will be like gods" (ib. 5); and finally that of disobedience. The first two clear the way for the last, and man falls by transgressing the divine command. Ensnared by deceiving words which he had not rebuffed, he did not resist the illusion of raising himself to the level of God, and by seeking a greatness for himself that was outside God's plan, he fell into ruin, dragging all his progeny down with him. But God knew that man had been deceived, and therefore, even while punishing him, promised him a Savior who would deliver him from error and sin.

To accomplish this work, the Son of God accepted being made like to man in all things save sin, not even refusing to be tempted by the devil, as we read in today's Gospel (Mt 4:1-11). The introductory sentence is striking: "Then Jesus was led by the Spirit into the wilderness to be tempted by the devil" (ib. 1). For Jesus the desert is not only a place of solitude and of face to face prayer with his Father, it is the battlefield where, before beginning his apostolic life, he takes a stand against the eternal enemy of God and man. Here too, as in Eden, the devil offers a triple temptation: against the dependence, the obedience, and the adoration owed to God alone. "If you are the Son of God, command these stones to become loaves of bread . . . Throw yourself down, for it is written, 'he will give his angels charge of you' . . . All these I will give you, if you will fall down and worship me" (ib. 3,6,9). Jesus is truly the Son of God and his power is infinite, but his Father does not wish him to use it for his own benefit. The Messiah must not be a conqueror, but "the servant of Jahweh," sent to save mankind with his humility, poverty, obedience, and the cross. Jesus does not deviate an iota from the path his Father has marked out for him. The victory won by the devil in the garden of Eden is turned into a full defeat in the desert of Palestine. "Begone, Satan! for it is written: 'You shall worship the Lord your God and him only shall you serve' " (ib. 10).

In the second reading (Rom 5:12-19) St. Paul sums up the whole history of salvation in a most effective synthesis: "As by one man's disobedience many were made sinners, so by one man's obedience many will be made righteous" (ib. 19). Disobedience, lack of faith in the word of God, and the pride of our ancestors have been remedied by the obedience of Jesus, by his attachment to the word and will of the Father, by the humility with which he repulsed every proposal of messianic glory and submitted, on the contrary, to the ignominy of the cross. The atonement will be completed on Calvary, but it already began in the desert when Jesus rebuffed Satan. Thus, "where sin increased, grace abounded all the more" (ib. 20), and salvation was offered to the whole of mankind. Through faith, humility, and obedience each of us can conquer the temptations of the enemy and enter into the way of Jesus the Savior.

O Lord, how could man who in paradise . . . had lost the path he was to follow, find the right path again without a guide in that desert where there are so many temptations, where it is so difficult to attain virtue, and so easy to fall into error? . . . What guide could he find to conduct him safely through the many snares of this world and the many deceits of the devil?

Who but you, O Lord, could be a guide great enough to be able to help us all, for who else is above all things? Who could put himself above the world, except you who are greater than the world? Who could be a guide so dependable that he could lead in the same direction, man and woman, Jew and Greek, ignorant and learned, slave and free, save you, O Christ, who alone are all in all? . . .

Give us the strength then to follow you, as it is written: "You will walk behind the Lord God and will be together with him" . . . Make us walk in your footsteps, and so be able to come back from the desert to paradise.

St. Ambrose, *Commentary on the Gospel of St. Luke,* IV 8-9,12

Almighty God, through our observance of this Lent, a sacramental sign of our conversion, help us to grow in understanding the mystery of Christ and to reflect it in a worthy way of life.

Roman Missal, Collect

YEAR B

May I serve you, O God, with a clear conscience through the resurrection of Jesus Christ. *(1 Pet 3:21)*

The Lenten Liturgy develops along a double track: on one side we have the fundamental stages of the history of salvation as seen in the Old Testament, and on the other the most salient facts of Jesus' life up to his death and resurrection as set forth in the gospel.

After Adam's sin destroyed the friendship between man and God, God himself initiated the series of his interventions which were aimed at leading man back to his love. There stands out among these the covenant made with Noah after the flood (Gen 9:8-15; 1st reading), when the patriarch, again standing on dry land, offered sacrifice to the Lord in thanksgiving for having been saved together with his children. "Behold I establish my covenant with you"'—said the Lord—"never again shall all flesh be cut off by the waters of a flood, and never again shall there be a flood to destroy the earth" (ib. 9,11). The punishments inflicted by God always carry within them the seed of salvation: when Adam had been expelled from Eden, he received the promise of a savior; Noah, saved from the same waters that had swept away untold numbers of people, received God's promise that a flood would never again overwhelm all mankind. As a sign of this covenant, God set his rainbow in the clouds (ib. 13), a bow of peace joining earth and heaven. But this is only a symbol of the immensely greater covenant which will be sealed with the blood of Christ.

St. Peter (2nd reading: 1 Pet 3:18-22), reminds the early Christians of "the ark in which a few, that is eight persons, were saved" and explains: "Baptism, which corresponds to this, now saves you" (ib. 20-21). While the baptismal waters destroy sin—as the waters of the flood destroyed sinful men—they save the believer "through the resurrection of Jesus Christ." The Christian, much more than Noah, is brought to salvation through water; not upon the wood of the ark, but upon the wood of the Lord's cross, through his death and resurrection. Lent seeks to reawaken the remembrance of our baptism in us, which, by cleansing us of sin, has bound us to live with "a clear conscience" (ib. 21), remaining faithful to our promise to renounce Satan and serve God alone.

To encourage us in this purpose, today's Gospel (Mk 1:12-15) opportunely puts before us the traditional scene of the desert where Jesus fights against Satan, rejecting all his suggestions. In contrast to the other synoptics, Mark does not stop to describe the various temptations, but sums them up very briefly, saying: "the Spirit immediately drove him out into the wilderness. And he was in the wilderness forty days, tempted by Satan" (ib. 12-13). This immediately followed his baptism in the Jordan: Just as Jesus had wished to fraternize there with sinners as if he needed purification like them, so in the desert he wanted to be like the rest of sinful men to the extreme limit his sanctity would permit, which was temptation. By agreeing to the contest with Satan, in which Jesus came out unquestionably the victor, he clearly demonstrated that he had come to free the world from the domination of the devil, and at the same time he merited for every man the strength to overcome Satan's snares. Even though he is baptized, the Christian is not immune from these; in fact sometimes the more he applies himself to serve God fervently, the more the devil tries to block his way, much as he tried to obstruct Christ and prevent his carrying out his mission as redeemer. We must resort, then, to the weapons that Jesus himself used: prayer and absolute conformity to the will of his Father: "Scripture has it: 'Man shall not live by bread alone, but by every word that proceeds from the mouth of God' " (Mt 4:4). Those who are faithful to the word of God and are constantly nourished by it cannot be overcome by the devil.

O water which washed the universe when it was drenched in human blood, and showed forth in figure our true purification! O water which merited to become the sacrament of Christ, washing everything without being yourself washed! You begin and you complete the perfection of the mysteries ... You gave your name to prophets and apostles, you gave your name to the Savior: they are clouds in the sky, the salt of the earth; he is the fount of life ...

When you gushed forth from the Savior's side, the executioners saw you and believed, and for this you are one of the three witnesses of our rebirth: indeed "there are three that give testimony, the water and the blood and the Spirit." The water is for purification, the blood for ransom, and the Spirit for resurrection.

St. Ambrose, *Commentary on Gospel of St. Luke* X:48

Christ, our Lord, who consecrated this holy Lenten season with a fast of forty days, and by rejecting the devil's temptations, taught us how to rid ourselves of the influences of sin, grant that we may share your paschal mystery in purity of heart until we come to its fulfillment in the eternal pasch of heaven (cf. Preface, 1st Sunday of Lent).

O Lord teach us to hunger for the living and true bread, and to learn to live by every word that comes from your lips (After Communion).

Roman Missal

YEAR C

No one who believes in you, Lord, will be put to shame.
(Rom 10:11)

On the First Sunday of Lent, we are transported for a moment of intense meditation into the desert (Lk 4:1-13) where Jesus was "tempted by the devil." In Holy Scripture, the desert is the privileged place of meeting with God; it was this for Israel who lived in it for forty years, for Elias who spent forty days there, and for the Baptist who retired thither from his youth. Jesus consecrates this custom; he also lives there alone for forty days. But for him the desert is not only a place of retirement and of intimate communion with God, it is also the place of the great encounter in which he was "tempted by the devil" (ib. 2). Satan suggests to Jesus a messianism of triumph and glory. Why suffer hunger? If he is the Son of God, let him change stones into bread. Why live like a miserable wanderer on the roads of Palestine, surrounded by people who were weighed down by poverty and political oppression? Let him but prostrate before Satan and he will receive from him dominion and power. Why endure the opposition of the priests and of the doctors of the law and of the leaders of the people? If he will cast himself down from the pinnacle of the temple; angels will bear him up and all will recognize him as the Messiah. No suggestions other than such as these can come from Satan who has been hurled into the depths because of his pride. But Jesus, the Son of God, who "emptied himself, taking the form of a servant" (Phil 2:7), knows only too well that to atone for the sins of mankind there is but one way: in place of rebellion and pride there must be humiliation, obedience and the cross. Precisely because he is the true Messiah he will save the world not by triumph but by suffering, becoming "obedient unto death, even death on a cross" (ib. 8). The temptations of the desert teach us that where we find ambitious schemes, and aspirations to power, success and glory, some trap of Satan is always hidden. To defeat his snares, like every other influence toward evil, we must hold fast to the words of Jesus: "You shall worship the Lord your God, and him only shall you serve" (Lk 4:8); that is, we must be determined to reject any proposition that may divert us from acknowledging and serving God as our only Lord.

The first two readings develop the concept of loyalty to God: the first (Deut 26:4-10) gives us the profession of faith of the ancient people of God, and the second (Rom 10:8-13) that of his new people. After he had arrived in the promised land, every Jew had to offer God the first-fruits of his harvest, pronouncing a formula which summed up Israel's history in three points: the appointment of the patriarchs and heads of families of a numerous people, their growth in Egypt and their exodus through the desert, and finally the gift of the promised land. In this way the pious Israelite revivified his faith in the God of his ancestors, and showed fitting appreciation for blessings received, as well as his own devotion and determination to serve him. It was a kind of "creed" expressed in word and in life.

Similarly, although in another context, St. Paul invites the Christian to express his faith: "because if you confess with your lips that Jesus is Lord, and believe in your heart that God raised him from the dead, you will be saved" (Rom 10:9). The Apostle draws our attention to two points: to believe that Jesus is the Lord, and to believe in his resurrection. Faith thus requires a twofold action: one interior: adherence to Christ in mind and heart—which justifies man; the other exterior: a public profession of faith—whether in liturgical prayer or in confessing Christ before the world as the martyrs did. Whoever puts his trust in Jesus need have no fear for "no one who believes in him will be put to shame" (ib. 11) and in his name he will be victorious in every struggle.

O Lord Jesus, who at the beginning of your public life withdrew into the desert, we beg you to teach all men that recollection of mind which is the beginning of conversion and salvation.

Leaving your home at Nazareth and your sweet Mother, you wished to experience solitude, weariness, and hunger. To the tempter who proposed to you the trial of miracles, you replied with the strength of eternal wisdom, in itself a miracle of heavenly grace.

It is Lent.

O Lord, do not let us turn to "broken cisterns," that can hold no water (Jer 2:13), or imitate the unfaithful steward or the foolish virgins; do not let us be so blinded by the enjoyment of the good things of earth that our hearts become insensible to the cry of the poor, of the sick, of orphan children, and of those innumerable brothers of ours who still lack the necessary minimum to eat, to clothe their nakedness, and to gather their family together under one roof.

John XXIII, *Prayers and Devotions* March 15

O Jesus we believe in your love and in your goodness; we believe that you are our Savior, that you can do what is closed to and unrealizable for any one else. We believe you are the light, the truth, the life; we have only one desire: to remain united to you, and to be Christians not only in name, but Christians who are convinced, apostolic, and full of zeal.

Paul VI, *Teachings* v.4

112 — NOT BY BREAD ALONE

Your words, O Lord are spirit and life *(Jn 6:63)*

1. Jesus said, in repulsing Satan: "It is written, man shall not live by bread alone, but by every word that proceeds from the mouth of God" (Mt 4:4). This warning is particularly suitable for Lent when the Christian, while mortifying his body by abstinence and fasting, must be preoccupied with nourishing his spirit with the word of God. He who lives by the Word and translates it into practice so that it inspires his thoughts, desires, and actions, will not perish through the assaults of the devil.

An attentive and serious listening to the Word, clarifies the way to salvation and to holiness. "You shall be holy, for I, the Lord your God, am holy" (Lev 19:1). It was not a man, not even the holiest of men, who built up such an ideal of holiness; instead, it was God who presented it to man as an invitation, even as a duty. Although sin deformed the creature who had been made to God's image, God does not relinquish making it anew so that it may become what he had intended: a reflection of his own holiness. With that in mind, man was given the divine law even in the Old Testament, where the commandments that deal with our duties toward God meet those toward our neighbor; they are summed up together in the supreme rule of love. If it is forbidden to do any harm to our brother, whether to his person, his reputation, or his goods, the sole purpose is to safeguard brotherly love. It is really beautiful to see how the old law often goes into minute details which are full of humaneness: "When you reap the harvest of your land, you shall not reap your field to its very border, nor . . . gather the fallen grapes; you shall leave them for the poor and for the sojourner . . . The wages of a hired servant should not remain with you all night until morning . . . You shall not curse the deaf, or put a stumbling block before the blind . . . You shall do no injustice in judgment . . . You shall not go up and down as a slanderer among your people . . . and you shall not stand forth against your neighbor" (Lev 19:10-16). Then all culminates on a very positive note: "You shall love your neighbor as yourself" (ib. 18). And every commandment ends with the same refrain: "I am the Lord" as if to say: I, the Lord your God, give you these orders because I am holy and want you to be holy; I am love and want you to be love.

2. When Jesus speaks of the perfection of his heavenly Father, he presents it under the form of love and of infinite mercy, exhorting us to imitate it in our dealings with one another: "Be merciful as your Father is merciful" (Lk 6:36). Why such insistence on love of neighbor? Because man is God's image, answers the Old Testament and the New one adds: Because the Son of God took human flesh and carried his brotherhood with mankind so far as to consider as done to himself whatever was done to any one. "Truly I say to you, as you did it to one of the least of these my brethren, you did it to me" (Mt 25:40).

These are the profound reasons why Jesus has put works of charity as the distinguishing criteria between the elect and the reprobate. The Lord's law cannot be separated: our duty toward God is not completely fulfilled unless, at the same time, our duty toward our neighbor is also fully observed. Vice versa, there cannot be a supernatural and lasting love of neighbor, if love of God is held in little account, or if our neighbor is loved simply out of human attachment, and not because he is made in the image of God, Christ's brother. This is the reason why during Lent the Church asks us not only for acts of prayer and of penance, but for works of charity also. The former more directly express our love of God; the latter, our love of our neighbor. Moreover, following an ancient rule, what we save through fasting, abstinence or other privation should be pledged to the relief of "our brothers who suffer from poverty and hunger" (Paul VI, Paen. 11). To devote ourselves to prayer and ignore our neighbor's needs, to protest that we love God but do not reach out a helping hand to one in need is to distort Christianity. God cannot be pleased with such prayers nor such declarations of love; and someday Jesus will say: "I was hungry and you gave me no food, I was thirsty and you gave me no drink" (Mt 25:42). Once again we see how only the word of God, listened to and wholly put into practice, is the source of life and salvation. "Man does not live by bread alone."

The law of the Lord is perfect, reviving the soul, the testimony of the Lord is sure, making wise the simple. The precepts of the Lord are right, rejoicing the heart; the commandment of the Lord is pure, enlightening the eyes; the fear of the Lord is clean, enduring for ever; the ordinances of the Lord are true, and righteous altogether. More to be desired are they than gold, even much fine gold... sweeter also than honey and drippings of the honeycomb. Moreover by them is your servant warned; in keeping them there is great reward...

Let the words of my mouth and the meditation of my heart be acceptable in your sight, O Lord, my rock and my redeemer.

Psalm 19:8-12,14

O charity, how good and how rich you are, how powerful! He who does not possess you, possesses nothing...

In order to clothe the naked, you are content to remain naked. For you hunger itself is filling, if one of the starving has eaten your food; your wealth consists in allotting all you own to mercy. Only you do not know what it is to need urging. You aid those who are oppressed without delay, whatever their need, even if they blame you. You are the eye of the blind, the foot of the crippled, the most faithful defender of widows. For orphans you do the work of parents—indeed you do it much better than they. Your eyes are never dry, for either compassion or joy prevents that. You love your enemies with a love so great that no one could tell the difference between them and those who are dear to you.

St. Zeno of Verona, On hope, faith, and charity 9

113 — WORDS OF POWER

O Lord, hear my prayer; give ear to my supplications in your faithfulness *(Ps 143:1)*

1. "So shall my word be that goes forth from my mouth; it shall not return to me empty, but it shall accomplish that which I purpose" (Is 55:11). God's word is living and effectual and always does what it expresses. Thus down through the centuries God's promises have all come true, without man's wickedness being able to turn aside the divine plans. His promises have become history and the vehicle of salvation for all who desire it.

In an analagous way, the word of God is a fertile seed which produces the fruit of holiness in all those who receive it with an open heart. No word of God is in vain; if some unfortunately reject it and thus waste it, it does not on that account lose its power; it will bear fruit elsewhere, and the will of God will still prevail.

The words of men are very different, they are empty and vanish in the air without leaving a trace. Yet even with men there are some which can become efficacious and powerful, not through their own merits, but by the goodness of God who welcomes them as a father welcomes the requests of his children and accedes to them.

Such are the words of the prayer that Jesus himself put into the mouths of his disciples: "Our Father who art in heaven" (Mt 6:9). Prayer that asks with sincerity and love for the glory of God, the coming of his kingdom, the fulfillment of his will, is always efficacious and always heard. In like manner he answers the prayer that asks with humility and trust for what is necessary to sustain life, provided his conditions are met: "Seek first his kingdom and his righteousness, and all these things shall be yours as well" (ib. 33). When prayer is a genuine expression of the feelings of the heart, and not a mechanical recitation of words repeated more out of habit than through intimate conviction, it is always heard and always effectual, even if the immediate result is not what we are expecting. God works in different ways than man; he builds his kingdom, carries out his will, provides for the welfare of his creatures in ways that are often mysterious and unrecognized by our human minds. Yet he unfailingly directs all things to their final end, the true good.

2. Just as bread is necessary for our physical life, so the forgiveness of sin is necessary for our spiritual life. "Since we all truly offend in many ways"—says Vatican II—"we all need God's mercy continuously, and must daily pray: 'forgive us our debts' (Mt 6:12)" (LG 40). Who can be dispensed from this humble prayer? It would be useless to pronounce the words without a repentant heart that is resolved on conversion and deeply convinced of its need for divine pardon. For man, made of body and soul, hunger can be a sharper thorn than sin; the need to have recourse to God to beg for food can be more deeply felt than the need to implore forgiveness. Yet even here the scriptural saying remains valid: "Man shall not live by bread alone, but by every word that proceeds from the mouth of God" (Mt 4:4), above all, by his words of forgiveness. If man, the sinner, is alive, it is precisely through God's forgiveness.

Jesus combined the asking for pardon with the condition required for this to be effective: "And forgive us our debts as we also have forgiven our debtors" (Mt 6:12). Our duty to God—to seek forgiveness—is linked to a duty to our neighbor—to forgive others—it is really this latter duty that makes the former effective. God who is the Savior of men and desires that all men be saved (1 Tim 2:4) is always ready to forgive, but he answers such a plea only if we have already done our duty toward our brother.

By calling for penance, Lent is urging us to beg God to pardon our sins and therefore pledges us to forgive each other, so that we may raise our prayer to the Lord without fear of rejection. Prayer that satisfies these requirements has a power guaranteed by the very words of the Lord: "Forgive and you will be forgiven; give and it will be given to you" (Lk 6:37-38). In this manner, prayer evokes divine mercy and atones for sins committed, especially when joined to the sacrament of penance, for then "it participates in a special way in Christ's infinite atonement" (Paen. 7), or when, in the Eucharistic Liturgy, it is united to the prayer and sacrifice of the Lord, who offers himself every day to the Father as the victim whose death has reconciled us to him (Euch Prayer III).

Our Father who art in heaven! . . . *O Son of God and my Lord! How is it that you can give us so much with your first word? It is so wonderful that you should descend to such a degree of humility as to join with us when we pray and make yourself the brother of creatures so miserable and lowly! How can it be that, in the name of your Father, you should give us all that there is to be given, by willing him to have us as his children—and your word cannot fail! You oblige him to fulfill your word, a charge by no means light, since, being our Father, he must bear with us, however great our offenses. If we return to him, he must pardon us, as he pardoned the prodigal son, must comfort us in our trials, and must sustain us, as such a Father is bound to do, for he must need be better than any earthly father, since nothing good can fail to have its perfection in him, and at the last he must make us participants and fellow-heirs with you.*

Forgive us our debts as we also have forgiven our debtors . . . *It is such a serious and important matter that God should pardon us our sins, which have merited eternal fire, that we must pardon all trifling matters which have been done to us . . .*

As I have so few, Lord, even of these trifling things, to offer you, your pardoning of me must be a free gift; there is abundant scope here for your mercy! . . .

How greatly the Lord must esteem this mutual love of ours, one for another! The good Jesus might have put everything else before our love for one another, and said: "Forgive us, Lord, because we are doing a great deal of penance, or because we are praying often, and fasting, and because we have left all for your sake and love you greatly." But he has never said: "Because we would lose our lives for your sake"; or any of these other things which he might have said. He simply says: "Because we forgive." *I believe the reason he said this was because he knew that our fondness for this dreadful (point of) honor made mutual love the hardest virtue for us to attain, though it is the virtue dearest to his Father. Because of its very difficulty he put it where he did, and offers it on our behalf to God.*

St. Teresa of Jesus, *Way* 27:2; 36:2,7 (Peers translation)

114 — SIN

Have mercy on me, O God, according to your steadfast love; according to your abundant mercy blot out my transgressions.
(Ps 51:1)

1. "The men of Nineveh will arise at the judgment with this generation and condemn it, for they repented at the preaching of Jonah, and behold, something greater than Jonah is here" (Lk 11:32). There is sorrow in these words of Jesus. The men of Nineveh had sinned, but at the preaching of Jonah they had done penance and amended their lives, whereas many children of Israel have rejected not simply a prophet, but the Son of God. It is the sin of pride which hinders believing in God, accepting his word, and obeying his law. It is the sin that still fills the world, the root of all the evils that afflict humanity and lacerate the Church. But while man abuses his freedom and voluntarily withdraws from God, God never ceases to call him back, to invite him to return. God's ways are the ways of infinite love: he calls man to participate in his divine life, to live in intimate, personal communion with him. The ways of man the sinner are directly the opposite: a rejection of love, a breaking off of relations of friendship with God. These are the consequences of mortal sin. But that is not all. "Sin has . . . diminished man, blocking his path to fulfillment" (GS 13), a fulfillment that can be realized only in communion with God, who is the one source of life, charity, and grace.

Since God is the cause of every creature, he is present in the sinner also, but not as Father, or Guest, or the Trinity which offers itself to the soul to be known and loved. Hence the sinner, though created to be the temple of the Blessed Trinity, makes himself incapable of living in the company of the divine Persons, closes off his road to union with God, and obliges God to break all ties of friendship with him. And all this is because, instead of the Supreme Good, he prefers the temporal, fleeting good of some wretched creature, some selfish satisfaction, some earthly pleasure. See here the malice of sin which rejects the divine gift and betrays the Creator, Father, and Friend.

2. Jesus has excluded no one from the benefits of his redemptive work; to the generation of those who had rejected him he said: "no sign shall be given to it except the sign of Jonah" (Lk 11:29). Just as Jonah, after spending three days in the belly of a fish, was ejected alive onto land and thence sent to preach to Nineveh, so Jesus, after passing three days in the tomb, will rise again from death to give life to all who believe in him. The death and resurrection of Christ are the greatest sign of his love for us who are sinners, and at the same time the utmost sign of his divinity. Whoever accepts him will be saved, will be able to wash away his sins in the blood of Christ, and will rise again with him to a new life.

However there are still many who refuse this sign, and look for others, and so remain in their state of sinfulness. By the law of solidarity, we are obliged not only to convert ourselves from sin, but also to fight, suffer, and pay for the sins of our brothers and to hasten their conversion through prayer and love.

O my God and my true Fortitude! What is this, Lord, that we are cowards about everything except being against you? In opposing you, all the strength of the children of Adam is used up. And if their reason weren't so blind, the reasonings of all together would not suffice for them to dare to take up arms against their Creator, and sustain a continual war against one who in a moment can plunge them into the abyss. But since they are blind, they are like madmen seeking their death because in their imagination it seems to them that by death they gain life. O incomprehensible Wisdom! How necessary is all the love you have for creatures in order to endure so much madness and to wait for our cure and strive to bring it about through a thousand ways and means and remedies!

It is something frightening to me when I consider that we lack the strength to be restrained in some very light matter (for they are truly convinced that they are unable to give up an occasion and withdraw from a danger where they may lose their souls), and yet we have strength and courage to attack a Majesty as great as yours. What is this, my God? What is this? Who gives this strength?

St. Teresa of Jesus, *Soliloquies,* XII, 1,2.

Narrow is the mansion of my soul; enlarge it that you may enter in. It is all in ruins; do you repair it. There are things in it which must offend your eyes; I confess and know it. But who shall cleanse me from my secret sins, and spare your servant from the sins of others? I believe, and therefore do I speak. Lord, you know. Have I not confessed against myself my transgressions against you, and you, my God, have forgiven the iniquity of my heart? Therefore I contend not in judgment with you; for if you, Lord, should mark iniquities, O Lord, who shall abide it?

Yet suffer me to speak unto your mercy, me, dust and ashes. Yet suffer me to speak, since I speak to your mercy, and not to a scornful man . . . You will return and have compassion upon me.

St. Augustine, *Confessions* I 5,6

115 — DELIVER US FROM EVIL

On the day I called, you answered me; my strength of soul you increased. (Ps 138:3).

1. "O my Lord, you only are our king; help me who am alone, and have no helper but you" (Esth 14:3). This was Queen Esther's prayer as she prepared to brave Ahasuerus to obtain favor for her people who were threatened with extermination. Prayer is the

great power of those who trust in God. The Christian knows he can pour out his tribulations to the Lord, and count on his help in any trouble, especially in the never easy enterprise of his own conversion. When a man enters into himself and considers his wretchedness and weakness, as well as the dangers that press on him from every side, "he finds that by himself he is incapable of battling the assaults of evil successfully" (GS 13). Only one way of salvation is open to him: recourse to God. "Lord, I have no helper but you".

We know by experience that we have not sufficient strength in ourselves to bring to a successful completion our chief Lenten duty, which is to die fully to sin in order to live fully in the risen Christ. But Christ himself, before leaving his own, prayed to his Father to preserve them from evil and from the evil one (Jn 17:15)—from the seductions of the world and the attacks of Satan. He had taught them to ask: "lead us not into temptation, but deliver us from evil" (Mt 6:13). Obviously he did not intend that his disciples be spared every kind of temptation and danger, for this would be impossible in this life; besides, God himself permits it to test our virtue, but he wanted to assure them sufficient strength to resist. The evil from which he desired to free them was sin, the only real disaster, because it separates us from God.

When we have made a firm resolution not to give in to temptation and sincerely call upon divine assistance, there is no doubt that our prayer is heard, because we are only asking what God desires even more than we do, since it was to save the world from sin that he sacrificed his only Son. But we should not forget that, besides prayer, mortification and works of penance are necessary, according to our Lord's admonition: "Watch and pray that you may not enter into temptation" (Mt 26:41). Vigils, like fasts, have always been considered among the more important penitential practices.

2. "If you then, who are evil, know how to give good gifts to your children, how much more will your Father who is in heaven give good things to those who ask him!" (Mt 7:11). Of the good things that we may ask of God, among the first are certainly conversion and deliverance from sin. But it can happen, even with those who are dedicated to the service of God, that we have a weary battle to fight in order to free ourselves from some misery which is never really conquered and is always reappearing; or we may find ourselves trapped in situations that threaten to sweep away promises we have made to God, holy purposes and resolutions. Perhaps we do not pray enough, or do not resort to God with full confidence: perhaps we do not ask, do not seek, do not knock, as the gospel requires, "for everyone who asks, receives; and he who seeks, finds; and to him who knocks, it will be opened" (ib. 8). Can these words of our Lord no longer hold?

Sin, however, must not be considered as only a personal evil; any sin—whether more or less serious, more or less obvious—weighs upon all society and upon all humanity, and attempts to upset God's order of things. To fight sin within oneself is to remove one heavy weight from the earth, and to heal one wound of the Church. Realizing this should make us more zealous in conquering sin within ourselves and more fervent in prayer so that every one may be freed of it. Following the prayer taught us by Jesus, the Church prays every day: "Deliver us, O Lord, from every evil . . . in your mercy keep us free from sin". (RM) The Church which teaches with Christ's own certainty assures us, her children, that no matter how serious the dangers that surround us, with God's help we can always be free from sin. If sin wreaks such havoc in the world, it is because we pray too little, we try to fight with means that are too human, we devise many initiatives, but too few of us pledge ourselves to bring prayer and penance into the battle. The Council particularly recommends for Lent "prayer for sinners" (SC 109); it is a warning not to be ignored.

I will give thanks, O Lord with my whole heart . . . and give thanks to your name for your steadfast love and faithfulness . . .

On the day I called you answered me; my strength of soul you increased . . . For though the Lord is high, he regards the lowly; but the haughty he knows from afar. Though I walk in the midst of trouble, you preserve my life; you stretch out your hand against the wrath of my enemies and your right hand delivers me . . . Your steadfast love, O Lord, endures for ever; do not forsake the work of your hands.

Psalm 138:1-3, 6-8

Lord, I have no salvation but in you; if you will not be my rest, my infirmity cannot be cured. Be for me a protecting God, a safe refuge in which I can be safe. If I chose another refuge I should not be safe . . . If I run from you, there is nowhere to go except to you; to avoid your wrath I will have recourse to your pardon. You are my strength and my refuge . . . to regain my steadiness when I begin to feel weak, I will seek refuge in you. May your grace make me firm and immovable before all the temptations of the enemy.

But I carry human frailty within me, I still bear the remnants of the first slavery, I have in my members a law which wars against the law of my mind and which seeks to enslave me in the toils of sin: the corruptible body still weighs down my soul. However resolute I feel, thanks to your grace, yet, as long as I continue to carry your treasure in this earthen vessel I must always live in fear because of that vessel of clay. In you I stand against all the temptations of this world, but if they multiply and make me afraid, you will be my refuge.

St. Augustine, *In Ps.* 70,15.

116—WHO THINKS HIMSELF TO STAND

Lord, consider my affliction and my trouble; and forgive all my sins *(Ps 25:18).*

1. "But if a wicked man turns away from all his sins which he has committed, and keeps all my statutes . . . he shall surely live; he shall not die . . . But when a righteous man turns from his righteousness and commits iniquity . . . for this he shall die" (Ez 18:21,24). God is speaking through Ezechiel. While sinners who are converted are promised salvation, the just who stray from the right path are threatened with perdition. If the merit of conversion is so great that it washes away all the sins previously committed, no less important is the harm of inconstancy in doing good, which can destroy a whole life of good works.

No one can be sure of himself. "Let any one who thinks that he stands take heed lest he fall." (1 Cor 10:12). Even those who habitually live in the state of grace—who perhaps have made profession of the life of perfection—can never relax their vigilance. We must not only guard against serious sins, but also against venial sins. The so-called "venial sin" is always an offense against God and opposed to charity, for if it does not destroy charity, it at least chills it, diminishes its fervor, and lessens and hinders its development. Venial sin does not break our friendship with God, but when committed habitually with our eyes wide open, it seriously endangers that friendship. It is not unusual to meet souls who having at first surrendered themselves to God with sincere fervor, afterwards let themselves fall into continual carelessness, indifference and voluntary omissions because they have given in to selfishness, laziness, and other passions, and do not know how to make a generous effort to control themselves. Their spiritual life is reduced to a kind of lethargy, which is not yet death, but has none of the freshness and vigor of strong, healthy life. The fervor of charity has been exhausted.

To put us on guard against such a state, St. Teresa of Jesus declares; "always fear when some fault you commit does not grieve you. For in regard to sin, even venial, you know that the soul must feel deep sorrow . . . For the love of God, take great care never to grow careless about venial sin, however small . . . There is nothing small if it goes against so great a Sovereign" (*Med.* 2:5,20; *Way* 41:3).

2. Quite different are the venial sins which we commit through frailty or inadvertence. Very often the soul is determined not to give in at any price; due to its weakness, however, it falls when temptation comes, especially if the attack is unexpected. Nevertheless, once aware of it, the soul feels sincere sorrow, repents at once, asks God's pardon, rises, and sets out again. Such sins cause no great harm to the soul; they are rather signs of its weakness and of spiritual immaturity. Moreover, if the soul sincerely

humbles itself after these falls, it will draw real profit from them and a more profound knowledge of its own misery, which will make it mistrust its own strength entirely and place all its confidence in God alone. It will experience in a practical way the great truth of the words of Jesus: "apart from me you can do nothing" (Jn 15:5). It is not unusual for God to permit such falls, and he does so precisely to give the soul this practical knowledge of its nothingness, and to anchor it firmly in humility, the foundation of all our spiritual life.

In regard to faults of this kind, St. Therese of the Child Jesus felt that we can be sure "they do not grieve our Lord," because they are not caused by bad will but rather spring from the weakness of human nature. Jesus gave us a simple way of checking to make sure that our will is good and really alienated from sin; at the same time it is a necessary condition for our prayer to be acceptable to God: "If you are offering your gift at the altar and there remember that your brother has something against you, leave your gift there before the altar, and go; first be reconciled to your brother" (Mt 5:23-24). Anyone who does not try to be at peace with his neighbor cannot consider himself free from voluntary sin; nor can his friendship with God be very warm since he is unable to push himself to accomplish so essential a duty. God does not make great account of certain failings that slip by due to human weakness, but he takes very seriously everything that harms peace and harmony among brothers.

Out of the depths I cry to you, O Lord! Lord, hear my voice! Let your ears be attentive to the voice of my supplications! If you, O Lord should mark iniquities, Lord, who could stand? But there is forgiveness with you, that you may be feared.

I wait for the Lord, my soul waits, and in his word I hope; my soul waits for the Lord more than watchmen for the morning. My soul, hope in the Lord! For with the Lord there is steadfast love, and with him is plenteous redemption. And he will redeem me from all my iniquities.

Psalm 130

"God, be merciful to me, a sinner!" Pardon me, Father, oh, pardon me, a miserable ingrate. I owe it to your goodness that I am still your spouse, even though I am unfaithful to you by my faults. "O God, be merciful to me, a sinner."

O my soul, what are you doing? Are you not aware that God sees you always? You can never hide yourself from his sight, for nothing is hidden from him . . . so put an end to your wrongdoing and rouse yourself.

O eternal God, Father of all goodness and mercy, have pity on us, because we are blind and in darkness, and I, more than anyone else, am miserable and to be pitied . . . O true Sun, enter my soul and illumine it with your brightness. Drive out the darkness and give me light; melt the ice of my self-love and kindle in me the fire of your charity.

St. Catherine of Siena, *Preghiere ed Elevazioni*

Lord, I have sinned: have pity on me, a poor sinner. Make the water of tears and sincere repentance penetrate my heart, that I may be able to cleanse my soul of its guilt before I leave you. Lord, give me your grace and your mercy that they may be to me adornment and glory, and that I may be pleasing to you, O Lord, give me good will and perseverance, so that I may be able to renew myself incessantly in your service and praise.

Ruysbroeck, *Works,* vol. 1.

117 — YOU SHALL OBEY HIS VOICE

Happy are they who keep his testimonies, who seek him with their whole heart. *(Ps 119:2)*

1. Moses said to the people of Israel: "You have declared this day concerning the Lord that he is your God, and that you will walk in his ways, and keep his statutes and his commandments ... and will obey his voice. And the Lord has declared this day concerning you that you are a people for his own possession ... a people holy to the Lord, your God, as he has spoken." (Deut 26:17-19). With this proclamation of the promises of the two parties the covenant between Israel and Jahweh was confirmed: fidelity and obedience on the part of Israel, fulfillment of the promises on the part of God. Through its obedience Israel will be a privileged people, consecrated, belonging to their God, who will take special care of them and save them.

For many centuries the Church, God's new people, has taken Israel's place, and today as yesterday, the requirement for being "God's people" is still obedience. The primary reason for obedience is the fact that man is a creature, and as such receives from God "life and breath and everything" (Acts 17:25), and therefore can in no way be independent of him. "Woe to him who strives with his Maker ... "—says the prophet—"Dare the clay say to him who fashioned it, 'What are you making?' " (Is 45:9). Obedience is the essential relationship of the creature with God, it ensures order, harmony and happiness. The rupture of this relationship was the ruin of mankind: "By one man's disobedience [Adam's], many were made sinners" (Rom 5:19), and Christ's obedience was needed to reestablish order. Disobedience is a break with God, an abandonment of his friendship, a refusal of his sovereignty, a proud pretension of living independently of him. Obedience is the practical recognition of God's absolute primacy, the realization that without him man can find no good, no happiness; it is humble submission to his wishes, loving and docile acceptance of his commandments, communion with him. For love of the Father and for our salvation, the Son of God was obedient even to death on the cross; that changed man's obedience from that of a simple creature, subject of necessity to its creator, to the obedience of a son, inspired by love.

2. In perfecting the old law Jesus showed that the relationship of man to God is not so much that of creature toward Creator, as that of son toward Father. In the Old Testament obedience to the divine law was dominated by the idea of God's sovereignty: "he will be your God, and you will obey his voice." This idea continues unchanged in the New Testament; the first commandment is still: "I am the Lord your God" (Deut 5:6); but it is completed and made much more loving through the idea of the fatherhood of God. Consequently obedience, the observance of the law, takes on a filial aspect. The figure of his Father is always present in Jesus' teaching: the duties of almsgiving, of prayer, and of fasting are to be carried out under the Father's eye, for he sees in secret (Mt 6:1-18), and the works of the disciples must be such as to give glory to the Father (Mt 5:16). This is particularly evident in the wording of the new law of charity: "Love your enemies and pray for those who persecute you, so that you may be sons of your Father who is in heaven" (ib. 44-45). While the ideal of the old law is the absolute holiness of God: "Be holy because I am holy" (Lev 11:44), the ideal of the new is God's holiness viewed especially in the aspect of fatherhood: "You must be perfect, as your heavenly Father is perfect" (Mt 5:48). This idea of fatherhood immediately brings to mind goodness and love, and it is precisely for this reason that Jesus places so much emphasis on the law of love, both as a response to the Father's infinite love, and as imitation of his kindness in our mutual relationships.

However, the fact that God is the Father, and man his son, does not lessen the duty of obedience, rather it makes it more of a duty since it springs not from servile fear, but from filial love. "Charity"—teaches St. Thomas—"is inconceivable without obedience . . . This is because friendship makes us want or not want the same things" (St. Thos 2-2,104,3). Obedience is the fruit of love, of friendship with God, and at the same time is their concrete witness. The more we renounce our own will and conform in all things to God's will, the more we are united to him in perfect communion.

I will praise you with an upright heart, when I learn your righteous ordinances. I will observe your statutes; O forsake me not utterly!

How can a young man keep his way pure? By guarding it according to your word . . . With my lips I declare all the ordinances of your mouth. In the way of your testimonies I delight as much as in all riches . . .

Behold I long for your precepts; in your righteousness give me life! Let your steadfast love come to me, O Lord, your salvation according to your promise; then shall I have an answer for those who taunt me, for I trust in your word . . . I will keep your law continually, for ever and ever; and I shall walk at liberty, for I have sought your precepts.

Psalm 119:7-9,13-14,40-45.

The sole aim of all our thoughts and actions and desires and prayers must be to please you, O Lord; and doing your will must be our way of perfection. You want each of us to love you with all our heart . . . One who loves you with all his heart can truthfully say to you what the Apostle said: "What shall I do, Lord?" (Acts 22:10). Lord, let me know what you want of me, for I am ready to do it. Make me understand that when I want what you want, then I am wanting what is best for me, for you certainly desire only the best for me . . .

My God, be then the only Lord of my heart; possess it entirely, and let my soul love and obey and seek to please only you . . . Do as you wish with me and with all that is mine; I consent to all and resign myself in all. O love that is worthy of infinite love, you have loved me so much that you died for me; I love you with all my heart, I love you more than myself and abandon my soul into your hands.

St. Alphonsus Liguori, *Practice of the Love of Jesus Christ* 13

118 — SECOND SUNDAY OF LENT

YEAR A

O God, you called us with a holy calling *(2 Tim 1:9)*

The theme of the first two readings of this Sunday could be entitled: the call of the faithful. In the Old Testament (Gen 12:1-4a) we read the history of the call of Abraham, who was the founder of the chosen people and the father of all believers. "The Lord said to Abram: 'Go from your country and kindred and your father's house to the land that I will show you!' " (ib. 1). The faith of this man was something wonderful and mysterious; he came from an idolatrous people, yet he believed in the one true God to the point of being ready to leave all—country and loved ones—to follow the voice of One who was urging him toward an unknown destination. Abraham set out and lived as a nomad, moving from place to place at God's indication, believing against all evidence that God would fulfill his promise: "I will make of you a great nation" (ib. 2).

In the second reading (1 Tim 1:8b-10), St. Paul speaks of the call of the Christian which finds its roots in that of Abraham, but is enlightened and elevated by the grace of Christ. "God has saved us and called us with a holy calling, not in virtue of our works, but in virtue of his own purpose and the grace which he gave us in Christ Jesus" (ib. 9). Abraham was called in view of Christ, for whom he was to furnish the people from which Christ was to spring; but we are called to follow Christ by virtue of the grace which flows from the paschal mystery of his death and resurrection. Abraham saw the day of Christ from afar (Jn 8:56); we see it from near, inserted as we are in time already sanctified by his coming. If Abraham answered the divine call so wholeheartedly, how much more are we not bound to do so now that Jesus has "abolished death and brought life and immortality to clear light through the gospel" (2 Tim 1:10).

Following an old tradition we read today the Gospel of the transfiguration (Mt 17:1-9), which is a synthesis of the mystery of our Lord's death and resurrection and a meaningful description of the Christian vocation. The event which took place six days after Peter's profession of faith at Caesarea, which had been immediately followed by the first mention of the Passion, is here shown to us as a reaffirmation of Peter's declaration: "You are the Christ, the Son of the living God" (Mt 16:16); at the same time it was an encouragement to the apostles that they might not lose hope on account of the sufferings that Jesus was to undergo. They had to understand that, instead of the Passion destroying the glory of the Son of God, it was the necessary road to attain it. "He was transfigured before them and his face shone like the sun, and his garments became white as light" (Mt 17:2). Confronted with such a spectacle, Peter burst out; he who had reacted violently to Christ's words on the passion, now, before the glory of his beloved Master, cries out enthusiastically: "Lord, it is well that we are here!" (ib. 4). He had been horrified by the cross; now glory makes him exultant and he would like to remain with it and ignore everything else. But the blessed vision on Tabor is only an anticipation of the glory of the resurrection, given as a "viaticum" for following Jesus courageously on the road to Calvary. All this is expressed by the voice from heaven: "This is my beloved Son with whom I am well pleased; listen to him" (ib. 5). The Father is pleased with the Son who, though sharing the divine nature with him, consents to hide its splendors under the guise of human flesh and still more under the ignominy of the cross. His disciples must always listen to him, especially when he talks of the cross and teaches the way to it. The Christian is called to conform himself to Jesus Christ, so that he may one day be made like to him in his glory.

God our Father, help us to hear your Son. Enlighten us with your word, that we may find the way to your glory.

Roman Missal, Collect 2nd Sunday of Lent

Pay all heed to my Son in whom I am well pleased, by whose preaching I am revealed, and by whose humility I am glorified. He is the truth and the life, my power and my wisdom. Listen to him, who was foretold in the mysteries of the law, priased by the tongues of the prophets. Listen to him, who ransoms the world with his blood . . . Listen to him who opens the way to heaven and through the torment of the cross prepares for you the steps that lead up to the kingdom . . .

In the preaching of the holy gospel all should receive a strengthening of their faith. No one should be ashamed of the cross of Christ, through which the world has been redeemed. No one should fear to suffer for the sake of justice; no one should lose confidence in the reward that has been promised. The way to rest is through toil, the way to life is through death.

Christ has taken on himself the whole weakness of our lowly human nature. If then we are steadfast in our faith in him and in our love for him, we win the victory that he has won, we receive what he has promised . . . When it comes to obeying the commandments or enduring adversity, the words uttered by the Father should always echo in our ears: "This is my Son, the beloved, in whom I am well pleased; listen to him."

St. Leo the Great, *Sermon* 51:7-8

YEAR B

I rely upon you, Jesus, who died and were raised from the dead, who are at the right hand of God, who indeed intercede for us.

(Rom 8:34).

This Sunday's Liturgy has a decided paschal quality, emphasizing Jesus' sacrifice and glorification. As usual, we begin with the Old Testament and consider today Abraham's sacrifice. In obedience to God's command, Abraham had had the courage, at seventy-five years of age, to give up country and home and customary routine; now in his old age he has carried his obedience even to sacrificing his only son. "Take your son, your only son, Isaac, whom you love, and go . . . offer him . . . as a burnt offering" (Gen 22:2). It was a terrible command for the heart of a loving father, and likewise an extreme test of faith for one who was not willing to doubt God. Isaac was his only hope for the fulfillment of the divine promises, yet Abraham obeyed and continued to believe that God would keep his word. Truly he deserves the title of "our father in faith" (Euch Pr I). But God was seeking not Isaac's death, but rather Abraham's unquestioning faith and obedience. Still, Isaac had a singular role to play in the history of salvation: he was to prefigure Jesus, the only Son of God, who would be sacrificed to redeem the world. What, through God's intervention, Abraham left incomplete, God himself would accomplish. "He who did not spare his own Son, but gave him up for us all" (Rom 8:32; 2nd reading). Isaac climbed the mountain, carrying the wood for the sacrifice on his back, and without murmur let himself be placed, bound, upon the piled wood; he is the figure of Christ who climbs Calvary carrying the wood of his cross, upon which he lets himself be stretched out, "freely offering himself to his sufferings" (Euch Pr II). Just as the divine promise were fulfilled in Isaac after he had been saved from death, so life and salvation for all mankind proceed from Christ, risen from the dead. No one can doubt this, since "Jesus, who died, yes, who was raised from the dead . . . is at the right hand of God and . . . intercedes for us" (Rom 8:34).

The Gospel of the day (Mk 9:2-10), which shows us Jesus transfigured on the mountain, offers us a preview of the glory of the risen Lord and of his power with his Father. Only the three closest disciples—Peter, James, and John—are privileged to witness it, the same ones who would be present later at the agony in Gethsemani, as if to indicate that glory and suffering are two inseparable aspects of the unique mystery of Christ. "He was transfigured before them and his clothes became glistening, intensely white—as no fuller on earth could bleach them" (ib. 2-3). These details, which are typical of Mark's account, express well the deep impression made upon the three, and especially on St. Peter, seeing the Lord resplendent in glory. They who had always seen him in his ordinary guise, a man like other men, now contemplate his divinity: they discover the shining face of the Son of God, who is "God from God, Light from Light" (Creed). Meanwhile the voice from heaven vouches for the vision: "This is my beloved Son; listen to him" (ib. 7); men must heed him in order to live according to his teachings, and God himself listens to him because through his sacrifice he will save mankind. But the divine so surpasses the human aspect that in revealing itself to man, it overwhelms and frightens him; the three disciples are overcome by fear, and Peter, without realizing what he is saying, suggests that they set up there three tents: "one for you, and one for Moses, and one for Elijah" (ib. 5). He did not realize that the vision was only given to encourage their faith, and that before arriving at the eternal vision, they would have to come down the mountain with Jesus, and hear him speak again of suffering, and follow him by carrying the cross with him. This is what it means to live the paschal mystery of Christ.

How wonderful Abraham's obedience was! What an example for us, O God . . . and all the more admirable because it was not only that he acted against the inclination of his heart . . . more was involved here than even a heartfelt sacrifice . . . You told him to do the opposite of what seemed right to him . . . But he trusted in you, and knowing that it was you who spoke, he obeyed, and with reason, for you are justice and holiness personified . . . How close faith is to obedience! Faith is the beginning of every good and obedience is its completion.

O Abraham, may you be blessed! Isaac, who so meekly allowed yourself to be bound to the altar, may you be blessed! My God, who make such virtues spring from men, may you be blessed from age to age for ever! Love means obeying you, obeying you with this promptness and this faith, in ways that rend the heart and turn the mind upside down . . . love is immediate, absolute sacrifice to your will and glory of what is most dear . . . It is what you did, in a wonderful way, O Abraham, getting up at once in the night to go to sacrifice your son. It is what you will do, O Son of God, coming from heaven to earth to live that life and die that death! . . . My Lord and my God, so may it be with me also, according to your most holy will.

C. de Foucauld, *Meditations*

Christ our Lord, you revealed yourself in glory on your holy mountain in the presence of your disciples. You had already prepared them for your approaching death. You wanted to teach them through the law and the prophets that you had first to suffer and so come to the glory of the resurrection.

Roman Missal, cf *Preface* 13

YEAR C

The Lord is my light and my salvation; whom shall I fear? Hide not your face from me. (Ps 27:1-9)

Today's Liturgy is lit up by the splendor of the Lord's transfiguration, a prelude to his resurrection, and a token of ours. As an introduction, the first reading relates God's covenant with Abraham (Gen 15:5-12,17-18). After foretelling for the third time that he would have numerous descendents: "Look toward heaven and number the stars . . . So shall your descendents be" (ib. 5), God shows him the land he will give him; and Abraham, with humble confidence, asks for a pledge of these promises. The Lord understandingly agrees and makes a covenant with him according to the custom of the nomads of that time. Abraham prepares a sacrifice of animals upon which God comes down during the night in the form of fire and finalizes the pact: "To your descendents I give this land . . . " (ib. 18). This is a figure of the new and definitive alliance that God will one day conclude in the blood of Christ through whch the human race will have the right, not to an earthly fatherland, but to a heavenly and eternal one.

On Tabor (Gospel: Lk 9:28-36), before the transfigured Jesus, God again pledges himself to men and presents his beloved Son: "This is my Son, my Chosen; listen to him" (ib. 35); He gives him to men as their Teacher, but on Calvary it will be as Victim. St. Luke tells us that the Transfiguration took place on the mountain as Jesus was praying: "The appearance of his face was altered and his raiment became dazzling white" (ib. 29). For a moment Jesus lets his divinity shine through his human features, and to the ecstatic eyes of his disciples appears as he really is: a reflection "of the glory of God, bearing the very stamp of his nature" (Heb 1:3). To see the face of God was the burning desire of the just of the old Testament and of the saints of the New. "I seek your face, O Lord. Do not hide your face from me" (Resp Ps). But when God grants such a privilege, it is for but one special, fleeting moment, like the vision on Tabor, to strengthen faith and infuse courage for carrying the cross. Two men are standing on either side of the transfigured Lord: Moses and Elijah; the first represents the law, the other the prophets—the law that Jesus has come to complete, and the prophecies he is to fulfill. The presence of these two great personages manifests the continuity between the Old and the New Testament, and their conversation foretells the passion of Jesus: "they spoke of his departure which he was to accomplish in Jerusalem" (Lk 9:31). As Moses and Elijah had suffered and been persecuted for God's sake, so will Jesus have to suffer. It is a vision of glory, then, interwoven with talk of suffering: two opposite but not opposing aspects of the one paschal mystery of Christ. Death and resurrection, the cross and glory.

The second reading (Phil 3:17;4:1) is a warm exhortation to carry Christ's cross with love, in order to share one day in his glory. "Many, of whom I have often told you and now tell you even with tears, live as enemies of the cross of Christ" (ib. 18). The Apostle laments over Christians who give themselves to worldly pleasures, to the pleasures of the flesh with minds fixed only on worldly matters. Then there is a sudden shift of thought that brings to his mind the vision on Mt. Tabor: "But our commonwealth is in heaven and from it we await a Savior, the Lord Jesus Christ, who will change our lowly body to be like his glorious body" (ib. 20-21). Our transfiguration will be complete only in eternal life, but it already begins here on earth through baptism; the grace of Christ is the leaven which transforms us from within and transfigures us into his image, provided we are willing to carry the cross with him.

Lord, I seek your face, your face, O Lord, I yearn to see. Therefore, O Lord my God, teach my heart now, where and how to seek you, where and how to find you. Lord, if you are not here, where shall I look for you? But then, if you are everywhere, why can I not see you? To be sure, you live in an inaccessible light... who will lead me, and take me where I may see you?

Lord, teach me how to look for you, and show yourself to me because I do seek you, and I cannot seek you if you do not show me how, nor can I find you if you do not show me yourself. O Lord, desiring, may I seek you; seeking, desire you; loving, find you; and finding you, love you.

St. Anselm *Proslogion* 1.

Now we lament, now we pray! We lament because we are miserable wretches, we pray because we are in need. Prayer will pass and give way to praise; tears will pass and joy will follow. Meanwhile in this time of probation, may our prayer to you, O God, never cease; we ask only one thing of you: Do not let us stop asking until through your gift and guidance, our prayer is granted.

I ask but one thing, however much I pray or cry or groan: only one thing... My heart has already told you: I have sought your face, Lord, your face will I seek. One thing I have asked of you, Lord, this I seek after: to behold your face.

St. Augustine, *In Ps.* 26, II 14,16.

119 — WE HAVE BEEN REBELLIOUS

Lord, with my whole heart I seek you; let me not wander from your commandments *(Ps 119:10)*

1. "O Lord... we have sinned and done wrong and acted violently and rebelled, turning aside from your commandments and ordinances" (Dan 9:4-5). Daniel's confession to God in the name of the people of Israel is still timely. Men of every age can repeat it to the end together with the prophet: "We have not obeyed the voice of the Lord our God by following his laws, which he set before his servants the prophets" (ib. 10).

The sin of disobedience to God, to his laws and to his representatives is among the most common, but also least heeded of sins. And yet we shall not find salvation except through obedience. It was the path frequented by the Son of God: "For I have come down from heaven, not to do my own will, but the will of him who sent me" (Jn 6:38). By freely acquiescing in the will of his Father who was sacrificing him for the salvation of the world, he accepted having to subject himself to all lawful authority, whether worthy or not, Jew or pagan, priests or officials of the Roman Empire.

It is God's way to govern men through other men who participate in his authority. "Let everyone be subject to the governing authorities"—warns St. Paul—"for there is no authority except from God" (Rom 13:1). Every form of rebellion against legitimate authority, every kind of anarchy really "rebels against the ordinance of God" (ib. 2). Therefore, not only for the sake of society, but also in conscience, the Christian must lend "obedience to just laws and reverence for legitimately constituted authorities" (CD 19; cf GS 74).

This is true with much greater reason for the shepherds of his flock, of whom Jesus said: "He who hears you, hears me; and he who rejects you rejects me" (Lk 10:16). From this perspective Vatican Council II exhorts all the faithful: "With ready Christian obedience laymen ... should accept whatever pastors, as representatives of Christ, decree in their role of teachers and rulers in the Church. So let laymen follow the example of Christ, who, by his obedience even at the cost of death, opened to all men the blessed way of liberty of the children of God" (LG 37).

2. There is no one in any station of life who is not bound to practice the virtue of obedience. "Be subject to one another out of reverence for Christ"—urges St. Paul—"Wives should be subject to their husbands as to the Lord . . . Children obey your parents in the Lord . . . Slaves, be obedient to those who are your earthly masters with fear and trembling, in singleness of heart as to Christ" (Eph 5:21-22; 6:1,5). Obedience in imitation of the Lord is always recommended to every category of persons; familial and social order is his will; hence the conclusion is clear: we should obey men as if we were obeying Christ. Christian obedience is characterized precisely by this supernatural spirit through which man, looking beyond the person who commands, fixes his gaze on God, to whom he pays the homage of submission. Such obedience is not reserved to those who have made a vow or special promise, but is of obligation for everyone. Indeed the Church exhorts all of us "to share the mind of Jesus Christ, who 'emptied himself taking the form of a slave . . . being born in the likeness of men' " (Phil 2:7-8) (LG 42).

Obviously our first obedience is due to God, and if any authority should impose anything contrary to the divine will, we would need to reply that it is not lawful to obey men above God (Acts 4:19). With this exception, obedience is to be practiced even when it goes contrary to our own will, especially if it involves the express will of God, his law, the good of the Church, dependence on religious superiors. Precisely because an individual is not an isolated being, but is part of the ecclesial community, the common good can sometimes require the renunciation of views, desires, and personal plans; but it is certain that this renunciation is more pleasing to God than any good deed or even act of devotion. "Has the Lord so great delight in burnt offerings and sacrifices, as in obeying the voice of the Lord? Behold, to obey is better than sacrifice" (1 Sam 15:22). These were Samuel's words to Saul who had offered the best of his flock in sacrifice to God, but had disobeyed his orders. Obedience is not a sacrifice of things, but of one's own will which is worth more than everything else.

O Lord, the great and terrible God who keeps covenant and steadfast love with those who love him and keep his commandments, we have sinned and done wrong and acted wickedly and rebelled, turning aside from your commandments and ordinances; we have not listened to your servants the prophets who spoke in your name . . . To you, O Lord belongs righteousness, but to us confusion of face . . . because we have sinned against you. To the Lord our God belong mercy and forgiveness; because we have rebelled against him . . .

Now therefore, O our God, hearken to the prayer of your servant and to his supplications, and for your own sake, O Lord, cause your face to shine upon your sanctuary, which is desolate. O my God, incline your ear and hear; open your eyes and behold our desolations . . . for we do not present our supplications before you on the ground of our righteousness, but on the ground of your great mercy. O Lord, hear; O Lord, forgive; O Lord, give heed and act!

Daniel 9:4-9, 17-19.

Oh! how sweet and glorious is this virtue of obedience, which contains all the rest, for she is conceived and born of charity; on her is founded the rock of the holy faith. She is a queen whose consort will feel no trouble, but only peace and quiet; the waves of the stormy sea cannot hurt her, nor can any tempest assail her . . . Such a one feels no hatred when injured, because he wishes to obey the precept of forgiveness; he suffers not when his appetites are not satisfied, because obedience has ordered him to desire you alone, Lord, who can and will satisfy all his desires . . . And so in all things he finds peace and quiet.

O obedience, you voyage without fatigue, and reach without danger the port of salvation! You are conformed to the only-begotten Son, the Word, you board the ship of the holy cross, forcing yourself . . . not to transgress the obedience of the Word, nor abandon his doctrine!

St. Catherine of Siena, *Dialogue* 136

120 — THEY SAY BUT DO NOT DO

Lord, give me understanding that I may keep your law and observe it with all my heart *(Ps 119:34)*

1. In regard to the scribes and Pharisees Jesus said: "Practice and observe whatever they tell you, but not what they do" (Mt 23:3). Jesus does not hesitate to recognize the authority of the doctors of the law in their position as religious instructors of the people, and he recommends that their teachings be followed; it is an example of how we are to obey those whose office is to guide or teach, even when they do not exercise their office worthily. But, on the other hand, Jesus openly warns against the conduct of such teachers and exposes their basic error: "they preach but they do not practice."

Everyone can be guilty of the sin of inconsistency, but, although it is blameworthy in anyone, it is especially so in those who, by reason of the office they hold or the way of life they have embraced, have a strict obligation to give witness in deeds to the doctrine they teach and profess. To have a certain amount of knowledge of spiritual matters without bothering to put it into practice creates real discrepancies; those who so act, discuss virtue and holiness, but base their behavior on unresisted passions and vices, so that they reach the point of no longer realizing the absurdity of their conduct, which denies in deed what they preach in word. Inconsistency particularly tempts "practicing Christians," not excluding consecrated souls, dragging them down to a mediocre way of life, which is despised by men and censured by God. "You are neither cold nor hot"—says the Lord—"because you are lukewarm . . . I will spew you out of my mouth" (Rev 3:15-16). The root of this problem often lies in a legalistic frame of mind, such as that of the Pharisees, which makes virtue consist in not overstepping the boundaries of sin, taking great care to include in this area everything that satisfies self, and not to do anything more than is strictly required. With this arrangement spiritual life loses its impetus and energy, levels out into a colorless state, shuts itself up within narrow horizons where the ideal no longer shines, and the flame of love is extinguished.

God has no wish to be served on the basis of cold legalism, but wholeheartedly, out of love; and real love gives without calculation or any holding back; it gives at its own expense.

2. The Council laments the fact that Catholics, who possess "all divinely revealed truth and . . . all the means of grace . . . fail to live by them with all the ardor they should. As a result, the radiance of the Church's face shines less brightly . . . before the world at large, and the growth of God's kingdom is retarded" (UR 4). This observation should make us think: inconsistency and mediocrity not only impede personal holiness, but do a great deal of harm to the entire Church. Criticisms and interpretations cause the gospel to be too little lived in the way that our Lord preached it. In the name of expediency and of prudence, the gospel message of charity and renunciation and poverty is often reduced to empty formulas of life which invite the criticism of the worldly and scandalize the simple.

We must open our hearts to accept the full gospel as Jesus preached it. We must meditate in depth upon the words of the Lord: "they do not do what they preach," and we must have the courage to compare these words with our actual lives. How many good ideas, how many truths we know and affirm, and yet never put into practice, simply relegating them to the sphere of ideas! To be doers of truth, livers of the gospel, witnesses to Christ—these are the goals toward which we should incessantly strive.

"Wash yourselves; make yourselves clean; remove the evil of your doings from before my eyes"—urges the Holy Spirit, speaking through Isaiah—"Learn to do good; seek justice" (Is 1:16-17). Our Lenten conversion demands a thorough cleansing from selfishness; it insists that we banish the evils of inconsistency and of pettiness from our actions and do good generously, that our justice be interior rather than exterior, and spring from love. A Christian cannot be like an acrobat, juggling back and forth between what is lawful and what is forbidden; or like a money-lender who weighs every penny on a scale; rather, we are called to be people who live the way of love (Eph 5:1), serving God with the devotion of sons, and our neighbor with the self-denial of a brother. Only thus can fervor be assured in the individual, in communities and in the entire Church, whose holiness "is unceasingly manifested as it ought to be through the fruits of grace that the Holy Spirit produces in the faithful" (LG 39).

God says: "What right have you to recite my statutes, or take my covenant on your lips? For you hate discipline, and you cast my words behind you . . . These things you have done and I have been silent; you thought that I was one like yourself. But now I rebuke you, and lay the charge before you . . . He who brings thanksgiving as his sacrifice honors me; to him who orders his way aright I will show the salvation of God!"

Psalm 50:16-17, 21,23

O Lord, you created spirits to be with you and to share your blessedness according to their degree; and the return they made you was at once to rebel against you. First a great part of angels, then mankind, have risen up against you, and served others, not you. Why did you create us, but to make us happy? Could you be made more happy by creating us? and how could we be happy but in obeying you? Yet we determined not to be happy as you would have us happy, but to find out a happiness of our own; and so we left you.

O my God, what a return is it that we—that I—make you when we sin! What dreadful unthankfulness is it!

You, O my God, have a claim on me, and I am wholly yours. You are the Almighty Creator, and I am your workmanship. I am the work of your hands, and you are my owner . . . my one duty is to serve you.

O my God, I confess that before now I have utterly forgotten this, and that I am continually forgetting it! I have acted many times as if I were my own master, and turned from you rebelliously. I have acted according to my own pleasure, not according to yours. And so far have I hardened myself, as not to feel as I ought how evil this is. I do not understand how dreadful sin is—and I do not hate it, and fear it, as I ought. I have no horror of it, or loathing. I do not turn from it with indignation, as being an insult to you, but I trifle with it, and, even if I do not commit great sins, I have no great reluctance to do small ones. O my God, what a great and awful difference is there between what I am and what I ought to be!

J.H. Newman, *Meditations* IV, 1

121 – THE BOAST OF THE CHRISTIAN

Far be it from me to glory except in the cross of our Lord Jesus Christ *(Gal 6:14)*

1. "The Son of Man will be delivered to the chief priests and scribes, and they will condemn him to death, and deliver him to the Gentiles to be mocked and scourged and crucified, and he will be raised on the third day" (Mt 20:18-19). This is the third time that he has told his followers of his coming suffering, and again he is not understood. The first time, Peter had strongly protested; the second time, the three chosen disciples had not grasped the meaning of his words, but did not have the courage "to ask him about this saying" (Lk 9:45); now, the third instance is followed by the presumptuous request that James and John put to him through the mouth of their mother: "Command that these two sons of mine may sit, one at your right hand, and one at your left, in your kingdom" (Mt 20:21). Jesus speaks of suffering, contempt, an ignominious death, and the apostles are preoccupied with assuring themselves of the first places. It is the perpetual tendency of pride—the sad heritage of original sin—which tries to establish itself in every field, including the religious. Before they can understand, these men will have to see their Master literally "mocked and scourged and crucified" and then raise up, as he had himself foretold. Still, Jesus warns them: "Are you able to drink the cup that I am to drink?" (ib. 22). Thus the lesson of Mt. Tabor is repeated: we do not attain to glory except by the narrow way of the cross. And, it must be added, without humility the mystery of the cross cannot be understood, much less lived. For anyone who seeks honor, success, and worldly fame, the cross is cause for scandal, an enemy which threatens his happiness and curtails his liberty. The proud man who wants to be the undisputed master of his own life rebels against every form of suffering, physical or moral, which impedes him from calling attention to his own talents, and, like the apostles, runs the risk of becoming an enemy of the cross of Christ. Only the humble, like Christ, are capable of submitting to the weight of the cross, of accepting, like him, insults, humiliations, and unjust treatment. Only in souls like these does the cross accomplish the work of purification and of destruction of sin that prepares them to rise again in Christ.

2. Jesus publicly condemned the conduct of the Pharisees who "love the place of honor at feasts and the best seats in the synagogues and salutations in the market places, and being called 'Rabbi' by men" (Mt 23:5-7). He speaks similarly to the Twelve in private: "You know that the rulers of the Gentiles lord it over them, and their great men exercise authority over them. It shall not be so among you" (Mt 20:25-26). The disciples of the Lord must not let themselves be contaminated by the mentality of the Pharisees nor by that of the great people of the world. Their con-

duct must be completely the opposite, and likewise their preferences: not to rule, but to serve; not to lord it over others, but to be one with them; in fact, to put themselves beneath others by choosing the last place. "Whoever would be great among you must be your servant, and whoever would be first among you, must be your slave" (ib. 26-27). James and John, who were aspiring to the first places in the kingdom of Christ, thus learn how they must behave if they are to acquire these: they must make themselves small, servants of their brothers, even to becoming their slaves. This is bewildering for anyone who judges according to the wisdom of the flesh, indeed it is absolutely incomprehensible and absurd; but for one who judges according to God, it is divine wisdom, enveloped in the mystery of Christ crucified. There is simply no other way to be a follower of him who "came, not to be served, but to serve, and to give his life as a ransom for many" (ib. 28). The whole life of Christ, particularly his Passion, is marked by a deep sense of service for the glory of God and the salvation of men. He "the first born of all creation, for in him all things were created in heaven and on earth" (Col 1:15,18), became servant to all men, their slave who was sold and given over to death in ransom for their sins. To drink of his cup means consenting to follow him along this road of humility and of the cross, it means giving ourselves to the service of God and of neighbor, with the conviction that we have to extend all our energies therein, even to total self-sacrifice. Then all notions of primacy and human distinction disappear and a Christian longs for only one glory: to become like his crucified God. "Far be it from me to glory except in the cross of our Lord Jesus Christ" (Gal 6:14).

O Jesus Christ, Son of the eternal Father, Our Lord, true King over all things! What did you leave in the world for your descendents to inherit from you? What did you ever have, my Lord, save trials, pains and insults? Indeed you had only a beam of wood to rest upon while drinking the bitter draft of death. Those of us, then, my God, who desire to be your true children and not to renounce their inheritance must never flee from suffering. Your crest is five wounds . . . Let that too be our device if we are to inherit your kingdom. Not by ease nor by comfort nor by honor nor by wealth can we gain that which you purchased for us by so much blood.

St. Teresa of Jesus, *Foundations* X:11 (Peers)

My God, make me always think of myself as the servant of all, servant of souls and of bodies, in order to do the greatest possible good to the one and the other, a servant in obeying every time I can do so, a servant when I take the last place . . . A servant when I do not allow myself to be served, but serve others instead, which is something that can always be done, whatever activity may be involved, as you yourself made evident; even though you were God, teacher, and Lord, you showed that you knew how to be in the midst of the Apostles as one who serves . . . Let me also give my soul, as you gave yours and together with you, for the redemption of the many . . . through prayer, penance, example and through the communion of the saints; . . . if it is pleasing to you, through martyrdom, through all the sacrifices it may please you to impose upon me at every moment of my life, which I offer to you for your greater glory . . . and in obedience to your will for the sanctification of men . . . O my God, I am your servant and your slave: make your will my food . . . Do whatever you want with me, for your glory, for the consolation of your heart . . . for the redemption of many . . .

C. de Foucauld, *On the Feasts of the Year,* Op. sp.

122 — THE RIGHTFUL PLACE

Lord, you search the mind and try the heart, to give to every man according to his ways *(Jer 17:10)*

1. "Cursed is the man who trusts in man . . . whose heart turns away from the Lord" (Jer 17:5). The proud, self-satisfied man who shuts God out and ignores him cannot be the beneficiary of divine blessings. Jeremiah compares him to a tree planted in unsuitable soil, which is therefore sterile and fruitless. He may seem to prosper, perhaps even to enjoy life for many years, but at some point his grandeur will crumble away, and his splendor will be changed into mourning. The rich man of the gospel parable (Lk 16:19-31), who feasted sumptuously while Lazarus groaned at his door, personifies this very well. Jesus is not condemning him simply because he possesses much wealth, but because he sets his heart on it and finds his whole happiness in enjoying it, completely oblivious of God and of his neighbor. "You shall not harden your heart, nor shut your hand against your poor brother" (Dt 15:7), says the Lord; but this man, disdainful of God, scorns his law also, and feels no pity for the beggar who vainly hopes to satisfy his hunger with table scraps. When death comes, the situation is reversed: the rich man is plunged into unending suffering, while the poor man is raised to everlasting happiness. The parable is a practical commentary on the "beatitudes" of the poor, of the hungry, of those who weep, because the kingdom of God is theirs: they shall be filled, they shall laugh (Lk 6:20-21); and of the "woes" hurled by Jesus against pleasure-seekers: "But woe to you that are rich, for you have received your consolation. Woe to you that are full, for you shall hunger . . . Woe to you that laugh now, you shall mourn and weep" (ib. 24-25).

On another occasion Jesus said that it was very difficult for the rich to be saved (Lk 18:24-25); the fact is that wealth very often engenders pride, from which comes impiety toward God and hardness of heart toward neighbor. It is rare that we find a rich man who is also humble. He who lives amid riches and honor is humble only when he understands their vanity and builds his life on God; such a one considers himself simply an administrator of the goods that Providence has entrusted to him so that he may share them with brothers in need.

2. It was not poverty in itself that saved Lazarus, but the fact that he accepted it from God with humility and patience, putting his trust in him. "Blessed is the man who trusts in the Lord" (Jer 17:7). Material poverty is a means of salvation when it is joined to poverty in spirit and to humility of heart. The poor man who is proud, rebellious against God and society, who smoulders with hatred and seeks to escape from poverty by unjust and violent means cannot be counted among those poor who will inherit the kingdom of heaven.

Essentially, salvation is for the humble, for those who, recognizing their total dependence on God, accept from him whatever condition of prosperity or adversity he sends—comfort or poverty, happiness or trials—without being either elated or irritated. Humility consists basically in accepting the condition proper to creatures who have nothing of their own, because whatever they do possess in the realm of being or of acting has come from God. Consequently we may never selfishly appropriate to ourselves the gifts we have received, nor boast of them as though they were ours, nor claim privileges or consider ourselves cheated if Providence has allotted to us a poor and humble place in life that is without honor.

Furthermore, humility consists in keeping within proper limits the love of our own excellence which inclines us to esteem ourselves more than we deserve and to put ourselves above others. Humility is truth, and for that reason it makes us take our rightful place, in accordance with the divine intentions, whether we are dealing with God or with our neighbor. Man, standing before God in his poverty, is conscious that he has nothing and can do nothing without divine help. "Apart from me you can do nothing" (Jn 15:5), says Jesus and St. Paul comments: "God is at work in you, both to will and to work for his good pleasure" (Phil 2:13). This, then, is the position of the man who is poor, but trustfully poor, aware of being loved by God as a son and of always being able to rely on his help. To his neighbor he is a brother, he is open to other's needs and eager to share his goods with them, more anxious to serve than to be served.

Cursed is the man who trusts in man and makes flesh his arm, whose heart turns away from the Lord. He is like a shrub in the desert, and shall not see any good come. He shall dwell in the parched places of the wilderness, in an uninhabited salt land.

Blessed is the man who trusts in the Lord, whose trust is the Lord. He is like a tree planted by water, that sends its roots by the stream, and does not fear when heat comes, for its leaves remain green, and is not anxious in the year of drought, for it does not cease to bear fruit.

Who can understand the human heart? You, O Lord, try the heart to give to every man according to his ways, according to the fruit of his doings.

cf *Jeremiah* 17:5-10

O Lord, I want to consider myself: what do I, a sinner, deserve? I who have scorned you? Nothing but punishment, nothing but eternal pain comes before my mind. I see clearly what was due me and what you have given me—given freely. To me, a sinner, you gave pardon, justification, and charity, that is, divine love, with which to do every good work; in addition you will give me eternal life, and the company of the angels; and all this through your mercy. May I never boast of my merits, because these same merits are your gifts! My God, my mercy! (In Ps 144:11)

Make me descend into my heart and confess to you: I have nothing that can please you except what I have received from you; whatever is from me, is displeasing to you. If I take stock of all I possess, what is there that I have not received? And if I have received it, why do I boast as though I had not received it? . . . Left to myself I could only get lost, and I would not have been able to find you again now, if you who made me had not come seeking me. (Ser 13:3)

St. Augustine

123 — THE LORD'S VINEYARD

Lord, wash me thoroughly from my iniquity; cleanse me from my sin (Ps 51:2)

1. Like the prophet Jeremiah who was persecuted by his people, so Joseph the Hebrew, who was also persecuted by his brothers, is a figure of the suffering Messiah. The Lenten Liturgy recalls the sorrowful vicissitudes of these Biblical personalities to help us to understand the mystery of Christ more thoroughly and the better to plumb the depths of human malice, with a view to salutary conversion. The story of Joseph's unhappy experience is dominated by the envy of his brothers who decided to free themselves of the young dreamer by killing him, but were held back from actually committing the crime by the compassion of one of them; they ended by selling him "for twenty shekels of silver" (Gen 37:28). This was a slightly lower price than would be agreed upon by Judas, many centuries later, for handing Jesus over to the Sanhedrin. Christ will also be the target of envy and of the hatred of his brothers: first the Nazarenes will attempt to stone him, then an apostle will sell him, and his own people, so favored by him, will crucify him. Jesus himself summarized the sad story in the parable of the wicked workers in the vineyard, who twice murdered their master's servants, and the third time

killed his son. The chosen people, the first to be called to salvation, not only rejected and slew the prophets sent by God, but treated the Son of God in the same way.

In the conspiracy against Joseph and still more in the one against Jesus, the passions that come into play are pride, envy, greed, and hatred. Joined to these are hardening of the heart and refusal of grace. It is not only the Jews who have been guilty of these passions and crimes, each of us has to recognize their germ within us, and perhaps, not too rarely, their worst fruits as well. Lent invites us to a sincere scrutiny of conscience in order to detect not only our actual faults, but everything—passions, bad habits, evil tendencies—that can lead to sin, everything that needs conversion.

2. The parable of the workers in the vineyard begins with a repetition of the famous allegory of Isaiah: the vineyard planted by God, the object of his loving care, which at harvest time yields only bitter grapes. God complains: "What more was there to do for my vineyard that I have not done in it?" (Is 5:4). It is a transparent image of the ingratitude of the chosen people who forget the great benefits received from God and turn their backs on him, reaching such hardness of heart that they will repudiate the Son of God, persecuting and crucifying him. Therefore the vineyard will be destroyed, says the prophet; entrusted to other workers, says the gospel. The vineyard of the gospel is the kingdom of God which is offered to Israel, but of which it makes itself unworthy, and so, concludes Jesus: "the kingdom of God will be taken away from you and given to a nation producing the fruits of it" (Mt 21:43).

History continues to repeat itself. Other men have been called by God to fill the places left vacant by the old Israel; God has given his kingdom to these, rewarded them with privileged vocations, surrounded them with loving solicitude, and made them into his new people, the Church; only a few bear the expected fruit, while many do not correspond with his graces. Passions continue to infiltrate the Lord's vineyard, transforming its workers from servants and faithful sons into ungrateful, greedy, rebellious, and traitorous men. Then, will not what happened to Israel be repeated?

The parable urges us to examine our consciences seriously, not to shut our eyes to the troubled ways of passion, to keep careful check on our conduct in order to forestall the inroads of evil. But however much we watch over ourselves and sincerely search into self, we are incapable of discovering every crease and shadow of our heart; we need a greater light which only God can give. This is why our examination of conscience must not be reduced to a cold introspection, but must rather consist in putting ourselves face to face with God to look at ourselves in him, to see ourselves in the light of his truth and infinite goodness, of his eternal love, of his grace and of his countless gifts. Then even the slightest flaws stand out in clearer light, and we feel more strongly urged to repentance and conversion, and at the same time are led to trust more in God than in self.

Come, Lord Jesus, take away scandals from your kingdom, which is my soul, and reign there, you who alone have the right. For avarice comes to claim a throne within me; haughtiness and self-assertion would rule over me; pride would be my king; luxury says, "I will reign"; ambition, detraction, envy, and anger struggle within me for the mastery. I resist as far as I am able; I struggle according as help is given me; I call on my Lord Jesus; for his sake I defend myself, since I acknowledge myself as wholly his possession. He is my God; him I proclaim my Lord; I have no other king than my Lord Jesus Christ!

Come then, O Lord, and disperse these enemies by your power, and you shall reign in me, for you are my King and my God.

St. Bernard *Super "Missus"* 4:2

O you who are full of grace and mercy, purify all sinners of their faults. Cleanse me with hyssop, have mercy on me! In your mercy, forgive me, as you forgave the publican and the sinful woman. O Christ, you who take away sins and welcome all who do penance; O Redeemer of mankind, in your mercy, save me . . .

My sins have crushed me to the ground, they have cast me down from my former heights. I am plunged into ruin as into an abyss. Who can restore my first beauty except you, O most wise Creator, who formed me in the beginning in your image and likeness? By my own will I have become an accomplice of the devil and a slave to sin. Deliver, me, Lord, in your mercy, have pity on me! . . .

I have heard your grace say to sinners: Call upon me and I will hear you, knock and I will open. I am calling now like the sinful woman of the gospel, I am begging like the publican and the prodigal son. I have sinned against heaven and against you . . .

O Savior, free my soul from sin, because my sins have aroused your anger; have pity on me in your mercy.

Hymn of Penance, from *Early Christian Prayers,* 274

124 — THE FATHER AND HIS SONS

"Father, I have sinned . . . I am no longer worthy to be called your son" (Lk 15:21)

1. "Who is a God like you, pardoning iniquity . . . you do not retain your anger forever, because you delight in steadfast love." Thus Micah praises the Lord and begs that "he will again have compassion upon us, . . . tread our iniquities under foot . . . cast all our sins into the depths of the sea" (Mic 7:18-19). This ancient prayer reveals a penetrating sense of God's mercy; nevertheless the Gospel examines it further and offers a vivid commentary in the parable of the prodigal son.

This parable shows that when a man sincerely repents of his sins, even when these are serious enough—abandoning his father's house and leading a dissolute life of impiety and disregard for all law—God wipes these out and forgets them like things that are trodden under foot or cast into the depths of the sea. God created man free, and when, in an act of independence and rebellion like the prodigal son, he leaves home to go and enjoy life in his own way, God does not constrain him to be good, nor hold him back by force, but waits for him, and continues to love him. Like the father in the parable, as soon as he sees him coming back he runs to meet him; in fact he does much more: he anticipates that return by arousing remorse and repentance in the heart of his wayward son—effects of his grace. And when the sinner, yielding to an interior impulse, decides to reform his life, and unburdens himself with a humble and sincere confession of his sins, God immediately welcomes him and makes ready a feast; he restores his rights as a son, clothes him with graces, readmits him to his friendship. "For this my son was dead and is alive again" (Lk 15:24). God rejoices in his life, rejoices to see him pass from the death of sin to the life of grace, rejoices when he returns to his love, the only source of life and of joy.

The parable tells of the immense mercy of God toward sinful man, and also indicates the dispositions the sinner must have to find mercy. The prodigal enters into himself, recognizes his failings and repents of them; he decides to put it all behind him and to go back to his father and confess his guilt; he knows he is unworthy to be welcomed as a son, yet he returns, trusting in his father's loving kindness. It is the same with every sacramental confession: if it is to bear fruit, it must be preceded and accompanied by repentance, and a resolve of amendment, by the humility of a contrite heart and by trust in divine mercy.

2. The parable also speaks of God's mercy for the sons who stayed at home, faithful to their duties, yet somewhat petty and lacking in love. Habit makes them insensible of the benefits of living in their father's house, and of enjoying his continual company. Thus they sin through their indifference to him. They are too sure that they are good sons, very different from the dissolute brothers who have gone off in search of adventure; therefore they sin also through lack of love for those far-off brothers. Since they feel no pain at the absence of these wayward ones, when these return repentant, those at home are surprised, and perhaps even irritated, to see them forgiven so quickly. It is the mentality of the pharisee who condemns the tax collector, and that of the workers of the first hour who are indignant because the last arrivals are treated like themselves.

These elder sons have need of God's mercy too, in order to be healed of their sin, which is so much the more insidious as it is the less recognized. God treats them with the same mercy as he does their prodigal brothers. See the father going out to meet the eldest son who is indignantly refusing to enter the house; he entreats him, listens as he pours out his grievances and protestations of having always been obedient, of having worked so much and yet never have been given even "a kid" with which to make merry with his friends. The father replies: "My son, you are always with me, and all that is mine is yours (Lk 15:31). The father's love is overflowing. When his son claims a kid, he answers simply: "all that is mine is yours"; the son feels unloved because there is no merrymaking for him, and the father answers: "You are always with me"; what festivity can be greater than that? The father would overcome with his own love his son's lack of love; he wants to make him understand that he is loved, but to make him understand also that he must love his brother for "it was fitting to make merry and be glad . . . for he was dead and is alive" (ib. 23). God wants his children alive with his love; it is for this reason that he pursues them, forestalls them, welcomes them and treats them with love. The essential thing is for them to learn to love from him.

The eldest son also needs to confess his sin, and it must be a confession that is made with a contrite heart, humbled at having lived so long in his father's house without having grasped the mystery of his love. To persevere in the service of God is indeed the ideal; but God does not want us to serve him as mercenaries but as sons, and sons must serve from love.

Who is a God like you, pardoning iniquity and passing over transgressions . . . not retaining your anger forever, but rather delighting in steadfast love? Have compassion on us again, Lord, and tread our iniquities under foot. Cast all our sins into the depths of the sea. Show your faithfulness . . . your steadfast love . . . as you swore to our fathers from the days of old.

Micah 7:18-20

Who am I, and what am I? How evil have not my deeds been, or if not my deeds, my words, or if not my words, my will? But you, O Lord, are good and merciful; your right hand has probed the depth of my death, and emptied out that abyss of corruption from the bottom of my heart that so I may no longer will what I myself have willed, but may only will what you have willed . . .

I will love you, O Lord, and thank you, and confess unto your name; because you have forgiven me these so great and heinous deeds of mine. To your grace I ascribe it, and to your mercy, that you have melted away my sins as it were ice. To your grace I ascribe also whatsoever I have not done of evil; for what might I not have done, who even loved a sin for its own sake? Yea, all I confess to have been forgiven me; both what evils I committed by my own wilfulness, and what by your guidance I committed not.

What man is he, who, weighing his own infirmity, dares to ascribe his purity and his innocence to his own strength; that so he should love you the less, as if he had less needed your mercy whereby you remit sins to those that turn to you? . . . Let him love you as much as I do, yea, and more, since he sees me to have recovered from such deep prostration in sin through him, by whom he sees himself to have been preserved from a like entanglement.

St. Augustine, *Confessions* IX 1:1; II 14

125 — THIRD SUNDAY OF LENT

YEAR A

Lord, give me this water that I may not thirst *(Jn 4:15)*

"Give us water to drink!" (Ex 17:2), said the people to Moses when they were irritated by thirst, while in the desert without water. At God's command Moses struck the rock and water gushed out in abundance. "The rock was Christ," affirms St. Paul (1 Cor 10:4); it was a figure of the Messiah who was to be a source, not of material water, but of spiritual water, "living water," offered not to one people only but to all people so that every man might slake his thirst and "never thirst again" (Jn 4:14).

This truth is illustrated in John's gospel by a specific incident. The Samaritan woman thought she was being made fun of when seated at the well Jesus told her: "If you knew the gift of God and who it is that is saying to you, 'Give me a drink,' you would have asked him and he would have given you living water" (ib. 10); she began to question. But the Lord asserted seriously: "Whoever drinks of the water that I shall give him will never thirst; the water that I shall give him will become in him a spring of water, welling up to eternal life" (ib. 14). Whoever receives this water will have within himself a permanent beginning of eternal life, the sanctifying grace that Christ communicates to all who believe in him. He is its inexhaustible source; we need only draw near him to obtain it. We obtain it first of all through baptism which repeats the symbolism of water in its sacramental sign. But in order to drink of this living and life-giving water we must believe. In fact Jesus prolongs his conversation with the woman until he leads her to believe, so much so that she, who had been distrustful at first, returns to her town, full of enthusiasm, to proclaim the Messiah. Baptism and faith are two gifts which are intimately connected: whoever believes may be baptized, and baptism infuses faith. Baptism immerses man in living water which pours out from the torn heart of Christ, water that purifies, quenches thirst, gives life, and becomes in the heart of the believer a "spring of water" which gushes out to eternal life and leads to it.

In speaking of the faith and grace which give man the right to look forward to a vital and eternal communion with God, St. Paul offers its surest guarantee: "hope does not disappoint us, because God's love has been poured into our hearts" (Rom 5:5). Grace, a participation in the divine nature, cannot be separated from God's love, which is the essence of his being, of his life. This love, which is poured out with grace in baptism, is not abstract, but concrete, and involves the faithful soul in that stream of infinite charity which led Christ to die for sinners. Is it possible to doubt such a love? "One will hardly die for a righteous man"—says the Apostle—"though perhaps for a good man one will dare even to die. But God shows his love for us in that while we were yet sinners Christ died for us" (ib. 7-8). The paschal mystery that the Liturgy is preparing to celebrate demonstrates that for man's sake Christ became a fountain of living water, springing forth unto eternal life, precisely through the infinite love which led him to die for man's salvation. To return this love a Christian can do nothing better than to allow himself to be invaded and transformed by grace and love, until he himself becomes like Christ crucified.

O Lord, in order to offer us the mystery of your humility, you sat at the well, and asked the Samaritan woman for a drink. You who were causing the gift of faith to be born in her, deigned to thirst for her faith; by asking her for water you lit within her the fire of the love of God. Therefore we beg of your immense mercy that we may have the strength to forsake the deep darkness of vice and to leave the waters of harmful passions, in order to thirst unceasingly for you who are the fountain of life and the source of goodness.

Ambrosian Preface, from *Early Christian Prayers,* 326

O compassionate and loving Lord of my soul! You likewise say: 'Come to me all who thirst, for I will give you drink.' How can anyone who is burning in the living flames of cupidity for these miserable earthly things fail to experience great thirst? There is an extraordinary need for water so that one might not be completely consumed by this fire.

I already know, my Lord, that out of your goodness you will give it. You yourself say so: your words cannot fail. Well, if those accustomed to living in this fire and to being reared in it, no longer feel it, or, like fools, do not succeed in recognizing their great need, what remedy is there, my God? You have come into the world as a remedy for needs such as these. Begin, Lord! Your compassion must be shown in the most difficult situations. (Soliloquies IX, 1)

Speaking to the Samaritan woman, you said that "whoever drinks of the water you will give will never thirst." How right and true as words coming from the mouth of Truth itself, that such a person will not thirst for anything in this life . . . although thirst for things of the next life increases much more than can ever be imagined through natural thirst. How thirsty one becomes for this thirst! For the soul understands the great value of this thirst. (cf. Way 19:2)

St. Teresa of Jesus

YEAR B

Lord, keep steady my footsteps according to your promise, and let no iniquity get dominion over me (Ps 119:133)

Soon after the Passover—that is, the passage to freedom of the people of Israel from Egypt through the desert to the promised land—God established a covenant with them which was finalized in the gift of the Ten Commandments. "I am the Lord, your God, who brought you out of the land of Egypt, out of the house of bondage. You shall have no other gods before me" (Ex 20:2-3). God's love for Israel, which was proved by his extraordinary intervention in his people's history, is the basis of their trust in their Lord. The Decalogue was not presented as a cold moral law imposed from above by pure authority, but as a law springing from God's love. After freeing his people from physical slavery in Egypt, he desired to free them from all moral slavery to the passions and to sin, in order to bind them to himself in a friendship which, on his part, was expressed in an all powerful and succoring goodness, and, on man's part, in fidelity to the divine will. Besides, the Ten Commandments only make more explicit that law of love—toward God and toward our neighbor—which God had impressed upon man's heart from the creation, but which man had quickly forgotten and distorted. Israel itself did not continue on in the fidelity promised on Sinai: there were many deviations, abandonments, betrayals. And down through the centuries there were many materialistic and formalistic superstructures which emptied the Ten Commandments of their real meaning.

Jesus had to come to restore the ancient law, to complete it, and to perfect it in its inner meaning, especially that of love. Christ's bold action in expelling those who were desecrating the temple has to be considered in this light. God must be served and adored with purity of intention; religion cannot be used as a means toward one's own interests, or selfish ambitions. "Take these things away; you shall not make my Father's house a house of trade" (Jn 2:16). Our relations with God, as with our neighbor, must be absolutely straightforward and sincere; it can happen that in divine worship or in the observance of some point of the Decalogue more attention is paid to the exterior, legalistic side than to the interior; in this case we can become, to a greater or lesser extent, desecrators of the temple, of religion, and of God's law. John notes that Jesus purified the temple by ridding it of the merchants and their goods as "the Passover of the Jews was at hand" (ib. 13). The Church at the approach of Easter, the Christian Pasch, seems to repeat his action by inviting the faithful to purify the temple of their hearts so that a purer worship of God may emerge. But Jesus also spoke of another temple of infinite dignity, the "temple of his body" (ib. 21), and was alluding to this when he said: "Destroy this temple and in three days I will raise it up" (ib. 19); these words, which scandalized the Jews, were understood by his disciples only after his death and resurrection. Through his paschal mystery, Jesus substituted his body for the temple of the Old Covenant—his was a living temple, worthy of the Trinity—which was offered in sacrifice for the salvation of the world, substituting for and annulling all the sacrifices of "oxen and sheep and pigeons" (ib. 14-15) that used to be offered in the temple at Jerusalem, which henceforth would have no reason for being. The heart of the New Covenant is no temple of stone, but "Christ crucified, a stumbling block to the Jews and folly to Gentiles; but to those who are called . . . the power of God and the wisdom of God" (1 Cor 1:23-24).

No insult or noisy condemnation could divert you from your chosen path, O merciful Lord, for you were restoring that which had been lost and brought to ruin. A special victim was being offered to God for the world's salvation, and it was your slaying, O Christ, true lamb, which had been foretold long centuries before, which was to bring the children of the promise to the liberty of the sons of God. The new Covenant was being ratified and the names of the heirs to the eternal kingdom were being written with your blood, O Christ. As supreme High-Priest you made your way into the holy of holies and under cover of your body entered, as the immaculate Priest, to placate God . . . This was the moment of the passage from the law to the gospel, from the synagogue to the Church, from many sacrifices to the one victim (Ser 68:3).

"The old has passed away, and the new has emerged to take its place": through you, O Christ, and, together with you, all who believe in you are one community in your passion and eternal resurrection and are reborn in the Holy Spirit, according to the words of the Apostle: "You have died and your life is hidden with Christ in God. When Christ, your life, is revealed, then you too will appear with him in glory." (Ser 69:4)

St. Leo the Great

YEAR C

Bless the Lord, O my soul, and forget not all his benefits
(Ps 103:2)

At the heart of this Sunday's Liturgy is an invitation to conversion. Its beginning is suggested by the story of Moses' call to be the guide of his people in organizing their departure from Egypt. It came to pass through a theophany, that is through a revelation of God, who showed himself in the burning bush and let Moses hear his voice and who called him by name: "Moses, Moses" (Ex 3:4), to whom he revealed his plan for liberating Israel and whom he commanded to take charge of the undertaking. Thus began the Jews' march across the desert which not only signified their emancipation from slavery to a foreign people but—what was more important—separated them from contact with idolatrous people, purified their customs, and detached them from earthly goods in order to lead them to a purer religion, a more intimate contact with God, and finally to possession of the promised land. The exodus of the chosen people is symbolic of the road of detachment and conversion which we are called upon to follow in a special way during Lent. At the same time the vicissitudes of these people who spent forty years in the desert without ever committing themselves to complete fidelity to God who had so favored them, should serve as a warning to us, the new People of God. St. Paul, recalling the extraordinary blessings which the Jews had enjoyed in the desert, wrote: "all ate the same supernatural food [manna], all drank the same supernatural drink [water which flowed freely from the rock]—nevertheless, with most of them God was not pleased, and they were overthrown in the wilderness" (1 Cor 10—3-5). Such was the unhappy ending of a history of infidelity and broken promises.

To belong to God's people, to have access to the living water of grace, the spiritual food of the Eucharist, and all the other sacraments is no guarantee of salvation if we do not embark upon an intense effort at conversion and total adherence to God. No one can take this for granted, neither in virtue of his position in the Church, nor on the basis of his own virtues or good services rendered: "let anyone who thinks that he stands, take heed lest he fall" (ib. 12).

The community of the faithful hear this same teaching from the mouth of Jesus. When someone referred to a political repression which had mowed down a number of victims, our Lord answered: "Do you think that these Galileans were worse sinners than all the other Galileans because they suffered thus? I tell you, No! But unless you repent you will all likewise perish" (Lk 13:2-3). Severe words, these, which make us understand that God is not deceived; and yet they are words which spring from God's love, for he promotes in every way the salvation of his creatures. Today, God is no longer speaking to his people through Moses, but through his divine Son; he is present, not in a bush which burns without being consumed, but in his only Son, who calls men to repentance and personifies never failing mercy. Because of mercy Jesus prays to his Father to give more time and to wait a little longer so that all may repent; just as the farmer does in the parable when he says to the overseer in regard to a barren fig tree: "Let it alone, Sir, this year also, till I dig about it and put on manure. And if it bears fruit next year, well and good; but if not, you can cut it down" (ib. 8-9). Jesus offers his grace to every soul, he gives it life through the merits of his passion, nourishes it with his Body and Blood, and implores the Father's mercy for it; what more can he do? It is up to each one not to abuse so many benefits, but always to use them better so as to bear the fruit of a genuine Christian life.

Bless the Lord, O my soul, and forget not all his benefits, who forgives all your iniquity, who heals all your diseases . . . The Lord works vindication and justice for all who are oppressed. He made known his ways to Moses, and his deeds to the people of Israel. The Lord is merciful and gracious, slow to anger and abounding in steadfast love . . . For as the heavens are high above the earth, so great is his steadfast love toward those who fear him.

Psalm 103:2-3,6-8,11

Turn around, O Lord, and free my soul . . . convert me, for I feel the difficulty and trouble involved in conversion . . .

It is written: he was in this world, and the world was made by him, and the world knew him not. Therefore if you were in the world and the world did not know you, it is because our impurity would not let us see you. But when we are converted, rather when, through transforming our former way of life, we are able to offer our spirit a new image, we experience how difficult and tiring it is, O Lord, to turn ourselves away from the darkness of earthly passions to the serenity and tranquility of your divine light. And so we say: Turn to us, O Lord, help us to accomplish that conversion within ourselves which will find you ready and waiting to offer yourself for the pleasure of those who love you . . .

Free my soul, which is as if tied to the irresolution of this century and pierced by the thorns of rending desires in the very act of being converted . . . so cure me, not because of my merits, but through your mercy.

St. Augustine, *In Ps.* 6:5

126 — THE LIFE OF BAPTISM

O God, you are light and in you is no darkness; let me walk in the light, as you are in the light *(Jn 1:5,7)*

1. In the history of Naaman, stricken with leprosy and miraculously cured in the waters of the Jordan, we see a figure of baptism, which cleanses man from sin. The waters of the Jordan, which will one day be sanctified by the baptism of Jesus, are a prelude to the baptismal waters which derive their regenerating power from Christ. Just as Naaman, washing in the river, saw his flesh become once again "like the flesh of a little child" (2 Kg 5:14), so in the water of baptism the Christian is reborn to a new life, resplendent in his innocence and grace, like to Adam on the first day of creation.

The sense of baptism's efficacy is so alive in St. Paul that he looks upon it as a definitive death to sin, and considers total abstention from sin itself normal for the Christian. He writes to the Romans: "You also must consider yourselves dead to sin . . . sin will have no dominion over you" (Rom 6:11,14).

However, baptism does not confirm us in grace; it washes away sin, but leaves us in our state of debility and frailty, so that abstention from sin is the fruit of continuous struggle against evil and of daily faithfulness to grace. Here we discover the need to employ to advantage the purifying and regenerative quality of baptism, by making room for it in our life, and letting it sink into the depth of our being. Wherever we detect vicious tendencies within ourselves—selfishness, pride, vanity, greed, laziness, envy, and such things—this is the area where we need to open ourselves to the grace of baptism, so that it may cleanse us; this is where we must cooperate with a generous effort of renunciation and detachment. "If any man would come after me, let him deny himself and take up his cross, and follow me. For whoever would save his life will lose it, and whoever loses his life for my sake will find it" (Mt 16:24-25). These requirements for the following of Christ involve us from the day of our baptism, and in the grace of baptism which makes us participants in the death of our Lord we find the strength to put them into practice.

2. Baptism has not only a negative efficacy, that of purifying us from sin, but a highly positive one as well: to form us into children of God. Those who are born again "of water and the spirit" (Jn 3:5) are the sons of God. Considering the fullness of this rebirth, St. John of the Cross writes: "To be reborn in the spirit during this life is to become more like God in purity, without any mixture of imperfection. Accordingly pure transformation can be effected—although not essentially—through the participation of union" (Asc. II 5:5). Here the mystical Doctor is pointing out the highest peak to which the full development of baptismal grace can lead. The first and fundamental requirement is an integral interior purity, because divine life, in which we participate through grace, cannot enter and completely transform a soul unless it finds it absolutely pure. The soul, says St. John of the Cross, is like a window pierced by a ray of sunlight; although the ray is brilliant of itself, capable of illuminating and penetrating the glass, it cannot do so unless the glass is totally clean and pure. Moreover, "the less film and stain are wiped away, the less the window will be illuminated; and the cleaner the window is, the brighter will be its illumination" (ib. 6). God is the divine sun which shines upon souls, anxious to invade them and penetrate them, even to transforming them through his light and his love; but for this to happen, man must resolve to rid himself of "every shadow and spot" of sin. At the moment that God finds a soul free from any attachment to sin, he quickly fills it with himself, with his own life; this is the beginning, the germ of the great transformation which the Lord wants to bring about in it. And the more we cleanse ourselves of every sin, of every faulty habit, of every imperfection, the more we make ourselves ready for total penetration and transformation by divine grace. In this way baptism gradually works in us that deep rebirth and full transformation that makes us like to God, living

by his very life, as a son is like to his father and lives by the life he has received from his father.

Lord our God, . . . bless this water; it makes the seed to grow, it refreshes us and makes us clean.
You have made of it a servant of your loving kindness: through water you set your people free, and quenched their thirst in the desert. With water the prophets announced a new covenant that you would make with man. By water, made holy by Christ in the Jordan, you make our sinful nature new in the bath that gives rebirth.
Let this water remind us of our baptism; let us share the joys of our brothers who are baptized in this Easter of Christ our Lord.

Roman Missal, Paschal Vigil, Blessing of Easter water

O Lord God, holy and true, my Creator and my Redeemer, who has signed me with the holy light of your countenance, redeemed me at the dear price of the blood of your only Begotten, and regenerated me unto the hope of life through baptism in the power of your Spirit, make me renounce Satan and all his pomps and all his works in very truth, with a sincere and perfect heart. Make me faithfully believe, with true and burning faith crowned with living works, . . . and cause me to cleave unto you and to go steadfastly with you unto the end.
O Lord Jesus Christ, high Priest, who by your precious death did give me life, deign with the power of your Spirit to rid me of all the wiles of the enemy by the efficacy of your presence. Rend asunder within me all the snares of the enemy and in your mercy banish from me all blindness of heart. O Christ, may your perfect charity make me triumph manfully over every temptation . . . May your radiant truth lead me onward and make me walk before you with a sincere and perfect heart.
Through your help may I so conduct myself that I may deserve to become the temple of God and the dwelling place of the Holy Spirit.

St. Gertrude *Exercises* 1

127 — HUMBLE AND TRUSTFUL

O Lord, there will be no shame for those who trust in you
(Dan 3:17)

1. "For we, O Lord, have become fewer than any nation, and brought low this day in all the world because of our sins . . . Yet with a contrite heart and a humble spirit may we be accepted" (Dan 3:14-16). During Lent the Church makes its own the prayer of Azariah who so humbly recognizes his people's offenses and with equal trust begs God's forgiveness and mercy. We Christians also need to acknowledge our offenses, and to confess that some of

the deviations of the modern world are due to our unfaithfulness, and the inconsistency of our way of living in relation to the principles of the gospel. We need to humble ourselves, individually and collectively, and to accept humbly, in a spirit of expiation, the consequences of our sins, but at the same time to turn trustfully to God, imploring for ourselves and for all the grace of pardon and of conversion.

Inspired by the prayer of Azariah, the priest says in the name of all the faithful after the presentation of the offerings: "Lord God, we ask you to receive us and be pleased with the sacrifice we offer you with humble and contrite hearts" (RM). Christian humility does not shut up a person within himself, nor lead to discouragement nor to doubt of God's mercy, but brings him to God with the confidence of a son. A son is sure of his father's love, he knows that his father is always ready to forgive him, provided he comes with a contrite heart, desirous of leading a better life. Azariah's prayer continues: "Now with all our heart we follow you, we fear you and seek your face . . . Deal with us in your forbearance and in your abundant mercy" (Dan 17-18). These are the dispositions God wants to see in his children after they have sinned: humility, purpose of amendment, trust in his mercy. Just because we have experienced that we cannot count on our own strength, we take refuge in God with full confidence, certain of finding in him the help we need to rise up from sin and to keep our resolutions. And in truth, although God resists the proud, "he leads the humble in what is right, and teaches the humble his way" (Ps 25:9).

2. "Humility, however deep it may be, neither disquiets nor troubles nor disturbs the soul; it is accompanied by peace, joy, and tranquillity . . . it enlarges it and makes it fit to serve God better." On the contrary, the devil's humility "only disturbs and upsets the mind and troubles the soul, so grievous is it. I think the devil is anxious for us to believe that we are humble, and, if he can, to lead us to distrust God." (*Way* 39:2). Lack of trust and anxiety lessen our capacity to love; the devil's purpose is precisely to draw us away from the path of love. He especially tempts in this way those who would never yield to open temptations to sin. In such a case our reaction should be to remember, as St. Therese of the Child Jesus teaches, that "what offends Jesus, what wounds his heart, is want of trust" (Let 71).

A lack of trust in God's mercy, even after serious falls, is never an indication of true humility, but rather of insidious pride and diabolical temptation. Had Judas been humble, instead of giving way to despair, he would have known, like Peter, how to beg forgiveness and to bewail his sins. Humility is the virtue that puts man in his proper place before God, which is that of a son, a weak and wretched one, yes, but one full of trust. When, after so many good resolutions, a soul find itself continuing to fall into the same faults, and after many more attempts still does not succeed in overcoming certain defects, it should humble itself, rather than be angry with itself. St. Teresa of Jesus says that "humility is the ointment for our wounds" (IC III 2:7). God let us experience our weakness precisely to give us a keener awareness of our indigence, so that we may be stripped of all presumptuous confidence in self, and turn to him with greater humility and trust.

Humility should also manifest itself in our relations with our neighbor, especially in our readiness to forgive. The proud man ties a string on his finger (as it were) as a reminder of every injury received and exacts amends for it, and when he does forgive it is with a gesture of condescension. On the other hand the humble man makes little of any wrongs done to him, he forgives even before he is asked, and realizing how much he himself needs mercy, he does not weigh things with his brother, nor count how many times he has already forgiven him. To him the words of the Lord will apply: "If you forgive men their trespasses, your heavenly Father also will forgive you" (Mt 6:14).

For your name's sake, do not give us up utterly, and do not break your covenant. Do not withdraw your mercy from us . . . For we, O Lord, have become fewer than any nation, and are brought low this day in all the world because of our sins . . . Yet with a contrite heart and a humble spirit may we be accepted . . . Such may our sacrifice be in your sight this day, and may we wholly follow you; for there will be no shame for those who trust in you. And now with all our heart we follow you, we fear you and we seek your face. Do not put us to shame, but deal with us in your forbearance and in your abundant mercy.

Daniel 3:11-19, *Prayer of Azariah*

Jesus, I repeat, filled with confidence, the publican's humble prayer. Most of all I imitate the conduct of Magdalene; her astonishing or rather her loving audacity which charms the Heart of Jesus also attracts my own. Yes, I feel it; even though I had on my conscience all the sins that can be committed, I would go, my heart broken with sorrow, and throw myself into Jesus' arms, for I know how much he loves the prodigal child who returns to him. It is not because God, in his anticipating mercy, has preserved my soul from mortal sin that I go to him with confidence and love . . .

St. Therese of the Child Jesus *Autobiographical Writings* p. 258

128 — PERFECT HOLOCAUST

I have come to do your will, O God *(Heb 10:7)*

1. God's word does not change. The Ten Commandments given to Moses are perfected, but also reconfirmed by Jesus when he declared: "not an iota, not a dot, will pass from the law until all is accomplished" (Mt 5:18). Jesus is teaching us to observe the law

with a new spirit of love and interiority, but the law still remains in its essential elements an expression of the immutable will of God. For this reason it is loving faithfulness to the law that will decide our eternal fate. "Whoever relaxes one of the least of these commandments . . . shall be called least in the kingdom of heaven; but he who does them . . . shall be called great" (ib. 19). We are great, not when we free ourselves from God, but when we carry out his will; when we adhere to the will of God, we partake of his holiness, his goodness and his wisdom. The law of God, said Moses to Israel, "is your wisdom and your understanding" (Dt 4:6).

In order to establish their lives in a continuous communion of love with God's will and hence with God himself, some of the faithful freely and spontaneously bind themselves to him by consecrating their wills to him. Their love is not satisfied with adhering to the divine will only when there is an obligation to do so, such as to observe the commandments or to accept circumstances dictated by providence; they desire to put their entire life at God's disposal for whatever he wishes. Here we see the vow of obedience, through which "religious . . . offer God a total dedication of their own wills as a sacrifice of themselves" (PC 14). In practice this demands continual renunciation of one's own will, not indeed through constraint but willed and freely offered to God "as a sacrifice of oneself," in view of an infinitely higher good: unceasing communion with God. Through his will, man controls himself and is capable of running his own life and making use of his freedom; therefore when he gives his whole will to God in an act of love, he is accomplishing a complete sacrifice of self. He no longer belongs to himself, he belongs to God, and he is no longer free to do as he chooses because he has chosen God as the one and only sovereign Lord of his life. The vow of obedience is a perfect holocaust, in which the sacrificial offering of the whole man is carried out.

2. While the other religious vows—poverty and chastity—offer God a part of man—worldly possessions and the use of sex—the vow of obedience takes hold of him at the root of his being—his will—and thereby completes and perfects his offering, his sacrifice. It is a sacrifice that can cost nature a great deal, but when carried out with fullness of love, it gives in exchange the greatest of blessings; it unites man to the will of God "with greater steadiness and security" (PC 14). Union with God is the precious fruit of the vow of obedience when lived faithfully. Furthermore, since obedience puts a man's entire life under the will of God, it opens it wide to the divine outpouring. St. John of the Cross says: "God communicates himself more to the soul more advanced in love, that is, more conformed to his will" (Asc II 5:4). Generous obedience is the surest and shortest way to reach this blessed conformity.

The will of God in regard to man is unescapably constant, it always seeks his salvation; God "desires all men to be saved" (1 Tim 2:4). It follows that to be united to the will of God is to be united to his "saving purpose" as the Council puts it (PC 14); it is to enter into the divine plan for the salvation of the world. Hence by its nature the vow of obedience has an apostolic dimension which establishes the individual before God in an attitude similar to that of Jesus. Through obedience the religious offers God the sacrifice of himself, following the pattern of Jesus Christ who came to "do the Father's will" (ib.) and gave his own life for the salvation of men. The offering of self in perfect obedience associates the religious with the work and redemptive immolation of Christ. This apostolic value is so intrinsic to the vow of obedience that it is present even when the religious exercises no exterior activity, whether because of having embraced the purely contemplative life or of some particular personal circumstances. The sacrifice of self through obedience has for its purpose putting one's life in God's hands in order to cooperate with Christ and in Christ for the salvation of our brothers. Each one achieves this end in proportion to the individual level of his union with the will of God.

Behold, O Lord, I give myself to you; for your good pleasure I join myself to Jesus in his entire submission to you in everything: "I do always the things that please you." Because I love you I will give you the homage that consists in submitting my whole being to your will whatever it may be. I wish to say in union with your Son Jesus: "I do as the Father has commanded me . . . (because) I love" (Jn 14:31). This will may perhaps be painful to my nature, to my tastes; it may be opposed to my personal ideal, hard to my spirit of independence, but I want to offer you this sacrifice as testimony of my faith in your word, of my confidence in your power, and of the love I bear to you and to your Son Jesus.

C. Marmion, *Christ, the Ideal of the Monk* 12:11 (p. 288)

O Jesus, who were "obedient unto death," you would not have one that loves you well take any other road than that which you yourself took.

O Lord, teach us to trust your words: "He who hears you, hears me" and to pay no further attention to our own wishes. You attach such great importance to this submissiveness (and rightly so, for it makes you Lord of the free will that you have given us) that if we practice it, now entirely annihilating our own desires, now winning only after a thousand battles, and thinking the judgment given in our case to be folly, we shall come, by means of this painful exercise, to resign ourselves entirely to doing what we are commanded. We shall do it in the end, whether it costs us pain or no, and you, for your part, will help us so much that, just because we submit our will and reason to you, you will make us masters of them. Then, being masters of ourselves, we shall be able to employ ourselves wholly in your service, making you a complete surrender of our will so that you may unite it with your own, beseeching you that the fire of your love may come down from heaven and consume this sacrifice . . . For there will be nothing more left for us to do, since we shall have laid our gifts on the altar.

cf St. Teresa of Jesus, *Foundations* 5:3, 12

129 — OBEDIENT WITH CHRIST

O Lord, may I follow you, becoming obedient even to death on a cross *(Phil 2:8)*

1. "This command I gave them: Obey my voice! . . . But they did not obey, or incline their ear, but walked in their own counsels and the stubbornness of their evil hearts and went backward and not forward" (Jer 7:23-24). Thus did God complain to Jeremiah about the disobedience of the old Israel. And the new Israel, to which God has spoken not through the prophets, but through his divine Son, is not immune from the same sin. Unfortunately it can also be said of many who call themselves Christians: "Truth has perished; it is cut off from their lips" (ib. 28).

When viewed in this framework, the vow of obedience is also seen as reparation for the resistance which the modern world opposes to the word of God, to his law and to his will. The Son of God was specifically sent to expiate this capital sin, and through their vow of obedience, religious associate themselves with his redeeming and saving expiation. "Christ"—says the Council—"to carry out the will of the Father . . . inaugurated the kingdom of heaven on earth . . . and by his obedience brought about redemption" (LG 3). Christ's life is wholly a mystery of obedience to his Father, of unconditional dedication to his will. We are not dealing with a joyful obedience, but with a difficult one that knows the bitterness of suffering. Christ wanted to become like man to the point of experiencing the pain of obedience when practiced under the most difficult and humiliating circumstances; "although he was a son, he learned obedience through what he suffered" (Heb 5:8), affirms St. Paul. Obedience made him accept Judas' betrayal, the agony of Gethsemani, abandonment by his closest friends; obedience handed him over to the soldiers, led him to judgment, burdened him with the cross, dragged him up Calvary, and finally made him, of his own will, stretch his arms upon the cross to die as a criminal. Having come into the world out of obedience, Christ wanted to live and to die in obedience, and thus "he became the source of eternal salvation to all who obey him" (ib. 9).

Religious obedience, which is communion with the salvific will of the Father, is also communion with the obedience of Christ, in whom that will is carried out. The gospel's counsel of obedience is the gift Jesus offers to those whom he wants to associate most intimately and effectively with his redemptive mission.

2. The vow of obedience means participation in the total submission to the Father for the salvation of the brethren. Obedience like this cannot be inspired by nature. God created man free; and man, although moving in the ambit of the divine commandments, has the right to rule himself as he likes. Liberty is so great a gift that no one may sacrifice it by subjecting himself to a life of unconditional obedience such as Christ's was, except by an intimate inspiration and motion of grace. The Council states very clearly that religious, following "the pattern of Jesus Christ . . . embrace obedience under the influence of the Holy Spirit" (PC 14). This expression echoes the words of the gospel that shows Jesus as "led by the Spirit" (Lk 4:1). Christ's obedience to the Father is never forced; if as the Word his will is but one with that of the Father, as man, he accepts the divine will with a wholehearted and loving adherence under the impulse of the Holy Spirit. Religious who are moved by that same divine Spirit, are being introduced to the mystery of Christ's obedience, so loving, spontaneous, and total. With this interior attitude, they "submit themselves to their superiors, whom faith presents as God's representatives, and through whom they are guided into the service of all their brothers in Christ. Thus did Christ himself, out of submission to the Father, minister to the brethren" (PC 14). The submission of Jesus to the Father is the model of the submission a religious owes his superiors. He accepts and respects his superior from a supernatural motive, in that he "takes the place of God", and is the mediator of the divine will. God makes use of superiors to manifest his will; and in obeying his superiors, the religious obeys God. Just as Jesus accomplished his earthly mission in full dependence on the will of the Father, so the religious carries out his activity "under the guidance" of superiors. The more he lets himself be led by the Holy Spirit in submitting to his superiors, the more his obedience acquires the gentleness of love.

O Christ, I love to contemplate your obedient charity, the purest, absolutely free, and completely spontaneous interior act, with which you offered yourself in obeying, in laying down your life, and in taking it up again, because such was the Father's commandment . . .

Both your charity and your obedience make me participate in your death and resurrection, and my soul is submerged in this ocean of charity and wholly taken into your obedience which I feel made mine within me; let this, my own obedience, be taken into and carried off in your offering, O my Master, so that I lose myself in you. O my Christ, O charity-obedience, living obedience, . . . what shall I say? Capture me, O Christ, in your obedience, like a leaf in a whirlwind . . . that I may disappear in you. I hide my life in you that it may be offered in your obedience, and be found again with you on the altar in heaven to which your holy Angel carries your Sacrifice.

G. Canovi; *Suscipe, Domine*

O Lord, how different are your ways from our clumsy imaginings! When a soul is resolved to love you and has resigned itself into your hands, you will have nothing of it save that it shall obey you and find out for itself how it may best serve you and desire to do so. It has no need to look for paths or to choose them, for its will is yours. You, my Lord, take upon yourself the task of guiding it in the way which is the greatest benefit to it. And even though our superior has no mind to our soul's profit . . . you, my God have a mind to our profit and dispose the soul and prepare things for it to do in such a way that, without knowing how, we find ourselves so much more spiritual and so greatly benefited that we are astonished.

St. Teresa of Jesus, *Foundations* 5:2 (Peers)

130 — RENUNCIATION AND DETACHMENT

O Lord, take me out of the net which is hidden for me, for you are my refuge (Ps 31:4)

1. "Return, O Israel, to the Lord your God; for you have stumbled because of your iniquity" (Hos 14:1). During the Lenten season, the Church continues to call her children to conversion with the words of the ancient prophets. Such an invitation concerns everyone: sinners hardened by evil, the lukewarm, the indifferent, and also those who are dedicated to the spiritual life, that all may attain to a deeper interior purification. Just as Israel, when exhorted by Hosea, promised God to return to the purity of its worship, abandoning all idols—"We will say no more 'our God' to the work of our hands"—so the Christian should welcome the invitation of the Church by resolving on total detachment from everything that might stand in the way of his giving himself to God. It remains true that man tends to create idols for himself, whether large or small, which rob his heart and his life of what should be given to God. The first of these idols is created within him according to the measure in which he seeks that which satisfies his selfishness, pride, vanity, greed, or inordinate desire for affection. At the same time his passions easily lead him to attach himself to persons and things which become other idols. Thus man remains divided in his affections and vital energies, and is therefore incapable of giving himself totally to God. If he is pledged by his vocation to a life of sanctity and union with the Lord, this condition blocks the way to it, and instead of making progress he remains stranded. Any voluntary attachment, however small, is a bond which holds us back from advancing toward God, and prevents us from reaching perfect union.

"For me"—says St. John of the Cross—"it makes little difference whether a bird is tied by a thin thread or by a cord. For even if tied by thread, the bird will be prevented from taking off just as surely as if it were tied by cord—that is, it will be impeded from flight as long as it does not break the thread. Admittedly the thread is easier to rend, but no matter how easily this may done, the bird will not fly away without first doing so." (Asc. 11:4) Many souls are in this condition; they desire to give themselves to God, they let themselves be entrapped by a multitude of petty attachments and imperfect habits. Only a generous renunciation can break these bonds and give full liberty of spirit.

2. "Although he was made by God in a state of holiness, from the very dawn of history man abused his liberty, at the urging of personified Evil. Man set himself against God and sought to find fulfillment apart from God" (GS 13). What is needed in order to reconquer our lost holiness and to reestablish our communion with God, is a pathway back to him, the path of detachment and total renunciation. This is demanded by baptism; for the grace of baptism really brings us to a new life in Christ, and makes it necessary for us to die to all that can lead to sin and is in any way in contrast with the holiness of Christ. It is demanded by the First Commandment, which was given by God in the Old Testament and confirmed by Jesus in the New: "The Lord our God is the Lord alone; and you shall love the Lord your God with all your heart, and with all your soul, and with all your mind, and with all your strength" (Mk 12:29-30). That word "all", so insistently repeated, means that "nothing" must stand in the way of, or lessen, our love for God. If our heart is occupied with inordinate affection for self or for others, it cannot love with all its strength. The law of charity reciprocally calls for the total renunciation of every affection which is not in accord with love of God and which cannot be absorbed into such love. Man "has only one will", says St. John of the Cross, which "if encumbered or occupied by anything will not possess the freedom . . . and purity requisite for the divine transformation" (Asc. I 11:6). When we are attached to created beings we become their slaves and instead of finding creatures a help in going to God, we find them an obstacle, an obstruction. This is why the Saint insists: "To come to possess all [God], desire the possession of nothing . . . When you turn toward something, you cease to cast yourself upon the all" (ib. 13:11,12).

Even the commandment to love our neighbor—"you shall love your neighbor as yourself" (Mk 12:31)—has analogous requirements, and, to be observed fully, exacts a generous renunciation of selfishness. Renunciation and detachment are not holiness, but they are indispensable conditions for attaining it, precisely because they make possible fullness of love.

Lord, seeing our wretchedness and your promise of a cure, we are quick to answer: Here we are, because you are the Lord our God . . . We were called and have answered: Here we are before you. We will show by our deeds that, since we have promised to be yours, we are subject to no one else but you, and so we say: Because you, O Lord, are our God. And indeed we recognize no other god: not the belly, like gluttons whose god is the belly. Not money, like the greedy, because avarice is idolatry. Nor do we deify and adore anything else as god, as many do; you, O God, are above all, through all, in all; and we are bound by the charity which unites us to you. Yes, charity unites us to God. Again we say: We are here before you, because you, Lord, are our God.

Origen from *Early Christian Prayers,* 64

It is a great evil when after you bring a soul to yourself it approaches and becomes attached to some earthly thing . . . When we do not give ourselves to you with the determination with which you give yourself to us, you do a great deal by leaving us in mental prayer and visiting us from time to time like servants in your vineyard. But these others [who are detached from everything] are favored children. You would not want them to leave your side, nor do you leave them, for they no longer want to leave you. You seat them at your table, you share with them your own food . . .

Oh, blessed renunciation of things so small and base that reaches so high a state . . . Your love for those who love you is not small. Why should we not show our love for you as much as we can? Consider what a wonderful exchange it is if we give you our love and receive yours. And what is it that we do for you, O Lord our Maker? We do hardly anything at all—just some poor weak resolution. And if you are pleased that by doing a mere nothing we should win everything, let us not be so foolish as to fail to do it.

St. Teresa of Jesus *Way* 16:8-10

131 — THOSE WHO HUMBLE THEMSELVES

O Lord, you deliver a humble people, but the haughty eyes you bring down (Ps 18:27)

1. Our Lord recounted the parable of the Pharisee and the tax collector "to some who trusted in themselves that they were righteous and despised others" (Lk 18:9). It is easy for man to fall into this temptation, and it can be particularly easy for those who profess a devout life. The fact that they observe God's law, practice exercises of piety, give alms, and perhaps also perform some penances can arouse in souls that are not cleansed of pride a certain sense of self-sufficiency. Such appear before God with head held high, with the secret conviction of having a kind of right to be listened to in preference to the many others who are "extortioners, unjust, adulterers" (ib. 11). But God thinks differently, and puts the publican, who is a sinner, but humble, ahead of the Pharisee, who is full of himself. This publican "would not even lift his eyes to heaven; but beat his breast, saying 'God, be merciful to me, a sinner!' " (ib. 13). Considering only external behavior the moral position of the Pharisee is without question superior to that of the tax collector; but in his heart there is the worm of pride which kills

charity: this man does not love either God or his neighbor. Instead of praising God and testifying to his love for him, he praises himself and loves his own excellence; instead of showing love for neighbor, he despises the tax collector. In the latter there is no charity either, for moral disorder has destroyed it; but there is humility: he is aware of his wretchedness, he is sorry for it and repents and calls upon God's mercy. And God, seeing the sincere feelings of his heart, justifies him; humility works the miracle: it reinstates him in charity. The opposite happens to the Pharisee: he remains locked in his pride and God's grace does not reach him. "For everyone who exalts himself will be humbled, but he who humbles himself will be exalted" (ib. 14). The parable is a powerful reminder of the value of humility which no other moral value can replace. Prayer itself is not pleasing to God unless it rises from a humble heart which recognizes, with simplicity and frankness, its own wretchedness before the Most High.

2. "God opposes the proud but gives grace to the humble" (Jas 4:6). In these few words is contained the great importance of humility, which rids the human heart of pride and of self-love, and opens it to God, his love and his grace. Holiness consists of love because only love can unite man to God; but humility is the foundation, because it prepares the ground for charity, and digs out space for it. Humility is to love what a foundation is to a building. Excavating the foundation of a house is not the same as building it, but it is the indispensable preliminary to doing so. The deeper and stronger the foundation, the higher can the house be built without fear of its collapsing. "This whole building"—says St. Teresa of Jesus—"has humility as its foundation. If humility is not genuinely present, for your own sake the Lord will not construct a high building lest that building fall to the ground." (IC. VII 4:8)

To the extent that humility empties the soul of the vain and proud pretenses of self, it makes room for God. And when the spiritual person "is brought to nothing, the highest degree of humility, the spiritual union between his soul and God will be effected. This union is the most noble and sublime state attainable in this life" (Asc. 7:11). It follows that the higher the ideal of sanctity and of union with God to which a soul aspires, the deeper it must descend to dig out in itself an abyss of humility to attract the abyss of infinite mercy. We must humble ourselves "under the mighty hand of God" (1 Pet 5:6), sincerely acknowledge our own nothingness, and become aware of our indigence; whoever wants to praise himself, let him do so—like St. Paul—only in regard to his weaknesses, so that God's power may rest upon him. Because when a man is weak and accepts it, then he is strong. (2 Cor 12:9-10)

The lofty ideal of union with God totally surpasses our human capacity; if a soul can aspire to it, it is not through reliance on its own virtues, but only because of confidence in God's help; for he has "exalted those of low degree, he has filled the hungry with good things, and the rich he has sent empty away" (Lk 1:52-53).

The greater you are, the more you must humble yourself; so you will find favor in the sight of the Lord. For great is the might of the Lord; he is glorified by the humble ... hasty judgment has led many astray.

There is one who is slow and needs help, who lacks strength and abounds in poverty; but the eyes of the Lord look upon him for his good; he lifts him out of his low estate and raises up his head, so that many are amazed at him.

Sirach 3:18-20,24; 11:12-13

O Lord, what good have I merited, I, a sinner? What good have I deserved? One Adam is descended from another, and in each Adam sins appear. I am a son of Adam ... and during my wicked lifetime I have added more wrongdoing to Adam's sin. Have I deserved anything that is good, I who was another Adam? Yet in your mercy you have loved me, not because I was in any way beautiful, but to make me so. (In Ps. 132:10)

If I seek what is my own, I find sin. If I seek what I have of my own, I find falsehood. Take away sin, and everything else you see in me is yours (Ser. 32:10).

Not to me, O Lord, not to me, but to your name give glory. Give me life for love of your name: according to your justice and not according to mine; not because I deserve it, but because you are merciful. If I should wish to pretend to some merit, except for you I would merit the utmost condemnation. You tore away my pretended merits and grafted on your gifts (In Ps. 142:18).

St. Augustine

O King of heaven, there is no queen like humility for making you surrender. Humility drew you from heaven to the womb of the Virgin, and with it ... we will draw you to our souls. And realize that the one who has more humility will be the one who possesses you more, and the one who has less will possess you less.

St. Teresa of Jesus, *Way* 16:2

132 — FOURTH SUNDAY OF LENT

YEAR A

Jesus, light of the world, following you may I not walk in darkness, but have the light of life (Jn 8:12)

The central theme of today's Mass is Jesus "the light"; consequently the Christian is "the son of the light". "I am the light of the world"—said the Lord—"he who follows me will not walk in darkness, but will have the light of life" (Jn 8:12); soon afterwards he demonstrated in practice the reality of this assertion by restoring the sight of the man born blind. Our Lord performed this miracle without being asked; the initiative was entirely his, and it was done with a definite purpose: "We must work the works of him who sent me while it is day . . . As long as I am in the world, I am the light of the world" (Jn 9:4-5). Jesus is the bright day, the light that drives away the darkness of the world, and the purpose of the miracle is to convince men of this. With saliva he made a little mud, spread it on the eyes of the man born blind, and sent him to wash in the pool of Siloam. "So he went and washed, and came back seeing" (ib. 7). This striking wonder was only the beginning of the profound transformation that Jesus desired to accomplish in this man. The physical light given to eyes in darkness was the sign and means of the light of the Spirit which our Lord instilled in him, to arouse in him an act of faith: " 'Do you believe in the Son of Man? . . . Lord, I do believe!' And he worshiped him" (ib. 35,38). Everything was changed for the man who had been born blind. For one who has always lived in darkness, acquiring sight was like a new birth, the beginning of a completely new existence: new acquaintances, new emotions, new viewpoints. And much more took place in his soul, which was now enlightened by such a strong faith that he resisted, unperturbed, the heckling and the insults of the Jews, who went so far as to "cast him out" of the synagogue (ib. 34).

All this is a figure of the radical transformation that takes place in the baptized. "For once you were darkness, but now you are light in the Lord" (Eph 5:8). By means of the sacrament we pass from the darkness of sin to the light of life in Christ, from spiritual blindness to knowledge of God through faith, which illuminates the whole of human existence, giving it new perceptions and new orientations. The result is that we "walk as children of light, for the fruit of light is found in all that is good and right and true" (ib. 8-9). The Christian must bear witness in his conduct to the baptism he has received, he must testify with deeds that for him Christ is not only the light of his mind, but the "light of his life." One who is baptized is no longer concerned with the works of darkness—sin—but with the works of light.

"Awake, O sleeper, and arise from the dead, and Christ shall give you light" (ib. 14). These words, quoted from St. Paul (and taken, it would seem, from a baptismal hymn) invited catechumens to rise from sleep, that is from the death of sin, to be enlightened by Christ. The same exhortation still applies—in fact with greater reason—to those who were baptized years ago; for everyone, the Christian life must truly be an incessant and progressive purification from every trace of sin, with the aim of opening us more and more to the light of Christ. Precisely because Christ is the light of the world, we are called to reflect his light and to make it shine in our own lives. This is the grace the community implores today at the conclusion of Mass: "O God, who enlighten every man who comes into the world, make the light of Christ shine in us, so that our thoughts may always be directed toward what is worthy of you and pleasing to you; that we may love you with all sincerity" (RM).

O Christ our Lord, through the mystery of your incarnation you became guide to man who was walking in darkness, and you led him to the light of faith. Through the sacrament of baptism you have freed us from the slavery of original sin in order to raise us to the dignity of children of God. For these marvels of your love we praise you.

cf *Roman Missal, Preface*

It is you, eternal light, light of wisdom, veiled in the flesh, who say to every one: "I am the light of the world; he who follows me, will not walk in darkness, but will have the light of life."

If I follow the earthly sun, no matter what I do to keep it in sight, it will leave me behind, since it must finish its appointed course each day. But you, our Lord Jesus Christ, although you are not revealed to all since you are veiled in the flesh, still you hold all things under the power of your wisdom. My God, you are everywhere whole and entire; and if I do not separate myself from you, you will never disappear from me.

O Lord, I burn with longing for the light, as you know, for my every desire is before you, and no groaning of mine is hidden from you. Who sees my desire, if not you, O my God? In order to have you, to whom can I turn but to you? Let my soul be enlarged through this great desire, make it stretch forward and become ever more capable of receiving what no eye sees, what no ear hears, and what no human heart has yet experienced!

cf St. Augustine, *In Io* 34:5-7

YEAR B

Give thanks to the Lord for he is good, for his mercy endures forever (Ps 36:1)

The Liturgy of the word continues to draw on the history of Israel for concrete lessons on the necessity of conversion and on God's mercy which ever pursues man in order to lead him to salvation. In spite of the continuing unfaithfulness of the Hebrews, even of their leaders and priests, God "sent persistently to them by his messengers, because he had compassion on his people . . . But they kept mocking his messengers and . . . scoffing at his prophets, till the wrath of the Lord rose against his people, till there was no remedy" (2 Chron 36:15-16). Then punishment followed, with the destruction of the temple and the deportation to Babylon. It is a history which, in spite of so many bitter experiences, is still repeated today in the life of nations, families and individuals. The more a man lets his passions dominate him, the more he closes himself to the word of God, rejects his messengers, distorts the truth, and suppresses the voice of his conscience, until he ends by living in discord with God, with himself, and with his neighbor. Out of all this come antagonisms, dissensions, struggles at every level. It is a real grace when we succeed in recognizing in such calamities the divine punishment of our excesses. "The wrath of the Lord" of which Scripture speaks is yet another manifestation of his mercy which punishes us in order to bring us to repentance.

However the New Testament makes it evident that now God punishes us only after he has exhausted the last resources of his infinite love. "God who is rich in mercy, out of the great love with which he loved us even when we were dead through our trespasses, made us alive together with Christ" (Eph 2:4-5). This is the supreme act of God's mercy; instead of punishing the sins of ungrateful man in man himself, who is always falling back into sin, he punishes man's sin in his only Son, so that by believing in Christ crucified, man may find salvation. "By grace you have been saved!" . . . —exclaims St. Paul—"By grace you have been saved through faith; and this is not your own doing, it is the gift of God" (ib. 5-8). It is an absolutely free gift, that no created being could ever have hoped for or deserved. Yet for two thousand years this gift has been at hand for all mankind; in order to benefit from it, we have only to believe in Christ, accepting salvation from him and adhering to his gospel. God had offered the free gift of salvation to the Jews also, as, for instance, when, in order to free them from poisonous serpents, he had ordered Moses to lift up a brazen serpent, so that when anyone who had been bitten by the serpents looked upon the brazen serpent, he was saved from death. But that was but a pale image of the salvation brought by Jesus, who was raised upon the cross "that whoever believes in him may have eternal life" (Jn 3:15). Today's Gospel continues: "God sent the Son into the world, not to condemn the world, but that the world might be saved through him" (ib. 17). There will still be judgment, but it will be one that man will bring upon himself, because just as "he who believes in (Christ) is not condemned," so also "he who does not believe is condemned already" (ib. 18). Whoever rejects Christ the Redeemer, whoever denies him, excludes himself by his own act from salvation, and God's judgment will only ratify his choice. "The immeasurable riches" of the grace and kindness of God, "shown to us in Christ Jesus" (Eph 2:7), indicate how serious is the responsibility of those who reject the divine gift or misuse it with levity. In actual fact we can never go too far in accepting it with the gratitude and faith and love it deserves.

Father, we acknowledge your greatness: all your actions show your wisdom and love. You formed man in your own likeness and set him over the whole world to serve you, his creator, and to rule over all creatures.

Even when he disobeyed you and lost your friendship, you did not abandon him to the power of death, but helped all men to seek and find you. Again and again you offered a covenant to man, and through the prophets taught him to hope for salvation.

Father, you so loved the world that in the fullness of time you sent us your only Son to be our Savior. He was conceived through the power of the Holy Spirit, and born of the Virgin Mary, a man like us in all things but sin. To the poor he proclaimed the good news of salvation, to prisoners freedom, and to those in sorrow joy. In fulfillment of your will he gave himself up to death, but by rising from the dead, he destroyed death and restored life.

Roman Missal, Eucharistic Prayer IV

YEAR C

This poor man cried and the Lord heard him, and saved him out of all his troubles. *(Ps 34:6)*

The thought of the Pasch, old and new, marked by the reconciliation of man with God, becomes ever more present in the Lenten Liturgy. The first reading shows us the chosen people, after its long purification of forty years of wandering in the desert, finally entering the promised land and festively celebrating its first Passover there. God has forgiven its unfaithfulness and is keeping his promise of old by giving Israel a country where it can raise up a temple for him.

But—says the second reading—"the old has passed away; behold, the new has come!" (2 Cor 5:17). The great new thing is the Christian Pasch which supplants the old, the Pasch in which Christ is sacrificed to reconcile men with God. No longer is it the blood of a lamb, nor the rite of circumcision, nor the offering of the fruits of the earth that renders them pleasing to God; it is God himself who personally intervenes for the salvation of mankind by giving his only Son. "God was in Christ reconciling the world to himself, not counting men's trespasses against them" (ib. 19). Only God could take this initiative, only his love inspire it, only his mercy achieve it. The innocent Christ is substituted for man the sinner; humanity is freed from the enormous weight of its guilt, which falls upon the shoulders of "him who did not know sin" and whom God made sin for us, "so that in him we might become the righteousness of God" (ib. 21). Once again Lent invites us to contemplate the divine mercy revealed in the paschal mystery through which man becomes "a new being" in Christ, liberated from sin, reconciled with God, back again in the house of the Father.

The two parables of the Gospel which Jesus uses to make himself understood by those who consider themselves just—the scribes and the Pharisees—again deal with the mystery of God's mercy. Since Jesus had come to give his life for sinners, he presented himself, with good reason, under the guise of a shepherd who leaves his flock to go in search of the lost sheep; "when he has found it, he puts it on his shoulders, rejoicing" (Lk 15:5). Each of us is the object of Christ's search, each is a creature pursued by his grace, by his love, and is redeemed by his blood, and each of us should let him overtake us, be caught and carried off to a better life.

Then follows the parable of the prodigal son who had abandoned his father's house; he had claimed his portion so he could live independent and free, but instead, had wasted his goods and his freedom, and was reduced to being a slave to his passions and a wretched keeper of unclean animals. Pangs of conscience, the echo of God's voice, roused him to return. God is always the father who waits untiringly for the children who have abandoned him, and uses the goad of disappointment and remorse to urge them to return. When at last he sees them on the road to repentance, he runs to meet them with the kiss of forgiveness and makes holiday for them. Those who have remained at home are also to take part in the celebration; these have been faithful to their duty, but perhaps more through habit than from love, which has made them incapable of understanding the Father's love for their brothers, incapable too of rejoicing in it and sharing in it. Thus they are also in need of pardon. Besides all men are sinners, though in different measure and form; blessed indeed are those who humbly acknowledge this and feel the need of reconciliation with God and of being always more converted to his love and to the love of their brothers.

O God, who so wonderfully work out our reconciliation by means of your Son, grant that your Christian people may walk with living faith and generous constancy toward Easter so near at hand.
Roman Missal, Collect

O Jesus, I am the lost sheep and you are the good shepherd, who hastened lovingly in search of me, found me at last and after a thousand caresses lifted me onto your shoulders and joyfully carried me back to the fold . . . I am, alas, the prodigal son who wasted your substance, your natural and supernatural gifts, and reduced myself to the most miserable state because I had fled far from you, you who are the Word by whom all things were made, and without whom all things turn to evil because they are nothing in themselves. And you are that most loving Father who welcomed me with a great feast when, repenting of my transgressions, I came back to your house and found shelter under your roof, in your embrace. You took me in again as your son, you set me once more at your table, made me share in your joys; you called me once more to take part in your inheritance.

You are my kind Jesus, the gentle lamb who called me your friend, who looked with love upon me, a sinner, who blessed me when I cursed you, who prayed for me on the cross, and from your pierced heart let flow a stream of divine Blood that washed away my impurities and cleansed my soul of its sins; you snatched me from death by dying for me, and by conquering death you gave me life.

You opened to me the gates of paradise. O the love of Jesus! and yet at last this love has conquered and I am with you, my Master, my Friend, my Spouse, my Father. Here I am in your heart! What then would you have me do?

John XXIII, *Journal of a Soul 1900,* p 68, 69

133 — JOY AND SORROW

O Lord, that I may suffer with you in order that I may also be glorified with you *(Rom 8:17)*

1. "Behold, I create new heavens and a new earth . . . Be glad and rejoice forever . . . No more shall be heard in it the sound of weeping and the cry of distress" (Is 65:17-19). The prophecy shows us in imaginative language the happiness of the messianic times when Israel's situation will be completely renewed and friendship between God and his people will be re-established. The Gospel also announces the coming of the Savior as "a great joy which will come to all the people" (Lk 2:10), a spiritual joy above all, but one of concrete repercussions in the relief and the comfort of so many human sufferings. The miracles by which Jesus cured the sick and raised the dead to life are its proof. Still, Jesus did not come to bring a message of earthly happiness nor to establish in this world an era which would banish all tears and grief. Rather, he came to take upon himself the full weight of human suffering in order to transform it into a means of salvation, and, therefore, of eternal happiness in that blessed land where alone "death shall be no more, neither shall there be mourning, nor crying nor pain" (Rev 21:4). The life of man redeemed by Christ is a beginning of this endless happiness. The "great joy" brought by Jesus is so real that it can pass through every kind of suffering without being smothered. In fact Jesus has pointed out that the way that leads to blessedness runs right through the way of tribulations embraced out of love for God: "Blessed are the poor, those who mourn, those who hunger, those who are persecuted" (Mt 5:3-10).

Christ's paschal mystery is a web of grief and joy, of death and resurrection; the life of the Christian, which springs from this mystery and is based upon it, reproduces its characteristics. And just as the paschal mystery is not exhausted in the passion and death of Christ, but through pain and death culminates in the joy of the resurrection, so Christian life, in spite of its earthly tribulation, is constantly oriented toward eternal joy. A Christian experiences the harsh reality of grief without taking a pessimistic view of life, because he knows that every suffering is a precious means of sharing in Christ's passion and hence in his resurrection also.

2. Man needs to be saved from sin and from its consequences as well, which are pain and death. Taken apart from the gospel,

these bitter realities constitute an enigma that crushes us; only Christ can shed light upon them and make them acceptable (GS 22). In taking responsibility for the sins of mankind upon himself, Christ wished to consume in himself their consequences also; thus his sacrifice has transformed pain and death—the heritage of sin—into instruments of redemption and salvation. "By suffering for us"—states Vatican II—"he not only provided us with an example for our imitation; he blazed a trail, and if we follow it, life and death are made holy and take on a new meaning" (ib.). Therefore we cannot look upon suffering as a disaster to be avoided by all means nor as an undesirable event to which we must submit out of necessity; nor solely as a punishment for sin, but as a means of salvation, because it is a means of communion with Christ who died and rose again to redeem sinful humanity. Suffering is the gate that introduces us into the paschal mystery of the Lord and lets us live it in its aspect of passion and death to prepare us for that of resurrection. It is impossible to share in the resurrection of Christ if we do not first suffer and die with him.

All the same, suffering is repugnant to us who have been created for happiness; and God does not disdain our groaning. Jesus never rejected those in trouble who had recourse to him; sometimes he tried their faith by treating them with apparent harshness, as he did with the royal official who begged him to cure his son (Jn 4:46-51), but in the end he intervened in their favor. In any case, even when God does not grant us relief, and permits the suffering to be prolonged, we must continue to trust in him. Only he knows what is for the real good of each of us. Certain tribulations which seem absurd and unfair from our human point of view have a very real place in his divine plans; our personal salvation, and that of many others, may depend on our acceptance of these. "In everything God works for good with those who love him" (Rom 8:28).

O Lord my God, I cried to you for help and you have healed me. O Lord, you have brought up my soul from Sheol, restored me to life from among those gone down to the pit. Sing praises to the Lord, O you his saints, and give thanks to his holy name, For his anger is but for a moment and his favor is for a lifetime. Weeping may tarry for the night, but joy comes with the morning . . . Hear, O Lord, and be gracious to me! O Lord, be my helper! You have turned for me my mourning into dancing; you have loosened my sackcloth and girded me with gladness, that my soul may praise you and not be silent. O Lord my God, I will give thanks to you for ever.

Psalm 30:2-5, 10-12

Emmanuel, God with us . . . you came down to be close to those whose hearts are overwhelmed with grief, to be with us in distress. The day will come when, drawn up into the clouds, we shall meet you face to face, and shall be always with you, provided that now we are anxious to have you with us, as a daily guide who will bring us to our heavenly homeland, or rather, be to us as the way, for then you will be the homeland itself.

It is good for me, Lord, to be in distress, as long as you are with me; I prefer that to being a king without you, or without you to be happy or in glory. It is better for me to draw close to you in my anguish, and to have you with me in the crucible of trial, than to be even in heaven without you. Whom have I in heaven but you? And there is nothing upon earth that I desire besides you (Ps 73:25). Gold is tried in the furnace and the just in the tribulation of distress. Here you are with them, O Lord, here you are present in the midst of those who are gathered together in your name . . .

Why are we afraid, why do we hesitate, why do we try to flee this crucible of suffering? It is true that fire rages; but you are with us in our trouble, O Lord. If you are with us, who can be against us? (Rom 8:31). And if you free us, who can snatch us from your hand? Who will be able to tear us away from you? And, finally, if you give us glory, who can condemn us?

St. Bernard, *In Psalm "Qui habitat"* 17,4

134 — A HEALING AND LIFE-GIVING POWER

O Lord, great is your love toward us, and your faithfulness endures forever *(Ps 117:2)*

1. Ezechiel saw in prophetic vision a spring of water gushing from the right side of the temple, which, as it flowed, became ever larger, with a vivifying power that brought life wherever it went. "Wherever the river goes, every living creature which swarms will live and there will be very many fish; for this water goes there, that the waters of the sea may become fresh" (Ezek 47:9). Even the Dead Sea, in contact with that water, became healthy and filled with fish, while the surrounding countryside was covered with trees of every kind. It is an image of the healing and life-giving power of grace which flows from the pierced side of Christ to purify and sanctify everyone who adheres to him with faith. Ezechiel's vision foreshadows the symbolism of water which is so frequent in the New Testament, particularly in St. John's Gospel. It calls to mind the living water promised by Jesus to the Samaritan woman and to the blind man at the pool of Siloe where he washed and regained his sight, or the waters of Bethesda near which Jesus healed the paralytic.

This last episode leads us to reflect upon the condition of powerlessness in which we find ourselves in regard to supernatural life. The paralytic man has been waiting for a cure for thirty-eight years, but he cannot reach the healing waters of the pool by himself and finds no one to put him into them. But the water is only a sign, the healing power is in Christ; he is the one who cures and saves. At his word "the man was healed, and he took up his pallet and walked" (Jn 5:9). Something similar happens in the sacraments, which are signs and vehicles of grace; the Church administers them, but it is Christ who works in them; it is he who saves and sanctifies. We can and must work to free ourselves from sin, but the most appropriate means for purification is the sacrament in which Christ washes us with his blood; we must pledge ourselves to acquire virtue, but nothing directly increases love within us like the Eucharist, in which Christ nourishes us with his own flesh. By means of the sacraments, the soul's good will is joined to Christ's action, and is strengthened by the sanctifying power of his grace.

2. Without grace we are held in the sterility of death, in the powerlessness of paralysis; but when grace touches us, life blossoms in us, and it is divine life, which is friendship, communion with God and holiness. In infusing grace into man, God himself, One and Three, makes his dwelling in us: "If a man loves me . . . my Father will love him; and we will come to him and make our home with him" (Jn 14:23). This is an inexpressible reality which takes place in each soul that is living in grace and love. However, God does not give himself completely to us, he does not transform us entirely in himself, nor perfect us in his unity, until he finds us empty of everything contrary to his will. Not only sin, but also the least voluntary defects, deliberate imperfections and infidelity, are contrary to God's will and perfection. God cannot want such things, nor can he admit to perfect union with himself a soul that is ensnared by any of these. It follows that our cooperation with the action of grace consists above all in freeing ourselves, with the help of grace itself, from everything that is contrary to God. St. John of the Cross teaches that we prepare for union with God by acquiring "purity and love, which is the stripping off and perfect renunciation of these things for God alone" (Asc II 5:8). Purity and love go together: the more we love God the more we become capable of renouncing any attachment to self and to other creatures, and of battling and conquering defects and imperfections, and so achieving great interior purity. On the other hand, greater purity is matched by more intense love; a soul that is purified is free to concentrate all its energies on God. Purity and love are intermingled and so integrated into each other, that they become inseparable, "for to love God is to labor to divest and deprive oneself for God of all that is not God" (ib. 7). This is an arduous program, but one that can be achieved when our will is strengthened by the healing and life-giving power of grace, because God present within us sustains our efforts; and while inviting us to communion with himself, at the same time, makes the way to it easy.

Blessed may you be, O my Creator and my Lord! Do not disdain me if I speak to you as a wounded man speaks to his doctor, or as one who suffers to one who can console him, or as a poor man to one who is rich and abundantly supplied with all kinds of goods.

The wounded man says: O doctor, do not despise me who am hurt, for you are my brother.

You who are the best of consolers, do not scorn me because I am in distress, but give my heart rest, and my senses consolation.

The poor man says: O you who are rich and need nothing, look at me, so very much weakened by hunger; behold me, who am naked, and give me some clothing to keep me warm.

Therefore I beg you: O most excellent and all powerful Lord, I consider attentively the scars of my sins, with which I have been wounded since childhood; I weep because time has gone by uselessly. My strength is not enough to sustain my weariness, because it has been exhausted in vanity. Since you are the source of all goodness and mercy, I implore you to have pity and mercy, I implore you to have pity on me. Touch my heart with the hand of your love, because you are the best doctor, console my soul because you are the good consoler.

St. Bridget, *Revelations and Prayers*

O my God, put me into that nakedness in which I take delight in the all, empty my spirit and memory of everything created, that I may enjoy only you . . . or rather not enjoy you, because this word recalls the senses, but that I may be in that emptiness, that bitter, solemn, mysterious nothingness in which is the all that is you, to whom the soul aspires and yearns to be united. O my God, I do not know how to say it, but I am dying of thirst for union with you, and I know that I can only be united to you in purity . . . your words are throbbing in my soul: "bring nothing," and I feel I bring too much and this causes me a sadness which would be desperate if I did not know that, in your mercy, you help any one who seeks you.

G. Canovai, *Suscipe Domine*

135 — THE WAY OF LIFE

Lord, you have turned my mourning into dancing, and renunciation into the resurrection of judgment (Ps 30:11; Jn 5:29)

1. "For as the Father raises the dead and gives them life, so also the Son gives life to whom he will" (Jn 5:21). Jesus, the Son of God, has the same power as the Father for giving life to man, lying prostrate in the death of sin. This is his mission as Savior: "I came that they may have life and have it abundantly" (Jn 10:10). But what can we do to receive the fullness of such life into ourselves? "He who hears my word"—says Jesus—"and believes him who sent me, has eternal life, (and) . . . has passed from death to life" (Jn 5:24). Two things are required. First of all, faith: to believe in God, to believe in Christ the Son of God; a faith that the Jews

refused, and, in refusing it, rejected and persecuted the Savior. Together with faith, we must listen to the Word, and this implies renunciation of self so as to adhere to the gospel, and to set out in the footsteps of the Lord. Our Lord points out what this following of him requires: "He who loves father or mother more than me is not worthy of me, and he who loves son or daughter more than me is not worthy of me . . . and he who loses his life for my sake will find it" (Mt 10:37,39). Jesus offers the fullness of life, but demands that we cleave freely to him; he asks the whole of our love, hence of renunciation also. He wants everything: our heart and will, our dearest affections, home, possessions, even life itself. His words cannot be interpreted as simply a way of speaking, they are concrete requirements for following him. We must not be afraid to listen to them, even if they turn our lives upside down. This will not be asked of everyone, nor in the same way of every Christian; but all of us are asked to be always ready to sacrifice any affection whatsoever, or anything, or even life itself, when this is necessary for being completely faithful to hearing and following our Lord. "The gate is narrow . . . and narrow the way that leads to life" (Mt 7:14), said Jesus, and he was certainly not speaking in parables. It is the narrow way of renunciation that leads to the fullness of life in God, because he who loses his life for God's sake will find it.

2. God did not create us for suffering and renunciation, but for happiness, for life; not for an ephemeral happiness during life in this world, but for an eternal and unfailing life, which can be found in God alone. However, God passes by, unnoticed by our senses, whereas the things of this world press upon us and entice us from all sides, leading us to seek our happiness in them. From this arises the necessity of controlling and mortifying their immoderate tendency toward pleasure, their looking for satisfaction in creatures. For those who desire to attain to the fullness of life in God, St. John of the Cross, in full accord with the gospel, suggests that they gradually accustom themselves to giving up "any sensory satisfaction that is not purely for the honor and glory of God . . . out of love for Jesus Christ. In his life, he had no other gratification, nor desired any other, than the fulfillment of his Father's will which he called his meat and food" (Asc I 13:4). Again it is a question of not seeking our joy and delight in pleasures of sense, which satisfy selfishness, self-love, and attachment to creatures, but in the will of God, in what pleases him. If we would be spiritual persons, we must force ourselves to change the direction of our inclination toward pleasure by detaching it from the goods of earth and turning it decisively toward God, until we can repeat with Jesus: "I always do what is pleasing to him" (Jn 8:29).

Jesus declared in speaking of his mission: "My judgment is just, because I seek not my own will, but the will of him who sent me" (Jn 5:30). By analogy, our way of judging, our choices, and our behavior are "just" as long as we seek the will of God in everything and in what pleases him and gives him glory, even when this is costly to our nature and requires detachment. In so acting, we deprive ourselves of a great many temporal satisfactions of the senses, and of earthly pleasures, but we thereby acquire an ever greater freedom of spirit, which makes us capable of using things and loving creatures without becoming their slave, and without allowing ourselves to be detained by them in our march toward God.

O Lord, to be your disciple means to be all yours, to belong to you fully, perfectly united to you, and to be one with you, no longer living in myself, but rather you living within me; this is what perfect union means. O my God, how I should like to be your disciple; it is the greatest glory I can attain to: "God's glory is this: that you become my disciples and bear fruit"; it is also my greatest good... O Lord, help me to do what is necessary for this... What does it mean to deny myself in order to follow you? It means to forget myself, not to consider self, not to be concerned with self any more than if it did not exist; then there is no longer interest, nor advantage, nor anything else; one ceases to be without the least concern for self... self is completely forgotten. But, O Lord, if I no longer seek my own good, will I then be seeking absolutely nothing?... This heart, this mind, emptied of self, will they stay empty?... No, not for even a moment. If I empty myself of self it is in order to be filled with you, my God; if I forget about myself, it is only to think of nothing but you.

C. de Foucauld, *Meditations on the Gospel.*

O Lord, a Christian is one who follows you. He is helped by your grace, but following your example, suffering is necessary for him, Lord; a religious, a priest, a Christian must be a friend of the cross. Walking in your light, I will keep continually in mind the thought that here on earth there is neither time nor place to look for satisfaction and pleasure.

As I move ahead as a Christian toward eternal happiness, I shall never succeed in finding happiness in this valley of tears. And yet, dear Master, our thoughts are sometimes confused; we are ever in hope of getting some personal compensation, hearing some word of praise, enjoying some measure of respect, of finding friendship in the circle about us, of tasting some consolation or some sweetness in prayer. Lord, give me consolation and satisfaction if they are of use for my salvation, but above all give me love and desire for mortification and the cross.

E. Poppe, *Spiritual Intimacies*

136 — FAITH AND HUMILITY

I thank you, O Father... that you have hidden these things from the wise and understanding, and revealed them to babes (Lk 10:21)

1. In his debates with the Jews, Jesus reprimanded them: "You search the Scriptures, because you think that in them you have eternal life, and it is they that bear witness to me. Yet you refuse to come to me that you may have life" (Jn 5:39). For the Jews the whole of perfection consisted in a minute and often arbitrary investigation of sacred Scripture, which they interpreted according to their personal opinions. In their pride they did not admit the possibility of error, and since they did not understand the meaning of the prophecies they were unwilling to admit that Jesus might be the Messiah whom these prophecies had foretold. Jesus sought to enlighten them, but the light did not penetrate their hearts which had been blinded by pride. "How can you believe, who receive glory from one another, and do not seek the glory that comes from the only God?" (ib. 44). The aim of these false teachers was not to penetrate the genuine spirit of the Scriptures, or to understand God's plan for the salvation of men and to conform to it, but only to be praised and honored by men. This was the great impediment to their faith in Christ. How could they accept a poor, humble Messiah who exalted the little, the simple, and the needy, while they were seeking "glory and praise from each other."

Both for faith in Christ and for the study of sacred Scripture we need humility. Jesus came to reveal God's mysteries to us, his plans for our salvation, and the authentic meaning of the Scriptures; but only the humble will let him teach them. One who thinks he is wise and just, wants to do things by himself; he accepts neither Master nor Savior. This situation has been perpetuated down through the centuries whenever proud men have rejected the magisterium and mediation of the Church, which is the official depositary of the word of God and of the sacraments of salvation. Jesus once asked: "When the Son of Man comes, will he find faith on earth?" (Lk 18:8) He will certainly not find it among the proud, nor in men who are puffed up with their knowledge, but he will find it among the humble and simple.

2. The Pharisees boasted of their belief in Moses, but they had not really understood his spirit, nor followed his example. Moses had refused to become the head of a great nation, desiring rather to save his people (Ex 32:7-14), whereas the Pharisees neglected the welfare of the people and were intent only on their own glory. Just as they did not understand Moses, neither did they understand the Messiah, who had been foretold by him and prefigured in his conduct; and for this reason Jesus admonished: "If you believed Moses you would believe me" (Jn 5:46). One cannot profess to believe in someone, and at the same time reject his teachings

and his example. Unfortunately this contradiction is not rare even among Christians, and can end in rejecting the gospel of humility and service.

We may be tempted to think that in order to do good, we must occupy privileged or prominent positions, whereas Jesus spoke and acted in absolutely the opposite manner. He taught his disciples to choose the last place, and to put themselves at the service of others, even when called upon to fill positions of responsibility. During the Last Supper itself our Lord was to say: "Let the greatest among you become as the youngest, and the leader as one who serves," and he added, as encouragement: "I am among you as one who serves" (Lk 22:26-27). Christ's whole life had been spent in rendering service to his Father and to men, but he wished to give a still more explicit example; the Apostles beheld him kneeling before them to carry out the most humble of menial tasks: that of "washing their feet" (Jn 13:5). The prophecies had spoken of the Messiah as "Servant of Yahweh," but Jesus here showed himself as servant of men as well, and asked his disciples to do the same.

Choosing the last place in the service of the brethren is a constant of the gospel; choosing to ignore this teaching is equivalent to rejecting the mystery of Christ: the mystery of him who "though he was in the form of God" did not wish to put forward his divinity in order to conquer men, "but emptied himself, taking the form of a servant" (Phil 2:7), becoming like the poorest and the most abject, bringing himself down to their level and fraternizing with them.

O Jesus, you are the light for those who open their eyes to see you; but for those who shut their eyes you are a stumbling block against which they break themselves. Because they did not want to learn the mystery of your weakness, the Jews stumbled and were broken and did not know you . . . You would have enlightened them with your truth if they had humbly asked you, but in their pride they did not welcome your light, and you who had come to enlighten them were a scandal to them . . . Because when your light is scorned, we no longer heed it; a dense fog covers it, and our passions completely hide it from our eyes.

When we walk in darkness, we do not know where we are going. We think we are going toward glory, pleasure, life and happiness, and instead we are headed toward perdition and death. O Lord, help us to keep going as long as the least spark of light remains!

cf Bossuet, *Meditations on the Gospel* III 17:1

O Jesus, when you were a wayfarer on earth, you said: "Learn of me, for I am meek and humble of heart, and you shall find rest to your souls." O almighty King of heaven! my soul indeed finds rest in seeing you condescend to wash the feet of your apostles, "having taken the form of a slave." I recall the words you uttered to teach me the practice of humility: "I have given you an example, that as I have done to you, so you do also. The servant is not greater than his master . . . "

O my Beloved, to teach me humility, you could not further abase yourself, and so I wish to respond to your love, by putting myself in the lowest place, by sharing your humiliations, so that I may have part with you in the kingdom of heaven. I implore you dear Jesus, to send me a humiliation whensoever I try to set myself above others.

And yet, dear Lord, you know my weakness. Each morning I resolve to be humble, and in the evening I recognize that I have often been guilty of pride. The sight of these faults tempts me to discouragement; yet I know that discouragement is itself but a form of pride. I wish, therefore, O my God, to build all my trust upon you. As you can do all things, deign to implant in my soul this virtue which I desire.

St. Therese of the Child Jesus, *Prayer 14* (Taylor, p. 317)

137 — WITH JESUS, HUMBLED

O Jesus, who humbled yourself and became obedient unto death, make me share in your feelings (Phil 2:5-8)

1. "Let us lie in wait for the righteous man, because he is inconvenient to us and opposes our actions . . . Let us test him with insult and torture, that we may find out how gentle he is and make trial of his forbearance. Let us condemn him to a shameful death" (Wis 2:12, 19-20). Christ is the just one, humiliated and persecuted by the wicked; the details described in the Book of Wisdom are startingly verified in his life and especially in his passion. The hatred of those who are offended by the holiness of his conduct and of his teaching is cast upon him, the most innocent one. "The world . . . hates me"—he will say, one day—"because I testify of it that its works are evil" (Jn 7:7).

The Son of God, who of his own will humbled himself even to being made man, even to being made "sin" so that he could take the place of sinful man, freely accepted being humiliated by the very ones he had come to save. Many times when the Jews tried to put him to death, Jesus escaped "because his hour had not yet come" (ib. 30), but he did not escape contradictions and humiliations. Eternal truth, he accepted being treated like a liar; infinite goodness, like an evil-doer; he who is uncreated wisdom is treated like a fool; perfect gentleness, like one who subverts the people; he is Son of God, and they treat him like one possessed by the devil. Christ's indignities are the price for ransoming mankind from pride, and at the same time are an encouragement to us to follow him along the way of humility. "Learn from me, for I am gentle and lowly in heart" (Mt 11:29).

Authentic humility stems from the heart, and from the deep, intimate conviction of one's own littleness before God. Whereas Jesus humbled himself by forgetting his dignity as Son of God, man, in order to be humble, must remember what he is: a creature that exists not through his own power, but only through the gifts received from God; a creature also that after sinning has fallen into a state of moral misery. The awareness of all this ought to make us profoundly humble, yet pride is so strong within us that it is always hard for us to humble ourselves, and even harder, to accept being humiliated. Only the grace which springs from the humiliations of Christ can help us establish ourselves in sincere humility of heart.

2. "Have this mind among yourselves which is yours in Christ Jesus, who, though he was in the form of God . . . emptied himself" (Phil 2:5-7). We never sufficiently meditate upon these words of the Apostle. All Christians are called to follow Jesus in the way of humility, and in order to do this must "become as nothing", that is, rid themselves of pride by accepting what destroys it: humiliations, especially the interior humiliation of noting our own deficiencies, shortcomings, and lack of faithfulness, and then the exterior humiliations which stem from the fact that our limitations and faults and errors are being observed by others. Many desire to be humble, but few welcome being humiliated; many beg for humility, but then in practice fly from humiliations. Yet, just as study is the means of acquiring knowledge, so humiliation is the way to acquire humility. Besides, humiliation is the just lot of sinful man. The Saints were so convinced of this that they considered no indignity too severe. "I have never heard anything bad said of me"—wrote St. Teresa of Jesus—"which I did not clearly realize fell short of the truth. If I had not sometimes—often indeed—offended God in the ways they referred to, I had done so in many others, and I felt they had treated me far too indulgently in saying nothing about these" (Way 15:3).

The Council particularly urges religious to practice the virtue of humility "through which we share in Christ's self-surrender" (PC 5). Whoever desires to be intimately associated with the mystery of Christ—as a religious vocation demands—must enter deeply into the way of his self-abasement. Of ourselves we are not capable of this; we need Christ himself to lead us into it, by making us share his humiliations. All the injustices, accusations, insults, misunderstandings and failures which we encounter in life are means to this; and by accepting them for the love of Christ, we open ourselves to the gift of his divine humility, and enter into the mystery of him who emptied himself for the glory of the Father and the salvation of mankind. By following Christ, humbled even to death on the cross, we take our place among those who give glory to God and help to save their brothers. Even the most stubborn are conquered and vanquished by humility.

O Christ, Son of God you took the lowest place and treated yourself as the last of men . . . throughout your whole life. This is how you wished to be treated by sinners, by demons, by the Holy Spirit and by your eternal Father. All this was in order to glorify your Father . . . to repair the dishonor given to him by our pride, to confound and destroy our arrogance, to make us hate vanity and love humility. How pride dishonors God and how horribly displeasing it must be to him since it was necessary that you, the Son of God, should thus humble yourself! What a dreadful vice is vanity when you had to lower yourself to such depths of abasement in order to destroy it! How precious is humility in the sight of God and how pleasing to him since you, his divine Son, wished to be treated in this way in order to make us love humility, to incite us to imitate you in its practice and to obtain for us the grace to practice it.

St. John Eudes, *Meditations on Various Subjects,* III 16

O loving Jesus, I kneel at your feet, sure as I am that you will know how to bring about what I cannot even imagine. I want to serve you wherever you wish, at any cost, at any sacrifice. There is nothing I can do; I do not even know how to humble myself. But I will say this to you and say it firmly: I want to be humble, I want to love humiliations and being treated with indifference by my fellows. I shut my eyes and hurl myself, with a sort of voluptuous delight into that flood of scorn, suffering and shame which you may be pleased to send me. I feel a great unwillingness to say this to you, it tears my heart, but I give you my promise: I want to suffer, I want to be despised for you. I do not know what I shall do—indeed I do not really believe myself—but I will not give up wanting this with all my heart and soul: "To suffer and be despised for you".

John XXIII, *Journal of a Soul,* Dec. 1903 p. 143

138 — THE MYSTERY OF THE PATIENT CHRIST

O Christ, who suffered for us, leaving us an example, that we should follow in your footsteps (1 Pet 2:21)

1. "But I was like a gentle lamb led to the slaughter; I did not know it was against me they devised schemes: 'Let us destroy the tree with its fruits, let us cut him off from the land of the living, that his name be remembered no more' " (Jer 11:19). Jeremiah, whom his fellow citizens sought to put to death, is a type of the persecuted Christ, the "Lamb of God"—as the Baptist was to name him—led to death to "take away the sins of the world" (Jn 1:29). But whereas Jeremiah did not know of the conspiracy hatched against him, Christ was perfectly aware of what was being plotted. The suffering which awaited him was no surprise, it was a free and conscious immolation of himself to the Father's will: "No one takes (my life) from me; but I lay it down of my own accord. I have power to lay it down, and I have power to take it up again; this

charge I have received from my Father" (Jn 10:18). These were the sentiments with which Jesus faced his passion and offered himself to it like a gentle lamb which makes no resistance and refuses nothing. His enduring is more than a passive endurance; it is a spontaneous, loving acceptance, sustained by the knowledge of his resurrection. Yet it is still real suffering which tortures heart and members.

The Son of God came into the world and saved mankind by assuming the weaknesses of our nature, through which he atoned for our sins; by his suffering he sanctified all the sorrow of the human race. In order to join him, we in our turn, must accept suffering. But the Christian endurance of suffering cannot simply turn into resigned patience—one almost forced upon us because we cannot get out of it. In imitation of Christ, Christian patience is the willing acceptance of whatever in our lives crucifies us, in loving conformity with God's will. The Christian becomes like the patient Christ through this willing adherence, and suffering becomes a participation in his mystery. When patience is understood in this way, it does not degrade a man, nor make him the slave of painful situations from which he either cannot, or does not know how to escape; instead it makes him capable of voluntarily embracing all the suffering that God permits in his life, with a positive attitude of love and of union with Christ, crucified and resurrected.

2. "Rejoice, in so far as you share Christ's sufferings"—says St. Peter—"that you may also rejoice and be glad when his glory is revealed" (1 Pet 4:13). The consciousness that we are sharing in the Lord's passion gives us courage, makes us serene and even happy in tribulations. Ours is not then a gloomy, desperate suffering, but one that is comforted and enlightened by hope. Those painful situations that have no human solution find support and explanation in the mystery of Christ, who intimately unites to himself all those who share his passion. Thus the sufferings of the innocent are no longer unreasonable, but symbolic of the innocent One who was crucified.

Seen from this perspective, Christian patience is not so much a moral virtue as a need to participate in Christ's mystery. Anyone who does not enter into the mystery of his passion and death will not enter either into that of his resurrection. And whereas eternal life will be the fullness of Christ's resurrection, life in this world is only its prelude, and entails a deep involvement in the suffering and death of our Lord. However, even now, the resurrection is already in progress through that divine life that Christ shares with those who have been baptized in his death and are linked to it.

We learn patience by keeping our eyes fixed upon the divinely patient One: "He committed no sin, no guilt was found on his lips. When he was reviled, he did not revile in return; when he suffered, he did not threaten . . . he himself bore our sins in his body on the tree" (1 Pet 2:22-24). Since it was man's sins that martyred the innocent Christ, it is not unjust that we who are guilty should feel their sting. Looking upon Christ crucified, each of us can know that we are not alone in our suffering; Christ took it upon himself to suffer our griefs, our distress and our anguish in order to make them less bitter for us, and to encourage us in tribulations. Strengthened by the example and grace of Christ, and sustained by his love for us, we learn to live with our personal suffering without losing heart, and we also learn to offer it up for the salvation of our brethren, as a humble contribution to the work of redemption. "In my flesh I complete what is lacking in Christ's afflictions for the sake of his body . . . the Church" (Col 1:24).

I looked at you, O my crucified Christ, and saw you offer yourself to your Father as victim for souls; reflecting on this great vision of your love, I have understood the vehemence of your soul's love, and desire to offer myself like you.

How I rejoice in the thought that from all eternity we have been known of the Father, as St. Paul says, and that he wishes to find in us the image of his crucified Son. Oh, how necessary suffering is in order that God's work may be done in a soul. O my God, you have an immense desire to enrich us with your grace, but it is we who determine the amount in proportion as we allow ourselves to be immolated by you—immolated like the Master in joy and in thanksgiving, saying with him: "The chalice which my Father has given, shall I not drink it?" O Master, You called the hour of your passion "your hour", that for which you had come, that for which you yearned with all your strength.

When a great suffering, or a very small sacrifice is offered me, I desire to think quickly that this is "my hour", the hour to prove my love for you, Lord, who loved me exceedingly.

Elizabeth of the Trinity, *Letter* 112
(Philipon, Spiritual Doctrine, p. 120)

O most sweet Jesus, what were the thoughts that induced you to suffer, and what immense charity you had in your passion! But tell me, my Jesus, could you not have redeemed us, and saved my soul without such an excess of love, with a milder punishment and a more moderate affection? O inexpressible sorrow of my Lord, O love so constant, unconquered and incomprehensible. My Jesus, when shall I be able to return your love as I ought and as I long to do?

Certainly for the future I shall have to live as though always dying . . . and still, however much I can suffer in this life, it will always be less than what I deserve by my sins. Indeed, this is the greatest cross, the greatest grief of all griefs, to have offended you, my God.

Jesus, my only love, do not abandon me; treat me in this life as it pleases you and with as many crosses as you want: I am here, resigned to your every wish. I only ask you never to let me separate myself from your grace by sinning.

Bl. Henry Suso, *Dialogue of Love, Life and Works*

139 — FIFTH SUNDAY OF LENT

YEAR A

O Jesus, you are the resurrection and the life; may I live and believe in you (Jn 11:25-26)

A Liturgy of resurrection characterizes this Sunday, which is dominated by the concept of Jesus as the source of life who has the power to bring even the dead back to life: "I will put my spirit within you and you shall live" (Ez 37:14). Ezechiel's prophecy directly concerned the moral and political renewal of Israel, which had been decimated and degraded by slavery; a renewal comparable to a resurrection that would make it again a free people and that became a reality after the return from Babylon. At the same time it foretold the messianic period which was to be marked by the spiritual and bodily resurrection of the Son of God as well as by the general resurrection of the body which will take place at the end of time.

Among the miracles of resurrection performed by Jesus, that of Lazarus is of capital importance, both because its subject was a man who had been dead four days and was already in the grave, and because it was accompanied by deeds and words which made it a particular "sign" of the messianic power of the Savior. Jesus' answer to the one who brought the news of Lazarus' illness: "This illness is not unto death; it is for the glory of God" (Jn 11:4); his delay in going over to Bethany, and finally his sudden declaration: "Lazarus is dead; and for your sake I am glad that I was not there, so that you may believe" (ib. 14-15)—all this tells us that the incident was intended to glorify Jesus, "the resurrection and the life", and at the same time to perfect the faith of those who believed in him, and to awaken it in those who did not (ib. 42). The Master insists on these two points in his conversation with Martha. She has faith: she is convinced that if Jesus had been present Lazarus would not have died; but he wants to lead her to recognize in his person the Messiah, the Son of God, who has come to give eternal life to as many as believe in him; "he who believes in me, though he die, yet shall he live; and whoever lives and believes in me shall never die. Do you believe this?" (ib. 25-26). This is the height to which faith must attain: to believe that the power of raising the dead belongs to Christ, and that, just as he can use it to bring Lazarus immediately back from bodily death, so he can also use it to assure eternal life to all who live in him through faith.

St. Paul takes up this theme again in his letter to the Romans: "If Christ is in you [through faith and love], although your bodies are dead because of sin, your spirits are alive because of righteousness" (Rom 8:10). Jesus did not abolish physical death—a consequence of sin—but by freeing man from sin, he made him share in his life, which is eternal life; so that death has no power over the spirit of one who lives "because of righteousness." Not only that, but the day will come—at the end of time—when even the bodies of those who have believed will rise again in glory, never to die again, sharing in the resurrection of the Lord. Then Jesus will be in the full sense "the resurrection and the life", exalted by the elect who are risen and living in eternity, through the grace flowing from the Easter mystery.

As Easter draws near, the story of Lazarus' resurrection is an invitation for us to free ourselves ever more from the bonds of sin, trusting in the life-giving power of Christ who wants to make us participate in his resurrection. May this indeed be true for every one for whom he is "the resurrection and the life", in time and in eternity!

Thanks be to you, Lord, holy Father . . . through Christ our Lord who, a man among men, wept for his friend Lazarus; God and Lord of life, he called him back from the grave. Full of compassion for all men, he causes them to pass, by means of the sacraments, from death to life.

Roman Missal, Preface

O true Friend, how badly he pays you back who betrays you! O true Christians, help your God weep, for those compassionate tears are not only for Lazarus but for those who were not going to want to rise, even though you call them. O my God, how you bear in mind the faults I have committed against you! May they now come to an end, Lord, may they come to an end, and those of everyone. Raise up these dead; may your cries be so powerful that even though they do not beg life of you, you give it to them so that afterward they might come forth from the depth of their own delights.

Lazarus did not ask you to raise him up. You did it for a woman sinner; behold one here, my God, and a much greater one; let your mercy shine. I, although miserable, ask life for those who do not want to ask it of you. You already know, my King, what torment it is for me to see them so forgetful of the great endless torments they will suffer, if they do not return to you.

St. Teresa of Jesus, *Soliloquies* 10:2-3

YEAR B

O Jesus, let me serve you and follow you; where you are, there I shall also be (Jn 12:26)

As Lent moves toward its close, the impending passion of our Lord fills the Liturgy. Today Jesus himself speaks of it through John's Gospel, which presents it as the mystery of his glorification and of his obedience to the Father's will. His words are occasioned by the request ot certain Greeks who wished to see the Lord. Their presence seems a substitution for the Jews, who had become definitely estranged from him and were now plotting to do away with him. Now Jesus can proclaim himself to be the Savior of all men: "The hour has come for the Son of Man to be glorified. Truly, truly, I say to you, unless a grain of wheat falls to the earth and dies, it remains alone. But if it dies it bears much fruit" (Jn 12:23-24). His glorification will come about through a death comparable to that the grain of wheat must undergo in order to give life to the new plant. In very fact, through his death there will be born the new people of God who will welcome Greeks and Jews and men of every nation, all equally redeemed by him. Jesus knows this and thus sees with joy the hour of the cross approaching, though at the same time his human nature feels its horror: "Now is my soul troubled, and what shall I say? 'Father, save me from this hour!' " (ib. 27). It is an anticipation of the lament of Gethsemane: "My soul is very sorrowful, even to death" (Mk 14:34). The words bring home to us the cruel reality of the passion of the Son of God, who, being true man, tasted all its anguish. But he did not retreat, for he had come into the world in a body capable of suffering, precisely to offer it to the Father in a sacrifice of atonement: "for this purpose I have come to this hour!" (Jn 12:27).

The voice of the Father answers his Son from heaven, confirming the hour of the passion as the hour of glorification. It is exactly at the time he is raised up on the cross that Jesus will draw all men to him, and at the same time give greatest glory to the Father.

St. Paul takes up this subject again in his Letter to the Hebrews, describing in very human terms the anguish of Jesus "in the days of his flesh" when he offered the Father "prayers and supplications with loud cries and tears" (Heb 5:7); a clear allusion to the lament of Gethsemane and to the cry of Calvary (Mk 15:34). He is "the Son", but the Father does not spare him because he "gave" him for the salvation of the world (Jn 3:16); the Son willingly accepts his Father's will, learning "obedience through what he suffered" (Heb 5:8). Being the Son of God, he had no need to taste death nor to obey through suffering, but he embraced them both so as to become "the source of eternal salvation to all who obey him" (ib. 9). Thus the passion reveals in the most eloquent way the sublimity of the love of the Father and of Christ for men; and also that in order to be saved by him who consummated the holocaust of his obedience by death on the cross, we must obey by renouncing ourselves.

Through his supreme act of self donation, Christ is the "high priest" (ib. 10) who reconciles men to God by his own blood, thus drawing up the "new covenant" of which Jeremiah speaks (31:1; 1st. reading). Through it man is renewed in his innermost self; God's law is no longer a simple external law engraved on tablets of stone, but an interior law written on the heart by love with the blood of Christ. Indeed it is through his passion that those days have come of which God had said: "I will put my law within them, and I will write it upon their hearts . . . I will forgive their iniquity, and I will remember their sin no more" (ib. 33-34).

We give you thanks, O holy Father, all-powerful and eternal God, through Jesus Christ, your Son, our Lord.

By fasting and penance we prepare to celebrate his passage to death; weeping we prostrate ourselves before him. For the day of our redemption is drawing near, the day of his passion, when he, our Savior and Lord, was handed over for our sake by the Jews and underwent the torment of the cross, when he was crowned with thorns, and buffeted, and made the object of multiplied physical sufferings in order to rise again at last, in virtue of his own power.

Eager to arrive at these holy days with hearts that are truly purified, we beg you, O God our Father, to wash us clean of every sin for the sake of his passion, clothing us again in the seamless garment which symbolizes the love you pour upon all.

By your love you prepare a sacrifice in us; by abstinence you will make us able to approach the holy altar in peace, freed of our sins.

Grant that Christ may obtain all this for us, for to him belongs praise, and power and glory for ever and ever.

Mozarabic Preface

YEAR C

O Lord, you have done great things for us (Ps 126:3)

The Liturgy of the Word today offers for our consideration the coming feast of Easter under the aspect of deliverance from sin. Although this had been merited for all men once for always by Christ, it must still be made actual for each of us; even more, it is matter that requires continual repetition and renewal, for we are always in danger of falling during the whole of our life, and no one can consider himself impeccable.

God, who once multiplied miracles in order to rescue his chosen people from slavery in Egypt, is now promising them new and greater ones to deliver them from the Babylonian captivity (1st. reading): "Behold, I am doing a new thing . . . I will make a way in the wilderness and rivers in the desert . . . to give drink to my people" (Is 43:19-20). The prophecy goes beyond the historical events of Israel and throws light on the messianic future in which God will work totally new wonders for the new Israel—the Church. Instead of a material road he will give the world his only Son to be the "way" of salvation; instead of water to quench the thirst of parched throats, the living water of grace flowing from Christ's sacrifice to purify us from sin and satisfy our thirst for the infinite.

This new order of things is concretely illustrated in the gospel episode of the adulterous woman, dragged before Jesus to be judged by him. "Teacher, this woman has been caught in the act of adultery. Now in the law, Moses commanded us to stone such. What do you have to say about her?" (Jn 8:4). The Savior did something absolutely new, something not contemplated in the old law; he pronounced no sentence, but after a silent pause, heavy with expectation on the part of the accusers and the accused, said simply: "Let him who is without sin among you be the first to throw a stone at her" (ib. 7). All of us are sinners; therefore no one has the right to set himself up as judge of others, save he who is the innocent one, the Lord; but not even he made use of his right, preferring to exercise his power as Savior: "Has no one condemned you? . . . Neither do I condemn you; go, and do not sin again" (ib. 10-11). Only Christ, who came to give his life for the salvation of sinners could free the woman from her sin and say to her: "Do not sin again". His word brings with it the grace that flows from his sacrifice. In the sacrament of penance, there is renewed, for each of the faithful, the liberating action of Christ which gives us the grace to fight against sin in order "not to sin again".

The second reading serves to deepen these reflections. St. Paul himself has sacrificed traditions, learning, and the whole way of life that bound him to his people, considering all these as "refuse" in order that he may gain Christ (Phil 3:8), and he encourages the Christian to renounce in like manner everything that does not lead to the Lord or that is contrary to him. This is the way to free ourselves completely from sin and to unite ourselves more and more to Christ until we "become like him in his death" in order to attain to the resurrection from the dead also (ib. 10,11). It is a road which provides us with ever new overcomings of self and of new deliverances through a deeper solidarity with Christ. No one can think he "has already attained this", but must press on to "make it his own": "because Christ Jesus has made him his own" (ib. 12).

Father, all-powerful and ever-living God, we do well always and everywhere to give you thanks through Christ our Lord. The days of his life-giving death and glorious resurrection are approaching. This is the hour when he triumphed over Satan's pride, the time when we celebrate the great event of our redemption.

By his redeeming passion, you brought life to the whole world, moving our hearts to praise your glory. In the mysterious power of the cross you judge the world and make the kingly power of Christ crucified shine upon it.

Roman Missal, Preface of Passion II, I

O my Jesus, what have I ever done? How could I abandon you and spurn you? How could I forget your name, trample upon your law, disobey your precepts? O my God, my Creator! My Savior, my life and my whole good! Unhappy miserable me; unhappy because I have sinned . . . because I have become like an irrational animal! My Jesus, tender shepherd, sweet Master, help me, lift up your fallen sheep, stretch out your hand to give me strength, blot out my sins, heal my wounds, strengthen my weakness, save me or I shall perish. I confess that I am unworthy to live, unworthy of the light, unworthy of your help . . . yet your mercy is indeed great; have mercy on me, O God who love men so much! You are my last hope, have pity on me according to the greatness of your mercy.

Louis de Blois (Blosius), works

140 — SIN NO MORE

Cleanse me with hyssop and I shall be clean; wash me and I shall be whiter than snow (Ps 51:7)

1. The experience of Susanna, who resisted the seductions of corrupt men at the cost of being falsely accused of adultery and unjustly exposed to death, was part of the ancient instruction of catechumens; those who were preparing for baptism were to learn from this strong pure woman how to be loyal to God's law and upright in conscience, no matter what risk was involved. At the same time, Susanna, who was freed from the intrigues of her slanderers by Daniel's intervention, was presented as a symbol of the baptized person who had been loosed from Satan's snares through the intervention of Christ. The Christian, saved by Christ from eternal death, is obligated to an even greater fidelity to God than the young Jewish maiden, both in the integrity of his faith and of his way of life. Confronted with the temptations and threats of the wicked, one who is baptized must have the courage to repeat with Susanna: "I choose not to do it and to fall into your hands, rather than to sin in the sight of the Lord" (Dan 13:23).

The New Testament also records an incident of a woman accused of adultery; unlike the innocent Susanna, this one is a sinner, but like Susanna is also dragged to trial by wicked men. Although an adulteress, she too is set free, not by a prophet this time, but by the Son of God who alone can remit sins. At the words: "Let him who is without sin be the first to throw a stone at her" (Jn 8:7), her malicious accusers went away "one by one", and the woman remained alone before the Lord. "There remain those two: misery and Mercy", says St. Augustine (In Io 33:5). And Jesus, who is Mercy even to the point of having come not to judge, but to save the world, absolves her: "Go, and do not sin again" (Jn 8:11). Susanna's liberation is a symbol of baptism, while that of the adulteress seems more related to the sacrament of penance. Even after being baptized, man always has the unhappy possibility of sinning; then the world shouts scandal and wishes to condemn him, but Jesus, who has paid for the salvation of sinners with his life, wants no one to be lost and grants pardon: "Go and do not sin again".

2. Baptism grafts us on to Christ and makes us live by his life, just as the branch lives by the sap that comes to it from the trunk. Penance strengthens the graft when sin has weakened it and removes the obstacles that impede the passage of the divine sap and increases its flow. The sacrament of penance is therefore the remedy for the moral ills of all the faithful, and like baptism, draws its power from Christ's paschal mystery.

"The repeated sacramental act of penance . . ."—affirms the Council—"greatly fosters the necessary turning of the heart toward the Father of mercies" (PO 18). Conversion of the heart is necessary not only for those who have fallen into serious sin, but also for those who, while living in grace, almost always need to free themselves from some sin in order to attain to the fullness of life in Christ. Although sacramental confession is necessary only in the first case, it is still very useful in the second, to bolster us in our efforts at purification and in our obligation of sanctity. Besides taking away sins, the sacrament of penance also has the function of healing wounds, of forestalling new falls, and increasing grace, so that the penitent may more easily overcome imperfections, resist temptations, and practice virtue. All this is assured by the action of Christ working in the sacrament: it is he who pardons, heals, and gives strength, "who loves us and has freed us from our sins by his blood" (Rev 1:5). We see from this the importance of frequent confession for those who are seeking perfection.

Such frequency, however, is not to be practiced at the expense of seriousness. The Council warns that for confession to be effective, it must be "prepared for by a daily examination of conscience", and be made with "contrite heart" (PO 18:5). The daily comparison of our own internal and external conduct with the gospel brings to light whatever is in contrast with Christ's teachings and example. This is the touch-stone which tests to what point our life is in fact "Christian", that is, moved by the authentic spirit of the gospel, or whether it is instead influenced by worldly vanity and the enticements of the passions. Making this examination of conscience in the presence of the Crucified spontaneously arouses heartfelt contrition; and the confession which follows will be a great help both for avoiding sin, and making progress in the spiritual life.

Do not, O Lord, withhold your mercy from me; let your steadfast love and your faithfulness ever preserve me . . . My iniquities have overtaken me till I cannot see; they are more than the hairs of my head; my heart fails me. Be pleased, O Lord, to deliver me; O Lord, make haste to help me! . . . As for me I am poor and needy, but the Lord takes thought for me. You are my help and my deliverer; do not tarry, O my God!

Psalm 40:12-14,18

Look upon me, O Jesus, infinite mercy; turn your face toward me, as I earnestly beg you, so that in your sight I may weep for my sins.

Once you looked upon Peter, who had fallen into sin; at your glance, and as a result of divine help, he wept bitterly; after regaining grace he remained in it forever. You also looked upon the thief, a criminal, so that he might humbly recognize you as the Lord of majesty, and thus he became worthy of passing through the gates of paradise with you.

You looked upon Mary the sinner, and she was suddenly wounded with remorse; without asking anything more, she prostrated herself at your feet and wept for her sins. She washed your feet with her tears, dried them with her hair to obtain your forgiveness, and with her precious perfume embalmed you in anticipation. Much was forgiven her because she loved much; she venerated the passion of him by whom she was loved and poured upon his head her perfumed ointment.

O holy will, O Creator, all goodness! O King who protect those who hope in you by snatching them from death! O good shepherd who carry your sheep on your shoulders! Be a shepherd also for this prostrate sinner who languishes in misery; raise me up, give me your hand and deign to set me on my feet again, so that I may remain thus in your presence, O most sweet Lord!

St. Leo IX, from *Prayers composed by the Popes*

141 – IN THE SIGN OF THE CROSS

All powerful and eternal God, you decreed that man should be saved by the wood of the cross, in order that where life was lost, life might be restored. (Roman Missal, Preface Exalt. Holy Cross)

1. After Jesus had tried to enlighten the Jews to lead them to faith, he was forced to say: "You will die in your sins unless you believe that I am he". They asked in return: "Who are you?" (Jn 8:24-25). Jesus did not answer this question immediately, but said, a little later: "When you have lifted up the Son of Man, then you will know that I am he" (ib. 28). If his words and his miracles are not enough to convince these obstinate men, his passion—the cross upon which he will be raised—followed by his resurrection, will be the supreme summons to their conversion and the most exhaustive answer to their questioning. On another occasion he said: "I, when I am lifted up from the earth, will draw all men to myself" (Jn 12:32). Jesus conquers men by his cross which becomes the center of attraction and of salvation for all mankind.

Whoever does not surrender to Christ crucified and does not believe in him, cannot attain salvation. It is in the blessed sign of the cross of Christ that we are redeemed; we are baptized, confirmed and absolved in that sign. The first sign that the Church traces upon the newborn infant, and the last with which she comforts and blesses the dying is always that of the holy sign of the cross. We are not dealing with a symbolic gesture, but with a great reality: Christian life is born of the cross; we are brought to life by the Lord crucified, and can be saved only by attaching ourselves to his cross and by placing our trust in the merits of his passion.

But faith in the crucified Christ must take us a step further. Since we have been redeemed by the cross, we must be convinced that our very life should be marked—and not just symbolically—by the cross of our Lord, that is, we must bear its living imprint. "If anyone serves me, he must follow me; and where I am, there shall my servant be also" (ib. 26), said Jesus. And he is on the cross. The same admonition is expressed in no less explicit terms by the synoptics: "He who does not take his cross and follow me is not worthy of me" (Mt 10:38). Since Jesus carried his cross and was sacrificed upon the cross, whoever wishes to be his disciple cannot choose any other way; it is the only one that leads to salvation, because it is the only one that makes us like the dead and risen Christ.

2. Reflection on the cross can never be separated from reflection on the resurrection which is its consequence and final conclusion. We are not redeemed by one who is dead, but by one who rose again from the death of the cross; therefore our carrying of the cross must always be fortified by the thought of Christ crucified and by that of Christ risen. "Pressing upon the Christian"—affirms the Council—"to be sure, are the need and the duty to battle against evil through manifold tribulations, and even to suffer death, but linked with the paschal mystery, and patterned on the dying Christ, he will hasten forward to resurrection with the strength which comes from hope" (GS 22). From this point of view, our daily cross becomes more than ever the sign and almost the sacrament of salvation, of redemption.

When the evangelist Luke refers to Jesus' words on the necessity of carrying the cross, he specifies that this must be *every day*. "If any man would come after me . . . let him take up his cross *daily*" (Lk 9:23). It is clear that Jesus was speaking not only of grave sufferings, but also of daily little ones. It is perhaps easier to accept, in one burst of generosity, great sorrows that happen only once, than some minute daily afflictions, which are connected with our state in life and with the fulfillment of our daily duties. These are troubles which are with us every day, always recurring, with the same intensity and insistence, through unavoidable situations which keep on, without change, for a long time. All this constitutes that specific cross which our Lord offers us daily, inviting us to carry it behind him; that humble daily cross that does not call for any great act of heroism, but before which we must each say our "yes", day after day, and meekly bend our back to carrying it with love. The gospel calls tribulations by the symbolic name of cross, as if to show that these troubles associate us with the real, and not symbolic, cross of Jesus, so that, united to his sufferings, they become a means of redemption just as the cross of our Lord was. Every suffering carries with it a redemptive grace which becomes ours when we embrace suffering in union with the crucified Christ.

O wondrous power of the cross! O ineffable glory of the passion! ... You have drawn all things to yourself, O Lord ... Your cross is the source of every blessing, the cause of all grace; through it faithful souls draw strength from weakness, glory from disgrace, life from death ...

The one only offering of your body and blood supplies with much more perfection for every other victim ... because you are the true "Lamb of God who take away the sin of the world". Thus you contain and perfect in yourself all mysteries, so that there may be one kingdom made up of all peoples, just as one single sacrifice substitutes for all victims.

St. Leo the Great, *Sermon* 59:7

Lord, give me your cross: through the multitude of my miseries, through your mercies, through your Calvary, through your crucified love, through your passion, as long as time endures. Lord Jesus, give me your cross, that invisible one that embraces all time and all eternity, the one that is made of crucified love, which is imprinted on the soul and constitutes its life.

Lord, I am crushed and consumed by the weight of my misery; I feel myself nothing, nothing but misery, and upon this misery of mine you imprint your adorable sign ... Lord, only your cross: to live it every minute, to feel it in everything, to find it in every thought. Jesus, oh! that I may no longer live without thinking of you crucified, that your cross may be the habitual dwelling-place of my soul, the place of my peace.

G. Canovai, *Suscipe Domine*

142 — THE SON WILL MAKE YOU FREE

In you, O Christ, we have redemption, the forgiveness of sins (Col 1:14)

1. When King Nebuchadnezzar commanded the three Jewish youths to adore the golden statue he had set up, under pain of being cast into a white-hot furnace, they answered: "If it be so, our God whom we serve is able to deliver us from the burning fiery furnace; and he will deliver us out of your hand, O King" (Dan 3:17). Their fearless faith was rewarded and they passed through the flames unharmed.

This marvelous event in the Old Testament is the figure of a still more marvelous act which is accomplished in the New: deliverance from the destructive fire of sin for those who believe in

Christ, who himself declared to the Jews: "If you continue in my word, you are truly my disciples; and you will know the truth and the truth will make you free" (Jn 8:31-32). The condition that Christ requires of men in order to free them from the slavery of sin is faith in him; a faith that is born of attentive, persevering listening to his word, the only word which contains the absolute truth, without any mixture of error or deceit. "I am the truth" (Jn 14:6), our Lord said; it is he who brings truth to the world, he is "the true light that enlightens every man" (Jn 1:9). His word is the vehicle of truth offered to men, so that, enlightened by it, they may be freed from the temptation of falsehood. The falsehood of the devil had led the human race astray at its very beginning, and had made man the slave of sin; Christ's truth shatters the old slavery and restores to man his freedom as a child of God. "The fruit of the tree tempted us; the Son of God redeemed us" (Rom. Missal, Good Friday).

In a world that is carried away by error, by false ideas, and corrupt customs, man is saved only by attaching himself to the gospel; only there can he find truth of doctrine and of life. Like the three Jewish youths, the Christian must have the courage to resist every kind of temptation, he must reject any theoretical or practical attitude which is not in keeping with the gospel, whether it openly contradicts it, or whether it alters it in some insidious way with interpretations that distort and minimize it. "Do not fear those who kill the body"—said the Lord—"but cannot kill the soul" (Mt 10:28).

2. Freedom belongs not to slaves, but to sons, "so if the Son makes you free, you will be free indeed" (Jn 8:35). Modern man who thirsts for freedom, needs to understand that true freedom is to be found only in Christ.

"Authentic freedom"—the Council teaches—"is an exceptional sign of the divine image within man" (GS 17). Man's freedom is nothing but a reflection of the infinite freedom of God. God is free in an absolute sense, man in a relative one; God's freedom consists in being able to do freely all the good he wishes; man's consists in the "free choice of good" (ib.). The more capable a man is of choosing and doing good, the freer he is. But sin has wounded him in his freedom; by clouding his mind it has made it difficult for him to know the truth, and to distinguish good from evil quickly; from this follows the deviation of the will, which is often inclined to choose evil rather than good. "Wretched man that I am! Who will deliver me from this body of death?" cries St. Paul, realizing how difficult it is for man to do all the good he would like to do. But he quickly adds, with much hope: "Thanks be to God through Jesus Christ our Lord!" (Rom 7:24-25). Only Christ can deliver us from this sad state of slavery, the result of sin, only he who "by dying destroyed death", a death caused by sin (RM).

But to enjoy fully the liberty that Christ offers us, we must trust in him, allow ourselves to be enlightened by him, incarnate Truth, and translate his words into our life and deeds. Freed from sin, we must make use of the freedom that God has given us and that Christ has restored to us, to serve God and Christ in love. God, infinite freedom, is love; we are free to the extent that we become love, that is, become capacity for loving God and our neighbor. "For you were called to freedom, brethren,"—writes St. Paul to the Galatians—"only do not use your freedom as an opportunity for the flesh, but through love, be servants of one another" (Gal 5:13). Liberty must be at the service of love, and authentic love is in its turn the generous and unselfish service of God and of our brothers.

My refuge and my fortress, my God, in whom I trust! For you will deliver me from the snare of the fowler and from the deadly pestilence. You will cover me with your pinions and under your wings I shall find refuge... No evil shall befall me... for you will give your angels charge of me to guard me in all my ways. Upon their hands they will bear me up, lest I dash my foot against a stone.

cf. *Psalm* 91:2-4, 10-12

As a doctor hates sickness and does everything he can to eliminate it and to help the sick person, so do you, my God, work in me with your grace to extinguish sin and free me from it... The first freedom, in fact, consists in being exempt from sin... When I begin to have fewer faults, then shall I begin to make a little progress toward freedom; but this will be only a beginning, not yet perfect liberty, because "I see in my members another law at war with the law of my mind"; and "I do not do what I want, but I do the very things I hate" (Rom 7:23,15)... On the one side there is freedom, on the other slavery; freedom is not yet complete, not yet unadulterated nor full, because we are not yet in eternity. I am still partly weak, partly free... In the extent that I serve you, O Lord, I am free, while in the measure that I serve the law of sin I am a slave...

What must I do, O Lord, about that weakness that remains in me? Nothing else but turn to you who said: "If the Son of God makes you free, you will be free indeed" (In Io 41:9-11).

O Lord I know it from yourself, that you will take care of my soul, because you say: "Do not fear those who kill the body, but cannot kill the soul" (Mt 10:28)... Let no one make me afraid: you who called me are the stronger because you are omnipotent; you are stronger than all the strong, higher than all the highest. You died for me: therefore I am sure of receiving your life, for your death is the pledge. For whom did you die? For the just, perhaps? I ask Paul and he answers: "Christ died for the ungodly" (Rom 5:6). So you died for me, when I was ungodly; now that I am justified, will you abandon me? (In Ps 96:17).

St. Augustine

143 — OBSERVANCE OF THE WORD

I promise, O Lord, to keep your words. *(Ps 119:57)*

1. "If you continue in my word . . . you will know the truth and the truth will make you free" (Jn 8:31-32). This assurance is completed by another: "If any one keeps my word he will never see death" (ib. 51). The word of the Lord is truth, it is life; the obligation to persevere in his word and to observe it guides us to a clearer and deeper understanding of the truth it contains, and leads us on to freedom from sin, and also from death, which is sin's gravest consequence. The observance of his word, the knowledge of truth, the conquest of liberty, and possession of eternal life are the progressive stages of Christian life which cross the frontier of eternity. All comes from the life-giving power of the Lord's words, which are "Spirit and life" (Jn 6:63), and "words of eternal life" (ib. 68).

The Jews did not understand this and protested: how could Jesus claim to free his disciples from death, when the prophets themselves and even Abraham were dead? In his reply our Lord pointed out the contrast between their incredulity and the faith of the Patriarch whose children they boasted of being: "Your father, Abraham, rejoiced that he was to see my day. He saw it and was glad" (Jn 8:56). Abraham who lived by faith in the word of God, and persevered in it to the point of heroism, had received the light to believe in the promised Messiah, and rejoiced in his advent from across the centuries. The Jews, on the other hand, although contemporaries of the Messiah, did not recognize him nor believe in him, because they rejected his word: "You seek to kill me, because my word finds no place in you" (ib. 37). The greatest blindness goes hand in hand with the greatest rejection of the word of Christ; blindness once drove the Jews to cry out for the death of their Savior, and in our own day it impels many people to persecute Christ in his Church. But Christ does not die, and he continues to say: "Before Abraham was, I am" (ib. 58). He is, today as yesterday, tomorrow and always; no power can prevail against him, and his disciples find light and life in him, even in their most trying moments. Their anchor of salvation is the eternal word of the Lord: "Any one who keeps my word will not see eternal death."

2. Observance of the word does not coerce nor destroy our liberty; on the contrary, it strengthens it. The Council declares in speaking of religious life that it has the advantage of offering to those who embrace it "liberty strengthened by obedience" (LG 43). Obedience to God is the great support of human freedom, tempted from within by the passions, and from without by the enticements of wickedness. Obedience defends us against the fickleness of our whims, against the weaknesses and uncertainty of our will, against the slavery of sin and the world; it makes us

totally free before the holy will of God for the full observance of his word. The more we enter by obedience into the will of God and live in it, the more we pass from a state of slavery to a state of freedom, and become sharers in God's own freedom. Then we can understand why religious obedience, which immerses our whole life in the divine will, "will not diminish the dignity of the human person but will rather lead it to maturity in consequence of that enlarged freedom which belongs to the sons of God" (PC 14).

When Jesus, the Son of God by nature, speaks of his relationship with the Father he always repeats: "I keep his word" (Jn 8:55); it is precisely by keeping God's word that we become more and more sons through the Son. And just as Jesus "by his obedience even at the cost of death, opened to all men the blessed way to the liberty of the children of God" (LG 37), so the more closely we imitate his obedience the more decisively we enter upon the way of liberty.

When the religious makes the vow of obedience, he is not destroying his liberty, but is pledging it in the greatest and most noble way to fulfill the will of God; he does not become an automaton in the hands of his superiors, but remains a living and free person who "for love of God" voluntarily submits to one like himself "in pursuit of an excellence surpassing what is commanded. Thus they liken themselves more thoroughly to Christ in his obedience" (LG 42). Religious obedience carries to the extreme the hearing and observance of the word in imitation of Christ who lived solely by the word of his Father.

My portion, O Lord, is to keep your words . . . When I think of your ways I turn my feet to your testimonies. I hasten and do not delay to keep your commandments.

Forever, O Lord, your word is firmly fixed in the heavens. Your faithfulness endures to all generations . . . If your law had not been my delight, I should have perished in my affliction. I will never forget your precepts, for by them you have given me life. I am yours, save me; for I have sought your precepts . . . The unfolding of your words gives light; it imparts understanding to the simple. With open mouth I pant because I yearn for your commandments.

Psalm 119:57-60, 89-94, 130-131

My Lord and my God . . . not only with my mouth, but from the depths of my heart I desire to do your will, your whole will, only your will, your will and not mine; make me know it, my God, and make me do it. Give me the faith and obedience of Abraham; make me listen to your voice. Your interior voice, the voice of those through whom you speak to me. Give me faith, my God, and give me obedience . . . which sacrifices the dearest affections of the heart and the strongest convictions of the mind in order to adhere solely to your holy and blessed will. My God, I beg this of you with all my heart, through our Lord Jesus Christ.

C. de Foucauld, *Meditations on the Old Testament,* Op Sp.

O delightful obedience, O pleasant obedience! O sweet, illuminating obedience which scatters the darkness of self-love. O vivifying obedience, you give the life of grace to the soul who has chosen you for spouse, slaying its own will which brings war and death to the soul ... You are benignant and kind, and meekly bear the greatest weights, for you are accompanied by fortitude and true patience. You are crowned with perseverance, because you do not fail on account of the great loads that are put upon you, but endure everything with the light of faith. You are so closely bound to humility that no creature can take this virtue from the soul who possesses you.

The good of obedience is seen in you, O Word, who taught us the way of obedience, being obedient yourself unto the shameful death of the cross. Our obedience is based on yours, which is the key that opened the door of heaven.

cf St. Catherine of Siena, *Dialogue* 144

144 — I CAST MY CARE ON YOU

I cast my burden on you, Lord, and you will sustain me *(Ps 55:22)*

1. "For I hear many whisperings: Terror is on every side! 'Denounce him! Let us denounce him!' All my familiar friends watch for my fall. 'Perhaps he will be deceived; then we can overcome him ... ' But the Lord is with me, as a dread warrior; therefore my persecutors will stumble, they will not overcome me" (Jer 20:10-11). The lament of the persecuted Jeremiah resounds in the Lenten liturgy as an expression of the suffering Christ, rejected, caluminated, and hated unto death. But, unlike Jeremiah, Jesus does not call for revenge, nor try to evade his enemies. If the Gospel records that many times he "escaped from their hands" (Jn 10:39), this is simply because the hour set by the Father had not yet come. Meanwhile, amid the threats and insults of the Jews, and their attempts to capture him, Jesus continued his work of preaching, and "many believed in him" (ib. 42). He knew the cross awaited him, he knew that his affirmations of his divinity, and the resurrection of Lazarus would irritate his adversaries all the more, and would hasten events, but he continues his work with supreme serenity and freedom. Trust in his Father sustained him: "For to you have I committed my cause" (Jer 20:12).

"To you have I committed my cause." It is this attitude of trust in God which must sustain us in our own hour of sorrow and persecution. "A servant is not greater than his master. If they persecuted me, they will persecute you" (Jn 15:20). Anyone who resolves to live according to the gospel, to defend truth, and to do good, will not be able to escape the contradiction of the same world that is opposed to Christ. And if God allows it, further sufferings and misunderstandings may be added from other sources, perhaps from good people or friends or even from family or those who are brothers in ideals. A true Christian is not scandalized; we know that the cross is an essential part of the heritage and of the following of Christ; we know that just as Christ saved us by his cross, so we enter upon the way of salvation and cooperate in the salvation of the world, by carrying our own cross.

2. "Cast all your anxieties upon him for he cares about you" (1 Pet 5:7). If we are turned back by suffering, we end up being irritated by it and being submerged in it, for we cut ourselves off from every generous impulse. But if, instead, we abandon ourselves to God, we keep our balance, and are able to think more of others than of self, and are always ready to give of self. "Resist [the devil] firm in your faith"—writes St. Peter to the persecuted Christians—"knowing that the same experience of suffering is required of your brotherhood throughout the world" (ib. 9). The thought of the sufferings of others, perhaps greater than our own, helps us to forget ourselves, and to go beyond our personal sufferings in order to dedicate ourselves to alleviating those of others, bearing our own cross in solidarity with our suffering brothers, and especially, in conformity with Christ crucified.

Yet sometimes anguish can be so deep that we are left as if overwhelmed by it. Then it helps to remember that Jesus too, in Gethsemane, was so weighed down by suffering that he sweated blood and moaned: "My heart is very sorrowful, even to death" (Mt 26:38). Even though he was the Son of God, and was himself God, he willed to experience within himself all the fright and terror and repugnance of human nature in the face of suffering. In the mortal sadness of Christ each of us finds his own anguish and anxieties sanctified and, at the same time, finds the strength not to succomb. Taking refuge with Jesus in his prayer to the Father: "Not as I will, but as you will" (ib. 39), we resist the assaults of grief, and are not shaken or exasperated by them; filial and trusting abandonment to the will of God makes us capable of facing the most tragic situations with simplicity and even serenity, because we know that those who trust in God cannot be put to shame (cf Dan 3:28).

"After you have suffered a little while, the God of all grace, who has called you to his eternal glory in Christ, will himself restore, establish, and strengthen you" (1 Pet 5:10). The tribulations of this life are always "a brief suffering" in comparison with the blessed eternity toward which the cross leads.

O God, you lead those whom you greatly love by the path of tribulation—and the more you love them the greater the tribulation . . . To think that you admit into your intimate friendship people who live in comfort and without trials is foolish . . .

It is not your will to give us riches, or delights, or honors, or all these earthly things. Your love for us is not that small... Do we want to know how you answer those who sincerely ask you to accomplish your will in them, we must ask your glorious Son who made this same prayer in the garden of olives... You accomplished your will in him through the trials, sorrows, injuries and persecutions he suffered until his life came to an end through death on a cross... See here what you gave to the one you loved most,... These are your gifts as long as we are in this world. You give according to the love you bear us: to those you love more, you give more of these gifts; to those you love less, you give less. And you give according to the courage you see in each of us and the love each has for you; whoever loves you much, will be able to suffer much, whoever loves you little will be capable of little.

St. Teresa of Jesus, *Way* 18:1,2; 32:6,7

O Jesus, you offer me a cup so bitter that my feeble nature cannot bear it. But I do not want to draw back my lips from the cup your hand has prepared... You teach me the secret of suffering in peace. The word peace does not mean joy, at least not felt joy; to suffer in peace, it is enough to will whatever you will. To be your spouse, Jesus, one must be like you, and you are all bloody, crowned with thorns!

How consoling it is to remember that you, the God of might, knew our weaknesses, that you shuddered at sight of the bitter cup, the cup that earlier you had so ardently desired to drink.

O Jesus, what it costs to give you what you ask! What happiness it costs! What unutterable joy to bear our crosses so feebly! Far from complaining of the cross you send me, I cannot fathom the infinite love which has brought you to treat me so... the greater my sufferings, the more limitless my glory... O Jesus, don't let me waste the trial you send me, it is a gold-mine I must exploit. I would set myself to the task without joy, without courage, without strength... I want to work for love.

St. Therese of the Child Jesus, *Letters* 63; 184; 59

145 – O CROSS, OUR ONLY HOPE

Far be it from me to glory except in your cross, O Lord Christ (Gal 6:14)

1. "Behold, I will take the people of Israel from among the nations ... and will gather them from all sides ... I will make them one nation ... I will save them from all their backslidings ... My servant David shall be king over them, and they shall all have one shepherd ... I will make a covenant of peace with them: it shall be an everlasting covenant with them" (Ez 37:21-26). Ezechiel's prophecy is touchingly paralleled in St. John's Gospel. Referring to the sentence by which Caiphas decreed the death of Jesus:

"You do not understand that it is expedient for you that one man should die for the people and that the whole nation should not perish" (Jn 11:50), the evangelist comments: "Being high priest that year, he prophesied that Jesus should die for the nation—and not for the nation only, but to gather into one the children of God who are scattered abroad" (ib. 51-52). Caiphas' intention was to rid himself of Christ in order to safeguard the political interests of the nation; but in God's plan the death of Jesus is an event of immensely greater and vaster bearing: upon it depends the spiritual salvation of Israel, and not that of Israel only, but of all the nations and of all God's children spread around the world. Ezechiel's prophecy is most fully and abundantly fulfilled in Christ's sacrifice: in the blood of Christ all men will be purified from sin, and the new and eternal alliance of peace between God and mankind will be established. Christ—dead and risen—will be the one king and shepherd who will reunite men into a single people to make them the people of God.

Once again it appears clearly how the cross of Christ stands at the center of world history: upon it depends the life, salvation and happiness of every creature. "Let us adore your Cross, Lord"—sings the Liturgy of Good Friday—"through the Cross you brought joy to the whole world" (RM). Just as the tree with forbidden fruit was the cause of sin and hence of death, so is the tree of the Cross the cause of redemption and life. This is why the Christian loves Christ's Cross, puts his hope in it, and salutes it: "Hail, O Cross, our only hope! . . . you increase grace for the just, and grant pardon to sinners" (Brev.).

2. The word of the cross is folly to those who are perishing, but to us who are being saved, it is the power of God" (1 Cor 1:18). For those who do not believe in Christ the cross is an unacceptable absurdity; but for those who follow him and love him "it is the power of God," a power that redeems, saves, and sanctifies. The more we aspire to holiness, the more we must love the cross, and not only the Cross by which we were redeemed, but also the personal cross that associates us with the mystery of Christ's death, in order to make us participants in the mystery of his life. "O souls who in spiritual matters desire to walk in security and consolation!"—exclaims St. John of the Cross—"If you but knew how much it behooves you to suffer in order to reach this security and state of consolation!" (Fl 2:28). We are so penetrated with selfishness and pride that we need to be purified and transformed to the depths of our being before we can attain to union with God. Only God can accomplish this work in us, and he does so by means of the cross. Therefore when God bursts into the life of one of his creatures with interior and exterior trials, afflicting it in body and soul, he does it one of the greatest favors, for it is a sign of his plans for love and holiness.

Christ accomplished the work of reconciling mankind with God when "he was most annihilated in all things: in his reputation before men, since, in beholding him die, they mocked him instead of esteeming him; in his human nature, by dying; and in spiritual help and consolation from his Father, for he was forsaken by his Father at that time." From all this, the spiritual person may "understand the mystery of the door and way which is Christ . . . and may realize that his union with God and the greatness of the work he accomplishes will be measured by his annihilation for God" (Asc II 7:11). When the soul is deeply convinced of this truth, it will not find the bold expressions about the cross of his Lord excessive, but will make them the blueprint of its own life: "Far be it from me to glory except in the cross of our Lord Jesus Christ, by which the world has been crucified to me, and I to the world" (Gal 6:14).

Hail, O life-giving Cross, O unconquerable trophy of piety, gate of paradise, comfort of believers, rampart of the Church; through you corruption has been annihilated, the power of death swallowed up and destroyed, and we have been raised from the earth to heavenly things. Henceforth, you are invincible, the adversary of demons, glory of the martyrs, true adornment of the saints, gate of salvation . . .

Hail, Cross of the Lord, through which the human race has been freed from the curse; you are the sign of true joy, who with your glorification have brought down all your enemies. Truly venerable, you are our succor, the strength of kings, the steadiness of the just, the dignity of sinners . . .

Hail, O precious Cross, guide of the blind, physician of the sick, resurrection of the dead, you raised us up again when we had fallen into corruption. Through you corruption has been ended and immortality has flowered, through you we mortals are made as gods, and the devil struck down . . . O Christ, today we kiss your precious Cross with our unworthy lips, sinners as we are.

We praise you, O Christ, who willed to be nailed to the cross; and like the thief we cry out to you: "Make us worthy of your kingdom!"

Oriental Liturgy, from *Days of the Lord*

O suffering God-Man, I beg you with all my soul, let me never take my eyes from you. If I keep on trusting in you, you will inflame me completely. I will try with all my strength to come back to you and to fix my eyes on you. I want to be continually returning to you and travel the ways of the Passion and of the Cross.

O afflicted God-Man, be my support. Who could reflect on you so poor and overwhelmed with such inexpressible and continual affliction, scorned and brought to nothing, and could have the grace to see this as in a vision, and not be ready to follow you, be it in poverty or in constant pain, or in abuse and scorn. For when we receive suffering it is a sign that we have been chosen by you, beloved Lord, who thus give us a pledge of your love. Let us then fix our gaze upon your sorrows and we shall find a remedy for every anguish. O Son of God, you took suffering as a blessing!

cf Bl. Angela da Foligno, *Book of the Divine Consolation*

146 — PALM SUNDAY

Of the Passion of the Lord

Blessed is he who comes in the name of the Lord, the King of Israel
(Jn 12:13)

1. Holy Week opens with the memory of the triumphant entrance of Christ into Jerusalem, which took place exactly the Sunday before his passion. Jesus had always opposed all public display and had fled when the people wanted to make him king (Jn 6:15); today he allows himself to be carried in triumph. Only now, when he is about to go to his death, does he accept public acclamation as the Messiah, the Redeemer, King and Conqueror. He accepts recognition as king, but as a king with unmistakable characteristics: humble and meek, he enters the holy city astride a donkey, he will proclaim his kingship only in the courts of justice, and will allow its inscription to be put only upon the cross. The festive entry into Jerusalem is the spontaneous homage of the people for Jesus who is announcing, through his passion and death, the full revelation of his divine kingship. The crowd that was singing hosanna was not able to grasp all the import of his action, but the community of the faithful who repeat that hosanna today can understand its full significance. "You are the King of Israel, you are David's royal son, who in the Lord's name come, the king and blessed One . . . To you before your passion, they sang their hymns of praise: to you now high exalted, our melody we raise" (Hymn, RM).

The Liturgy invites us to look upon the glory of Christ the eternal king, so that we may be prepared to understand better the value of his humiliating passion, which is the necessary road to his highest glorification. Therefore it is not a matter of accompanying Jesus on a momentary triumph, but of following him all the way to Calvary, where, by his dying on the cross, he will triumph forever over sin and death. These are the sentiments expressed by the Church when, in blessing the branches, it prays that the Christian people may fulfill the external rite "with utmost devotion, triumphing over the enemy and honoring with all their heart the . . . merciful work of salvation" of the Lord. There is no more beautiful way to honor Christ's passion than to become part of it in order to triumph with him over our enemy, sin.

2. The Mass brings us fully into the theme of the passion. The prophecy of Isaiah and the responsorial psalm anticipate certain details with startling precision: "I gave my back to the smiters, and my cheeks to those who pulled out my beard. I hid not my face from shame and spitting" (Is 50:6). Why such submissiveness? Because Christ, foreshadowed in the servant of Jahweh described by the prophet, is wholly stretched out to the will of the Father, and with him desires the sacrifice of himself for the salvation of men. "The Lord God has opened my ear, and I was not rebellious,

I turned not backward" (ib. 15). So we see him dragged before the tribunal, then to Calvary, and there stretched out on the cross: "They have pierced my hands and my feet; I can count all my bones" (Ps 22:16-17). The Son of God was reduced to this condition for one single reason: love; love for the Father whose glory he wants to restore, love for mankind whom he wants to reconcile with the Father.

Only infinite love can explain the disconcerting humiliations placed on the Son of God. "Christ, who though he was in the form of God did not count equality with God something to be grasped at, but emptied himself, taking the form of a slave" (Phil 2:6-7). In his passion Christ carried to the extreme limit his renunciation of claiming the rights due to his divinity; he not only hid them under the appearance of human nature, but stripped himself of them to the point of submitting to the torture of the cross and exposing himself to the bitterest of insults: "He saved others, he cannot save himself. Let Christ, the King of Israel, come down now from the cross that we may see and believe" (Mk 15:31-32). Like the evangelist, the Church too does not hesitate to propose to the faithful the consideration of Christ's passion in all its cruel reality, so as to make it clear that he who is true God is also true man, and suffered as such; by eliminating from his tortured humanity every trace of his divinity, he became brother to men to the point of sharing death with them that they might share his divine nature. "For us Christ became obedient unto death, even death on a cross. Therefore God has highly exalted him, and bestowed on him the name which is above every name" (RM). From extreme annihilation springs highest exaltation; even as a man, Christ is established as Lord of all creatures and exercises his sovereignty in reconciling them with God, ransoming them from sin and conferring his divine life upon them.

Increase the faith of those who hope in you, O God, and listen to our prayers. Today we honor Christ, our triumphant King, by carrying these branches; grant that we may remain united to him, to bear the fruit of good works.

Roman Missal, *Blessing of Palms*

O Jesus, foreseeing the multitude that was coming to meet you, you mounted an ass and gave a wonderful example of humility amid the applause of the people who were coming to you, and were cutting down branches and strewing the street with their garments. While the crowd sang songs of praise, you, ever mindful of compassion, lamented over the destruction of Jerusalem. Rise now, O handmaid of the Lord, and go in the procession of the daughters of Zion to see your true king . . . Accompany the Lord of heaven and earth, sitting on the back of the colt, follow him with olive branches and palms, with works of piety and triumphant virtues.

St. Bonaventure, *The Tree of Life* 15.

How you loved us, good Father, who did not spare your only Son, but delivered him up for us! How you loved us, for whom he that thought it no robbery to be equal with you, was made subject even to the death of the cross, He alone, free among the dead, having power to lay down his life, and power to take it up again. For us he was victor and victim in your sight, and victor because a victim; for us he was priest and sacrifice before you, priest because he was sacrifice; where we were slaves, he made us your children by being your Son and becoming our servant! So I hope steadfastly in him that you will cure all my infirmities, for he sits at your right hand and makes intercession for us; else should I despair. For many and great are my infirmities, but your medecine is mightier.

St. Augustine, *Confessions* X, 43

147 — TOWARD BETHANY

Monday of Holy Week

O hail, our King, only you have had compassion for our sins (RM)

1. The first of the celebrated songs of the "Servant of Jahweh" (Is 42:1-7), leads to a study of Christ's demeanor during his passion. Meek in his silence "he does not cry . . . or make (his voice) heard in the street," nor does he complain about the insults, the accusations, or his condemnation; he is meek in dealing with his enemies, "bruised reeds" which he will not break, "dimly burning wicks" he will not quench, but whom he forgives and tries until the very end to enlighten and save. Christ's gentleness toward sinful men, upon whom he has compassion and for whose sins he is preparing to atone, is changed into fortitude as he fulfills his mission, and preaches truth and justice even to his death: "he will not fail or be discouraged till he has established justice on the earth." Jesus labors for the coming of his Father's kingdom, to affirm God's rights over men, and to re-establish men in justice and holiness. He does not surrender in this; his death itself will be his supreme act of fortitude in accomplishing the work entrusted to him by the Father. Since Christ's strength is divine, not even death will overcome it; on the contrary, he will conquer death in order to give life to men. Jesus is truly the "Servant of God" prophesied by Isaiah, called "in righteousness" and "given as a covenant to the people, a light to the nations." In him all men find mercy: "Hail, our King: you alone showed mercy for our sins" (Verse at Gospel). Christ fought against sin and condemned it, but he punished it only in himself, while he gave the guilty his pardon and obtained his Father's for them also.

"The Lord is my light and my salvation; whom shall I fear? The Lord is my life's refuge; of whom should I be afraid?" (Ps 27:1). The Liturgy recognizes in these words the voice of Christ appealing trustfully to his Father for help during his passion; we also can use them to express to our Savior our own gratitude and unfailing trust. In Christ crucified the christian finds the remedy for his sins, as well as a haven in life's troubles and strength to carry the cross.

2. Before entering into the depths of the mystery of the passion, the Liturgy presents us with an intimate and delightful picture: "Six days before the Passover, Jesus came to Bethany, where Lazarus was, whom Jesus had raised from the dead" (Jn 12:1-11). The banquet in that hospitable home, given by his faithful friends at the beginning of the week that will see his death, has all the appearance of a last farewell and almost of anticipation of what is about to happen. This is expressed in a special way in Mary's loving action; without regard to cost, she anoints the feet of Jesus with "a pound of costly ointment of pure nard." It is the supreme homage of a faithful heart which seems to want to make up to the Master for the betrayal that awaits him; at the same time, it is a foreshadowing of his death, for, according to Jewish custom, only the feet of corpses were anointed. On the other hand, in the presence of Lazarus—whom Jesus had raised from the dead—there is a portent of the resurrection. One who had brought back to life a man dead for four days and had said: "I am the resurrection and the life" (Jn 11:25), could not remain a victim of death. Such a portent is not lacking in Mary's action if the ointment was also poured over the Lord's head, as the synoptics say (Mk 14:3); the anointing of the head, which was reserved for kings signifies a recognition of the divine kingship of Christ, which the resurrection will make known in its full glory.

But in this intimate episode the dark shadows of malicious criticism are not lacking, a prelude to his betrayal. "Why was this ointment not sold for three hundred silver pieces and given to the poor?" Concern for the poor is but a pretext on the lips of Judas who "was a thief; and as he had the purse he used to take what was put into it" (Jn 12:5-6). This is the attitude of many who are scandalized at valuable things being consumed solely for God. In their eyes, prayer, adoration, and what is much more, human lives spent in the love and praise of God, are a useless waste; time, money and life are well used only if employed in the direct service of men. They forget that although concern for the poor is a great obligation, which no one emphasized more than Christ, love and worship of God are still greater obligations. Besides, it is not only bread that the poor need, they also need people—those who by spending themselves in prayer will sustain their faith and remind them that material well-being is of little worth if God is not sought above everything.

O Jesus, you were led to death like a lamb, like a sheep that does not open its mouth before its shearers. You utter no word of complaint to your Father who sent you, nor against the men whose debt you are paying . . . not even against the people who belong especially to you, and from whom, in exchange for such great benefits, you receive unheard of wrongs . . .

When I study your behavior carefully, I discover not only the mildness, but also the humility of your heart... We saw you, and you had neither attractiveness nor beauty before men, but were become a disgrace to them, like a leper; the last among men, truly a man of sorrows, stricken and humiliated by God... O Jesus, lowest and loftiest, humble and sublime, the disgrace of men and the glory of the angels! No one more sublime than you, and no one more humble...

Great are your mercies, O Lord, but great also the miseries you suffer! Will these conquer mercy, or will mercy overcome the miseries?... You cry out: "Father, forgive them because they know not what they are doing." O Lord, how wide is your forgiveness, how deep the abyss of your sweetness! How different are your thoughts from ours, and how unchangeable your mercy, even for the wicked!... O charity, that bears all things and has compassion on all!

St. Bernard, *In Feria IV Holy Week* 2,3,9

My God, on that evening... of love and of grief, that evening of sweetness because you are present, of sorrow because you are so close to death and suffering, Mary spreads perfume upon your feet and upon your head... She pours it over your feet, spilling the perfume and breaking its container, and she gives you her whole being, body and soul, heart and mind: she gives you all that she is: she pours out the perfume and breaks its container... She saves nothing, she gives all, all that she is and all that she has... O Jesus, I want to give myself to you as that holy woman gave herself, without holding back anything either of myself or for myself... "Behold, I come to do your will." Lord, make my gift complete, so that I give you my whole self and everything that belongs to me as well: the perfume, the container, my soul and body, everything.

cf C. de Foucauld, *Meditations on the Gospel,* Op Sp.

148 — GLORY AND BETRAYAL

Tuesday of Holy Week

O Lord, be to me a rock of refuge, a strong fortress to save me (Ps 71:3)

1. After the comforting respite in Bethany, Jesus returns to Jerusalem, where he faces the final heated debates with the Pharisees and continues to teach the people. "He made my mouth like a sharp sword... He made me a polished arrow"; the introduction that the Servant of Jahweh made of himself through Isaiah (49:1-6), may be applied to Christ in the grip of his adversaries, not because he is a sword or arrow that is bent on destroying them, for he came not to judge but to save (Jn 3:17), but because he denounces their errors and condemns their malice with divine freedom. In fact there will always be people like the

Pharisees, who will reject the message and the love of Christ. This is the cause of the bitterest anguish of his passion, of which we can catch a hint in the words of the prophet: "But I said 'I have labored in vain, I have spent my strength for nothing and vanity' " (Is 49:4). But Christ's anguish is always accompanied by trust in the Father who has concealed him "in the shadow of his hand" and in him "will be glorified" (ib. 2-3); this is infinite compensation for all the rejections of men. God will certainly not abandon his beloved Son to humiliation and death forever, but will lead him away from it through the resurrection, thus showing the world his own glory and that of his Christ.

Jesus will also express himself in this vein during the evening of the Last Supper, immediately after declaring that he was about to be betrayed. "Now is the Son of Man glorified, and in him God is glorified" (Jn 13:31). "Now," because the betrayal begins Christ's passion, and his passion leads to the glory which the Father has prepared for him; which will in turn bring about the glorification of the Father himself and the salvation of men. The passion is always shown as the gateway to Christ's exaltation and the world's salvation. The prophet too had had a glimpse of it in this aspect when he concluded his references to the sufferings of the Servant of Jahweh with the magnificent declaration: "It is too light a thing for you to be my servant, to raise up the tribes of Jacob, and restore the preserved of Israel. I will give you as a light to the nations, that my salvation may reach to the end of the earth" (Is 49:6).

2. The passage of John's Gospel which the Liturgy proposes for our consideration today brings together those most sorrowful remarks that Jesus made to his disciples: "Truly, truly, I tell you solemnly, one of you will betray me . . . The cock will not crow till you have denied me three times" (Jn 13:21,38). Jesus knew that betrayal was awaiting him, but this foreknowledge did not make him insensitive; the approach of that hour moved him to the point whereof John gives witness: "he was troubled in spirit" (ib. 21). It was the shuddering of the Redeemer's humanity, for, although God, he loved and suffered with the heart of a man. That agitation had a special echo in Peter, the ardent and impetuous apostle who wanted to find out right away who the betrayer was, perhaps to reprove him and prevent him from carrying out his infamous plan. It never entered his mind that he, too, could fall into the snare of temptation. His love for the Master was great and sincere, but presumptuous; he was too sure of himself; Peter needed to learn that no one can consider himself better than others, not even better than traitors. Indeed, this very night, just a few hours after declaring to the Lord: "I would give my life for you," came the bitter experience of his weakness: first at Gethsemane where, while Jesus agonized, he let sleep overtake him as it did the others; and then when he fled, full of fear, when Jesus was captured; and a third time, still more painful, took place in the courtyard of the palace of Caiphas. A servant recognized him as a disciple of the

Nazarene, and Peter, overcome by panic, denied it: "I neither know nor understand what you mean" (Mk 14:68); three times he denied it, and the last time the most emphatically of all, since, as Mark relates, "he began to curse and to swear: 'I do not know this man of whom you speak' " (ib. 71). Mark is the evangelist who describes Peter's denial the most minutely; the humble confession of his fall that the head of the Apostles makes through the lips of his disciple should serve as warning to all of us. No one can consider himself sure of not falling. Probably when the cock crowed, and more surely when Jesus turned and looked at him (Lk 22:61), Peter came back to his senses, and at the same time remembered the words his Master had spoken that night, together with that earlier warning: "Apart from me you can do nothing" (Jn 15:5). Peter no longer had any need for the Master to insist; now he understood and "he went out and wept bitterly" (Lk 22:62). Blessed tears of repentance which wash away and dissolve presumption in humility.

O God of my soul, how we hasten to offend you and how you hasten more to pardon us! What reason is there, Lord, for such deranged boldness? Could it be that we have already understood your great mercy and have forgotten that your justice is just?

"The sorrows of death surround me"—Oh, oh, what a serious thing sin is, for it was enough to kill God with so many sorrows! And how surrounded you are by them, my God! Where can you go that they do not torment you? Everywhere mortals wound you.

Oh, great blindness, my God! What extraordinary ingratitude, my King! that we serve the devil with what you yourself give us! Shall we repay the great love you bear us by loving the one who so abhors you and must abhor you forever? After the blood you shed for us, and the blows and great sorrows you suffered, and the severe torments you endured, do we . . . accept as companions and friends those who disrespectfully treat you? O Lord, why do we see you bound and tied by the love you bear us? What more did those who delivered him to death do? . . . Oh, my God, how much you suffer for one who grieves so little over your pains!

St. Teresa of Jesus, *Soliloquies* X:1; XII:3-5

Remember, my Jesus, how dearly I have cost you! Remember, O merciful God, what a price you paid upon the wood of the bitter cross for me, a sinner! Remember, my compassionate Redeemer, what I have desired to do and not what I have done! . . .

O sweet Lord Jesus Christ, how many times I have given you bitter gall in exchange for the honey which you gave me! How many sins for so many gifts! How much evil for so many benefits! O how many times, while I enjoyed things that were yours . . . I offended you with these same things of yours.

O how many times, accepting your wages, I fought under the banner of the devil and the world. Give me now the grace to render you . . . good and not evil, gratitude and not ingratitude, and that I may always grieve when I do or think anything against your majesty; grant that in the future I may repay love for love, blood for blood, and life for life.

B. Camilla da Varona *Letters,* Op. Sp.

149 — THE HOUR OF DARKNESS

Wednesday of Holy Week

O Lord, be gracious to me; heal me, for I have sinned against you (Ps 41:4)

1. "Truly I say to you, one of you will betray me" (Jn 13:21; Mt 26:21); These same words quoted by John, are also reported by Matthew, who adds other details. It was not only Peter who wanted to know who the traitor was; the others were anxious too, and "were very sorrowful, and began to say to him one after another: 'Is it I, Lord?' " (Mt 26:22). Even Judas dared to ask the question. Jesus had already secretly pointed him out to John: "He to whom I shall give the morsel when I have dipped it in the dish" (Jn 13:26), and to the queries of all had given an indirect answer: "He who has dipped his hand in the dish with me will betray me" (Mt 26:23). But Judas with cynical coolness was seated at the table as a friend, while planning the betrayal. He accepted the revealing mouthful without a quiver, but could not remain hidden; he himself provoked his denunciation: "Is it I, Master?" Jesus answered: "You have said so" (ib 25). What the Master had veiled with compassionate delicacy, he was now constrained to say openly. Although he knew what Judas' end would be, he had chosen him and loved him like the others, and had also warned him; about a year before he had said: "Did I not choose you, and one of you is a devil?" (Jn 6:70); this had been said for Judas' benefit, to put him on guard. During supper, in order to point him out, the Lord made use of a gesture of friendship—the morsel dipped and offered—which was intended as a tacit admonition; and then, in the Garden of Olives, he made one last attempt to save him from his fall when he accepted, rather than rejected, the traitor's kiss. But by this time Judas was in the clutches of the devil, to whom he had given himself in exchange for thirty pieces of silver. And Jesus is forced to declare: "The Son of Man goes as it is written of him, but woe to that man by whom the Son of Man is betrayed" (Mt 26:24). These are serious words that throw light on the traitor's tremendous responsibility. Judas had not followed the Master out of love, but out of selfishness, looking for material gain; greed had made him a thief: he began by pilfering small money, and then for small money betrayed him who was of no more interest to him, because he (Christ) was offering little hope of worldly gain. Thus the words of the psalm were verified: "Even my bosom friend who . . . ate of my bread, has lifted his heel against me" (Ps 41:9).

2. "It is for your sake that I have borne reproach, that shame has covered my face . . . Insults have broken my heart, so that I am in despair. I looked for pity, but there was none; and for comforters, but I found none" (Ps 69:8,21). In these days, consecrated to the mystery of the passion, the words of the psalmist echo the lament of Christ exposed to infamy, maligned and tortured, abandoned by all, and betrayed by his friends: "This is your hour and the power of darkness" (Lk 22:53), the Lord had said at the moment of his capture. This is the hour when betrayal becomes a handing over to the authorities, to condemnation to death and to crucifixion. But it is also the hour fixed by the Father for the consummation of his sacrifice and therefore the hour to which Jesus has looked forward with such burning desire: "I have a baptism to be baptized with, and how I am constrained until it is accomplished" (Lk 12:50). And further: "I have earnestly desired to eat this Passover with you before I suffer," (ib. 22:15); this would be his Passover, the sacrifice that would be anticipated in the Eucharistic Supper.

Christ's sacrifice supposes a traitor: this had been foreseen in the Scriptures, which did not, however, determine the betrayal, but simply announced it because it was going to happen. For though everything has been preordained by God, who so loved the world as to give his Son for its salvation, this did not exempt from guilt the man who of his own will became a traitor. "What does Judas have, if not sin?"—says St. Augustine—"In handing Christ over to the Jews, he certainly was not thinking of our salvation, which was the reason for which Christ gave himself into the hands of enemies; Judas was thinking of the money he would gain, and therein found the ruin of his soul" (In Io 62:4). God's plan made use of this infamous act to bring Christ to his passion. "Judas handed Christ over, and Christ handed himself over on his own: Judas did it to carry out his horrible bargain, Christ to achieve our redemption" (ib.). Christ's passion is an inexpressible mystery, even in this concurrence of divine and human causes; it is better to contemplate it in prayer than to analyze it with human logic. It contains a warning for each of us, for in each of us a traitor can in some measure be hidden. But the pardon granted to Peter and to the good thief is proof of the infinite love of Jesus' crushed heart, a love that can wipe out any sin whatsoever, once it has been confessed and bewailed.

O Jesus, how exceeding was your kindness toward your stubborn disciple! . . . Even without going into the details of the traitor's godlessness, I am struck infinitely more by your tender mildness, O Lamb of God! Your gentleness is given to us as a model . . . Behold here, Lord, a man you held in particular trust, who seemed so united with you, your adviser and close friend, who tasted your bread, and ate sweet dishes with you at the holy supper—he it was was who struck you with the blow of wickedness. And yet . . . most gentle

Lamb, you did not hesitate to offer yourself to that most malicious mouth, which kissed you at the hour of betrayal... You held back nothing that could possibly tame the obstinancy of an evil heart. (The Tree of Life 17).

Good Jesus, how many they are who smite you! Your Father smites you, for he did not pardon you, but gave you over as a victim for us all. And you smite yourself, by offering your soul to death, for this is something no one can take away from you without your permission. In addition, the disciple who betrays you with a kiss smites you; the Jews smite you with kicks and blows; the Gentiles smite you with whips and nails. See how many people, how many humiliations, how many executioners!

And how many your betrayers! The heavenly Father betrayed you for our sake; you betrayed yourself, as St. Paul joyously sings: "He loved me and he gave himself over for my sake." The exchange is truly amazing! The Master betrayed himself for the servant, God for man, the Creator for the creature, the Innocent for the sinner (Mystical Vine 5:5).

St. Bonaventure, *Mystical Booklets*

My kind Lord, how I thank you for bearing with me, who have been a thousand times worse than Judas! You made him your disciple and you have made me your bride and daughter... O my Jesus, I have betrayed you not just once, as he did, but an almost infinite number of times...

Who crucified you? I did. Who struck you at the pillar? I did. Who crowned you with thorns? I did. Who gave you vinegar and gall to drink? I did. My Lord, do you know why I tell you all these things that I have done? Because I have seen... in your light, that the mortal sins I have committed have afflicted and grieved you much more than all those tortures did.

Bl. Camilla da Varona *Mental sorrows of Jesus* 8, Op. Sp.

150 — THE LORD'S SUPPER

Holy Thursday

What shall I render to the Lord for all his bounty to me? I will lift up the cup of salvation and call upon the name of the Lord. (Ps 116:12-13)

1. The celebration of the paschal mystery, the center and summit of the history of salvation, begins on Holy Thursday with the celebration of the evening Mass which commemorates the Lord's Supper.

The readings all concentrate on the theme of the Passover supper. The passage from Exodus (12:1-8;11-14) records its institution which took place when God ordered the Hebrews to sacrifice in each family "a lamb without blemish," and to sprinkle the doors of their houses with its blood so that they might be spared from the slaughter of the first-born, and then to consume it hurriedly in the manner of travelers. That very night, saved by the blood of the lamb, and nourished by its flesh, they were to begin their march toward the promised land. This same rite was then to be repeated every year in memory of the event. "It is the Lord's Passover" (Ex 12:11), which commemorates his "passage" in the midst of Israel to free it from the slavery of Egypt.

Jesus chose the celebration of the Hebrew passover for establishing the new Passover, his Pasch, in which he is the true "lamb without blemish," sacrificed and consumed for the salvation of the world. He began the new rite while sitting at the table with his disciples. "The Lord Jesus on the night in which he was betrayed took bread"—so we read in the second lesson (1 Cor 11:23-26)—"and when he had given thanks he broke it and said: 'This is my body, which is for you . . . ' In the same way also the cup, after supper, saying, 'This cup is the new covenant in my blood.' "

That bread, miraculously transformed into the Body of Christ, and that chalice that no longer contained wine, but the Blood of Christ, each offered separately that night, were the announcement and the anticipation of the death of the Lord in which he would pour out all his blood, and are today its living memorial. "Do this in remembrance of me," is St. Paul's way of presenting the Eucharist to us: "Each time you eat this bread and drink of this chalice, you proclaim the death of the Lord." The Eucharist is "living bread" which gives eternal life to men (Jn 6:51), because it is the "remembrance" of Christ's death, because it is his Body "given" in sacrifice, his Blood "poured out . . . for the forgiveness of sins." (Lk 22:19; Mt 26:28). Nourished by the Body of Christ, and sprinkled and washed by his Blood, we are enabled to bear the harshness of our earthly journey, to pass from the slavery of sin to the freedom of the children of God, from the weary crossing of the desert to the promised land: to the Father's house.

2. "Take this all of you, and eat it: this is my Body . . . Take this all of you, and drink: this is the cup of my Blood" (RM). Lest habit have deadened the keenness of our faith, today's Liturgy invites us to rouse ourselves and to penetrate deeply and lovingly the inexpressible reality of the mystery that took place for the first time in the upper room before the astonished eyes of the disciples, and which is renewed on the altar today with the same concreteness. It is always the Lord Jesus who accomplishes the act of consecration in the person of his minister, and today, the anniversary of the institution of the Eucharist and of the eve of his death, it takes on a moving actuality.

Jesus, "having loved his own who were in this world, . . . loved them to the end," says John in beginning his account of the Last Supper (3rd reading: Jn 13:1-15); "on the night when he was betrayed," adds Paul, referring to the institution of the Eucharist.

The contrast is tremendous: on the part of Christ, infinite love "to the end," until death; on the part of men betrayal, denial, abandonment. The Eucharist is the Lord's answer to betrayal by his creatures. He seems so impatient to save men, who are so weak and unfaithful, that he mystically anticipates his death by offering them as nourishment that body which he will soon sacrifice upon the cross and that blood which he will shed even to the last drop. Although death will shortly wrest him from the earth, his presence will be living and real in the Eucharist until the end of time.

Together with the sacrament of love, Jesus left his Church the witness of love: his "new commandment." Suddenly the Twelve saw the Master kneeling before them in the manner of a servant: "he poured water into a basin, and began to wash the disciples' feet" (ib. 5). The scene ended with a warning: "If, I . . . your Lord and Teacher, have washed your feet, you also ought to wash one another's feet" (ib. 15). It was not so much a matter of imitating his physical act, as of their attitude of sincere humility in their relations with one another; they were each to consider and behave to each other as though each were the servant of the other. Only humility like this will make it possible to fulfill the command that Jesus is about to give: "A new commandment I give to you that you love one another; even as I have loved you, that you also love one another" (ib. 34). The washing of the feet, the institution of the Eucharist, and his death on the cross indicate how and to what point we must love our brothers in order to fulfill the Lord's command.

O good Jesus, to awaken our love, you resolved to remain with us here below . . . You knew beforehand the death they would make you die and the dishonors and insults you would suffer . . . O eternal Father, how could you consent that your Son remain among us every day to suffer? . . . Oh, God help me, what great love from the Son, and what great love from the Father!

O eternal Father, how is it that you consented? Why do you desire to see your Son every day in such wretched hands? How can you in your compassion now see him insulted day after day? . . . Why must all our good come at his expense? . . . Should there not be some one to speak for this most loving Lamb?

O holy Father in heaven . . . since nothing remained for your divine Son to do and he left sinners a gift as great as this most holy Eucharist, be pleased, O most merciful Lord, to provide a remedy that he may not be thus badly treated and that, since he provided a means so good that we may offer him many times in sacrifice, this precious gift may avail; that there will be no advance made in the very great evil and disrespect committed and shown in places where this most Blessed Sacrament is present.

cf St. Teresa of Avila, *Way* 33:2-4; 35:3

Praise to you, blessed Father, through Christ our Lord. He, the true and eternal priest, instituted the rite of the everlasting sacrifice; he offered himself to you first as the victim of salvation, and commanded us to perpetuate the offering in memory of him. By eating the flesh that he sacrificed for us, we are strengthened; and by drinking the blood he shed for us, we are purified.

Grant O Father, that in this great mystery, we may find the fullness of love and of life.

cf *Roman Missal, Preface and Collect*

O Jesus come, my feet are dirty. Become a servant for my sake. Pour water into the basin; come, wash my feet. I know that it is presumptuous to speak like that, but I fear the threat in your words: "If I do not wash your feet, you have no part in me." So, wash my feet that I may have part with you. But what am I saying: wash my feet? Peter could say that, for he needed to have only his feet washed and be completely clean. But as for me, once I have been washed, I still need that baptism of which you say, O Lord; "As for me, I have a baptism with which I must be baptized."

Origen, from *Early Christian Prayers,* 63

151 — PIERCED FOR OUR SINS

Good Friday

Into your hands I commit my spirit; you have redeemed me, O Lord, faithful God *(Ps 31:5)*

1. The liturgy of Good Friday is a moving contemplation of the mystery of the Cross which seeks not only to commemorate our Lord's sorrowful Passion, but to make it come alive again for each of the faithful. Two texts are offered to us: the prophetic one attributed to Isaiah (Is 52:13; 53:12), and the historical one of John (18:1-19, 42). The enormous distance of more than seven centuries that separates these two accounts is annulled by the impressive coincidence of the facts, related by the prophet as a description of the sufferings of Jahweh's Servant, and by the Evangelist as an account of the last day on earth of Jesus. "Many were astonished at him"—says Isaiah—"his appearance was so marred, beyond human semblance . . . He was despised and rejected by men, a man of sorrows, and acquainted with grief" (Is 52:14; 53:3). And John, with the other evangelists, tells of Jesus betrayed, insulted, slapped, crowned with thorns, ridiculed and presented to the populace as a mock king, condemned and crucified. The reason for so much suffering is defined by the prophet: "He was pierced for our offenses, crushed for our sins," and its expiatory merit is also pointed out: "Upon him was the chastisement that made us whole, and with his stripes we are healed" (Is 53:5). There is even a sign of an anguished sense of

repulse on the part of God—"We esteemed him stricken, smitten by God, and afflicted" (ib. 4)—which Jesus expressed on the cross in the cry: "My God, my God, why have you forsaken me?" (Mt 27:46). But what stands out clearly above everything else is the voluntariness of his sacrifice: the Servant of Jahweh spontaneously "makes himself an offering for sin" (Is 53:7-10); Christ gives himself up to the soldiers freely, after having made them fall to the ground by a single word (Jn 18:6), and freely allows himself to be led to his death, he who had said: "No one takes (my life) from me; I lay it down of my own accord" (Jn 10:18). Even the glorious conclusion of this voluntary suffering was foreseen by the prophet: "He shall see the fruit of the travail of his soul . . . because he poured out his soul to death"—says the Lord—"I will divide him a portion with the great" (Is 53:11,12). Alluding to his passion Jesus had said: "When I am lifted up from the earth (I) will draw all men to myself" (Jn 12:32). All of this demonstrates that the Cross of Christ stands at the center of the history of salvation, already foreshadowed in the Old Testament by the suffering of the Servant of Jahweh, the symbol of the Messiah who was to save mankind, not through an earthly triumph, but by sacrificing himself. It is the route we must each travel in order to be saved and to be a savior.

2. Between the readings of Isaiah and John, the Liturgy inserts a passage from the Letter to the Hebrews (4:14-16; 5:7-9), in which Jesus, the Son of God is presented in his character as the highest and only Priest, yet not so distant from men that "he is unable to sympathize with our weaknesses, but one who in every respect has been tempted as we are, yet without sin." It was in the trials of his earthly life, especially in those of his passion that he experienced in his innocent flesh all the bitterness, sufferings, anguish, and weakness of human nature. Thus he is at the same time a Priest and a Victim, one who offers in atonement for man's sins not the blood of goats and calves, but his own blood.

"In the days of his flesh he offered up prayers and supplications with loud cries and tears to him who was able to save him from death." It is an echo of the agony in Gethsemane: "O Father, all things are possible to you. Remove this cup from me. Yet not what I will, but what you will" (Mk 14:36). In obedience to the will of his Father, he gives himself up to death, and having tasted its bitterness, he will be freed from it by his resurrection, thus becoming "the source of eternal salvation to all who obey him" (Heb 5:9). Obeying Christ, Priest and Victim, means accepting, like him, the cross, and abandoning ourselves, like him, to the will of the Father: "Father, into your hands I commit my spirit" (Lk 23:46; cf Responsorial Psalm).

Christ's death is immediately followed by his glorification. The centurion on duty exclaimed: "Certainly this man was innocent!" and all who were present "saw what had taken place; (they) returned home beating their breasts" (Lk 23:47-48). The Church follows the same path, and after having mourned the Savior's death bursts forth in a hymn of praise and prostrates in adoration; "We adore your cross, Lord, and praise and glorify your holy resurrection; since only through the cross has joy entered into the entire world." With these same feelings, the Liturgy invites the faithful to eat of the Eucharist, which, never so much as today, shines brilliantly in its reality as a memorial of the Lord's death. The words of Jesus re-echo in our hearts: "This is my body to be given for you. Do this as a remembrance of me" (Lk 22:19), and those of Paul: "For as often as you eat this bread and drink this cup, you proclaim the death of the Lord until he comes!" (1 Cor 11:26).

O Christ Jesus, prostrate beneath your cross, I adore you, "Power of God," you show yourself overwhelmed with weakness so as to teach us humility and confound our pride. O High Priest, full of holiness, who passed through our trials in order to be like unto us and to compassionate our infirmities, do not leave me to myself, for I am but frailty. May your power dwell in me, so that I fall not into evil.

C. Marmion, *Christ in His Mysteries,* 14

Hail, bloody head, crowned with thorns, broken, struck by a rod, and covered with spit. Hail! There is a foreboding of death upon your gentle face; its color is gone, but under that frightening pallor the heavenly court adores you.

O holy Face, so struck, so bruised and condemned because of our sins, brighten the eyes of this unworthy sinner with a sign of your love! I have sinned, oh forgive me! Do not reject me. While death draws near, bend your head a little toward me and let it rest in my arms.

When my time shall come to die, come quickly, O Jesus! In that dread hour let your blood be my protection, O Jesus! Protect me and deliver me! I will go whenever you want, my dear Jesus, but only be near me then! Hold me tight to you because you love me; then show yourself to me upon the cross that saved us!

(attributed to) St. Bernard, PL 184

O Cross, unspeakable love of God, O Cross, glory of heaven, eternal salvation, terror of the wicked.

Buttress of the just and light of Christians, O Cross, in this world, through you God made man became a slave; in heaven through you man in God was made king; through you the true light arose and cursed night was overcome . . .

You are the bond of peace, which unites men in Christ the mediator. You become the ladder by which man climbs to heaven.

Be always an anchor and support for us, your faithful people. Rule over our dwelling, guide our ship. In the cross make steadfast our faith, in the cross make ready our crown.

St. Paulinus of Nola *Poem* 19

152 — AWAITING THE RESURRECTION

Holy Saturday

The Lord God is my strength and my song, and he has become my salvation *(Is 12:2)*

1. It is most fitting, on Holy Saturday, to reflect upon the whole mystery of Easter: the passion, death and resurrection of our Lord, toward which the entire history of salvation converges and in which it is accomplished. The Liturgy invites us to this by offering us a series of scriptural readings which touch upon the most important stages of this wonderful history in order to concentrate them on the mystery of Christ. First of all, the work of creation is presented (1st reading), coming forth from the hand of God, and looked upon with satisfaction by him: "God saw everything that he had made, and behold, it was very good" (Gen 1:31). Only good things can come from God, who is infinite goodness, and although sin came only too quickly to upset all creation, God, ever faithful in his goodness, at once provided a plan of restoration which would be accomplished through his divine Son. We are shown a prophetic figure of him in Isaac, whom Abraham prepared to sacrifice in obedience to the divine command (2nd reading); and just as Isaac was set free, so Christ, after suffering death, would gloriously rise again. Another prominent point is the miraculous "passage" through the Red Sea (3rd reading) which was carried out by the people of Israel through God's intervention, a symbol of baptism through which those who believe in Christ "pass" from the slavery of sin and death to the freedom and life of God's children. Then follow very beautiful prophetical texts on the redeeming mercy of the Lord, who in spite of continued infidelity on the part of men, never ceased desiring their salvation. After punishing the sins of his people God will call them back to himself with the affection of a faithful husband for the wife who has betrayed him. "For a brief moment I forsook you, but with great compassion I will gather you back . . . ; with everlasting love I will have compassion on you, says the Lord, your Redeemer" (Is 54:7-8). Hence comes the pressing invitation not to let the hour of mercy go by in vain: "Seek the Lord while he may be found, call him while he is near. Let the wicked forsake his way . . . Let him return to the Lord that he may have mercy on him, and to our God for he will abundantly pardon" (Is 55:6-7). If all this was true for the people of Israel, it is so much more so for the Christian people, for whom God's mercy reached its apex in Christ's paschal mystery. And Christ, "our Passover," the Lamb immolated for the salvation of the world, urges us all to give up sin and return to his Father's house, by walking toward "the shining of his light" in the joy of knowing and doing "what is pleasing to God" (Baruch 4:2,4).

2. The history of salvation, which culminates in Christ's Easter mystery, becomes the history of each human being through baptism, which inserts him into this mystery. In fact "we were buried with him [Christ] by baptism into death, so that as Christ was raised from the dead . . . we too might walk in newness of life" (Rom 6:4). This explains why baptism has such an important place in the liturgy of the Easter Vigil: in the scriptural texts and in the prayers, and especially in the rite of the blessing of the water, of administering the sacrament to new converts, and finally in the renewal of baptismal promises. To celebrate Easter means "to pass over" with Christ from death to life; it is a "passage" begun with our baptism which must be carried out in an ever fuller way during our entire lifetime. "If we have been united with him [Christ] in a death like his"—insists St. Paul—"we shall certainly be united with him in a resurrection like his" (ib. 5). It is not a matter of beautiful phrases, but of an immense reality, of radical transformations wrought through baptism, of which we are too forgetful and too little aware. Participation in Christ's death means crucifying the old man, the man of sin; it means dying "to sin, once for all with him" (ib. 10), and therefore dying every day to our passions, our inclinations to evil, to selfishness, to pride; it means—according to the triple renunciation of our baptismal promises—ever more and more to renounce Satan, his works, his vanities. All this is not in words, nor for the space of a liturgical function, but in our whole way of life. "You must also consider yourselves dead to sin"—cries the Apostle—"and alive to God in Christ Jesus" (ib. 11).

By virtue of baptism, when not only received but lived, the Christian people are seen to be the people foretold by Ezechiel (36:25-26 7th reading), sprinkled and purified with "clean water"—the water which flowed from the pierced side of the crucified Christ—the people who receive from God "a new heart" and "a new spirit," which are preeminently the gifts of Easter. So prepared, each of us is ready to sing the Alleluia, and to take part in the Church's joy in proclaiming the resurrection of the Lord; each of us also is risen with [Christ] to live in him for the glory of God.

O all-powerful Father . . . you are God eternal and incomprehensible; when all mankind was dead through the wretchedness of its frailty, moved only by love and your most merciful pity, you sent us your Son Jesus Christ our Lord, true God, clothed in our mortal flesh. It was your will that he should come, not in the pomp and glory of this passing world, but in distress, poverty and suffering, understanding and doing your will for the sake of our redemption . . .

And you, O Jesus Christ, our Redeemer . . . you punished our iniquity and Adam's disobedience in your own body, being obedient even unto your infamous death on the cross. Upon the cross, my sweet love, Jesus, . . . you atoned for us, and at the same time made amends for the insult to your Father in your own self.

I have sinned, O Lord, have mercy on me. *Wherever I turn, I find your ineffable love: and I cannot excuse myself for not loving, because only you, God and Man, are the one who loved me without being loved by me; in very fact, I was not, and you made me. All that I want to love, I find in you . . . If I want to love God, I have your ineffable Godhead; if I want to love man, you are man . . . if I want to love the Lord, you have paid the price with your Blood, snatching us from the servitude of sin. You are our Lord, our Father and our Brother through your goodness and boundless love.*

St. Catherine of Siena, *Prayers and Elevations*

O God, through the paschal mystery we have been buried with Christ in baptism, grant that we may walk with him in newness of life. So, accept the renewal of our baptismal promises, by which we rejected Satan and his works, and now promise to serve you faithfully in the holy Catholic Church.

O all-powerful God, Father of our Lord Jesus Christ, who have forgiven all our sins and given us new birth by water and the Holy Spirit, keep us faithful to his grace for eternal life.

cf *Roman Missal, Easter Vigil*

153 — EASTER SUNDAY

Give thanks to the Lord for he is good, his steadfast love endures forever (Ps 118:1)

1. "This is the day the Lord has made; let us rejoice and be glad, alleluia" (Resp. Ps.). Easter is the most joyful day of the year because "the Prince of life, who died, now reigns immortal" (Sequence). If Jesus had not risen, his incarnation would have been in vain, and his death would not have given life to men. "If Christ has not been raised, your faith is futile" (1 Cor 15:17), exclaims St. Paul. Who indeed can believe in and hope in a dead man? But Christ is not dead, he is living. "You seek Jesus of Nazareth, who was crucified"—the angel said to the women—"He has risen, he is not here" (Mk 16:6).

At first this announcement caused fear and alarm, so much so that the women "fled . . . and said nothing to anyone for they were afraid" (ib. 8). But with them, or perhaps a little ahead of them, was Mary Magdalen who, as soon as she saw "that the stone had been taken away," ran immediately to notify Peter and John: "They have taken the Lord out of the tomb, and we do not know where they have laid him" (Jn 20:1-2). They both ran in haste, and when they entered the tomb they saw "the linen cloths lying, and the napkin which had been on his head . . . rolled up in a place by itself" (ib. 6-7); they saw and believed. This was the newborn Church's first act of faith in the risen Christ, evoked by the solicitude of a woman and the sign of the wrappings lying in the empty tomb. If some one had tried to take away the body secretly, who would have troubled to strip the corpse and remove the linens so carefully? God was using simple things to enlighten the disciples who "as yet did not know the Scripture that he must rise from the dead" (ib. 9), nor what Jesus had himself foretold concerning his resurrection. Peter, the head of the Church, and John, "the one whom Jesus loved" (ib. 2), have the merit of accepting "the signs" of the risen Lord: the news brought by a woman, the empty tomb, the wrappings left there.

"Signs" of the resurrection are still to be found in the world, although in other forms: the heroic faith and evangelical life of so many humble and hidden persons, the vitality of the Church which no external persecutions and internal struggles have been able to weaken, the Eucharist, which is the living presence of the risen Christ who continues to draw men to himself. It is for each of us to accept these signs, to believe as the Apostles believed, and to strengthen our faith continually.

2. In the second reading the Easter Liturgy recalls one of Peter's most moving speeches on the resurrection of Jesus: "God raised him on the third day and made him manifest to us who were chosen by God as witnesses . . . who ate and drank with him after he rose from the dead (Acts 10:40-41). These words still vibrate with the emotion of the Head of the Apostles over the great deeds of which he was witness through his intimacy with the risen Christ, with whom he had sat at table, eating and drinking with him.

Easter calls all the faithful to the table with Christ risen, a table where he himself is food and drink. "Christ has become our paschal sacrifice, let us feast with joy in the Lord" (Gosp. verse). This passage is taken from the first letter to the Corinthians, in which St. Paul refers to the rite that prescribed eating the paschal lamb with unleavened bread—that is, made without yeast—and urges Christians to cleanse out "the old leaven, the leaven of malice and evil," in order to celebrate the Passover with "the unleavened bread of sincerity and truth" (1 Cor 5:7-8). We must approach the table of Christ, the true Lamb sacrificed for the salvation of mankind, with a heart that is cleansed of all sin, renewed in purity and truth; in other words, with the heart of one who is raised up from the dead. The resurrection of the Lord, his "passage" from death to life, must be mirrored in the resurrection of the faithful, effected through an ever more radical "passage" from the weaknesses of the old man to new life in Christ. This resurrection is reflected in a deeper yearning for heavenly things. "If then you have been raised up with Christ"—says the Apostle—"seek the things that are above, where Christ is seated at the right hand of God. Set your mind on things that are above, not on things that are on earth" (Col 3:1-2). The necessity of being concerned with earthly realities must not impede those who are "risen with Christ" from having their hearts set on eternal realities, the only sure ones. There is always a hidden temptation to settle down here on earth as if this were our only homeland. The resurrection of the Lord is a powerful summons which reminds us that we are always on a journey, travelers on the road toward our heavenly homeland. Christ rose again to draw all men into his resurrection and to lead them to his eternal dwelling place, even making them participants in his glory.

It is Easter, the Passover of the Lord . . . not a figure, nor a story, nor shadow, but the Lord's own Pasch . . .

Truly, O Jesus, you have protected us from utter ruin and stretched out your fatherly hands to us; you have hidden us under your fatherly protection. You shed your divine blood here on earth through that covenant which was so bloody and so full of love for us. You drove away the threats of wrath and restored to us our original peace with God, the most High . . . You are indeed totally unique and wholly in all! Let the heavens welcome your spirit . . . but let earth have your blood . . .

O divine Pasch, come down from heaven to earth, and rising again from the earth to heaven! . . . You are the joy, the honor, the food, the delight of us all; the shadows of death were dispelled for you and life was extended to everyone, the gates of heaven thrown open. God showed himself, and man was made as God . . .

O divine Pasch, God of heaven, in your generosity, you now unite yourself to us in the Spirit: through him the great wedding hall is filled, and all are wearing the wedding garment . . . The lamps of our souls will no more be extinguished; in a divine and spiritual way, fed from the oil of Christ, the flame of grace burns brightly in all of us, in our bodies and in our souls.

We beg you, O Lord God, eternal King of souls, O Christ, hold out your hands over your holy Church and over the holy people who are always yours: defend them, guard them, preserve them; fight, challenge, lay low all enemies . . . Grant us to sing with Moses the canticle of victory, for yours is the glory and the power, world without end!

St. Hippolytus of Rome, from *Early Christian Prayers,* 44

O Christ, risen on high, we must rise with you. You have gone away out of sight, and we must follow you. You are gone to the Father, we, too, must take care that our new life "is hid with you in God" . . . It is then the duty and the privilege of all your disciples, O Lord, to be exalted and transfigured with you; to live in heaven in our thoughts, motives, aims, desires, likings, prayers, praises, intercessions, even while we are in the flesh . . . Teach us to "set our affection on things above"; and to prove that we are yours, in that our heart is risen with you, and our life hid in yours. cf. J.H. Newman, *Parochial and Plain Sermons VI* Ser. 19 (pp 213,214,220)

154 — ABOUT THE RISEN ONE

Easter Monday

The Lord is risen as he said: let us all rejoice and be glad, for he reigns for ever (RM)

1. While Mark refers only to the amazement of the women when they hear of the resurrection, Matthew completes the story by noting that their fear was coupled with "great joy, and (they) ran to tell his disciples" (Mt 28:8). Driven by their love, the women were the first to go to the tomb that Sunday at break of dawn; the first to see it open and empty, and the first to learn of the resurrection; however, they are not to be the only ones to receive the great news, but rather to be its messengers. It was important for the Church, which then consisted of the little group of disciples gathered around Peter, to be informed of it: "Go quickly and tell his disciples that 'he has risen from the dead, and, behold, he is going before you to Galilee; there you will see him' " (ib. 7). Angels announced the birth of Jesus to the shepherds, angels proclaimed his resurrection to the women. This is God's chosen way; for his great messages he chooses by preference the humble and the simple: "He chose what is low and despised in this world, even things that are not, to bring to nothing things that are, so that no human being might boast in the presence of God" (1 Cor 1:28). On the other hand, the Church is the depositary and dispenser of the mysteries of faith; everything must be given through her and be guaranteed by her authority, which is particularly aided by the Holy Spirit.

While the women were hurrying along with the good news, "suddenly without warning Jesus stood before them and said 'Peace' " (Mt 28:9); once again they were the first: they saw the risen Master before the apostles did, perhaps in reward for their faithfulness in having followed him to Calvary, helping in his burial, and then returning to offer their respects to his body. Jesus greeted them and repeated what the angel had already said: "Do not be afraid! Go and tell my brothers to go to Galilee, and there they will see me" (ib. 10). This is the first time Jesus has directly called the Apostles by the name of brothers; now that he was risen from death and about to return to his Father, they were more than ever his brothers: by the grace of adoption, the fruit of the paschal mystery, and by virtue of the mission that they were to spread throughout the world, continuing the Savior's work. Meanwhile the women prostrated before the risen Lord and embraced his feet: an action which expressed their love and reverence for him who is always God, even though he was raising men to the dignity of being his brothers.

2. Matthew refers to another detail, which was the shabby machinations of the high priests to keep the Lord's resurrection

hidden; a real fraud perpetrated through money. While they had offered the traitor a few coins to get their hands on Jesus, now in order to corrupt the guards at his tomb, they do not hesitate "to give a sum of money" (Mt 28:12). However attached men may be to money, they are quite capable of spending it when it can help them to maintain wicked positions which they are unwilling to renounce. The Jews who had not believed in Jesus while he was alive and working miracles in their midst did not believe the evidence of his resurrection either, and propagated falsehood. Jesus risen has conquered the devil, for the powers of hell shall not prevail (Mt 16:18); but the devil does not cease obstructing the truth by sowing lies, for he is "a liar and the father of lies" (Jn 8:44). This is still true today, for although Christ's victory is complete in itself, it does not dispense his disciples from temptation and struggle. It always remains true that any one who does not want to believe because of a position already taken, is not going to budge even in the face of evidence. Jesus said so: "If they do not hear Moses and the prophets, neither will they be convinced if some one should rise from the dead" (Lk 16:31).

The attitude of the disciples was completely different. In the beginning, stunned by the greatness of the fact, they had trouble in believing in the resurrection. which some of them considered women's imagination (Lk 24:11), but after they had ascertained the facts, they became its most ardent witnesses. The incredulity of the Jews, originating in pride, was incurable; but that of the disciples was rather due to the bewilderment of the human mind when faced with the divine, and changed quickly into ardent faith. In fact, the testimony of the fourth evangelist, confirmed by Luke, is significant: for if some were doubting the message of the women, Peter quickly came to his senses; he "rose and ran to the tomb" (ib. 12), and, like John, "he saw and believed" (Jn 20:8). On the very day of Pentecost, Peter himself, in the name of all the disciples, would bear witness to the resurrection before those who had condemned Jesus and whom he himself had feared so much: "You crucified and killed (him) by the hands of lawless men. But God raised him up, having loosed the pangs of death" (Acts 2:23-24). Any one whose heart is humble and upright, though he may pass through doubts, will always attain the truth, which God never ceases to offer to all men.

Where are you going, O Mary Magdalen, in company with the holy women? Where are you headed in such a hurry? You are going to the tomb. You arrive there, and then: the earth trembles, the tomb is opened, an angel appears . . . Jesus is no longer there: he has risen as he had said . . . You are seeking as dead, One who is alive . . .

Here I am at your feet, O my Jesus . . . I also see you risen! You have risen and will never die again . . . you are blessed for all eternity: never again will you see the shadow of suffering . . . You are immovably settled in the highest happiness . . . O my God, I too am blessed because you are blessed... Of course I want to be blessed, to be together with you one day in heaven, but, my God, what matters more than my blessedness is yours ... the blessedness of heaven consists in loving you and in seeing you blest ...

In your resurrection and in your infinite and eternal happiness, I have a source of inexhaustible happiness, a foundation of happiness that nothing can take away from me ... For all eternity I possess the essential of what constitutes my happiness ... a good that surpasses every other good, the most desired of my desires, that which is the substance of the angels' and saints' happiness, that which will make my life a heaven... on the one and only condition that I love you!

C. de Foucauld, *On the Feasts of the Year, Op. sp.*

O Jesus, rising from the dead by divine power, you opened eternity to us and taught us the ways of life... First, before all others, you appeared to the timid women because their intense devotion merited it. Then you showed yourself successively to Peter, to the two disciples on the road to Emmaus, and to the apostles gathered together ... By thus appearing in many ways during forty days, both eating and drinking with them, you enlightened us in faith, and raised us up to hope, that you might finally enkindle us in love ...

Most blessed were the eyes that saw you, O Lord! But I too shall be happy if one day I may be able to see your shining brightness, more brilliant than the sun.

cf St. Bonaventure, *The Tree of Life* 34-35, Op. myst.

155 — MESSENGERS OF THE RISEN LORD

Easter Tuesday

My soul waits for the Lord; he is my help and my shield
(Ps 33:20)

1. During Easter week the Liturgy of the Word gathers together the principal testimonies of the resurrection and offers them for our meditation and for the strengthening of our faith. The story of Magdalen is taken up today, "Mary Magdalen, from whom he [Jesus] had cast seven demons" (Mk 16:9); she stood out in the group of holy women because of her ardent love and her persistence in searching for the Lord. After having first run to inform Peter of the empty tomb, she retraced her steps; when the disciples returned home after verifying the fact, she remained "weeping outside the tomb" (Jn 20:11). She did not rest content: she wanted to find that blessed body at any cost. She was so preoccupied by her thoughts and by her grief that she was neither moved nor frightened by the vision of the angels. When they asked the reason for her tears, she explained: "Because they have taken away my Lord, and I do not know where they have laid

him" (ib. 13). When Jesus appeared to her, she did not recognize him, but, mistaking him for the gardener, said to him: "Sir, if you have carried him away, tell me where you have laid him and I will take him away" (ib. 15). Mary was not thinking of the resurrection, and was so upset that the carefully placed linens in the empty tomb had made no impression on her. Neither did it occur to her that it would be impossible for a frail woman like herself to carry away a dead body. The intensity of her grief prevented her from thinking clearly. She was seeking the dead Jesus; he was alive and standing in front of her, and she did not recognize him. But he called her by name: "Mary!" and hearing his voice was enough to make her understand everything: "Rabboni!" (ib. 16). It was the cry of her love and of her faith. She would have liked to stay at the feet of her Lord, now that he was found at last, but he commissioned her to "go to my brothers" (ib. 17).

The good news of the resurrection must not be allowed to stop, but must be spread abroad as quickly as possible in order to reach all men, all the "brothers" of the risen Jesus. Like Mary Magdalen, every Christian must be its messenger, not so much by word as by the signs he carries in himself. The faithfulness, the love, and solicitude of Mary Magdalen and her readiness to go to the "brethren" hold a lesson for us.

2. Peter's first discourse to the people, culminating in his testimony of the Lord's resurrection and of his glorification—"God has made him both Lord and Christ, this Jesus whom you crucified" (Acts 2:36)—ends with a peremptory invitation: "Repent, and be baptized . . . every one of you in the name of Jesus Christ, for the forgiveness of your sins" (ib. 38). Conversion and baptism immerse us in Christ's Easter mystery, and involve us in his death and resurrection. Easter calls for the reborn, the resurrected; the rebirth and the resurrection of which baptism is not only the beginning, but also offers the grace for its progressive and complete fulfillment. As Christians we are never finished being converted, reborn and risen again; the condition of our life on earth is the tension of a continual regeneration in Christ, conforming us more and more to his death and resurrection. A Christian's striving is never ended; "we ourselves"—says the Apostle—"who have the first fruits of the Spirit, groan inwardly as we wait for the redemption" (Rom 8;23). We shall have full and complete redemption only in heaven, for only then shall we be assimilated in an enduring way into Christ's paschal mystery, and die "to sin, once for all . . . (and be) alive to God in Christ Jesus" (Rom 6:10-11).

Meanwhile as long as we live on earth as pilgrims, we must bear within us the marks of the death and resurrection of the Lord: the mark of his death through our rejection of sin, the overcoming of our passions, the generous renunciation and mortification which makes us like our crucified Lord; the mark of his resurrection by a life that is bright with purity and love. Each of us must make room for the Lord, so that we may rise and live again in him; so that within us, Christ may continue to dwell among men and do good: by consoling the afflicted, strengthening the weak, enlightening the blind, aiding the poor, helping the young, giving love and truth to all. The Apostle had this in mind when he said: "Always carrying in our body the death of Jesus, so that the life of Jesus may also be manifested in our bodies" (2 Cor 4:10).

O Jesus, hiding so that you can be sought with ever greater ardor and be found with keener joy, and held on to with ever growing care . . . This is the game, O divine Wisdom, that you play with the universe, you who are happy to be with the children of men.

Woman, why are you weeping, whom are you seeking? *He whom you are seeking is with you, don't you know that? You possess the truth, eternal happiness, and you still weep? You have within you what you are looking for without—and you really are outside, weeping beside a tomb. [But Christ says to you:] Your heart is my tomb: I am not lying there dead, I live eternally. Your soul is my garden . . . your weeping, your love and your desire are my work: you possess me within you without realizing it, and that is why you seek me outside. Then I will appear to you exteriorly, to bring you back into yourself, and make you find within what you look for without.*

Mary, I know you by name, you must learn to know me by faith . . .

Do not touch me . . . for I have not yet ascended to the Father: *You have still not believed that I am equal, coeternal, and consubstantial with the Father. Believe this and it will be as if you had touched me. You see the man, which is why you do not believe, because one does not believe what he sees. You do not see God: believe, and you will see him.*

St. Bernard (attributed) *On the Passion and Resurrection* 15:38

O Christ, risen for the glory of the Father, make me begin to live a new life. As you freed yourself from your bindings and came forth from the sepulcher, living and glorious, so may I free myself from my passions and bad habits so as to live a life of perfect grace. O Jesus, glorious Conqueror, let me share in your passion, so that I may also share in your resurrection. Let me rise to life with you, not as Lazarus or the others did, only to die again, but in the way you rose: make me lead a new life and nevermore die the death of sin.

cf L. Da Ponte *Meditations* V 2:4

156 — STAY WITH US

Easter Wednesday

Stay with us, Lord, for it is toward evening—and the day is now far spent *(Lk 24:29)*

1. On the very day of Easter, toward evening, the risen Jesus, under the guise of a wayfarer, joined two of the disciples on the road to Emmaus, who were discussing the disturbing happenings of the preceding Friday in Jerusalem (Lk 24:13-35). Like Mary Magdalen, they too did not recognize him; not because they were overcome by emotion, but because they were convinced that all was ended for ever. They had been thinking that Jesus was "the prophet, powerful in word and deed before God and all the people," but his condemnation to death and his crucifixion had disappointed them. "We had hoped that he was the one to redeem Israel . . . Besides all this, it is now the third day since this happened" (ib. 21). They had heard of the women's "vision of angels," and knew about the empty tomb, but this was not sufficient to reawaken their hopes because "him, they did not see," and they did not realize that he himself was walking beside them. Jesus intervened to enlighten them: "O foolish men, and slow of heart to believe all that the prophets have spoken! Was it not necessary that the Christ should suffer these things and enter into his glory?" (ib. 25-26). Their idea of a political Messiah, who would bring about Israel's prosperity, prevented the two from recognizing in the suffering Christ the promised Savior. How could one hope for salvation from a dead man hanging on a cross? Any one who does not believe in the resurrection of the Lord cannot grasp the mystery of his redeeming death. The prophets had spoken of it, the Lord Jesus himself had foretold it; the two disciples knew it; what is more, the Lord was with them and they heard him unfold the Scriptures: "Beginning with Moses and all the prophets, he interpreted to them in all the Scriptures the things concerning himself" (ib. 27); they listen gladly, but still do not believe. But for Mary it was enough to hear herself called by name for her to recognize him who was risen; for the two disciples, neither his voice nor their long conversation nor his interpretation of the Scriptures sufficed.

It is true: we can have the Lord near us, walk beside him, and still not recognize him; we can have an excellent knowledge of the Scriptures, yet not grasp the deep meaning that reveals God to us. That is the reason many do not succeed in making the leap from knowing to believing, from knowing a great many things to understanding the one thing necessary. Even seeing the Savior is not enough for belief, if faith does not enlighten us interiorly. "Lord, increase our faith!" (Lk 17:5).

2. When the mysterious traveler was about to take his leave, the two disciples begged him: "Stay with us for it is toward even-

ing, and the day is now far spent." This was not so much a gesture of courtesy toward the stranger as a need to remain in his company and to hear again the word which inflamed their hearts with such unaccustomed ardor. Their prayer was heard far beyond the asking. Not only did the Lord accept their invitation and enter the house, but "when he was at table with them, he took the bread and blessed and broke it, and gave it to them. And their eyes were opened and they recognized him" (Lk 24:30-31). This act of breaking bread was typical of Jesus when he ate with his disciples; but this does not exclude the possibility of its being a repetition of the Eucharistic act of the Last Supper, at which these two disciples were perhaps also present. In any case, Jesus let himself be known in a climate of prayer and intimacy. The ground had been prepared by the unfolding of the Scriptures, but faith springs from prayer and from intimacy with the Risen One.

If in many of us faith is cold, as it were asleep and incapable of guiding and transforming our lives, the reason can often be traced to a lack of serious prayer and of personal intimacy with Christ. Many believe in Jesus, even to acknowledging him as an historical person, and to accepting what Scripture and the Gospels say of him, yet they do not believe in him as a person who is always alive and present, who wants to be our companion on the road, our friend, and the guest of our heart. We have not yet met him in the intimacy of prayer, and of sitting together at the table to break bread. For such people, the Eucharistic banquet is a simple symbolic rite, not a feeding on Christ, dead and risen again for our salvation; not a living and throbbing welcoming of him to our hearts in order to keep him company in friendly intimacy. "Stay with us!" The beautiful Easter prayer expresses the desire for such an intimate personal meeting with the Lord, because only in this way are faith and love kindled and made capable of enkindling the hearts of others. Peter, who had had this intimate encounter with the Lord, was able to say to the crippled beggar at the temple gate: "I give you what I have! In the name of Jesus Christ of Nazareth, walk!" (Acts 3:6). He gave him the gift of his own faith, a faith so great that it performed the miracle of his recovery.

O Lord, you appeared to two disciples who did not yet believe in you, but were nevertheless talking about you as they walked along. However, you hid your face from them: you wanted to appear exteriorly to their physical sight just as you did interiorly to the eyes of their hearts. In the depths of those hearts they loved you, yet with doubts. You granted them the blessing of your presence because they were talking about you; but because of their hesitation, you hid your face from them by which they would have recognized you. You opened to them the mysterious meaning of the Scriptures; but since you were still a stranger in their hearts as regards their faith, you pretended to go on farther . . . It was necessary to test them to see if, although not loving you as their God, they would at least love you in the guise of a stranger.

And then, see, they offer you hospitality . . . They set the table, serve you food and drink, and though they had not recognized you when you were explaining the Scriptures, they know you in the breaking of bread. Hearing your precepts, they were not enlightened, but in observing them, they knew you. O Lord if I want to understand the things I hear from you, I must put them into practice at once.

St. Gregory the Great, *Homilies on the Gospels,* 23:1-3

O Lord, do not let my faults so blur the eyes of my spirit that I do not see you when you are near, and that I do not recognize you when I hear your voice in my heart. If by your secret providence you should wish to hide yourself, do not let me lack the presence of your grace, so that I may not fail in my duty through my own weakness.

O good Jesus, stay with me, for the light of faith is growing dim in my soul, and the fervor of my charity is cooling; if you go away I shall become a cold, dark night. Stay with me, Lord, because the day of my life is setting, and I need your company more than ever . . . Stay with me, Lord, so that I may attain my desire and reach eternal life, and remain with you always.

L. Da Ponte, *Meditations* V 7:1,4

157 — AMONG HIS OWN

Easter Thursday

The Lord has risen indeed! To him be glory and power for ever and ever! (Lk 24:34; Rev 1:6)

1. After appearing to Mary Magdalen and the other women, to Peter and to the disciples at Emmaus, Jesus showed himself on the very evening of Easter to the Eleven and to the others who were gathered together with them in Jerusalem (Lk 24:35-48). They believed in the resurrection and were talking about it: "The Lord has risen indeed. He has appeared to Simon"; furthermore they have just heard the account of the two from Emmaus. Still, when Jesus stood in their midst, "they were startled and frightened, and supposed they were seeing a spirit." The manifestation of the divine so dazzles the human mind that doubt arises spontaneously: Can it be true? Is it my imagination? But blessed be the doubts of the disciples! They bear witness that their faith in the Risen Lord did not spring from credulity or enthusiasm, nor from suggestion, but was based on objective data examined with realistic perception. Jesus helped them himself to realize the truth of things: "See my hands and my feet, that it is myself. Handle me, and see; for a spirit has not flesh and bones as you see that I have." They not only saw; they touched: what can be handled can-

not be imaginary. But the joy of finding their Teacher alive again is so great that they still do not dare to believe. And the Lord, adapting himself more and more to their way of thinking, said: "Have you anything here to eat?" He took fish and "ate before them." His state of glory freed him from all physical need, but he took food to prove the concrete reality of his Person. He is there in their midst in his glorified body, and if his body has special powers, such as unexpectedly appearing and disappearing, it is still his own real body, as is proved by the mark of the nails in his hands and feet (Jn 20:25-27).

The risen Lord adapted himself in his appearances with wonderful condescension to the state of mind of those to whom he showed himself. He did not treat all the same, but by different ways and methods led them all to the certainty of his resurrection. This was what mattered. The resurrection is the key to the whole of Christianity, and he wanted to give the newborn Church every guarantee of it, so that down through the centuries the faith of the faithful might rest upon a solid foundation. "The Lord is risen indeed!" Upon this great truth we can each base our own life.

2. Jesus expounded the Scriptures to the Eleven while they were gathered in Jerusalem. It was not enough for them to recognize him and to believe in his resurrection; they had to understand the intimate connection between the facts they had been witnessing, and what was written of him "in the law of Moses, and the prophets, and the psalms" (Lk 24:44). There was complete identification between the Messiah of the prophets and the historical Jesus with whom they had lived and whom they had seen die on the cross, and now find risen again. It is this identity that makes their faith and their hope valid. During his earthly life, Jesus had explained these things: "These are my words which I spoke to you while I was still with you" (ib.), but the disciples had not understood. Jesus, risen, had to "open their minds" before they could finally comprehend what the Scriptures had proclaimed, namely that "the Christ should suffer and on the third day rise from the dead" (ib. 46).

If we do not understand the passion, neither can we understand the resurrection; and, conversely, the latter explains and justifies the former. For any one who believes in the resurrection of Christ, in which is included and foretold the resurrection of the faithful, the cross is no longer a cause of bewilderment or scandal, neither in regard to the passion of Christ, nor to the suffering that enters into each one's personal life.

The Apostles' preaching follows the lines traced out by Jesus; an example of this is found in Peter's discourses, in which there is always a connection made between the Old Testament, the life of Christ, and his resurrection. "The God of Abraham and of Isaac and of Jacob, the God of our fathers, [that is to say, the God of the promises], glorified his servant Jesus, [the Savior presented as the servant of Jahweh], whom you delivered up and denied . . . whom

God raised from the dead. To this we are witnesses . . . What God foretold by the mouth of all the prophets, that his Christ should suffer, he thus fulfilled" (Acts 3:13,15,18). This is a synthesis of the history of salvation: from the promises made to Abraham up to the coming of the Savior, and to his passion, death, and resurrection. In his great love, God prearranged and fulfilled all this for the salvation of men "so that those who live, might live no longer for themselves, but for him who for their sake died and was raised" (2 Cor 5:15).

O Lord, come into my soul and say to my powers and senses: "Peace be with you." Lord, give me the peace that the world cannot give; make peace between my flesh and my spirit, between my interior and my exterior powers; put me at peace with your Father and with my brothers. O Lord, say to my soul: "It is I, fear not," because if you are with me, all fear disappears.

I thank you, sovereign Master, for the great favor you showed your disciples, and, through them, to us as well. You let yourself be seen and touched, communicating life and joy to them. Blessed was he who was able to be present at that happy meeting: who was able to see your beauty, hear your voice, and touch your precious wounds. O sweet Jesus, I present myself in spirit before you, I adore your sovereign majesty, and prostrate, I approach to kiss your precious wounds, fully trusting that they will heal mine.

Finally, O Lord, I beg you to reveal to me, as you did to your disciples, the secrets of Holy Scripture. I confess that my sins make me incapable of understanding them; but remember that through the merits of your passion you opened the book sealed with seven seals. Lord, open for me the book of your mysteries and open my intellect, so that I may understand them and be all inflamed in the fire of your love.

cf L. Da Ponte, *Meditations* V 8:2-4

Stretching out your hands upon the Cross, O Christ, you filled the world with your Father's tender love and for this we intone a song of victory.

At your command, O Lord of life, death approached you with fear, like a slave, and through its means, you won for us eternal life and resurrection.

Byzantine Liturgy, Canon of the Resurrection

158 — IT IS THE LORD

Easter Friday

Lord God, you are my God, and I will give thanks to you; you are my God, I will extol you *(Ps 118:28)*

1. John tells us (21:1-14) of another appearance of Jesus, which took place at the sea of Tiberias, after a night of fruitless fishing on the part of the Apostles. They did not recognize him; still they accepted his suggestion to cast out their net again; and it was so filled that "they were not able to haul it in." Immediately "the disciple whom Jesus loved" recognized the "sign" of the Master's presence in the extraordinary catch, and said: "It is the Lord!" Love made John more discerning than the others, but the same love made Peter react more quickly: at once he jumped into the water in order to reach the Lord sooner. "Each of them"—comments St. John Chrysostom—"remained true to his character; the one had greater penetration, the other a greater animation. John was the first to recognize Jesus, but Peter was the first to go to meet him" (In Io 87:2). The delicacy with which John, the protagonist and reporter of the event, emphasized Peter's primacy, here, as at the tomb, is significant: he willingly recognized in him the primacy that Jesus himself had conferred on him.

"It is the Lord!" With this term, familiar to the disciples, John recognized and pointed out Jesus, but now that he is risen the words take on a new meaning, a deeper and more vital one. Easter, in fact, is the full crowning of Jesus' lordship: now all creatures belong to him because he has bought them back at the price of his blood, by the full giving of himself, and by his obedience even to death on the cross. "Therefore, God has highly exalted him and bestowed on him the name which is above every name; . . . so that every tongue may confess that Jesus Christ is Lord, to the glory of God the Father" (Phil 2:9-11). Every tongue must joyfully proclaim that the risen Jesus is "the Lord." From the prophecies to the Apocalypse, all Scripture proclaims his glory: "Worthy is the Lamb who was slain to receive power and wealth and wisdom and might and honor and glory and blessing!" (Rev 5:12). We must join this universal chorus and sing the glories of the risen Christ by letting his dominion triumph in us; we must yield every privilege, every place, we must deliver ourselves to him without reserve, so that he may be the only Lord of our life.

2. Jesus is the Lord, but although he is risen, nothing has changed in his manner: he is always the one "who came not to be served, but to serve" (Mt 20:28). On the shore Jesus had prepared "a charcoal fire . . . with fish lying on it, and bread," and when his friends arrived, tired after spending the night on the lake and dragging their net to shore with great effort, he invited them to refresh themselves: "Come and have breakfast." "He took the bread and gave it to them, and so with the fish" (Jn 21:10-13). Did

the Apostles perhaps think of the Last Supper, when Jesus took bread, blessed it and gave it to them, and said: "Take, eat, this is my body" (Mt 26:26). Although we are not dealing with the Eucharist here, the comparison comes easily and spontaneously.

The risen Lord continues to prepare his table for men, and instead of serving them bread and fish, he goes so far as to give them his Body as food and his Blood as drink. In this way he sustains in those who believe in him that divine life to which he has begotten them by his death and resurrection. The Eucharist is therefore the perfection of baptism, and is, like baptism, an essentially paschal sacrament. Although the Eucharist is the memorial of the Lord's death, it is also that of his resurrection, because the Body and Blood offered in the sacrament are not the body and blood of a dead man, but of one who is alive, who has risen and lives eternally, and has the power to share his immortality with those who are nourished by him. "He who eats my flesh and drinks my blood has eternal life, and I will raise him up at the last day" (Jn 6:54). Then the lordship of the risen Lord will reach its highest manifestation, having taken into his own resurrection that of all who believe in him.

Peter, the vigilant witness to Christ's dominion, will be the first to defend it before the tribunal; when questioned about the cure of a cripple, he will declare with all his zeal: It was done "by the name of Jesus Christ of Nazareth, whom you crucified, whom God raised from the dead, by him this man is standing before you well . . . There is salvation in no one else" (Acts 4:10,12). Only Jesus has the power to save, only he is Lord of life and of death, and is capable of healing and of making us rise again.

O Peter, you run everywhere eagerly, and not content with having seen what you saw, you look again, and burning with desire to see the Lord, are never satisfied with seeing him. You see him alone, you see him together with the Eleven, you see him with the seventy, you see him when Thomas believes. You also see him while you are fishing; but not content with having seen him, and impatient with eagerness, you abandon your net and ignore any danger; to you it seems too long to wait to get there by boat with the others. Once before, when the Lord walked upon the water, you forgot your nature and ran to meet him upon the water's waves. So too here, while the Lord stands on the shore, you hasten to pay him homage by the shortest and most hazardous route.

It is certain that you believed, and that you believed because you loved, and that you loved because you had believed. This is why you were sad when Jesus asked you for the third time: "Do you love me?" But the Lord was not doubting your love, he was not asking for information, but wanted to teach you that, at the moment of his ascension into heaven, he would leave you as vicar of his love. You answered: "Lord, you know well that I love you." Conscious of the dispositions of your soul, you made manifest the love that God had known about for a long time. Who else could say "yes" to him so easily? O Peter, who declare your love in that manner before all the others, you are preferred before the others because charity is the greatest of all.

cf St. Ambrose, *Commentary on the Gospel of St. Luke* X, 174-175

It is you, O divine Risen Lord, who come to me; you who after having expiated sin by your sufferings, have vanquished death by your triumph; you, henceforth glorious, live only for your Father. Come to me "to destroy the works of the devil," and to destroy sin and my infidelities; come to me to detach me more from all that is not you; come to make me a partaker of that superabundant perfect life which now overflows from your sacred humanity. I will then sing with you a hymn of praise to your Father, who has crowned you as our Head upon this day of honor and glory.

C. Marmion, *Christ in His Mysteries,* 15

159 — GO AND PREACH

Easter Saturday

O Lord, who can utter your mighty doings, or show forth all your praise? (Ps 106:2)

1. All the appearances of the risen Jesus end with an apostolic command: to Mary Magdalen the Lord said: "Do not hold me . . . but go to my brothers and say to them: 'I am ascending to my Father and your Father' " (Jn 20:17); to the other women he said: "Go and tell my brothers to go to Galilee, and there they will see me" (Mt 28:10). Although the disciples of Emmaus did not receive such a command, as soon as Jesus disappeared, they felt obliged to go back to Jerusalem, to inform the Eleven of what had taken place (Lk 24:35). According to Mark's brief relation of this appearance, the disciples "would not believe it" (16:11,13). Luke, also, says of the women's message, "the words seemed to them an idle tale and they did not believe them" (Lk 24;11).

It is precisely upon this refusal to believe that Mark dwells in his succinct account of Jesus' appearance to the Eleven: "He upbraided them for their unbelief and hardness of heart, because they had not believed those who saw him after he had arisen" (Mk 16:14). It was the same rebuke that had been given to the disciples at Emmaus: "O foolish men and slow of heart to believe all that the prophets have spoken" (Lk 24:25). The Lord's reproach was justified by the fact that many times he had predicted to his disciples what was going to happen; this is a further proof that the Apostles' belief in the Resurrection was not born in a moment of religious exaltation, but was based upon personal experience, through which each of them could say he himself had been an eyewitness.

Only after making sure of the firmness of their faith did Jesus give his disciples the great mandate: "Go into all the world and preach the gospel to the whole creation" (Mk 16:15). Now that their risen Lord had given them every proof of the reality of his resurrection, they must go out and preach to all men. Indeed, with the resurrection, "the good news" of universal salvation accomplished by God in Christ is now complete, and must be spread throughout the world to become the story of every man.

2. "Go and preach." The command sown in the hearts of the disciples by the risen Lord and made fruitful on Pentecost by the life-giving power of the Holy Spirit, became an irrevocable resolution to consume their lives in preaching the gospel.

"When they saw the boldness of Peter and John" in attesting the resurrection of Jesus and in attributing the miraculous recovery of the cripple to the power of the risen One, the leaders of the people and the high priests "charged them not to speak or teach at all in the name of Jesus." But they replied with holy boldness: "We cannot but speak of what we have seen and heard" (Acts 4:13-20). How could they keep silent about the truth, of which they had been witnesses? They had learned it from the lips of Jesus, the Son of God, during the years of their life together; they had its proof in his many miracles, and finally the supreme verification in his resurrection from the dead. It was impossible for them to repudiate through silence what each of them had seen and touched with his own hand. Like Peter and John, the other Apostles also began the preaching which, in a short time, would extend beyond Palestine and reach Asia Minor, Greece, and Italy, winning for Christ men of every culture, class, and race.

The Church was born from Jesus' paschal mystery, born as an apostolic power that was destined to transform the world. There was the ferment of a new life here, a divine life which was derived from the risen Lord and sought to permeate the entire mass of human society in order to transform it into a Christian society, living from the very life of Christ. We are each bound to this undertaking; it is an obligation that springs from baptism, from the gift of faith freely received from God, which must not remain a personal privilege, but must be shared with our fellowmen. We shall propagate our faith and preach the gospel to the extent that we carry within us, in all the facets of our life, the imprint of the risen Christ; whoever meets us and deals with us should be able to say: "I have seen the Lord" (Jn 20:18).

God, you have desired your Church to be a sacrament of salvation for all people, and that it should extend, down through the centuries, the saving work of Christ the Redeemer; Lord, rouse the hearts of your faithful, make them all feel the urgency of their missionary vocation and work together for the salvation of the entire world, so that through you, from all the people, one single family and one people may take shape and grow.

Roman Missal, Mass for the Evangelization of People B

O Jesus, in spite of my littleness, I would like to enlighten souls as did the prophets and the doctors. I have the vocation of the apostle. I would like to travel over the whole earth to preach your name and to plant your glorious cross on infidel soil... but one mission alone would not be sufficient for me. I would want to preach the gospel on all the five continents simultaneously and even to the most remote isles. I would be a missionary, not for a few years only but from the beginning of creation until the consummation of the ages. But above all, O my beloved Savior, I would shed my blood for you even to the last drop.
St. Therese of the Child Jesus, *Autobiographical Writings* B p. 193

Christ Jesus, crucified, dead, risen, glorious: you are the only truth, the only reality in the world! O Christ, I beg you... make your gospel the essential thing for me, as also your word and your peace. Your ideal, O Christ, is the only reality.

I shall not be able to build anything without you; nor offer anything to others without you; I do not want to give men anything outside of you, because they are not seeking this reality, lost as they are in their poor "realities," so little real that they vanish quickly like shadows. How shameful if I, your priest, were not always present to tell them that there is only one reality that endures, an eternal life, an infinite love, a divine person, a Man-God in whom they are going to be made partakers of the divine nature. This reality is you, O Christ, peace of the world, because you reconcile them with the heavenly Father, because you give consciences unity, purity, justice, and charity.

O Christ!... I want only you; you are my all; I want to proclaim to the world only you, your eternal love, your crucified and glorious love. Because man was made to sing and bring love.

P. Lyonnet, *Spiritual Writings*

160 — SECOND SUNDAY OF EASTER

O Lord, do not let me be faithless but believing *(Jn 20:27)*

1. The account in John's Gospel (20:19-29) of the appearance of Jesus to the Apostles who were gathered in the Cenacle is enriched by details of particular importance. On the evening of the resurrection, Jesus entrusted to them the mission he had received from the Father. "As the Father has sent me, even so I send you." Then he gave them the Holy Spirit: "He breathed on them and said to them: 'Receive the Holy Spirit. If you forgive the sins of any, they are forgiven; if you retain the sins of any, they are retained.' " It was not a gift of the Spirit in a visible and public way as would come to pass at Pentecost, but it was indeed significant that on the very day of his resurrection, Jesus poured out his

Spirit upon the Apostles. The Holy Spirit thus appears as the first gift of the risen Christ to his Church at the moment he established it and sent it forth to prolong his mission in the world. Together with the outpouring of the Spirit he instituted penance, which with baptism and the Eucharist is a typically Easter sacrament, an efficacious sign of the remission of sins and of the reconciliation of men with God, brought about by Christ's sacrifice.

But Thomas was absent that evening, and when he returned he refused to believe that Jesus was risen: "Unless I see . . . and place my finger in the mark of the nails, and place my hand in his side, I will not believe." He must not only see, but absolutely had to put his hand in the wounds. Jesus took him at his word: "Eight days later" he came back and said to him: "Put your finger here, and see my hands; put out your hand and place it in my side; do not be faithless, but believing." The Lord had compassion on his apostle's lack of belief, and with infinite kindness offered him the proof that he had so boldly demanded. Thomas was won over, and his incredulity dissolved into a great act of faith: "My Lord and my God!" This valuable lesson warns those who believe not to be surprised at the doubts and difficulties which others may experience in believing. Instead, we need to sympathize with the doubtful and unbelievers, and to surround them with prayer, remembering that "the charity of Christ urges us to act lovingly, prudently, and patiently in our dealings with those who are in error or are in ignorance with regard to the faith" (DH 14).

2. "Have you believed because you have seen? Blest are those who have not seen and yet believe" (Jn 20:29). Jesus here praised the faith of all those who were to believe in him without the consolation of perceptible experience. The Lord's praise re-echoes in the voice of Peter when he was moved by the lively faith of the early Christians, who believed in Jesus as if they had known him personally. "Without having seen him, you love him; though you do not see him, you believe in him, and rejoice with unutterable and exalted joy" (1 Pet 1:8). This is the blessedness of the faith proclaimed by the Lord; it must be the happiness of the faithful of every age. In the face of difficulty and trouble in believing, we need to remember the words of Jesus, in order to find in them the support for a bare and naked faith, but still a faith that is certain, because it is founded on the word of God.

Faith in Christ was the cohesive force which united the early Christians in a compact society, based on a deep communion of feeling and life. "The company of those who believed were of one heart and soul" (Acts 4:32). This was the fundamental characteristic of the first Christian community, born from the "power" with which "the apostles gave their testimony to the resurrection of the Lord Jesus" (ib. 33), and from the corresponding power of the faith of each believer. It was a faith so strong that it caused them to renounce their material possessions spontaneously, and to hold them in common for the benefit of the more needy, who were considered true brothers in Christ. It was not a theoretical or ideological faith, but one so concrete and active that it gave a totally new character to the life of the faithful, not only in the area of relations with God and of prayer, but also in their relations with their neighbors, even in the field of concerns about which men in general are extremely jealous. This kind of faith is a rarity today; for too many of us, faith has no effect on our habits; it transforms little or nothing in our lives. Christianity of this sort neither convinces nor converts the world. We need to reinvigorate our faith from the example of the early Church, we need to beg of God the grace of a profound faith, for the victory of the Christian depends on the strength of his faith. "This is the victory that overcomes the world, our faith. Who is it that overcomes the world but he who believes that Jesus is the Son of God?" (1 Jn 5:4-5)

With the apostle Thomas, I adore you, O my God! If I have, like him, sinned through unbelief, I adore you the more... "My Lord and my God" (Jn 20:28). To have you is to have everything I can have.

Thomas came and touched your sacred wounds. O will the day ever come when I shall be allowed actually and visibly to kiss them? What a day will that be when I am thoroughly cleansed from all impurity and sin, and am fit to draw near to my incarnate God in his palace of light above! What a morning, when having done with all penal suffering, I see you for the first time with these very eyes of mine, I see your countenance, gaze upon your eyes and gracious lips without quailing, and then kneel down with joy to kiss your feet, and am welcomed into your arms. O my only true Lover, the only Lover of my soul, you will I love now, that I may love you then.

What a day, a long day without ending, the day of eternity, when I shall be so unlike what I am now, when I feel in myself a body of death, and am perplexed and distracted with ten thousand thoughts, any one of which would keep me from heaven... O my Lord, what a day when I shall have done once for all with all sins, and shall stand perfect and acceptable in your sight, able to bear your presence, nothing shrinking from your eye, not shrinking from the pure scrutiny of angels and archangels, when I stand in the midst and they around me.

O my God, though I am not fit to see or to touch you yet, still I will ever come within your reach, and desire that which is not yet given me in its fullness.

J.H. Newman, *Meditations on Christian Doctrine* VI 2:1-3

O Lord Jesus Christ, we have not seen you in the flesh with our mortal eyes, yet we know and believe and profess that you are truly God. O Lord, we beg you: let this profession of our faith lead us to glory; let our faith save us from the second death; let this hope be our comfort when we are driven to weep in the midst of so many af-

flictions, and conduct us to eternal joy. And after the trial of this life, when we arrive at the goal of our heavenly calling and see your body glorified in God . . . oh, grant that our bodies too may receive glory from you, O Christ, our Leader.

Mozarabic Liturgy

161 — DIALOGUE WITH GOD

O Father, let my fellowship be with you and with your Son in union with the Holy Spirit (1 Jn 1:3)

1. John's first letter begins with the precious affirmation: "that which we have seen and heard we proclaim also to you so that you may have fellowship with us; and our fellowship is with the Father, and with his Son Jesus Christ" (1:3). The whole history of creation and redemption converges into this one purpose: the establishment of an intimate friendly communion between man and God. "An outstanding cause of human dignity"—states the Council—"lies in man's calling to communion with God. From the very circumstance of his origin, man is already invited to converse with God" (GS 19). This is our highest calling, which differentiates us from all other creatures, which, no matter how big or beautiful, are incapable of entering into a relationship with God, and of responding to him who made us out of nothing. When God made us, he created us in his image and likeness, intelligent and free, capable of responding to his love. Thus began the dialogue, as it were, between God and man. God spoke: he revealed himself to the patriarchs, and to the prophets, unveiled to them his plans of generous salvation, that they might transmit them to the people of Israel, and evoke from them a response of adherence and fidelity. Then, when men alienated themselves from God, failing to abide by his conditions and his law, God fell silent: there were no more prophets to proclaim his word. Divine silence is the punishment of sin, and man, created to speak with God and to live in communion with him, felt abandoned. Then, in the fullness of time, when God wanted to activate his plan for the salvation of the world, he sent his own Word, the eternal Word, to take flesh and become a man among men. "Lo, I have come to do your will, O God" (Heb 10:7), says the Word as he becomes incarnate, and from that moment God receives from the man, Christ, the most perfect answer to his love; the dialogue between the Most High and mankind now develops in a most sublime way. From that moment every believer is drawn up into the dialogue between Christ and his heavenly Father, in fact is called to take part in it with personal prayer.

2. Christian prayer is fundamentally a participation in the sublime conversation between the Father and the Son in love and in communion with the Holy Spirit. When the Gospel relates that

Jesus often "withdrew to the wilderness and prayed" (Lk 5:16), or spent nights in prayer (Lk 6:12), it is referring precisely to his private, intimate communion with the Father, a communing whose mystery man cannot penetrate, but concerning which Jesus himself has revealed some part for the instruction of his disciples. Thus we have his prayers to the Father, spoken aloud, in which he always delights to manifest his position as son. "Father," he repeats in every appeal. He is the only Son of God, absolutely equal to the Father in his divine nature; the Father expresses himself fully in the Son, and the Son expresses the Father fully in an eternal colloquy, so perfect that it pours itself out in that principle of mutual communion that is the Holy Spirit. Indeed, in this colloquy, from the moment of the incarnation, there is not only the word, but the incarnate word, there is Jesus, true God and true man, and in him there is all humanity in as much as he associates it with his whole mystery. In fact, Jesus lets man share through grace in his divine sonship, and makes him a child of God. "To all who received him . . . he gave power to become children of God . . . who were born, not of blood . . . but of God" (Jn 1:12-13), so that we "should be called children of God; and so we are" (1 Jn 3:1). Having made us his children, Jesus invites us to take part in his eternal colloquy with his Father. When the disciples said to him: "Lord, teach us to pray" (Lk 11:1), Jesus immediately introduced them to this dialogue, and first of all taught them to call God by the name of "Father." All too often this name is mentioned without thought, out of habit, but it truly epitomizes the whole substance of Christian prayer and expresses its most basic attitude, that of sons in the Son.

Lord, make me capable and worthy to understand this highest gift of your goodness; because of it you deigned to create us in your likeness, when you made us rational and clothed us with yourself and with your powers of reason. You gave us intelligence so that we might know you, my God! You offered us the gift of your wisdom. Truly the gift of all gifts is to savor you in truth!

Finally you gave us the gift of love. O supreme Being, make me worthy to understand this gift, which is above every other, since all the angels and the saints have no other gift than that of seeing you loved, of loving and contemplating you! O supreme Good, you deigned to let us know you as Love, and you make us love this Love. O most wonderful Lord, what wonderful things you accomplish in your children!

Above everything else you gave us the gift of your Son, sent to death to give us life: he is the gift above all gifts . . . O Jesus Christ, you put us in possession of God, your Father.

Bl. Angela da Foligno, *Book of the Divine Consolation* III

How great is your mercy, O Lord Christ, how great your favor and your goodness in showing us how to pray thus in God's presence, and even to call him Father! Like you who are the Son of

God, we are also called his children. None of us would ever have dared to use this word in our prayer; we needed you to encourage us. O Jesus, help us to remember that when we call God, our Father, we must act as children of God. If we delight in God our Father, he must also be able to be pleased with us.

Our Father, make us temples in which men can recognize your presence. Let our conduct not betray your Spirit; you have made us heavenly and spiritual, help us to think and act in a way that is entirely heavenly and spiritual.

cf St. Cyprian, *On the Lord's Prayer,* 11

162 — OUR FATHER

Let the words of my mouth and the meditation of my heart be acceptable in your sight, O Lord (Ps 19:14)

1. In the Our Father (Mt 6:9-13) Jesus has given us the essential outline of Christian prayer. In it first place belongs to the concept of the fatherhood of God. He is the Father who shares his divine life with us, who comes close to us, who makes his home in those who love him: "If a man loves me . . . my Father will love him, and we will come to him and make our home with him (Jn 14:23). At the same time he is the most high God "who is in heaven," infinitely superior to every creature, to whom we owe the homage of adoration, praise, and submission. The first part of the "Our Father" is an exact statement of the rights of God's sovereignty and of his transcendence, which in no way take anything away from his fatherhood. True prayer does not put God at the service of man, but man at the service of God; to serve him is to make holy his name, to make use of every means to spread his reign, in order to accomplish his will. These are the great values toward which Jesus directs Christian prayer in the first place. He who was the perfect adorer of the Father wishes to raise us to his own attitude of adoration, praise, and dedication to the cause of his Father.

Jesus teaches that prayer is also a humble, trustful recourse to God in all the necessities of our earthly life, from the more material things such as our daily bread to the more spiritual like the forgiveness of sins, the strength to overcome temptation, and deliverance from evil. Just as a son turns to his earthly father with assurance in every need, so must we trustingly direct ourselves to our heavenly Father.

The "Our Father" is a compendium of all Christian prayer, from the simple vocal prayer of a baby to the solemn liturgical prayer of the Church; from interior prayer, an intimate conversation with God, to the community prayer in which the faithful join to praise their common Father. When we say the "Our Father," it should so take hold of our hearts that we experience at least a little of what St. Therese of the Child Jesus felt: she was moved even to tears when she called God by the sweet name of Father; it was enough to immerse her in contemplation. (Counsels and Remembrances).

2. Jesus rebuked the Pharisees who had reduced divine worship to a mere exterior formalism, devoid of all soul, saying of them: "This people honors me with their lips, but their heart is far from me" (Mt 15:8). Instead he taught his disciples to pray "in Spirit and truth" (Jn 4:23), that is, that the lifting of the mind and heart to God must precede any verbal expression, for prayer is essentially an expression of desire and of interior love. St. Therese used to say: "For me prayer is an aspiration of the heart, it is a simple glance directed to heaven, it is a cry of gratitude and love in the midst of trial as well as joy" (Auto Mss p. 242). Without this deep undergirding, prayer loses its real meaning and becomes simply a mechanical recitation which gives no honor to God and does not bring us close to him.

St. Teresa of Jesus teaches us to accompany vocal prayer with mental prayer, and explains her thought thus: "If while speaking I thoroughly understand and know that I am speaking with God and I have a greater awareness of this than I do of the words I am saying, mental and vocal prayer are joined" (Way 22:1); that is, the interior dialogue of the heart and mind sustains and gives life to the exterior dialogue of the lips. This is why the Saint insists: "it is good that [in your need to speak to God] you consider whom you are speaking with, as well as who you are, at least if you want to be polite" (ib.). This obligation contributes toward making prayer alive and life-giving: it becomes a true dialogue with God which opens up into communion and gives it sustenance. Before teaching the "Our Father," Jesus himself pointed out with what interior inclinations we need to apply ourselves to simple vocal prayer: "Whenever you pray, go into your room, and shut your door" (Mt 6:6); obviously these words are not to be understood only in their physical sense, but also in the spiritual sense of recollection and interior application, because only in this way can we find God and offer him a prayer pleasing to him.

My God, how good you are to let us call you "Our Father!" Who am I that my Creator, my King, my supreme Master permits me to call him "my Father?" And not only permits me, but bids me to do it! My God, how good you are! How I ought to remember this sweet command at every moment of my life! What gratitude, what joy, what love, and especially what trust it ought to inspire in me. Since you are my Father, O my God, how much I must always hope in you! And since you are so good to me, how good I should be to others! Since you will to be Father to me and to all men, how much I ought to feel myself the loving brother of every one, no matter who, and no matter how wicked he may be!...

O Father, our Father, teach me ever to have your name upon my lips as Jesus did, and in him and thanks to him, let saying it be my greatest happiness. O Father, our Father, may I live and die saying, "Our Father!" and through my gratitude, my love and my obedience, be truly your faithful son, a son pleasing to your heart.

C. de Foucauld, *Meditations on the Pater,* Op. sp.

O my God, do you ever permit one who is about to speak to you (to) consider it good to do so only vocally? . . . Just because you are good does not mean that we should be rude. At least, in order to thank you for the bad odor you must endure in consenting to allow one like myself to come near you, we should strive to be aware of your purity and of who you are . . .

Oh, our Emperor, supreme Power, supreme Goodness, Wisdom itself, without beginning, without end, without any limit to your works; they are infinite and incomprehensible, a fathomless sea of marvels, with a beauty containing all beauty, strength itself! O God help me, who might possess here all human eloquence and wisdom together in order to know how to explain clearly—insofar as is possible here below . . . a number of the many things we can consider in order to have some knowledge of who this Lord and God of ours is.

St. Teresa of Jesus, *Way* 22:1,4,6

163 — INTERIOR LISTENING

Speak, Lord, your servant hears *(1 Sam 3:10)*

1. The sacred liturgy is "the summit" of divine worship and the "source" of the sanctification of men (SC 7:10). "The spiritual life, however, is not confined to participation in the liturgy. The Christian is assuredly called to pray with his brethren, but he must also enter into his chamber to pray to the Father in secret" (SC 12). The doctrinal treasures contained in the sacred liturgy, and the same divine mysteries which the liturgical acts celebrate and offer to the faithful, need to be assimilated in silence and reflection, in that intimate communion with God that is the form of mental prayer commonly known as "meditation." From Old Testament times on, Sacred Scripture has called "blessed" those who "meditate day and night" upon the law of the Lord (Ps 1:1-2), that is, on his word, his teachings and his mysteries in order the better to probe their meaning and to translate them into the concreteness of daily life. In this connection we have in the Gospel the example of the Blessed Mother, of whom St. Luke twice says that she "kept all these things" that she saw and heard about her divine Son, "pondering them in her heart" (2:19; cf 51). Without this interior deepening, God's word does not penetrate the soul, but stays on the surface without becoming part of daily life. Then follows what Jesus pointed out regarding "those who, when they

hear the word of God, receive it with joy, but have no root ... in time of temptation they fall away" (Lk 8;13); while those "who, hearing the word, hold it fast in an honest and good heart, and bring forth fruit with patience" (ib. 15). Just to listen with our external ears is not enough, this is but the first step; what is needed then is the interior listening of the heart, which, by allowing itself to be permeated by the divine word, acquires those deep convictions which can be translated into everyday life. Jesus not only emphasized the need for this vital listening, but proclaimed it a beatitude: "Blest are they who hear the word of God and keep it" (Lk 11:28).

2. Speaking of the importance of the word of God as nourishment for the spiritual life, Vatican Council II says: "Prayer should accompany the reading of Sacred Scripture, so that God and man may talk together, for we speak to him when we pray; we hear him when we read the divine sayings" (DV 25). The reading serves as a beginning, a point of departure for the interior dialogue: the written word then becomes a living word which God himself lights up in the depths of the recollected soul, making it understand its meaning and its practical application for daily life. Thus, the soul advances from reading to the attitude of Mary of Bethany, who, "seated at the Lord's feet, listened to his teaching" (Lk 10:39). This is the precious listening which Jesus calls the "one thing needful ... the good portion" (ib. 42); meaning that an hour spent listening to the words of eternal life is worth more than a thousand worldly accomplishments. Then spontaneously, the listening opens into prayer, which is the response of the soul to the Lord's word and light: adherence, acceptance, renunciation, and an impulse of love for God, renewed fervor in serving him, resolution to do good, and thanksgiving. Sacred Scripture, particularly the Gospel, texts of the missal and breviary offer most beautiful and useful themes for meditation, precisely because they are the word of God, and the word of the Church. Turning to religious, the Council says: "They should take the Sacred Scripture in hand each day by way of attaining 'the excellent knowledge of Jesus Christ' (Phil 3:8) through reading these divine writings and meditating on them" (PC 6); to clerics, it recommends that they "always grow in understanding of God's revealed word, and may know how to grasp it through meditation" (OT 4); and it does not speak differently to the laity when it declares that "only ... by meditation on the word of God" (AA 4) will they learn to seek and see Christ in every circumstance of life. The purpose of meditation is to know God better so as to love him more, or, as St. John of the Cross says, to acquire some "knowledge and love of God" (Asc II 14:2).

O Lord, my God, give ear to my prayer ... let your Scriptures be my pure delight: let me not be deceived in them, nor deceive others about them ... O my God, light of the blind, and strength of the weak; yes also light of those who see, and strength of the strong, hearken to my soul, and hear it crying out of the depths ... Not in vain would you have the darksome secrets of so many pages written ... Perfect me, O Lord, and reveal them unto me. See, your voice is my joy; your voice exceeds all other joys. Give what I love: for I do love; and this love is your gift. Forsake not your own gifts, nor despise this blade of thirsty grass. Let me exalt you for whatever I shall find in your books; let me hear the voice of your praise, and drink of you, and meditate on the wonderful things of your law from the beginning, when you made heaven and earth, until we reign everlastingly with you in your holy city.

St. Augustine, *Confessions* XI 3

O Lord, all my greatness is in listening to you: hearing you in the external word of your law, and hearing you in the interior inspiration of your Spirit, in the multi-faceted ways by which your providence speaks. Listening to you in the quiet depths of my heart, in the inflamed but beautiful desire of my will, in the humble and devoted fidelity of everyday work, and in deep sincere uprightness of life ...

It is more precious and more important to hear just one of your words, and to establish with you a current of interior attention, than the many things that my love would like to offer you. This is Mary's great merit, the one thing necessary, the best part, which she has attained and cannot lose. May I also listen, and know how to listen to you, O my Teacher.

cf G. Canovai, *Suscipe Domine*

164 — THE LIVING WATER

As the hart longs for flowing streams, so my soul longs for you, O God (Ps 42:1)

1. "They have forsaken me, the fountain of living waters; and hewed out cisterns for themselves ... broken cisterns, that can hold no water" (Jer 2:13), thus was God complaining of his people through the mouth of Jeremiah. God is a most pure source of life-giving water, the only one capable of satisfying the craving of man's heart for the infinite; he has always invited us to quench our thirst at his spring, but like Israel, we have continued to stray far from him by turning to the pleasures of the world, which like broken cisterns, cannot satisfy our thirst. When the Son of God came into the world, he renewed the invitation more explicitly: "Whoever drinks of the water that I shall give him will never thirst," and, "if any one thirst, let him come to me and drink ... Out of his heart shall flow rivers of living water" (Jn 4:14; 7:37-38). Jesus is the inexhaustible source of the living water of grace, which, by giving men a share in divine life, satisfies

our longing for love and happiness, letting us "taste and see that the Lord is good" (Ps 34:8). In this sense, the saints have understood by the living water promised by Jesus, not only sanctifying grace, but also that light and love which proceed from grace, and are obtained particularly through prayer, especially contemplation.

Commenting upon Jesus' invitation, St. Teresa of Avila says: "The Lord invites us all. Since he is Truth itself, there is no reason to doubt. If this invitation were not a general one, the Lord would not have called us all . . . But since he spoke to all without limitations . . . I hold it as certain that all those who do not falter on the way will drink this living water" (Way 19:15). Just as a life of grace is offered to all, so, at least in some form, contemplation is also offered to all; it is prayer's delicious fruit, inasmuch as God calls us to communion with himself in order to make us enjoy, even here, a first taste of his infinite goodness and love.

2. Every one is called to listen to God's word. For God was speaking to all when he pointed to his only begotten Son and said: "This is my beloved Son . . . listen to him" (Mt 17:5). When we listen to Jesus, we listen to the eternal Word, the Word that reveals the Father. When we look at Jesus, when we know him, we see and know God: "He who has seen me has seen the Father" (Jn 14:9), said Jesus, and then he added: "He who loves me will be loved by my Father, and I will love him and manifest myself to him" (ib. 21). This knowledge of God is reached through the assimilation of Sacred Scripture and through listening to the teachings of the Church, but even more through an interior listening to the intimate voice of God, who secretly reveals himself to those who love him and seek him with a desire that is keen, sincere, and constant. Then a light and a love heretofore unknown, the fruit of the gifts of the Holy Spirit, are progressively infused into us, by means of which we come to know God in a new way: we intuitively sense that God is truly the One, totally the Other, completely different from all other beings and infinitely superior; that he deserves all the love and self-surrender of his creature. This profound sense of the divine, this new way of knowing and loving God is the living water which satisfies the thirst of the human spirit. It is the initial stage of contemplation, God's precious free gift, which he will, however, not deny to anyone who seeks him with love and purity of heart.

Contemplation is not synonymous with revelations, visions, or ecstasy, but consists essentially in that secret experience which uncovers and lets us taste God's greatness and his mysteries. Viewed in this light, we can say that every Christian is called to contemplation, or, as St. Teresa of Jesus puts it, that God does not exclude anyone "from striving to come to this fountain of life" provided that he searches for it "as it should be sought" (Way 20:1; 19:15).

As the hart longs for flowing streams, so my soul longs for you, O God. My soul thirsts for God, for the living God. When shall I come and behold the face of God?...

Why are you cast down, O my soul? And why are you disquieted within me? Hope in God; for I shall again praise him, my help and my God. My soul is cast down within me, therefore I remember you...

By day the Lord commands his steadfast love, and at night his song is with me, a prayer to the God of my life.

Psalm 42:1-2,5-6,8

O Lord you invite all... (and say) "I will give you to drink."

Your mercy is so great you excluded no one from striving to come to this fount of life to drink. May you be blessed forever! How rightly might you have excluded me!... No, since he did not stop me when I started to walk along this path, nor order me to be thrown into the abyss, surely he excludes no one; rather, he calls us publicly, crying aloud.

O Lord, when you satisfy this thirst, the greatest favor you can grant the soul is to leave in it this same need—and a greater one—to drink the water again. (Way 19:15; 20:1-2; 19:2).

O Life, who gives life to all! Do not deny me this sweetest water that you promise to those who want it. I want it, Lord, and I beg for it, and I come to you. Do not hide yourself, Lord, from me, since you know my need and that this water is the true medicine for a soul wounded with love of you...

O living founts from the wounds of my God, how you have flowed with great abundance for our sustenance, and how surely he who strives to sustain himself with this divine liqueur will advance in the midst of the dangers of this life. (Soliloquies, 9:2).

St. Teresa of Jesus

165 — THE FOUNT OF LIFE

For with you is the fountain of life ... (Ps 36:9)

1. The Church has always been "dedicated to the contemplation" of divine things, and continues to recommend it to her children through the voice of the Council. She especially proposes it for priests by inviting them to nourish and sustain "their own activities with the fullness of contemplation" (LG 41), and for members of institutes of perfection, so that by its means they may adhere "to God, in mind and in their hearts" (PC 5).

Having received in baptism the virtue of faith, which is the beginning of all supernatural knowledge of God, and the gifts of the Holy Spirit, which are supernatural dispositions that perfect the virtues and make us capable of detecting the divine light and motions, we have the way to contemplation open to us. The theological virtues and the gifts of the Holy Spirit constitute the normal structure of the life of grace; therefore their workings should not be looked upon as extraordinary, but rather as innate to the normal development of Christian life. It follows that if any one freely seconds the action of grace, does not reject the practice of virtue, and is totally open to divine inspiration, the Lord will not deny that soul at least a sip of the living water—that is, some form of contemplation. St. Teresa of Avila is convinced of this and declares that "in many ways the Lord gives to drink to those who wish to follow him, so that no one will go without consolation or die of thirst" (Way 20:2). The way and the measure and the level of contemplation depend solely upon God's pleasure, for he is master of his gifts and distributes them "when he desires, as he desires, and to whom he desires. Since these blessings belong to him he does no injustice to any one" (IC IV 1:2). We cannot, then, advance any claims; in this case the words of Jesus carry more weight than ever: "When you have done all that is commanded you, say, 'We are unworthy servants.' " (Lk 17:10). But God loves the humble, and he will exalt them in due time (cf 1 Pet 5:6).

2. The way that disposes the soul for contemplation is that of deep humility, entire generosity and total availability. "Reflect"—writes St. Teresa to her daughters—"that he does not want you to hold on to anything, so that you will be able to enjoy the favors we are speaking of. Whether you have little or much, he wants everything for himself" (IC V 1:3). Besides, "Since he does not force our will, he takes what we give him, but he does not give himself completely, until we give ourselves completely" (Way 28:12). This is why the Saint in her works, before discussing contemplation, lingers long on the virtues, in particular upon humility, detachment, and charity, which she wants to see practiced without half-measures, in the most generous and perfect way.

This spirit of totality is clearly evangelical. Jesus compared the kingdom of heaven to "a treasure hidden in a field"; to acquire it the finder did not hesitate "to sell all he has" (Mt 13:44); he spoke of the faithful servant who zealously and profitably invested for profit all the money he had received, and who was told: "Come, enter into the joy of your master!" (Mt 25:21). And he spoke especially of the essential condition for being true friends of God: those who would be admitted to intimacy with him, and be introduced to his secrets: "You are my friends if you do what I command you" (Jn 15:14). The Lord reveals himself and gives himself to his sincere friends so that his words may be verified in them: "that my joy may be in you and that your joy may be full" (ib. 11). But any one who is not prepared to give himself totally to God will never arrive at experiencing the joy of his friendship and of his intimate secret communications. Graces like these are reserved for his "favored children. He would not want them to leave his side nor does he leave them, for they no longer want to leave him" (Way 16:9).

"How precious is your steadfast love, O God"—sings the psalmist—"The children of men take refuge in the shadow of your wings . . . You give them drink from the river of your delights for with you is the fountain of life" (Ps 36:7-9). These words attain their full meaning in those who, by giving themselves to God with full generosity, are permitted to satisfy their thirst at the living source of contemplation.

O Lord, I run to the spring, I desire the sources of the water. In you is the fountain of life, an inexhaustible source; in your light there is a light which will never be darkened. I long for this light, this fountain . . . Seeing this light, my inner eye grows keener and drinking from this fountain my inner thirst becomes more acute. I run to the fountain, panting for its water, but I do not run at random . . . I run like a deer . . . not a slow running, but with all speed I run to the source with untiring longing . . .

O Lord, I am panting at the fountain; you have power to refresh me, and you fill to overflowing those who come to you thirsting . . . My soul thirsts for the living God . . . as the deer thirsts for the springs of water, so my soul thirsts for you, my God.

St. Augustine *In Ps.* 41:2-5

My God, my soul rejoices and leaps with joy and gratitude because you have let it share in the only life, and continually slake its thirst at that spring of "water gushing forth to eternal life" . . .

O my Friend, my hidden Guest, my God, you are my life, you are everything, my everything; in fact I would say you are the true me, so much do I feel taken up and possessed by you . . . O embrace of God, joy, tranquil peace, continually diffused and exultant, O marvel of your love, O communion of every moment! Only this is to live! . . . You are never satisfied and you are infinite, unreachable, continually pursued and yet continually possessed; satiated with yourself, yet you leave me in insatiable hunger, and unquenchable thirst. O my God, take me, consume me, burn me . . .

G. Canovai, *Suscipe Domine*

166 — INTIMACY WITH GOD

O Lord, you have not called us servants, but friends (Jn 15:15)

1. Every form of prayer is an encounter between man and God, and as prayer becomes deeper, the encounter becomes more intimate, a true communion "with the Father and with his Son Jesus Christ" (1 Jn 1:3). St. Teresa of Jesus looked at prayer in this perspective: "Mental prayer is nothing else than an intimate sharing between friends; it means taking time frequently to be alone with him who we know loves us" (Life 8:5). Prayer is not a solitary meditation in which we are alone with our thoughts, it is a sharing; the soul has a companion in its solitude: God, and treating intimately with him, reflects, prays, believes, and loves. It

will normally be necessary to take some pious consideration as a starting point to support meditation and to reanimate our awareness of God's love, so that the soul recollects itself and the will feels drawn to love. Having thus reached the center of prayer, the soul remains "heart to heart" with God. According to the impulse of grace and the state of the soul, it will pour itself out in intimate spontaneous conversation, expressing its gratitude and its desire to return the divine love; or perhaps it will expose its troubles and needs to the Lord, asking forgiveness, confiding its sorrows, invoking his help and offering its resolutions. Every so often it leaves off its conversation to listen: to perceive any inspirations or movements of grace through which God may be speaking to the soul, making it understand his mysteries, drawing it to himself, and urging it on to good. But when we notice our thoughts are beginning to wander and our will is cooling off, we return to considerations for as long as is necessary to arouse our love and awaken devotion. Thus, by alternating the dialogue with pauses of silence, with moments of meditation, or even of vocal prayers recited slowly and devoutly, we learn how "to be alone" with God and "to reach that special friendship with him" that is prayer (St. Ter. of Jesus, Life 8:6).

2. Friendship requires knowledge, love, and reciprocal exchange; this is also the case in prayer. Through faith we are made capable of knowing God in the mysteries of his intimate life and in particular in the mystery of his infinite love. Basing itself upon the facts of revelation, faith has the precise duty of nourishing our knowledge of God so that it may bring forth greater love. "We know and believe the love God has for us" (1 Jn 4:16): here is the fruit of prayer enlightened by faith, a most precious fruit, because when we are profoundly convinced of the love God has for us, we are totally open to reciprocating it. This is brought about through charity, which makes us capable of loving God for himself, and of finding joy in his friendship. It was God who first loved us and by giving freely of his love, put us in a position to love him in return. "We love because he first loved us" (ib. 19). The theological virtues of faith and charity are the basic elements of prayer understood as a relationship of friendship with God. Tender feeling is not excluded and may sometimes even be strong, but it is not essential; we must learn to base our intimacy with God much more upon faith and charity than upon our feelings. In such a way our converse with the Lord becomes less lively, but deeper; the movement of our will toward him grows more sober, but also more resolute and more practical. Rather than giving vent to many expressions of love, we prefer to be silent and to concentrate ourselves on an all-embracing look at God, contemplating him in faith and love. From time to time communication becomes silent and contemplative: a simple glance penetrates God's truth and the truth of his mysteries, and causes them to be savored. This is true communion and mutual friendship: the more the soul con-

templates its God, the more it becomes enamored and feels the need of giving itself to him with complete generosity; on the other hand God gives of himself, enlightening the soul with his light and drawing it more powerfully to him by his love and grace. "If a person is seeking God, his Beloved is seeking him much more" (Fl 3:28).

Lord Jesus, here I am with my cowardice and my foolish desires: grant me your merciful love and your help; I need your infinite goodness: forget that I have been a bad friend; I would like to begin a new friendship with you in which everything is in common, a friendship for life and for death.

Give me a new heart, a faithful heart, humble like your Mother's, ardent and indomitable like Paul's.

Dearest Mother, obtain this rehabilitation for me from Jesus . . . do not let his grace fail me, nor his strength. Mother, make me generous: while you are accepting my offering, at the same time change my heart . . .

Jesus, make me ready for anything your friendship may demand of me.

I want to sacrifice everything for my friendship with you, Jesus: Jesus and I; all the rest is vanity. I have renounced everything; this is not just an empty formula.

P. Lyonnet, *Spiritual Writings*

My God, you tell us that in order to pray, we do not have to feel obligated to recite vocal prayers, it is enough to talk to you interiorly in mental prayer; in this manner of praying it isn't even necessary to say any words at all, even interiorly, it is enough to stay lovingly at your feet, contemplating you—kneeling before you with feelings of admiration, compassion, surrender and desire for your glory . . . feelings of charity, with the utmost desire to see you—in short, all the feelings that love inspires. This prayer, so ardent even when silent, is excellent . . . As St. Teresa says, prayer consists not in talking much but in loving much; this follows from your words also . . .

O Jesus, may I learn to love and practice this solitary, secret prayer every day, this prayer in which no one sees us except our heavenly Father, in which we are absolutely alone with him . . . a secret and delightful colloquy in which we pour out our hearts freely, far from the eyes of everyone.

C. de Foucauld, *Meditations upon the Gospel*, Op. Sp.

167 — THIRD SUNDAY OF EASTER

YEAR A

You ransomed us, O Lord, with your precious blood *(1 Pet 1:18-19)*

The fifty days that elapse between Easter and Pentecost are an uninterrupted celebration of the paschal mystery, with its highpoints on the Sundays, each of which is regarded as another Easter Sunday. On each, the Liturgy continues to proclaim the resurrection of the Lord, deepening its various aspects. Today, with the exception of the Gospel which gives us again the episode of the disciples of Emmaus, upon which we already meditated on Easter Wednesday (Meditation #156), we listen to Peter, the first preacher of the resurrection.

The Acts relate a passage of his courageous discourse on the day of Pentecost in which he declares to the "men of Israel" that the Jesus they condemned to death is risen: "You crucified him and killed him at the hands of lawless men; God raised him up, having loosed the pangs of death, because it was not possible for him to be held by it" (Acts 2:23-24). How could one who had accomplished such "mighty works and wonders and signs" (ib. 22) be swallowed up by death, one who had snatched the prey from death itself, restoring life to the young man of Naim, to the daughter of Jairus, and to Lazarus after four days in the tomb? Peter appeals moreover to the Scriptures in which he now knows how to read the mysterious prophecies of the resurrection: "You will not abandon my soul to Hades, nor let your Holy One see corruption" (ib. 27). The words of the psalmist who hopes not to remain a prisoner in Hades—the land of the dead—are applied to Jesus, the preeminently "holy One," whose body suffered no dissolution even in death.

In this speech Peter is defending the resurrection; in his first letter he explains the value of the paschal mystery and offers it to the faithful as the determining motive for holiness in their lives: "You know that you were ransomed . . . not with perishable things such as silver, or gold, but with the precious blood of Christ, like that of a lamb without blemish or spot" (1 Pet 1:18-19). The consciousness of having been ransomed from shame and from the slavery of sin by means of the blood of the Son of God is, for Peter, one of the strongest arguments to impel men to love their Savior and to live in such a way as not to make his passion in vain. That "precious blood" is a very concrete reality for Peter: he saw it being shed during the time of the passion, saw its traces on the cloths found in the tomb, saw the wounds of the risen Christ whence it had been poured out to the last drop. The joy of the resurrection did not make him forget the sorrowful passion which had preceded it, without which Jesus would not have risen again, nor have saved sinful humanity. It is truly by virtue of his blood that we receive the gift of faith: we believe that God "raised him from the dead and gave him glory, so that your faith and hope are in God" (ib. 21): the hope of eternal resurrection.

From where did Peter, a rough fisherman, derive such a profound doctrine of the Easter mystery? He also, like the disciples at Emmaus,—and more than they—had been taught by Jesus. When Jesus appeared to the Eleven on Easter evening, he not only explained the Scriptures, but "opened their minds," so that they might understand them (Lk 24:45). Only the grace of Christ, lived in intimate relationship with him, could transform a man interiorly and infuse into him so convinced a faith and so intense a love as to make him an apostle.

O Christ, our paschal sacrifice, when you offered your body on the cross, your perfect sacrifice fulfilled all others. As you give yourself for our salvation, you show yourself to be the priest, the altar, and the lamb of sacrifice. The joy of the resurrection renews the whole world.

cf Roman Missal, *Easter Preface* V

O Christ Jesus, although God of all majesty, you humbled yourself even to accepting the torment of the cross in order to save mankind. From the distance of centuries, Abraham saw you prefigured in his son, as the people of Moses also saw in the paschal lamb they sacrificed. You are the one of whom the prophets declared: he will bear the sins of all men, he will annul all our misdeeds.

This is the great pasch, O Christ, which your blood has covered with glory; the pasch that inebriates the Christian people with immense joy, which we celebrate in profound adoration! O mystery of grace, the inexplicable mystery of divine munificence! O most venerable of all feasts, on which you gave yourself up even to death to save us, mere servants!

O blest be your death that broke the chains of our death! Now can the prince of hell consider himself beaten, and we, saved from falling into the abyss, exult with great joy because you, O Lord, brought us back to the road to heaven.

Ambrosian Preface, from *Early Christian Prayers* 328

YEAR B

O Jesus, you are our peace *(Eph 2:14)*

During the Sundays of Easter, the Old Testament readings are replaced by the Acts of the Apostles, which give us the primitive apostolic preaching and bear witness to the resurrection of the Lord, showing how the Church was born in the name of the risen One.

In the first reading today, Peter presents the resurrection of Jesus by inserting it into the history of his people as the fulfillment of all the prophecies and promises made to their fathers: "The God of Abraham . . . the God of our fathers, has glorified his servant Jesus, whom you delivered up and denied in the presence of Pilate . . . But God raised him from the dead. To this we are his witnesses" (Acts 3:13, 15). If this testimony and that of those who have seen the risen Christ is not sufficient, we are given a "sign" in the miraculous recovery of the cripple as soon as he had come to the temple gate. To emphasize the resurrection, Peter does not hesitate to recall the painful events that had preceded it: "You denied the holy and righteous One, and asked for a murderer to be granted to you, and killed the Author of life" (ib. 14-15). The accusations are pressing, almost merciless; but Peter knows very well he himself is included, because he, too, has denied the Master; all men are included who by their sinning continue to deny "the holy One" and reject the "Author of life," preferring their own passions instead, which bring death. Peter has not forgotten his offense, for which he will weep all his life, but at the same time he keeps in his heart the sweetness of the Lord's forgiveness. This enables him to pass from accusation to excuse: "I know, my brothers, that you acted out of ignorance, as did also your rulers" (ib. 17); hence he invites them to conversion: "Repent therefore and turn again to God, that your sins may be blotted out" (ib. 19). Just as he had been forgiven, so will his people also be—and all other men as well—provided they all acknowledge their faults and resolve to sin no more.

At this point, (in the second reading), we link up with John's touching admonition: "My little children, I am writing this . . . so that you may not sin" (1 Jn 2:1). How could any one who has grasped the meaning of the Lord's passion have the audacity to return to sinning? At any rate, conscious of human frailty, the Apostle continues: "But if any one does sin, we have an advocate with the Father, Jesus Christ, the righteous" (ib.). John, who heard the dying Lord on Calvary implore the Father's forgiveness for those who had crucified him, knows how far he went to defend sinners. An innocent victim of the sins of mankind, Jesus is also their worthy advocate because he himself "is the expiation for our sins" (ib. 2).

We can glean the same thought from the Gospel of the day.[1] Appearing to the apostles after his resurrection, Jesus greeted them with the words: "Peace to you" (Lk 24:36). The risen Lord offered peace to the Eleven who are amazed and frightened by his appearance, and certainly not the less confused and repentant for having abandoned him during his passion. He, who had died to destroy sin and reconcile men with God, offered them peace to assure them of his forgiveness and unchanging love. Before he left them, he made them messengers of conversion and forgiveness for

[1]See also Easter Thursday, Meditation #157.

all: "Repentance and forgiveness of sins should be preached in his name to all nations, beginning from Jerusalem" (ib. 47). And so Jesus' peace is to be carried throughout the world precisely because "he is the propitiation for our sins." It is the mystery of his infinite love!

O Christ, our Pasch, you offered yourself for our salvation. O King of glory, continue to immolate yourself for us, be the advocate who always pleads our cause; you are the victim who dies no more, and the Lamb once slain, who lives for ever.

cf *Roman Missal, Easter Preface* III

O Lord, what will you give us? "Peace I leave you, my peace I give you!" It is enough for me. I thankfully receive what you leave me... I am happy this way; I am sure it is for my best interests... Peace I want, peace I desire and nothing more. He that is not satisfied with peace is not satisfied with you. For you are "our peace who have made us both one." This is necessary for me, this is enough: to be reconciled to you and to be reconciled to myself. For when there is a dividing wall of hostility between us, I am become burdensome to myself. I will be cautious henceforth not to appear ungrateful for the gift of peace you have given me. To you, O Lord, the glory... as for me, I shall be well content if I can but preserve peace...

Deliver me, O Lord, from a haughty eye and an insatiable heart, that is impatiently covetous of the glory that belongs to you alone, and so loses peace without attaining to eternal glory.

cf St. Bernard, *On the Canticle of Canticles* 13:4-5

YEAR C

To the Lamb be blessing and honor and glory and might for ever and ever *(Rev 5:13)*

This Sunday's Liturgy offers a triple testimony to the resurrection: the appearance of Jesus on Lake Tiberias; the declaration of Peter and the Apostles before the Sanhedrin; the prophetic vision of John of the glory of the Lamb.

The appearance of Jesus on the Lake[1] is accompanied by remarkable details: the miraculous catch of one hundred and fifty three large fish, the meal prepared by the risen Lord on the shore, the bestowal of the primacy on Peter. Impelled by his love for Jesus, Peter was the first to run to meet him, and when their meal was finished, the Lord examined him in particular about his love. It must have been painful to be thus questioned three times on such a delicate point, but Jesus was quietly leading him to make amends in this way for his triple denial and to bring him to understand that, rather than feeling sure of his love for God, he must entrust this certainty to God. Peter sensed this, and after

[1]See Easter Friday Meditation #158.

the third questioning, "grieved," but more humble, he answered: "Lord, you know everything. You know that I love you" (Jn 21:17). Upon this foundation of humility and self-renunciation, the Apostle is made head of the Church. And to make him understand that there was no question of an honor here, but of a service similar to that which Jesus had given in offering himself for man's salvation, he is told: " . . . when you are old, you will stretch out your hands, and another will gird you and carry you where you do not wish to go" (ib. 18).

The Acts (first reading) show Peter at his place as the head of the Apostles, as they are dragged before the Sanhedrin, accused of preaching the name of Jesus. After declaring that "we must obey God rather than men" (Acts 5:29), Peter resumed his open preaching of the resurrection: "The God of our fathers raised Jesus whom you killed by hanging him on a tree" (ib. 30). Though scarcely out of prison and knowing that worse could befall him, he was unafraid, because all his confidence rested in the risen Christ, and by now he has understood that he must follow him in his sufferings. He strengthened his discourse with an unusual affirmation: "We are witnesses to these things [passion-resurrection] and so is the Holy Spirit whom God has given to those who obey him" (ib. 32). This was the same as saying that the Holy Spirit speaks through the mouth of those who, in obedience to God, preach the gospel at no matter what risk. For the Apostles the risk quickly became reality for they were made to undergo scourging, which they suffered joyfully: "rejoicing that they were counted worthy to suffer dishonor for the name" (ib. 41). This is the testimony that the Lord expects from every Christian, devoid of human respect, free from the fear of danger. The courageous faith of the believer is more convincing to the world than any kind of defense.

Joined to the testimony of the Church militant, which is always imperfect because of human weakness, is that of the Church triumphant (second reading), which gives loud praise to the glory of the risen Christ: "Worthy is the Lamb who was slain, to receive power and wealth and wisdom and might and honor and glory and blessing!" (Rev 5:12). It is a song of gratitude and love on the part of all creatures for him who, in saving man, redeemed the whole universe. It is a magnificent fragment of the heavenly Liturgy, of which the Eucharistic Liturgy here on earth repeats the motif: "For yours is the kingdom and the power and the glory for ever and ever." We are called to join the elect in praising and adoring the Lord in glory not only in tongue and gesture, but still more by our lives and actions.

O God, we have come in these days to know the full greatness of your love; grant us to welcome your offer of salvation with open hearts, so that, freed from the darkness of sin, we may firmly adhere to your teachings.

Roman Missal, *Collect*—3rd Thursday of Easter

O Lord, in return for so much tenderness you ask me anxiously one thing only: My son do you love me? Lord, Lord, how can I answer you? See my tears, my throbbing heart . . . What can I say? "Lord, you know that I love you."

Oh, if I could love you as Peter loved you, with the fervor of Paul and all the martyrs! My love must be joined to humility, a low opinion of myself and scorn for the things of this world—and then make of me what you will: an apostle, a martyr, O Lord!

At the sight of my most gentle Jesus humbling himself and, like a meek lamb, submitting to persecution, torture, treachery and death, my soul is bewildered, ashamed, prostrated; I can find no words—even my pride hangs its head in shame. "O most sweet Jesus, comfort of the pilgrim soul, with you I am voiceless, but my very silence speaks to you!" (year 1902, pp. 91-92).

Oh, after so many graces, showered upon me during my long life, there is nothing now that I can refuse. You have shown me the way, O Jesus. "I will follow you wherever you go," to sacrifice, to mortification, to death (year 1961, p. 318).

John XXIII *Journal of a Soul*

168 — WITH JESUS

The Lord is my shepherd; he restores my soul (Ps 23:1,3)

1. Just as Christ is the center of prayer and of liturgical worship, so must he also be the center of our personal prayer, "I am the way and the truth and the life"—said Jesus—"no one comes to the Father but by me" (Jn 14:6). In order to lead men back to friendship with him, God chose to make use of his divine Son, and if we are to go to God, we must follow the same way: seek Christ and attach ourselves to him who is our Mediator, our Redeemer.

In speaking of prayer, St. Teresa says: "This method of keeping Christ present with us is beneficial in all stages and is a very safe means of advancing quickly" (Life 12:3). This advice is as useful for beginners as it is for proficients, because Jesus is Master, the guide as well as the object of prayer. He is our Master: "The Master is here and is calling for you" (Jn 11:28); he alone has the words of eternal life. Through prayer he instructs his friends, and reveals himself and the divine mysteries to them: "All that I have heard from my Father, I have made known to you" (Jn 15:15). He teaches us to pray in secret to his heavenly Father and to adore him in the intimacy of our hearts "in Spirit and truth" (Jn 4:24). He offers us the living water which quenches our thirst and inflames us with divine love: "If you knew the gift of God, and who it is that is saying to you 'Give me to drink,' you would have asked him, and he would have given you living water" (ib. 10). St. Teresa concludes: "The Lord helps us, strengthens us, and never fails; he is a true friend . . . God desires that if we are going to please him and receive his favors, we must do so through the most sacred humanity of Christ, in whom he takes his delight . . . We must enter by this gate if we desire God to show us great secrets: (Life 22:6). Indeed Jesus himself said: "I am the door; if any one enters by me, he will be saved and will go in and out and find pasture" (Jn 10:9). Whoever takes Christ as the guide of his prayer walks by a very sure path, and can repeat with the psalmist: "The Lord is my shepherd; I shall not want; he makes me lie down in green pastures. He leads me beside still waters, he restores my soul" (Ps 23:1-3).

2. When St. Teresa was teaching her daughters to pray, she said: "Since you are alone, strive to find a companion. Well, what better companion than the Master himself? . . . Indeed, I am not asking you . . . to make long and subtle reflections . . . I am not asking you to do anything more than look at him . . . If you are joyful, look at him as risen . . . If you are experiencing trials or are sad, behold him burdened with the cross on his back . . . If he has moved your heart to pity at seeing him thus, not only will you desire to look at him, but you will also delight in speaking with him . . . not with ready-made prayers, but with those that come from the sorrow of your own heart, for he esteems them highly" (Way 26:1-6). This is a very simple and efficacious method of prayer, which helps us to become one with Christ, to live his mysteries not only at prayer, but in daily life. The Church itself, in distributing the mysteries of the life of Christ throughout the liturgical year, invites us to follow that same direction. Inspired by the Liturgy and using the means it offers, we shall have the best of guides for centering our mental prayer on Jesus, and at the same time will be able to follow the development of the liturgical year with better understanding. Liturgical life and the life of prayer will complement each other, finding their common center in Jesus. That ardent lover of Jesus, St. Paul, wrote to the Ephesians: "I bow my knees before the Father . . . that he may grant you . . . to have the power to comprehend with all the saints, what is the breadth and length and height and depth, and to know the love of Christ . . . that you may be filled with all the fullness of God" (Eph 3:14-19). The knowledge of the mystery of Christ of which the Apostle speaks does not come from study, but from prayer; from prayer at the feet of Jesus, contemplating him and loving him, because he has said: "He who loves me . . . I will love him and manifest myself to him" (Jn 14:21).

You loved us, O Lord Jesus Christ, fathomless Love, from the depths of your love; you became man for us; you abased yourself to raise us up; you bent down to lift us up; you shed your majesty to fill us with your divinity; you came down to us, so that we might rise up to you.

There is no father, no mother, no friend nor any one else who has loved us as much as you, O Lord, who created us . . .

What a good and happy thing it is, and how desirable, to feel the violence of your love, O Lord Jesus Christ; you enlighten our souls every day with the rays of such burning charity, heal our soul's wounds, light up the secrets of the heart; you nourish and warm our minds by infusing into the soul a strengthening enthusiasm!

Oh! how sweet the merciful sweetness and tenderness of your love, O Lord Jesus Christ, you who give liberally of that charity which those enjoy who love nothing, nor seek nor desire to think of anything, except you.

You invite us, you enrapture us, and attract us to your love by going before us, so strong is the force of your affection.

R. Giordano, *Contemplation on Divine Love* 5

O Christ, you are not one truth among other truths. You are Truth, and all that is true in this world is you. You are not one love among other loves. You are Love, in which all authentic loves are purified, sanctified, and united—not diminished but rather completed. You are not one means among other means, a means to be used beside other means, whose usefulness can be doubted... no, you are the only way, and at the same time, the true end, you are life...

O Lord, what could I do without you, since you have taken everything in me, since you are whatever is most intimately me, since you are my greatness, my life, my everything?

O Christ I recognize you as my only Lord for ever. Woe to me if I should offer my heart and soul to another master! Because there are no other masters for man or other loves outside of Love.

Here are all my energies, all my useful talents... I do not want to hide anything from you, or take anything away from you, or rob you of anything... I abandon everything to you... This pledge between you and me is an engagement between two persons, between your love and mine, whose only stipulation is never to speak of a limit to giving... Between us, everything is for life and for death.

P. Lyonnet, *Spiritual Writings*

169 — THE PRAYER OF RECOLLECTION

You are my Lord. I have no good apart from you *(Ps 16:2)*

1. The foundation of interior prayer is the presence of God in us. First of all the *presence of immensity* by which God is present with his action in all his creatures. "He is not far from each one of us"—says St. Paul—"for in him we live and move and have our being" (Acts 17:27-28); this divine presence is so essential that if it were to cease, we should cease to exist. Moreover, there is the *presence of friendship* which is realized only in the faithful in the state of grace; in it, God already present as Creator, is present also

as a Father, as a Friend, as a sweet Guest; he is present in the mystery of his Trinitarian life, inviting us to dwell with the three divine Persons: with the Father, the Son, and the Holy Spirit. This is the consoling promise of Jesus to the soul who loves him: "If a man loves me . . . my Father will love him, and we will come to him and make our home with him" (Jn 14:23). One who is conscious of this sublime reality and recollects himself to speak with God, present, living, and acting in his heart, who seeks God there, loves him, and is united to him and lives in intimacy with him, has here a most excellent method of mental prayer. "Be joyful and gladdened in your interior recollection with him, for you have him so close to you!"—exclaims St. John of the Cross—"Desire him there, adore him there. Do not go in pursuit of him outside yourself. You will only become distracted and wearied thereby and you shall not find him . . . nor have him more intimately than by seeking him within you" (Sp C 1:8). In the measure in which the sense of God's presence within us becomes living and deep, interior prayer becomes an easy, spontaneous, real "spring of water, welling up to eternal life" (Jn 4:14). "Do you think"—says St. Teresa—"that it matters little for a soul with a wandering mind to understand this truth and see that there is no need to go to heaven in order to speak with one's heavenly Father or find delight in him? Nor is there any need to shout. However softly we speak, he is near enough to hear us. Neither is there any need for wings to go to find him. All one need do is go into solitude and look at him within oneself" (Way 28:2).

2. Speaking of the prayer of recollection—the prayer in which the soul is recollected in God present within it—St. Teresa observes that it depends on us to acquire it "because this recollection is not something supernatural [i.e. not an infused recollection which is a pure gift of God], but something we can desire and achieve ourselves with the help of God" (Way 29:4). The first step toward attaining it consists in recollecting ourselves, gathering our powers together and retiring within ourselves with God, a practice which is not always easy because our senses, imagination, and intellect tend spontaneously toward external things. Therefore it requires a certain effort that calls for decision and energy. "The soul"—counsels the Saint—"should get used to this recollection; although in the beginning the body causes difficulty because it claims its rights without realizing that it is cutting off its own head by not surrendering" (Way 28:7). As with all Christian life, prayer, too, is the fruit of struggle and conquest, which is required by God as proof of the good will of his creature and is consequently rewarded by growing facility in interior recollection. "Then, the gain will be clearly seen. We will understand when beginning prayer, that the bees are approaching and entering the beehive to make honey" (ib.). We shall then be free to concentrate on God, present within us, and to converse with him there. The whole time of prayer may be passed in acts of faith, love and

adoration, never tiring of admiring and contemplating the Trinity dwelling within us and of offering it our humble homage. But if this is not enough, we can also use other practices: "Centered there within itself, the soul can think about the passion, and represent Christ Jesus to itself, offering him to the Father," or else, more simply, it may linger with its divine Guest "like a father, or a brother, or a teacher, or as with a spouse, sometimes in one way, at other times in another; he will teach you what you must do in order to please him . . . (The soul) may tell him all about its sufferings, and ask for their solution, always mindful that it is not worthy to be called his child" (ib. 2-4). St. Teresa concludes: "Those who by such a method can enclose themselves within this little heaven of our soul, where the Maker of heaven and earth is present . . . are following an excellent path and they will not fail to drink water from the fount" (ib. 5).

O Word, Son of God, you make me understand that together with the Father and the Holy Spirit, you are hidden in the innermost being of my soul. If I want to find you I should enter within myself in deepest recollection.

Well then, my soul, since your beloved Bridegroom is the treasure hidden in your field, for which the wise merchant sold all his possessions [Mt 13:44] in order to find him you should forget all your possessions and all creatures and hide in the interior, secret chamber of your soul. And there, closing the door behind you (your will to all things), you should pray to your Father in secret [Mt 6:6].

Grant, O Lord, that remaining hidden with you, I may be able to love and enjoy you, and delight with you in hiding, in a way transcending all language and feeling.

cf St. John of the Cross, *Spiritual Canticle* I 6,9

O Lord, grant me the grace to know how to enclose myself within this little heaven of my soul, where you are present. There you let me find you, there I feel you are closer to me than anywhere else, and there you prepare my soul quickly to enter into intimacy with you. Then the soul, understanding that all the things of the world are but toys, seems all of a sudden to rise above everything created and escape it, like one who takes refuge in a fortified castle to be safe from enemies.

O Lord, may I make every effort to recollect myself within me; then I shall travel far in a short time, I shall be safe from so many dangers and your love will be enkindled more quickly. Being so close to the fire, a little breath will be enough and the tiniest spark will set everything ablaze.

cf St. Teresa of Jesus, *Way* 28:4-8

It seems to me that I have found my heaven upon earth, because my heaven is you, my God, and you are in my soul.

"You in me, and I in you"—may this be my motto. What a joyous mystery is your presence within me, in that intimate sanc-

tuary of my soul where I can always find you, even when I do not feel your presence. Of what importance is feeling? Perhaps you are all the closer when I feel you less. You are there nevertheless, and I love to seek you there. I wish never to leave you alone, let my life be one continual prayer.

Elizabeth of the Trinity, *Letters 107; 45*

170 — UNDER TRIAL

Be gracious to me, O Lord, for I am in distress . . . But I trust in you (Ps 31:9,14)

1. "Your face, Lord, do I seek. Hide not your face from me; turn not your servant away in anger" (Ps 27:8-9). Man seeks his God in prayer, but faith is not yet vision, charity in exile is still not full possession, and therefore he suffers and laments because he cannot find God and be united to him as he would like. It seems as though the Lord is hiding his face, and abandoning his creature, and even while it ardently desires to remain with him, it feels as though rebuffed, alone, arid, and incapable of a good thought or impulse or affection. Yet God is there: he is immutably present in the soul in grace, and is waiting for proof of its fidelity, notwithstanding the hardships of the trial. St. Paul said well: "Likewise the Spirit helps us in our weakness, for we do not know how to pray as we ought" (Rom 8:26). Prayer is a gift of God; only God can make us capable of praying as we should, and before embarking upon a life of prayer, we should be conscious of our weakness and of our inability to pray. When the Holy Spirit assists us by the movement of grace, prayer then becomes easy and spontaneous, but when he apparently suspends this action of grace, we experience our poverty, insufficiency, and our coldness of mind and heart. To engage in prayer inevitably means to encounter these problems, which in the designs of God serve the purpose of purifying us of the childishness of sensible comfort through forcing us to proceed with a stronger and more resolute will. Thus we learn to turn to prayer with greater purity of intention, not in order to find pleasure therein or spiritual consolation, but to please God, to prove our allegiance to him, and to tell him by our actions that we love him more than ourselves, and know how to seek him and to wait for him even in the bitterness of aridity and solitude. "I wait for the Lord, my soul waits, and in his word I hope; my soul waits for the Lord more than watchmen for the morning" (Ps 130:5-6).

2. "Humble yourselves therefore under the mighty hand of God, that in due time he may exalt you" (1 Pet 5-6). This is the attitude we should take during prayer in the time of aridity. As we experience our inability to pray and feel ourselves reduced to

nothing, we are despoiled of a certain self-assurance and complacency which unconsciously insinuate themselves when prayer comes easily and pleasantly. This spontaneously leads us to approach the Lord in deep humility. "God be merciful to me, a sinner" (Lk 18:13). "Lord, I am not worthy to have you come under my roof" (Mt 8:8), I am not worthy to speak with you, I am not worthy of your friendship. Similar sentiments of sincere and convinced humility, springing from the depths of the heart, are not meant to mortify or disturb us, nor to stifle our trust in God, nor to shake our faith in his love, but rather to make us face the truth: the truth of our nothingness before the all of God. The Lord causes us to pass through the trial of humility to make us understand through experience that when he offers us intimacy and calls us to communion with himself, this is a pure gift of his infinite love, of a promise that is not due to the creature's merits, but solely to divine liberality. In this way, notes St. John of the Cross, the soul "communes with God more respectfully and courteously, the way one should always converse with the Most High" (M I 12:3), an indispensable quality for progress in prayer. "The whole groundwork of prayer is based on humility"—says St. Teresa of Jesus—"the more a soul lowers itself in prayer, the more will God raise it up" (Life 22:11). Although very bitter and mortifying, we should accept aridity with good will, since such precious fruits come from it, and gently humble ourselves under God's hand for as long as it pleases him, persevering in prayer in the attitude of the true "poor one of Israel," who waits for his Lord with humble confidence.

O Lord, blessed be your name for ever, because you willed me to suffer this tribulation. I cannot escape it, so I have recourse to you, that you may help me to profit by it. O Lord, I am deeply afflicted, my heart can find no rest, and it suffers much on account of this hard trial. What can I say to you, O beloved Father? I am in anguish; Lord, save me! This happens to me in order to glorify you by my very humiliation, but later, you will deliver me. May it please you to deliver me, O Lord, for alone and wretched, what can I do or where can I go without you?

Give me once more the grace of patience! Help me, O God, and I shall fear nothing, even if the burden is heavy. And now, what shall I say in all these misfortunes? Lord, your will be done. I well deserve the tribulation which is crushing me. I must bear it. May I do so patiently until the storm is past and calm re-establish.

Imitation of Christ III 29:1-2

Lord, have pity on me, not according to my sinfulness and the severity of your divine justice, but according to the greatness of your infinite mercy. I alone have sinned, and done much evil in your sight, and therefore I am not worthy to enter into the sanctuary of sweet converse with you; but, O my Creator, remembering that I was conceived in iniquity, you will be the more inclined to feel sorry for me, since I am your creature, redeemed by your blood. Give me, O most merciful Lord, the joy and happiness that you used to give me when you were drawing my soul to you in a divine manner into the ocean of your compassionate goodness.

But, if you know that it is advisable, O Lord, for me to be so arid and dry in this pool of abnegation of self, where suffering purifies love for you in the souls of your servants, may your holy will be done always and for all eternity.

St. Charles da Sezze, *Autobiography* VII 30, Op. v. 2

171 — PERSEVERANCE AT ANY COST

The Lord is my strength and my shield. In him my heart trusts (Ps 28:7)

1. "No one who puts his hand to the plow and looks back is fit for the kingdom of God" (Lk 9:62); and whoever recoils from the difficulties encountered along the road to prayer will never conquer that particular kingdom of God that is intimacy with him. St. Teresa says: We "must have an earnest and most determined resolve not to halt until we reach the goal," the source of the living water promised by Jesus to those who, thirsting for him, seek him with perseverance. We need to give ourselves to prayer, not only in moments of joyful transport and sensible devotion, but also in times of dryness, discomfort and repugnance; and all this, not just for a certain period, but at all times, every day, all our life. "Come what may, happen what may, whatever work is involved, whatever criticism arises, whether they arrive or die on the road . . . persevering to the end" (Way 21:2). Without a great and very resolute determination it is only too easy to find pretexts for neglecting prayer. Powerlessness and aridity can cause us to think that it is a waste of time to devote ourselves to prayer and that we would do better to work, all the more so when we are urged on by many obligations. Or perhaps the feeling of our wretchedness and unworthiness may lead us to the conviction that it is a rash illusion to aspire to intimacy with God and therefore useless to persevere in prayer. But all these are suggestions of the enemy who tries every means to dissuade us from prayer. "This was the greatest temptation I had"—declares St. Teresa—"it nearly brought about my ruin" (Life 7:11;8:7 Peers) Even if dryness were to blame, or it were the result of unfaithfulness or a lack of generosity or of dissoluteness, we must not desist on account of any of these. "In spite of any wrong he who practices prayer does, he must not abandon prayer, since it is the means by which he can remedy the situation; and to remedy it without prayer would be much more difficult. May the devil not tempt him the way he did

me, to give up prayer out of humility . . . If we are truly repentant and resolve not to offend God, he will return to the former friendship" (ib. 5).

2. In speaking of the temptations of the devil, St. Peter says: "Resist him, firm in your faith" (1 Pet 5:9): this is exactly what we must do to persevere in prayer in the face of aridity. Faith makes us strong in our belief in God's love even when he tests us: "For the Lord reproves him whom he loves, as a father the son in whom he delights" (Prov 3:12). Faith assures us that God is with us even when he seems to abandon us, and listens to us although he seems to be deaf to our groaning, because "his steadfast love endures for ever" (Ps 118:2). It assures us that God rejects no one even if he be a wretch or a sinner; he sent his Son "not to call the righteous, but sinners" (Mt 9:13); in fact the one remedy for human wretchedness lies precisely in God, who, because he loves men, infuses goodness and grace into them. The more the one who prays knows how to believe in God's love with unshakeable faith, the more closely he is united to him. It is not through experiencing sweet and consoling prayer that we are introduced to friendship with God, but through the practice of the theological virtues, which can be more intense and unifying in spite of the weariness of keeping on in darkness and dryness, without the least feeling of comfort. "Not every one who says to me 'Lord, Lord,' shall enter the kingdom of heaven, but he who does the will of my Father who is in heaven" (Mt 7:21). The aim of prayer is not so much impulses of affection, as full adherence to the will of God. When we believe in God we put our trust in him, and trusting in him we rely upon his guidance, and let ourselves be led where he wishes. Faith thus leads to charity which binds us to choose, to will, and to do all that God wills. "You are my friends if you do what I command you" (Jn 15:14). True friendship leads progressively to only one single willing or not willing, which can come about even in the dryest prayer. Unable to express our love through words of affection, we concentrate our energies on conforming ourselves to the will of God, seeking to know it constantly better, to accept it more willingly and to carry it out with greater generosity. Thus prayer overflows into life and transforms it.

O Lord, in order that love be true and the friendship endure, the wills of the friends must be in accord. The will of the Lord, it is already known, cannot be at fault; our will is vicious, sensual, and ungrateful, so that we do not yet love you as you love us . . .

O infinite goodness of my God, for it seems to me I see that such is the way you are and the way I am. O delight of angels, when I see this I desire to be completely consumed in loving you! How certainly you do suffer the one who suffers to be with you! Oh, what a good friend you make, my Lord! How you proceed by favoring and enduring. You wait for the other to adapt to your nature, and in the meanwhile you put up with his! You take into account, my Lord, the times when he loves you, and in one instant of repentance you forget his offenses.

I have seen this clearly myself. I do not know, my Creator, why it is that every one does not strive to reach you through this special friendship, and why those who are wicked, who are not conformed to your will, do not, in order that you make them good, allow you to be with them at least two hours each day, even though they may not be with you, but with a thousand disturbances from worldly cares and thoughts . . . Through this effort they make to remain in such good company (for you see that in the beginning they cannot do more, nor afterwards, sometimes) you force the devils not to attack them, so that each day the devils' strength against them lessens; and you give them the victory over the devils. Yes, for you do not kill—life of all lives!—any of those who trust in you and desire you for friend.

St. Teresa of Jesus, *Life* 8:5-6

O Lord, what does it matter, when I can retire within myself, enlightened by faith, whether I feel or don't feel, whether I am in light or darkness, enjoy or do not enjoy? I am struck by a kind of shame at making any distinction between such things and, despising myself utterly for such want of love, I turn at once to you, my divine Master, for deliverance. Help me to exalt you . . . above the sweetness and consolations which flow from you, because I have resolved to pass by all else in order to be united with you.

Elizabeth of the Trinity, *Second Retreat* 4

172 — LIGHT FROM DARKNESS

I will look to you, Lord; when I sit in darkness, you will be my light (Micah 7:7-8)

1. "O God . . . my flesh faints for you and my soul thirsts for you as in a dry and weary land where no water is" (Ps 63:2). Just as in a land that is parched by the sun, where water is absolutely lacking, thirst increases beyond measure, so in the trial of aridity the soul that loves God becomes faint with thirst. Privation increases its desire, and while it continues to search for him in prayer, it finds no pleasure or comfort. Nor can it even obtain any help from meditation, for it has become incapable of that; in fact reasoning and discourse no longer help at all. Its trust in God does not permit it to seek compensation or to ask for earthly consolations: created things do not attract it, and no longer satisfy. Its attention remains directed toward God and it turns to him "solicitously and with painful care" (N I 9:3), because seeing itself deprived of joy in spiritual matters, it is afraid it no longer knows how to love and serve God. Yet St. John of the Cross shows how all this, rather than indicating a lack of love, is the fruit of a more intense love. Because if charity were extinguished and dryness

were to blame, we would not be anxious about not loving God, nor so constant in seeking him and pledged to remain faithful to him amid all this suffering. In addition, when these states are simultaneous and lasting, the Saint recognizes in them the signs of that crisis which progressively leads to contemplation (cf N I:9). "Suffering produces endurance"—says St. Paul—"and endurance produces character, and character produces hope. And hope does not disappoint, because God's love has been poured into our hearts through the Holy Spirit who has been given to us" (Rom 5:3-5). Something similar happens in the life of prayer: when the affliction of aridity is borne with constancy, it disposes us to attain more fully to that which we hope for: to be loved by God and to be able to love him in return. This is a hope which cannot be deceived because, without realizing it, divine love has already been infused in us by the Holy Spirit from the day of our baptism.

2. In actual fact, the Holy Spirit is working secretly in the soul that has been placed by God in this purifying aridity, through which he is preparing it to receive a deeper, purer, more delicate knowledge and love of God. We know God through the understanding illuminated by faith, but by a human procedure founded on reason, and distinct concepts and thoughts. But no matter how lofty, these concepts and thoughts are always circumscribed, and can therefore only imperfectly tell us something about God, who is infinite, without any limit. And here, while a man suffers in aridity and can no longer find profit in meditation, the Holy Spirit is infusing into him a new way of knowing: a general knowledge, indistinct and undefinable, but which begets a very deep sense of the transcendance of God, of his infinite being, his supreme majesty, and his boundless goodness. We then perceive by intuition that the divine Being is an "unfathomable abyss," that the mysteries and the ways of God are "inscrutable and unsearchable" (Rom 11:33); esteem, respect, and reverence for God grow spontaneously, and there is born in the soul the need to adore, and to acknowledge the divine sovereignty. "I am the Lord your God . . . you shall have no other gods before me" (Ex 20:2-3): the first commandment is no longer a law imposed from without, but an imperative that comes from within, something living, experienced in the depths of the soul; something that takes possession of the whole man and makes him adhere with all his energies to God, the highest Truth, the supreme Good—the Truth and Good which infinitely surpass our human capacity and at the same time draw us along through the divine attraction that God himself exercises over us in obscure prayer, that is shorn of distinct concepts, but is all the more luminous because it infuses a reflection of the divine light. Thus under the guidance of the Holy Spirit, who activates his gifts, we can sing with the psalmist: "In your light do we see light" (Ps 36:9); and likewise: in your love we shall learn to love.

O God, you are my God, I seek you; my soul thirsts for you and my flesh faints for you, as in a dry and weary land where no water is. So I have looked upon you in the sanctuary, beholding your power and your glory. Because your steadfast love is better than life . . . so I will bless you as long as I live; I will lift up my hands, and call on your name . . . My soul is feasted . . . my mouth praises you with joyful lips.

When I think of you upon my bed, I meditate on you in the watches of the night; for you have been my help, and in the shadow of your wings I sing for joy. My soul clings to you; your right hand upholds me.

Psalm 63:1-8

O God, who will give me to rest in you? Who will make you enter my heart and inebriate it, so that I shall forget my misfortunes and embrace you, my only Good?

What are you to me? In your goodness, permit me to speak. What am I to you, that you enjoin me to love you, and are disturbed if I do not love you, and threaten me with all kinds of ills? If I do not love you, does that mean that I am slighting you? Poor creature that I am, tell me, in your mercy, Lord my God, tell me what you are to me. Say to my soul: "I am your salvation!" Say it so that I shall hear it. The ear of my heart is turned toward you. Open it, O Lord, and say to my soul: "I am your salvation!" I shall follow your voice and adhere to you . . .

When I shall be united with my whole self to you, I shall nowhere have sorrow or labor; and my life shall wholly live, as wholly full of you. Now you raise on high those whom you fill; because I am not full of you I am a burden to myself. Lamentable joys strive with joyous sorrows, and I know not on which side is the victory . . .

Lord, have pity on me! See, I do not hide my wounds from you. You are the physician, I the sick; you are merciful, I miserable.

St. Augustine, *Confessions* I 5:5; X 28,39

173 — LOVING ATTENTION TO GOD

Send out your light and your truth; let them lead me on (Ps 43:3)

1. "God's word is living and active" (Heb 4:12), says St. Paul, and the same can be said of the general knowledge of God, infused into the soul by the Holy Spirit. It is so effective that it captures not only the understanding, but also the will, which is borne toward God in order to adhere to him in faith and love. Then, we spend prayer with our intellect and will open to God, turning to him with a loving advertance that occupies us in a way that is almost imperceptible, yet effective. St. John of the Cross notes that at the beginning, this knowledge is so "delicate and almost

imperceptible" (Asc II 13:7) that we who have become habituated to the exercise of well-defined considerations and sentiments, hardly perceive it; and even when we do begin to have a certain awareness of it, we have the impression that we are doing nothing, and wasting time; this is why we are so tempted to return to the meditations or the affective colloquies of before. But if we hold firm, and persevere in remaining in God's presence in the simple attitude of faith, content to stay near the Lord, to keep him company, and to look upon him in silence, with a little time we become able to look at God without the crutch of ideas or feelings or special exercises, in a delicate relation of spirit to spirit. It is a loving attention to the Someone who is present, whose presence is not perceived in a tangible way, yet is intuitively perceived as the only Presence, before which all other presences disappear. God is there; in fact, God alone! This suffices, and it becomes so dear to us that we would not give it up for anything in the world: "Whom have I in heaven but you? . . . God is the strength of my heart and my portion for ever" (Ps 73:25-26). Then, progressively, the words of St. John of the Cross are verified: "The soul likes to remain in interior peace, and quiet, and repose" (Asc II 13:4).

2. According to St. John of the Cross, this "general and loving attention to God" results from practicing the three theological virtues, with the help of a gentle and hidden inflowing of the Holy Spirit. The soul that has long practiced faith and love has acquired the habit of this, so that without resorting to continual repetition of distinct acts, it can remain in God's presence in a delicate and prolonged act of faith and love. By means of this effort, he thus reaches the point where he treats with God with loving advertence like one who looks lovingly upon the beloved object it is seeking. The Holy Spirit intervenes to invite it to this practice and to support it in doing so, and by a secret actuation of his gifts, infuses into it a loving knowledge of God. St. John of the Cross puts it well: "Since God . . . communes with it through a simple and loving knowledge, the soul, also, communes with God through a simple and loving knowledge or attention, so that knowledge is thus joined with knowledge, and love with love" (Fl 3:34). Through the practice of the theological virtues, we prepare ourselves to receive the divine inflowing; we put ourselves, so to speak, in God's way, and through this very action receive and accompany the action of the Holy Spirit. But in the beginning the influence of the Holy Spirit will not always be constant, and there will be times when we will realize the need of recourse to some ingenuity in order to remain recollected. A return to meditation, reading, or vocal prayer is not to be excluded, in fact it will sometimes be necessary, but the most effective practice will always be that of renewing our acts of faith and love, because it is really the theological virtues that prepare the mind and heart for the divine inflowing. "So faith, hope, love abide, these three" (1 Cor 13:13), says St. Paul; they are the essential values of Christian life and in particular of

the life of friendship and of fellowship with God. The deeper and the more intense the practice of the theological virtues becomes, the more the soul clings to God, and opens itself to his action, and God overflows into him in a way far beyond man's way of acting.

Your treasure, my God, is like an infinite ocean, yet a little wave of feeling, passing with the moment, contents us. Blind as we are, we hinder you and stop the current of your graces. But when you find a soul permeated with a living faith, you pour your graces plenteously into it; they flow into the soul like a torrent, which after being forcibly stopped against its ordinary course, has found a passage, and spreads its pent-up flood with great impetuosity (2nd Letter).

O Lord, grant that I may make it my only business to persevere always in your holy presence, keeping myself there in a simple attention and a most loving regard . . . in a silent and secret conversation of my soul with you. O Lord, I contemplate you as my Father, present in my heart; and there I adore you . . . keeping my mind in your holy presence and calling it back every time I surprise it wandering in distraction (6th and 9th Letters).

Br. Lawrence of the Resurrection, *Practice of the Presence of God*

O Lord, let me not be attached to anything, neither to any sensible or spiritual joy, nor any other apprehension. Make my soul completely free regarding all things, so that I may persevere in the profound silence that is necessary for deep and delicate listening to your word, since you speak to the heart in solitude, in supreme peace and tranquility.

cf. St. John of the Cross, *Living Flame* III 34

With bold surrender, I wish to remain gazing upon you, O Lord, my divine Sun. Nothing will frighten me, neither wind nor rain, and if dark clouds come and hide you from my gaze, I will not change my place because I know that beyond the clouds you still shine on and your brightness is not eclipsed for a single instant. Even if you remain deaf to the sorrowing of your creature, even if you remain hidden, I accept being numb with cold and rejoice in this suffering. My heart is at peace and continues its work of love.

cf. St. Therese of the Child Jesus, *Autobiographical Writings* (B (198, 199)

174 — FOURTH SUNDAY OF EASTER

YEAR A

The Lord is my shepherd; I shall not want *(Ps 23:1)*

The figure of the Good Shepherd dominates today's Liturgy. The Gospel and the second reading speak specifically of him, while the first does so indirectly. In the Old Testament God was already thought of as the Shepherd of Israel, governing it through kings, judges, and priests. But these men often drew the divine wrath upon themselves, because instead of promoting the welfare of their flock, they either led it by the false ways of idolatry, or were only concerned with feeding themselves (cf Ez 34:20). Finally, taking pity on his people God sent his Son, the one true shepherd who was the incarnation of all his love for men.

In John's Gospel, Jesus himself points out the sharp contrast between the conduct of false shepherds and his own. The former are thieves who treacherously gain entry to the flock in order to "steal, and kill, and destroy" (Jn 10:10), spreading disorder and fear everywhere. Unfortunately, plunderers of this kind are never lacking; in the guise of shepherds they insinuate themselves into the Church, upset it with false theories, and scatter and bewilder the faithful. May it please God that the words of the Gospel be true for them: "The sheep did not heed them" (ib. 8). On the other hand, Jesus is the true shepherd: the sheep trust him, they "hear his voice and he calls his own sheep by name and leads them out" (ib. 3). When they follow him they have nothing to fear, nor will they lack anything; he indeed came "that they may have life and have it abundantly" (ib. 10), to the point where he was ready to sacrifice his own life to make theirs safe. By accepting death in order to save his flock, Jesus is at the same time both shepherd and door for his sheep. "I am the door"—he said—"If any one enters by me he will be saved and will go in and out, and find pasture" (ib. 9). No one enters the sheepfold of Christ—the Church—without believing in him, without passing through the mystery of his death and resurrection. Baptism is precisely the sacrament which, immersing us in Christ's Easter mystery, leads us into his sheepfold, where we shall find salvation.

The first Church community was born upon this foundation on the day of Pentecost. Peter's solemn declaration: "God has made him both Lord and Christ, this Jesus whom you crucified!" (Acts 2:36) so profoundly impressed the people who were listening, that "about three thousand souls" asked to be baptized "in the name of Jesus Christ" (ib. 38). After they had scorned and rejected him, even to condemning him to death as a criminal, they were now recognizing him as their only savior. The scattered sheep of Israel were entering the Church through its only door, Christ.

Later, in order to exhort the persecuted Christians to patience, Peter reminded them of what Jesus had done and suffered for them; his mildness in the face of insult, the love with which he took upon himself their sins, bearing them "on the tree" to destroy them by his death (1 Pet 2:23-24). He concluded with saying: "By his wounds you have been healed. For you were straying like sheep, but have now returned to the shepherd and guardian of your souls" (ib. 25). The Shepherd's sacrifice has restored life to his sheep and led them back into the fold. Therefore the people of God rejoices in celebrating his resurrection: "The good shepherd is risen, he who gave his life for his sheep, who died for his flock" (RM, Com ant—A).

The Lord is my shepherd; I shall not want; he makes me lie down in green pastures; he leads me beside still waters; he refreshes my soul. He leads me in paths of righteousness for his name's sake. Even though I walk through the valley of the shadow of death, I fear no evil; for you are with me; your rod and your staff, they comfort me.

You prepare a table before me . . . You anoint my head with oil; my cup overflows. Surely goodness and mercy shall follow me all the days of my life.

Psalm 23

O Christ, good Shepherd, who gave your life for your flock, you went looking for the lost lamb over mountain and hill . . . and found it. After finding it, you carried it on those same shoulders that were to bear the wood of the cross, and, taking it along with you, you brought it back to the life of heaven . . .

O God, we needed you to take our flesh and to die for us in order to give us life. We died with you in order to be justified; we are risen again with you, because we were crucified with you. And since we rose again together, we are glorified with you.

St. Gregory Nazianzen, *Prayer* 45:26, 28

YEAR B

O Jesus, good Shepherd, you know your sheep; may I also know you (Jn 10:14)

Today we look at the paschal mystery in the figure of Jesus, the good Shepherd and cornerstone of the Church.

In the hour of peril, the good shepherd does not abandon his flock like a mercenary, but in order to lead them to safety, hands himself over to the enemy and to death: "The good shepherd lays down his life for the sheep" (Jn 10:11). It is the spontaneous gesture of Christ's love for us: "No one takes (my life) from me; but I lay it down of my own accord" (ib. 18). In this mystery of infinite mercy Jesus' love is interwoven and blended with that of the Father. The Father sent him so that we might have in him a shepherd who would take care of us and assure us of true life. In the second reading John says: "See what love the Father has given us, that we should be called children of God; and so we are" (1 Jn 3:1). The Father has given us such love through his Son, who has freed us from sin through his sacrifice and has shared with us, not a name, but a new way of being, a new life: the being and life of the children of God. By virtue of the redeeming work of Christ each of us is called to belong to a single family that has God as its father, and a single flock that has Christ as its shepherd. This family and this flock are identified with the Church, of which, as Peter says in the first reading, Jesus is the cornerstone. "This is the stone which was rejected by you builders, but which has become the head of the corner" (Acts 4:11). The Synagogue rejected him, but through the mystery of his death and resurrection, Jesus has become the support of a new building: the Church.

Christ the good Shepherd, and Christ the cornerstone, are two separate images, which express the same reality: he is the only hope of salvation for the whole human race. "For there is no other name under heaven given to men by which we must be saved" (ib. 12).

Hence the urgency for all men to belong to the one Church ruled by Christ, to the one flock he governs. Jesus repeats today what he has said before: "I have other sheep that are not of this fold. I must bring them also" (Jn 10:16). In very truth, there are still innumerable sheep who are far from the fold, but it was just these whom Jesus meant when he said: "They will heed my voice" (ib.). Yet how can they heed unless there is some one to preach the gospel to them? Every believer is involved in this pressing duty: each must work with prayer and sacrifice to lead to Christ's fold the sheep who are ignorant, far-off, scattered, and wandering, so that all may become "one flock" and all may have "one shepherd" (ib.).

A final reflection is suggested by today's Gospel. "I know my own"—says Jesus—"and my own know me, as the Father knows me and I know the Father" (ib. 14-15). This is not a matter of simple theoretical knowledge, but of a vital consciousness which implies relations of love and friendship between the good Shepherd and his sheep, a relation that Jesus does not hesitate to compare to that which exists between the Father and himself. From the humble rustic simile of the shepherd and his sheep, Jesus rises to his life in communion with the Father, and inserts his own relationship with us into such a perspective. This is the true love of God's children; it begins here on earth, in faith and love, and culminates in heaven where "we shall be like him for we shall see him as he is" (1 Jn 3:2).

O Lord, you say: "As the Father knows me, I know the Father, and I give my life for my sheep" (Jn 10:15). It is as if you said: the fact that I give my life for my sheep makes it clear that I know the Father and that I am known by him . . . The charity that makes you die for your sheep, shows how much you love the Father . . .

Again you say: "My sheep hear my voice, and I know them, and they follow me; and I give them eternal life" (ib. 27-28). Shortly before that you had said: "If any one enters by me he will be saved, and will go in and out and find pasture" (ib. 9). He will enter through faith, and then go out, passing from faith to vision, from ease in believing to contemplation, and will find pasture in the eternal feast.

Your sheep will find pasture, because whoever follows you with a simple heart is nourished by eternally fruitful pasture. And what indeed is the pasture of these sheep if not the intimate joys of a forever verdant paradise? In truth, the pasture of your elect is the face of the ever-present God. While we contemplate him without ceasing, our minds are fully satisfied with the food of life . . .

O Lord, make me seek these pastures to enjoy them with all the heavenly citizens . . . Fill me with ardent longing for the things of heaven, that I may love them and really set out on my way.

St. Gregory the Great, *Homilies on the Gospel* 14:4-6

YEAR C

The Lord is God; it is he that made us, and we are his; we are his people and the sheep of his pasture. (Ps 100:3)

The Fourth Sunday of Easter is dedicated to the good Shepherd: it shows us under this figure, which was so dear to the primitive Church, an expression of Christ's love for mankind. All belong to him in the way that sheep belong to the shepherd; he watches over them with jealous care, and he is their source of life and salvation: "I give them eternal life and they shall never perish. No one shall snatch them out of my hand" (Jn 10:28). This is a great privilege, but it exacts a condition on our part: "My sheep hear my voice . . . and they follow me" (ib. 27). The ones who hear the voice of Jesus are those who accept the gospel and grasp its true meaning, those who heed the voice of the Church—popes, bishops, superiors—and obey it, those who pay attention to the voice of conscience and of interior inspiration; by listening to all these voices, and translating them into life and work, we follow the Lord faithfully and with growing diligence.

But belonging to Christ's flock is not a privilege that is reserved only to some; it is rather a gift that is offered indiscriminately to all those who are willing to accept it. By God's design the first fruits of the gospel were reserved for the Hebrew people among whom Jesus exercised his ministry, but after the resurrection the apostles were commanded to preach it "to all nations" (Lk 24:47). Israel's opposition then became the reason for the apostles' turning their attention to the pagans. "It was necessary that the word of God should be spoken first to you"—said Paul and Barnabas to the Jews—"since you thrust it from you and judge yourselves unworthy of eternal life, behold, we turn to the gentiles" (Acts 13:46; 2nd reading). The good Shepherd who has given his life for all excludes no one from his flock, but if we knowingly reject Christ's message, we are excluding ourselves; we are judging ourselves "unworthy of eternal life." Nevertheless, those who believe should always extend their hand to their incredulous brothers, and to those who are stubborn or who run away, and make it easy for these to enter and to return to the one only fold. His fold must not be thought of as a closed place that is meant to welcome and take care of only those who believe, but as a wide space open to all who wish to enter. Its gate is wide and inviting, like the heart of Jesus which he wished to define as "the door of the sheep" (Jn 10:7). Whoever consents to enter through this door will always be welcomed and will find salvation: "If any one enters by me, he will be saved" (ib. 9). This attitude of openness preserves in the Church that character of universality that her Founder imprinted upon her, and that dynamism which makes her alive and fruitful.

The second reading shows us the eternal glory of the Lamb surrounded by "a great multitude which no one could number from every nation, from all tribes and peoples and tongues" (Rev 7:9); it is a most beautiful and comforting assurance of the universality of salvation. At the center of John's prophetic vision, Jesus appears under the figure of the Lamb-shepherd who has washed the robes of the elect and made them white in his blood. Then "those who have come out of the great tribulation"—the painful labor of preserving and defending their faith in the midst of the sufferings of this life—will suffer no more "because the Lamb . . . will be their shepherd and he will guide them to springs of living water" (ib. 17). This is the eternal life which the good Shepherd promises his sheep.

Make a joyful noise to the Lord, all you lands: serve the Lord with gladness; come into his presence, singing. Know that the Lord is God! It is he that made us, and we are his; we are his people, and the sheep of his pasture . . . For the Lord is good; his steadfast love endures for ever, and his faithfulness to all generations.

Psalm 100:1-3,5

O Jesus, you said: "I am the door. If any one enters by me, he will be saved" . . . I do not want to content myself with reading your words, meditating upon them; help me, Lord, to apply them, to live them, to make them a part of my life . . . Help me to live by faith, leaving aside human reason, which is folly before you, and regulating my life according to the words of your divine wisdom, which is folly in the eyes of men. Oh, that I may "enter through you" by loving you with all my heart . . . "enter through you" by imitating you . . . "enter through you" by obeying you. Sheep are united to their shepherd, because they look to him, follow him, and obey him; may I follow you and love you, my divine Shepherd, by copying their example; may I gaze on you in contemplation, and follow you by imitating you, and oh! may I obey you.

C. de Foucauld, *Meditations on the Gospel* Op. Sp.

175 — MARY OUR GUIDE AND MODEL

O Mary, he who finds you finds life and obtains favor from the Lord (Prov 8:35)

1. Vatican Council II urges all the children of the Church to see "that the cult of the Blessed Virgin be generously fostered . . . it charges that practices and exercises of devotion towards her be treasured as recommended by the teaching authority of the Church in the course of centuries" (LG 67). The month of May which has been consecrated to Mary from early days occupies a special place among these devotional practices. In this month the heart of every Christian turns spontaneously toward our heavenly Mother, with a desire to live in closer intimacy with her and to strengthen the ties which bind us to her. It is a great comfort on our spiritual way, which is often fatiguing and bristling with difficulties, to meet the gentle presence of a mother. Near her, everything becomes easier; the weary, discouraged heart, disturbed by storms, finds new hope and strength, and continues the journey with fresh courage.

"If the winds of temptation arise," sings St. Bernard, "if you run into the reefs of trials, look to the star, call upon Mary; in danger, sorrow, or perplexity, think of Mary, call upon Mary" (Missus 2:17). There are times when the hard road of the "nothing" frightens us, miserable as we are; and then, more than ever, we need her help, the help of our Mother. First among Christians, Mary the most holy Virgin has trodden the straight and narrow path which leads to sanctity; first among us all, she has carried the cross and has known the ascents of the spirit through suffering. Sometimes, perhaps, we do not dare to look at Jesus the God-Man, who because of his divinity seems too far above us; but near him is Mary, his Mother and our mother, a privileged creature surely, yet a simple creature like ourselves, and therefore a model more accessible to our weakness.

The Blessed Virgin "invoked in the Church under the titles of Advocate, Benefactress, Helper and Mediatrix" (LG 62) stretches out her hand to us to lead us to her Son, to make our way to holiness easier and to introduce us into the secret of her own interior life, so as to be, after Jesus and subordinately to him, our way and model and rule.

2. St. Therese of the Child Jesus, referring to certain discourses on the Blessed Virgin, said: "She is spoken of as unapproachable, whereas she should be represented as imitable" (NV 23-VIII). Mary is inaccessible, it is true, in the sublime privileges which flow from her divine maternity, and it is right to consider these prerogatives in order to admire and contemplate them, to praise our Mother's greatness and hence to love her always more and more; but, at the same time, we should consider Mary in the concrete picture of her earthly life. It is a simple, humble picture, which never leaves the framework of the ordinary life common to all mothers of a family; under this aspect, Mary is truly imitable. Our program for the month of May must be to contemplate Mary "who shines forth to the whole community of the elect" (LG 65).

We especially need to consider Our Lady as the ideal and model of the interior life. No one has understood, as she did, the depth of meaning in the words of Jesus: "But one thing is necessary" (Lk 10:42), and no one has lived by these words better than she. From the very first moment of her life, Mary was entirely God's and lived only for him. Consider the years of preparation spent in silence and prayer, the months passed at Nazareth in recollection and in adoration of the eternal Word incarnate within her, the thirty years lived in sweet intimacy with Jesus, her Son and her God; the sharing of his apostolic life, the union with him in his passion, and finally, her last years with St. John, during which, by her prayers, she was the support of the infant Church. Although the scenes in which she moved changed in appearance, although the external circumstances varied, her life remained unchanged in its substance, in her interior search for the "one thing necessary," and in her adherence to God alone. The succession of events and her exterior activity did not hinder her from persevering in that attitude of continual prayer in which St. Luke presents her to us: "Mary kept all these things, pondering them in her heart" (2:19).

If, in imitation of Mary, our heart is firmly anchored in God, nothing can distract us from our interior occupation: to seek and love the Lord and live in intimacy with him.

O Mary, you are the clear and shining star . . . twinkling with excellencies, and resplendent with example, needfully set to look down upon the surface of this great, wide sea. When I find myself here, not so much walking upon firm ground as battered to and fro by the gales and storms of this life's ocean, I keep my eyes fixed on this star's clear shining. If the hurricanes of temptation rise against me, or I am running on the rocks of trouble, I look to the star and call upon you, O Mary. If the waves of pride or ambition or slander or envy toss me about, I look to the star and call upon you, O Mary. If the billows of anger or avarice, or the enticements of the flesh beat against my soul's bar, I look to you, O Mary. If the enormity of my sins trouble me, if the foulness of my conscience confound me, if the dread of judgment appall me, if I begin to slip into the deep of despondence, into the pit of despair, I think of you, O Mary. In danger, in difficulty, in doubt, I think of you, O Mary, I call upon you. O Mary, be ever in my mouth and in my heart, and that I may not lack the succor of your prayers, let me not turn aside from the example of your teaching. Following your example, I shall never go astray; praying to you, I shall never lose hope; keeping you in mind, I shall never fall into error. If you hold me, I shall never slip; under your protection I shall fear nothing; with you for guide, I shall not weary; if you help me, I shall arrive safely in port, and so I shall experience in myself the truth of the words: "And the Virgin's name was Mary."

St. Bernard, *On the "Missus Est"* 2:17

Now 'tis at Nazareth, O Virgin full of grace,
In poverty abiding, you never knew desire;
Nor ecstasy nor miracle nor rapture there had place,
To fill your life with splendor, O Queen of heavenly choir!
Ah! countless are the little ones that throng the earth today,
Unfearing, without tremor, to you they lift their eyes,
Incomparable Mother, 'tis by the common way
It pleases you to go, that you may lead them to the skies.
Throughout this exile sad I long, O Mother mine,
To dwell with you, to follow each day your path above.
In contemplating you, enraptured, I divine
In your pure, gentle heart the deep abyss of love;
Your gentle gaze maternal will banish all of fear;
It teaches me to weep, it teaches happiness.

St. Therese of the Child Jesus, *Poems*

176 — THE HANDMAID OF THE LORD

O Mary, you said: "I am the handmaid of the Lord" (Lk 1:38); teach me to place my life at his service.

1. All the splendors—divine filiation, participation in divine life, intimate relations with the Trinity—which grace produces in our souls, are realized in Mary with a prominence, a force, a realism, wholly singular. If every soul in the state of grace is an adopted child of God and a temple of the Holy Spirit, the Blessed Virgin is so par excellence and in the most complete manner, because the three Persons of the Blessed Trinity communicated themselves to her in the highest degree possible for a simple creature. Mary, indeed, "is endowed with the supreme office and dignity of being the Mother of the Son of God, and as a result, she is also the favorite daughter of the Father and the temple of the Holy Spirit. Because of this gift of sublime grace, she far sur-

passes all other creatures, both in heaven and on earth" (LG 53). Chosen and loved by God from all eternity as the mother of his Son, Mary occupies the first place among those that the Father "chose in (Christ), before the foundation of the world, to be holy and blameless before him" (Eph 1:4). She has first place on account of the singular fullness of grace and holiness with which God adorned her from the moment of her immaculate conception; she has first place because she was foreseen by God before every other creature in view of the incarnation of the Word. "The Lord created me . . . at the beginning of his work"—Mary can say—"the first of his acts of old" (Prov 8:22). When Adam, deprived of the state of grace, was driven out of Paradise, only one ray of hope illumined the darkness of fallen humanity: "I will put enmity between you and the woman"—God said to the serpent—"and between your seed and her *seed; he* shall bruise your head" (Gen 3:15). Here Mary appears on the horizon as the Mother of the Savior, immaculate and spotless, as she who will never be for a single moment a slave of the devil, but always inviolate, belonging wholly to God, the beloved daughter whom the Most High will always look upon with sovereign complacency.

2. Mary lived her divine filiation in a profound sentiment of humble dependence and loving adherence to God's every will. We have the best example of this in her reply to the angel's message: "I am the handmaid of the Lord" (Lk 1:38). Mary was aware of her position as a creature in relation to the Creator, and although she had been raised to such high dignity that "after God's, it is the greatest that can be imagined" (Pius XI, *Lux veritatis*), she could find no better way to express her relations with God than to declare herself his "handmaid." This word describes the interior attitude of the Virgin toward God; it was not a passing attitude, but one that was permanent and constant throughout her whole life, like that of Jesus, the "Servant of Jahweh," who, when he came into the world, announced: "I have come to do your will" (Heb 10:9). In like manner Mary, who was to be the most faithful likeness of Jesus, offered herself to the will of her heavenly Father when she said: "I am the handmaid of the Lord. Let it be to me according to your word" (Lk 1:38). Faithful to her word, she would accept without reserve not only every manifest will of God, but also every circumstance permitted by him: the long, inconvenient journey which would bring her far from home, just when she was about to bring into the world the Son of God; the poor, humble shelter of a stable; the flight into Egypt by night, the privations and inconveniences of exile, the labor and weariness of a life of poverty, the separation from her Son when he would leave her to begin his apostolate, the persecutions and insults he would endure and of which her maternal heart would be well aware, and finally, the disgrace of the passion and death of her beloved Son on Calvary. We have good reason to believe that in each of these events, her interior dispositions were the same as on the day of the Annunciation: "I am the handmaid of the Lord." What an exam-

ple for us of humble dependence on God, of absolute fidelity to his will, and of perseverance in our vocation, in spite of the difficulties and sacrifices we shall have to encounter.

O Mary, purest of virgins and most fruitful of mothers . . . present before God from eternity . . . Truly you were there, uncreated, in the mind of God before all creation, just as you afterward merited to be created.

This is why at the beginning when all things were to be created, you stood out in the sight of God, bringing him greatest joy. Indeed God the Father rejoiced because of the fruitful work you would accomplish with his help; the Son for your upright constancy; and the Holy Spirit for your humble obedience. But the joy of the Son and of the Spirit was also that of the Father; and that of the Son was likewise the joy of the Father and the Spirit; and again the joy of the Holy Spirit was that of the Father and the Son. And even as they felt one single joy because of you, so they all had for you one single love.

St. Bridget of Sweden, *Revelations and Prayers*

O Mary, full of faith in the heavenly word and entirely submissive to the divine will that has just been manifested to you, you reply: "I am the handmaid of the Lord. Let it be to me according to your word." This fiat *is your consent to the divine plan of redemption; this* fiat *is like the echo of the fiat of creation; but it is a new world, an infinitely higher world, a world of grace that God himself creates after this consent: for at this moment the Divine Word, the second Person of the Holy Trinity, becomes incarnate in you: "the Word was made flesh."*

C. Marmion, *Christ the Life of the Soul* II 12

O Daughter, listen and hear, you who were worthy to merit to become the daughter of the Son, and the handmaid of him who begot you, the Mother of the Lord and of the Savior, the Son of the Almighty. The King, enraptured by the splendor of your loveliness, was pleased to choose your earthly flesh for his immaculate home; so may he, who chose you for his Mother with so much love, grant us the happiness and the fullness of his grace, so that while we are yours in love while on earth, O holy Mother, so after death, we may go without fear to meet him whom you brought forth.

Visigothic Prayer 222, from Pieta Mariana nelle antiche liturgie

177 — SPOUSE OF THE HOLY SPIRIT

O Mary, filled with the Holy Spirit, reveal to me the secret of your obedience.

1. "The Blessed Virgin Mary"—says St. Augustine—"was the only one who merited to be called the Mother and Spouse of God" (Ser 208:4). She was the true mother of God because she was the mystical spouse of the Holy Spirit, who had come upon her with a superabundance of grace from the first moment of her immaculate conception, "fashioned by (him) and formed as a new creature" (LG 56). The Holy Spirit had prepared her, with most loving care, to be the living tabernacle of the Son of God; and when the angel appeared to her with his great announcement, he saluted her at once with: "Hail, full of grace!" (Lk 1:28). Already possessed by the Holy Spirit, already overflowing with grace, she was still to receive a most singular new fullness: "The Holy Spirit will come upon you and the power of the Most High will overshadow you" (ib. 35).

Stirred by Mary's greatness, the Church prays: "O almighty, everlasting God, by the cooperation of the Holy Spirit, you made ready the body and soul of the glorious Virgin Mother Mary to be the fit dwelling place for your Son" (Brev). "By the cooperation of the Holy Spirit": he is the architect of this miracle of grace and love, and the Blessed Mother belongs wholly to him as his bride, his temple, his exclusive property. To her the divine Paraclete addresses the words of the Canticle: "A garden enclosed is my sister, my bride, a garden enclosed, a fountain sealed" (Song 4:12). A garden locked against all profane entry, never violated by the shadow of sin, never ruffled by the wind of unruly passion, never taken up with any worldly affection. Mary was ever the most faithful spouse of the Holy Spirit, totally consecrated to him, attentive and docile to all his impulses and inspirations.

Looking upon her, our most loving Mother, we feel impelled to keep our own hearts always attentive and docile to the action of the Holy Spirit.

2. "All who are led by the Spirit of God are sons of God" (Rom 8:14). No creature was ever more completely moved and guided by the Holy Spirit than was the Blessed Mother: "The most glorious Virgin, Our Lady"—says St. John of the Cross—"was always moved by the Holy Spirit" (Asc III 2:10). Uniquely endowed with grace from the beginning, Mary lived in this attitude of unbroken openness and availability to the action of the Holy Spirit, which is characteristic of sanctity and of perfect union with God. Her course began at the point to which the saints arrive, with less perfection, at the end of their lives; furthermore, by her free faithful correspondence to grace she advanced to towering heights in this lofty state.

After Jesus, the Virgin Mary is the surest model and guide for those who aspire to union with God; her very creaturehood makes her more accessible to us, and more easily imitable. Mary lived only for God. Studying her life in the Gospels, we never see her influenced by selfish motives or by reasons of personal interest; only one thing moves her: the glory of God and the interests of Jesus and of souls. In her humble, hidden life, in her work, in her poverty, in all the privations and sufferings she had to undergo, there was never a thought of self; but forgetful of her own suffering and totally given to God, she was wholly given to fulfilling his will. It was the Holy Spirit who guided her, who urged her, who sustained her, and her secret was that she let herself be ruled and moved by him in everything. Just as she had conceived the Son of God by the operation of the Holy Spirit, so all her actions were begun by his inspiration.

Although Mary's sublime privileges are reserved to herself alone, we can all seek to imitate her dispositions by eliminating from our lives everything that is the fruit of egoism, self-love, or pride, and by doing only those things that are inspired by grace, under the impulse of the Holy Spirit.

O Mary, you are holy in body and mind. You can say in a special way: "my conversation is in heaven" (cf Phil 3:20). You are the garden enclosed, the sealed fountain, the temple of the Lord, the sanctuary of the Holy Spirit. You are the wise Virgin who not only provided herself with oil, but filled her lamp with it. O Mary, how were you able to reach the inaccessible majesty of God, except by knocking, asking, and seeking? Yes, you found what you were looking for, and the Angel said to you: "You have found favor with God." Yet, how could you, who were already full of grace, find more grace? Oh! you were truly worthy to find grace, because you were not satisfied with the fullness which you had, but asked for a superabundance of grace for the salvation of the world! "The Holy Spirit will come upon you," said the angel, and this precious balm was poured over you in such abundance that it flowed from you over the whole earth.

St. Bernard, from the "*Aqueduct*" 9:5

O Mary, the Holy Spirit always dwelt in the immaculate sanctuary of your soul; he alone was the director you always obeyed and followed in every interior or exterior action. It can be said of you more than of any other of the faithful, that the Holy Spirit is the sweet guest of your soul. Who can imagine the heavenly colloquies and the reciprocal outpourings of love between your immaculate heart and your sweet Guest? (Mary, Angels, and Saints)

O Mary, who always left to the Holy Spirit the control and direction of your mind and of your heart and actions . . . make us understand well how happy are the souls who let the Holy Spirit rule them, and thus run in the way of perfection; who pray to him, respect him, heed him, obey him, and submit their spirit to the Spirit of God in everything (To the Holy Spirit).

Bl. Elena Guerra

178 — MOTHER OF GOD

Blessed are you, O Virgin Mary, who carried the Creator of the world in your womb; you gave birth to your Creator, remaining a virgin forever. *(RM Mass BVM #2)*

1. "At the message of the angel, the Virgin Mary received the Word of God in her heart and in her body, and gave Life to the world. Hence she is acknowledged and honored as being truly the Mother of God and Mother of the Redeemer" (LG 53). Vatican II thus presents the figure of the Blessed Mother in synthesis. The divine maternity is the source of all her privileges; all her greatness and glory and her very existence are only explained by her predestination to this high office. If God had not decreed that the incarnation of his Son should take place in the womb of a virgin, we should never have had that masterpiece of grace and loveliness, the most blessed Virgin; we should never have had her smile or her maternal caresses. Therefore the Church teaches us to love and honor Mary because she is the Mother of God, the Mother of Jesus; and loving her in her relation to God, our devotion to her only makes our love for God, for Jesus, deeper and more tender.

"Mother of God, Mother of our Creator," we invoke her in the litany. These two titles which seem to be contradictory, actually express a unique synthesis because Mary, although a creature, is really the Mother of her Creator, the Mother of God's Son to whom she has given a human body: the fruit of her womb and of her blood. Here we understand more than ever how her dignity reached the threshold of the infinite. "Because the Blessed Virgin Mary is the Mother of God, she has a kind of infinite dignity which is derived from the infinite good, which is God" (St. Thos 1,25,6). We cannot imagine a higher dignity, for, except for Christ, no human creature has been united to God in so intimate and sublime a manner as Mary, who is his Mother. If any one wonders why so little is said about Mary in the Gospel, St. Thomas of Villanova replies: "What more do you want? Is it not enough for you to know that she is the Mother of God? . . . It would have been sufficient to say, 'Jesus was born of her' " (In fest BVM 8:9). In fact, O Mary, all I need to know in order to love you is that you are the Mother of my God.

2. Although God, from all eternity, had predestined Mary to be the Mother of his Son, he would not have her unaware of this, and so, when the time came for carrying out his plan, he asked the humble Virgin's consent. The Angel's message revealed to Mary

the sublime vocation which God had reserved for her: "Behold, you will conceive in your womb and bear a son, and you shall call his name Jesus" (Lk 1:31). Mary asked and the Angel explained the mystery of the divine maternity which would take place in her, without prejudice to her virginity. What could God have asked that Mary would have refused? It was not the first time that she gave up her own will for God's: from the beginning of her existence, she had lived in the state of perfect union with God, and her chief characteristic was simply this full conformity of her human will with the divine will. That is why Mary gave her consent with all the love of her soul, said her fiat, accepted voluntarily, and voluntarily abandoned herself to God's action. "By thus consenting to the divine utterance, Mary . . . became the Mother of Jesus, and embracing God's saving will with a full heart . . . she devoted herself totally as a handmaid of the Lord to the person and work of her Son" (LG 56). From this moment the mystery was accomplished, and the Virgin Mary bore God present within her. The Word of God was present in her by the life of the body which Mary communicated to her Son; he was present in her by the superabundance of supernatural life which the Son communicated to his Mother; between the Mother and the Son there was an exchange of life, an identity of affections, desires and sentiments which the heart of Christ implanted in the heart of Mary. No one could ever say more truly than Mary: "It is no longer I who live, but Christ who lives in me" (Gal 2:20).

Immense, marvelous mystery! And in the depths of this mystery we find the *yes* of a humble, human creature. God has created man free, and that is why, although he wants to work great things in him, he will not do so without his consent. God wants to transform us by his grace and to sanctify us, but before he does so, he waits for our assent. When this *yes* is complete and total, as Mary's was, God will accomplish his work in us.

"Hail, full of grace, the Lord is with you; not only is there with you God the Son, whom you clothed with your flesh, but also God the Holy Spirit, through whom you conceived, and God the Father, who from all eternity begot him who is to be your Son. The Father is with you, who makes his Son yours; the Son is with you who, wishing to accomplish a prodigious mystery, is hidden in your womb, while preserving your virginity; the Holy Spirit is with you and together with the Father and the Son sanctifies you. Truly the Lord is with you.

"Blessed are you among women . . . and blessed is the fruit of your womb." Not that, because you are blessed, the fruit of your womb is also blessed, but because he prevented you with the blessings of sweetness, therefore you are blessed. Truly blessed is the fruit of your womb, in whom all nations are blessed, of whose fullness you have received as others have, but in a fuller measure.

St. Bernard, *On the Missus est* 3:4-5

If I look at you closely, O Mary, I see that the hand of the Holy Spirit wrote the Trinity upon you when he formed within you the incarnate Word, the only-begotten Son of God. He wrote the wisdom of the Father, that is, the Word; he wrote his power, because he was the power that accomplished the mystery; he wrote the mercifulness of the Holy Spirit, because only through divine grace and mercy was such a mystery prepared and carried out . . . O Mary, I see the Word given to you, living in you.

In you, O Mary, man's strength and freedom are also made manifest, because after the decision of the great heavenly council, he sent the Angel to you to announce the secret of the divine council, and to ask your will; for the Son of God would not come into your womb until you had given the free consent of your will. He waited at the door of your will for you to open it to him; he wanted to come to you, but he would never have entered if you had not opened to him, saying: "I am the handmaid of the Lord; let it be to me according to your word."

St. Catherine of Siena, *Prayers and Elevations*

179 — OUR MOTHER

O Blessed Virgin Mary, you are the mother of grace, the hope of the world; hear your children who cry to you (RB)

1. When she consented to become the Mother of the Son of God, Mary bound herself by very close bonds not only to the person of Jesus, but also to his work. She knew that the Savior was coming into the world to redeem the human race; hence when she agreed to become his Mother, she also agreed to become the closest collaborator of his mission. "The holy Fathers rightly see Mary used by God not merely in a passive way, but as cooperating in the work of human salvation through free faith and obedience" (LG 56). And in fact, by giving us Jesus, the source of grace, Mary cooperated most effectively and most directly in the diffusion of grace in the souls of all who believe. Mary "gave to the world that very life which renews all things . . . and is"—states the Council—"a mother to us in the order of grace" (LG 56, 61).

As one woman, Eve, had cooperated in the losing of grace, so by a harmonious disposition of divine Providence, another woman, Mary, would cooperate in the restoration of grace. It is true that all grace comes from Jesus, who is the *only source* of grace and the *one and only Savior;* but, inasmuch as Mary gave him to the world, and was intimately associated with his whole life and work, we can truly say that grace also comes from Mary. If Jesus is its source, Mary, according to St. Bernard, is its channel, the aqueduct which carries it to us. Since Jesus willed to come to us through Mary, so all grace and all supernatural life come to us through her. "This is the will of him who decreed that we should have *everything* through Mary" (St. Bernard). *All* that Jesus merited for us by strictest right, *condignly,* Mary has merited for us fittingly, *congruously.* The Blessed Virgin is then truly our Mother. When she brought forth Jesus, she brought us forth at the same time to the life of grace; we can address her in all truth: "Hail holy Queen, *Mother* of mercy; our *life*, our sweetness, and our hope!"

2. The "union of the Mother with the Son in the work of salvation was manifested from the time of Christ's virginal conception up to his death" (LG 57); from the moment that Mary became the Mother of the Savior, she devoted herself to us like a most loving mother. Even as the redemptive mission of Jesus, begun at the moment of his incarnation, was consummated on Calvary, so too Mary's maternity found its fullest expression at the foot of the cross. While Jesus was dying in the midst of the most atrocious torments, his loving heart was preparing a truly exquisite gift for us. On earth his dearest possession had been his Mother; now he would leave her to us as a most precious inheritance. "Behold your Mother" (Jn 19:27), he said to St. John, thus giving her to the apostle who, at that moment, represented the whole human race. These words of Jesus expressed the great truth which had had its beginning at the first moment of his incarnation in the Virgin's womb and which was now fulfilled at the foot of the cross: this is the truth of Mary's spiritual motherhood of all mankind. Mary saved our souls together with Jesus, for as he was offering himself in sacrifice for us, Mary was offering him, her Son, as the divine Victim for our redemption. As co-redemptrix, she procured the life of grace for us; therefore she is the woman who in the supernatural order gives us life: she is our mother. She " 'is clearly the mother of the members of Christ . . . since she cooperated out of love so that there might be born in the Church the faithful, who are members of Christ their Head' . . . Therefore . . . taught by the Holy Spirit, the Church honors her with filial affection and piety as a most beloved mother" (LG 53).

"God so loved the world that he gave his only Son . . . that it might be saved through him" (Jn 3:16-17), says the evangelist, and similarly, St. Bonaventure declares: "it can be said that Mary so loved the world that she gave her only Son, in order that, through him, all might have eternal life" (St. Bon. Ser. 1 on B.V.M.). See at what price Mary has become our mother and we have become her children.

O most holy handmaid and mother of the Word, whose motherhood shows you a virgin, and whose virginity attests you a mother, welcome the people who are seeking you with your loving embrace. In your mercy, lead to abundant pastures the flock that has been redeemed by the blood of the Son you bore; you who gave food to your Creator, offer food to those who are yet to be created; glorify the devoted ones you see at your feet because of the devout homage they pay you; care for and protect us who rejoice to carry the sweet yoke of your queenship. May all who in any way sing the praises of your immaculate conception, always live as your subjects, O Queen, and purified of all sin attain one day to him, whose mother they proclaim you by their faith. Preserve us in your love as long as we are on earth, so that he who was born of you may possess us for all eternity.

"*Visigothic Prayer*" 233 from Ancient Liturgical Marian Piety

O Mary . . . my Mother! For my sake you offered your virginity, for my sake defended it and accepted the angel's word; for my sake you made offering in the temple, for me you received Simeon's prophecy, for me suffered in Bethlehem, for me were an exile in Egypt; for my sake you were poor and weary at Nazareth, for me searching in Jerusalem, silent in the temple, entreating help at Cana; for me you were uneasy at Capharnaum, and alone in his absence; for me you were in anguish before the tribunal, and desolate but strong on Calvary; for me you prayed with the Twelve, for me exulted in the Spirit and for me were triumphant in heaven . . . All this was for my sake, chosen on my account; you loved me, gave birth to me, welcomed me to your motherly arms, in the image of God's providence, before I was made, all for my sake . . . O most loving Mother!

Blessed Virgin, who not only gave his human features to the adorable Word, Son of God, but likewise offered to God the Father in the temple that same Word, become man, consecrating him to the fulfillment of the Father's will, receive my soul in your motherly embrace and present it to your divine Son, unite your prayer to mine so that I may be chosen to carry out the will of the Father.

G. Canovai, *Suscipe Domine*

180 — MARIAN LIFE

O Lord, grant that, through the intercession of the Virgin Mary, we may merit to share in the fullness of your grace (RM, Mass B.V.M.3)

1. The high place which Mary, as the Mother of God, occupies in the work of our sanctification fully justifies our desire to live intimately with her. As children love to be near their mother, so we as Christians want to live with Mary, and in order to do this, we resort to little means of keeping her in our thoughts. For instance, we may have her picture before us and greet her affectionately every time we look at it. Then, with a glance of faith, we can go beyond the picture, and reach Mary living in glory—Mary who, by means of the beatific vision, sees us, follows us, knows all our needs, and helps us with her maternal aid; "for"—teaches the Council—"taken up to heaven, she did not lay aside this saving role, but by her manifold acts of intercession continues to win for

us gifts of eternal salvation" (LG 62). Thus, by means of faith, our soul remains in continual contact with Mary. Spontaneously throughout the day, we increase our little pious practices in her honor, our prayers and ejaculations; all these combine to intensify our relations with Mary. The liturgical feasts of Mary, Saturdays, the month of May, the several feasts of Mary are for us so many occasions of remembering her especially, of meditating on her prerogatives, contemplating her beauty, and continually increasing our love for her. In fact, it is impossible to bear the sweet picture of Mary in our mind and heart without feeling moved to love her, without feeling the need of showing her the reality of our love by trying to please her, that is, by living like true children of hers. In this way the "Marian" life, or rather the life of intimacy with Mary, can permeate the whole of our "Christian" life and make us more faithful in the fulfillment of all our duties, for nothing can please Mary more than to see us lovingly accomplishing her Son's will. Furthermore, Christian life lived under Mary's maternal eye acquires that special gentleness and sweetness which arise spontaneously from the constant companionship of a most loving mother who lavishes attention on us.

2. "True devotion (to Our Lady) does not consist in fruitless and passing emotion . . . but proceeds from true faith, by which . . . we are moved to a filial love toward our mother and to the imitation of her virtues" (LG 67). Imitation of Mary is itself one of the principal aspects of the Marian life. Jesus alone is the "Way" that leads to the Father, he is the only model; but who is more like Jesus than Mary? Of whom more than Mary can it be said that she has the same thoughts as Christ? "O Lady"—exclaims St. Bernard—"God lives in you and you live in him. You clothe him with the substance of your flesh, and he clothes you with the glory of his majesty." (De duod. praerog. 6). While Jesus dwelt in the virgin's pure womb, he clothed her with himself, communicated his infinite perfections to her, filled her with his sentiments, desires, affections, and divine wishes; and Mary, who gave herself up entirely to his action, was completely transformed into him, so that she became a faithful copy of him. The former liturgy sang of her that "Mary is the most perfect image of Christ, formed truly by the Holy Spirit." The Holy Spirit, the Spirit of Jesus, took full possession of Mary's pure, gentle soul, and traced in it, very delicately and perfectly, all the features and characteristics of the soul of Jesus. Therefore we can well say that to imitate Mary is to imitate Jesus. This is why the Church chooses her for our model. We do not love Mary for herself alone, but because she is the mother of Christ, whose most faithful image she is. By incarnating in himself the perfections of the Father, Jesus made it possible for us to imitate them; by retracing Jesus' perfections in herself, Mary has made them more accessible to us, has brought them within our very reach. None can say as well as she: "Be imitators of me as I am of Christ" (1 Cor 11:1). Since

Jesus came to us through Mary, it is wholly appropriate that we should go to Jesus through her.

O loving Mother, you say: blessed are they who with the help of divine grace, practice my virtues and walk in my footsteps in life. Yes, O Mother, they are happy throughout their life here in this world, through the abundance of the graces and sweetness that you communicate to them from your fullness . . . happy in death that is sweet and tranquil, at which you are present so that you yourself can introduce them to the joys of heaven; happy for eternity because no faithful servant of yours who has imitated your virtues, has ever been lost.

O Virgin Mary, my good Mother, how happy they are—I repeat from the full transport of my heart—how happy they who do not let themselves be deceived by false devotion to you, but faithfully journey in your footsteps, follow your advice, and obey your commands!

St. Louis de Montfort, *Treatise on True Devotion* 6:1

Love for you, O Mary, brings with it a wonderful tenderness in the spiritual life . . . and causes a sense of confidence and submission in the heart. Without our realizing it, love for you disposes us to bear our many hardships and crosses with joy, and to recognize and love them. O Mary, I am indebted to you for so much, for everything. God gave me everything when he gave me you. How could I ever be ungrateful? O Mary! . . . I love you . . .

Any one who loves you, O Mary, is walking on a good road . . . Any one who does not love you is not deserving of trust, even if he works wonders. How can any one who sincerely loves you be afraid, O Mary? Any one who has let himself fall into your net is safe for all eternity, O Mother of God. The more the devils attract and draw me, the more indissolubly the meshes of your net, O Mary, intertwine themselves around me. I know no mother like you, O Mary. O Mother most admirable, pray for us!

Oh! how sweet you are! Why are your servants so uncomplicated, O Mary, and why do they obey so joyfully? How does it happen that your servants feel a childlike tenderness in their relations with God, and that they adapt themselves to even the most wicked with such courtesy and indulgence? The reason is that in your relations with them, O Mary, you really make them, though unconsciously, share in your own deep humility and incomparable meekness.

E. Poppe, *Spiritual Intimacies*

181 — FIFTH SUNDAY OF EASTER

YEAR A

O Jesus, the way and the truth and the life; lead me to the Father
(Jn 14:6)

The Liturgy of the final Sundays of Easter concentrates our attention on teachings of Jesus taken from his discourse at the Last Supper, the priceless testament he left his apostles before setting out on his passion.

Today the first place is given to the great declaration: "I am the way and the truth and the life" (Jn 14:6), which was provoked by Thomas' question; he had not understood what Jesus meant about returning to the Father, and so had asked: "Lord, we do not know where you are going. How can we know the way?" (ib. 5). The apostle was picturing a physical road, while Jesus was pointing out a spiritual one, so lofty that he identified it with his person: "I am the way"; and he not only shows him the way, but also the end to which it leads: "the truth and the life," which is himself. Jesus is the way which leads to the Father: "No one comes to the Father but by me" (ib. 6); he is the truth that reveals him: "He who has seen me has seen the Father" (ib. 9); he is the life that communicates divine life to men: "For as the Father has life in himself," so does the Son have it and gives it "to whom he will" (Jn 5:26,21). We find salvation on one condition only: by following Jesus, heeding his word and letting ourselves be invaded by his life which he shares with us through grace and love. In that way we not only live in communion with Christ, but also with the Father, who is not far away from Christ nor separated from him; indeed he is within him since he is one and the same with the Father and the Holy Spirit. "Believe me that I am in the Father and the Father in me" (Jn 14:11). The life of the Christian and of the entire Church is founded upon this faith in Christ, true God and true man, the way which leads to the Father and is equal to the Father in everything.

The first and second readings show us the development and the life of the early Church under the influence of Jesus "the way, the truth and the life." The Acts (6:1-8) make us present at the rapid increase of the faithful which followed the disciples' preaching, and then at the choice of their first co-workers who, by taking over the works of charity, left the Apostles free to devote themselves entirely "to prayer and the ministry of the word" (ib. 4). This concerned liturgical worship—the celebration of the Eucharist and communal prayer—but certainly also private prayer, in which the Apostles had been instructed by the teaching and example of Jesus. Since the Master used to spend long hours in solitary prayer, the apostle was conscious of the need to strengthen himself with personal prayer in intimate union with Christ, for only in that way would his ministry be successful and bring to the world the word and love of the Lord.

While the Acts speak of the Apostles' ministry and that of their co-workers, the second reading treats the priesthood of the faithful. "You are a chosen race"—writes St. Peter to the first Christians—"a royal priesthood, a holy nation" (1 Pet 2:9). No one is excluded from this spiritual priesthood; it is bestowed on all who are baptized, associating them with Christ's priesthood. Jesus, the only way leading to the Father, is also the only priest who of his own power reconciles men with God and offers him a worship that is worthy of his infinite majesty; by binding them closely to himself, the faithful too are raised up to "a holy priesthood, to offer spiritual sacrifices acceptable to God through Jesus Christ" (ib. 5). Jesus is the only source of life for the Church, the only source of the ministerial priesthood and of that of the faithful; there is no worship or sacrifice worthy of God if not united to Christ's, just as there is no personal holiness nor apostolic fruitfulness except inasmuch as these are derived from him.

O Father, the Savior and the Spirit of adoption come from you: look upon the children of your love with benevolence, in order that all who believe in Christ may be given true liberty and their eternal inheritance.

Roman Missal, *Collect*

O Jesus, help me walk the way of humility so that I may reach eternity. You, O God, are the homeland toward which we are traveling; as man, you are the way upon which we travel. We are coming to you, coming through you. Why should we be afraid of making a mistake? You did not go away from the Father when you came to us... you are God and man... God, because you are the Word; man, because being the Word, you took flesh. Every man is poor and a beggar before you, O God. What am I worth? If I only knew my poverty... And yet O Jesus, you say to me: Give me what I gave you... I ask for what is mine: give it to me and I shall return it... for the little that you give me, I will restore much more. You give me things of this world, I will give you heavenly things in return. You give me temporal things, I will pay you back in those of eternity. I will restore you to yourself, when I call you to myself.

St. Augustine, *Sermon* 123:3,5

YEAR B

O Lord, that I may abide in you, and you in me *(Jn 15:4)*

Today the Liturgy of the Word gives us a synthesis of the

Christan life: conversion, insertion into the mystery of Christ, and development of charity.

The first reading (Acts 9:26-31) refers to Saul's arrival in Jerusalem, where "they were all afraid of him, for they did not believe that he was a disciple" (ib. 26). But Saul on the way to Damascus "had seen the Lord, who spoke to him" (ib. 27); suddenly struck by an extraordinary grace, he was changed from a fierce enemy to an ardent apostle of Christ. Conversion is not so sudden for everyone; in fact it normally requires a long persistent work to overcome passions and bad habits, and to change our way of thinking and behaving. But conversion is possible for everyone, not only as a passage from disbelief to faith, and from sin to a life of grace, but also as the practice of virtue, the development of charity, in ascents toward holiness. Considered in this way it is not simply a passing incident, but something that involves our entire life.

Conversion, confirmed by the sacrament, inserts man into Christ so that he may live in him and live his very life. This is the theme of today's Gospel (Jn 15:1-8). "Abide in me and I in you"—says the Lord—"As the branch cannot bear fruit by itself, unless it abides in the vine, neither can you unless you abide in me" (ib. 4-5). The branch can live and bear fruit only if it is attached to the trunk; likewise, only by remaining in Christ can a Christian live in grace and love and produce the fruit of sanctity. This shows the powerlessness of man regarding supernatural life, and the necessity of total dependence on Christ; it also shows Christ's positive desire to make man live from his own life. This is why as Christians we are never disheartened; whatever resources are lacking in ourselves, we find in Christ; the more we experience the truth of his words: "apart from me you can do nothing" (ib. 5), the more we put our trust in the Lord who wants to be all things to us. Baptism, and the incorporation in Christ which results from it, are free gifts, but it is our duty as Christians to live them, keeping ourselves united to Christ by personal faithfulness as the many times repeated expression indicates: "live in me." The great means for living in Christ is for his words to abide in us (ib. 7) through the faith which makes us accept them, and the love which makes us put them into practice.

Among the statements of our Lord there is one in the second reading (1 Jn 3:18-24) which is of particular importance: "This is his commandment: we . . . should love one another just as he has commanded us" (ib. 23). The practice of brotherly love is our distinctive mark as Christians, precisely because it attests to our vital communion with Christ; indeed it is impossible to live in Christ, whose life is essentially love, without living in love and producing the fruits of love. Just as Christ loved the Father and loved all men in him, so our love for God must be translated into sincere love for our fellow men. Therefore St. John so warmly recommends: "Little children let us not love in word or speech, but in deed and in truth" (ib. 18). Whoever loves his neighbor in this way—both friend and foe—has nothing to fear before God, not because he is without sin, but because God "is greater than our hearts, and he knows everything" (ib. 20); seeing our charity toward our brothers, he will pardon all our sins with great mercy.

O Truth, you declare: "I am the vine, you are the branches. Whoever lives in me and I in him will bear much fruit, because without me you can do nothing"... You do not say: without me you can do little, but rather: "without me you can do nothing." Make me believe that whether it be little or great, I cannot do it without you, since without you no one can do anything... Indeed... if the branch does not remain joined to the vine and does not draw its sustenance from the root, it cannot of itself produce any fruit...

If I live in you, what else can I desire except what is in conformity with you? By abiding in you who are the Savior, what else can I desire except what is oriented toward salvation? In fact, I want one thing inasmuch as I abide in you; and something else inasmuch as I am still in this world... Your words remain within me when I do what you have commanded and I desire what you have promised me; but, when your words stay in my memory without being reflected in my life, then the branch is no longer part of the vine, for it is not drawing its life from the root.

St. Augustine, *In Io* 81:3-4

YEAR C

Lord, make us love one another, as you have loved us (Jn 13:34)

We meditate today on the totality of the mystery of Easter: from Christ's passion to his glorification, from the presence and influence of the Risen Lord in the Church to its participation in his eternal glory.

The Gospel (Jn 13:31-35) begins with the moment in which Jesus, after announcing Judas' betrayal, speaks of his glorification as though it were an already present reality, linked to his passion. "Now is the Son of Man glorified and in him God is glorified" (ib. 31). The contrast is strong, but only in appearance, for in consenting to be betrayed and delivered to death for the salvation of men, Jesus was fulfilling the mission the Father had entrusted to him, and this is the precise reason for his glorification. He therefore considers it already begun, just as he already considers as fact the glory he is about to render to God by his redeeming death.

First the passion, and then his glorification, will separate Jesus from his disciples, and before leaving them he assures them of his invisible presence in love. He wants to remain in their midst through the love with which he has loved them, and which he leaves them as a heritage so that they may live it and find it again in their mutual relationships. "A new commandment I give to you that you love one another, even as I have loved you, that you also love one another" (ib. 34). Reciprocal love modeled upon the love of the Master, indeed arising from it, assures the Christian community of the presence of Jesus and is its sign. At the same time it is the badge of true Christians: "By this all men will know that you are my disciples" (ib. 35). The life of the Church thus began, sustained by an absolutely new cohesive and expansive force of extraordinary power, because it was not founded on human love, which is always fragile and deficient, but upon divine love: the love of Christ re-lived in the mutual relationships of the faithful.

This love is the secret of the untiring apostolic zeal of Paul and Barnabas, of whom today's first reading speaks (Acts 14:20b-27). One journey followed upon another; after they had founded new Churches, they returned to visit them, to urge their disciples "to continue in the faith" (ib. 22); in each Church they chose and ordained priests; they left to evangelize other countries, and afterwards returned to Antioch to render an account to the congregation there "of all that God had done with them" (ib. 27). The love of Christ which sustained them and their awareness that he himself was working in them and with them, did not dispense them from tribulations, just as the new converts to Christianity were not exempt from them, since "through many tribulations we must enter the kingdom of heaven" (ib. 22).

To encourage the Church on its way, John, in the second reading (Rev 21:1-5a), gives it a glimpse of the glory of the heavenly Jerusalem—the Church triumphant—which is shown to us "as a bride adorned for her husband" Christ. She will be "the dwelling of God with men" (ib. 2,3), where the Son of God will set up his permanent dwelling, no longer rejected as in this world, but welcomed by all the elect as their Lord and Comforter. Then he will "wipe away every tear from their eyes, and death shall be no more" (ib. 4). Through his passion and resurrection Christ has sanctified pain and death, though without eliminating them; but in eternal life where men will share fully in the glory of his resurrection, "there shall be no more mourning nor crying nor pain" (ib.). Everything will be renewed in the glory and love of the risen Christ.

O Christ, our paschal sacrifice, through you, we children of the light are reborn to a new life; you have opened the gates of the kingdom of heaven to those who believe in your love. Your death is our ransom from death, and in your resurrection all life rises again. Through this mystery all humanity is inundated with the joy of the resurrection and there is rejoicing over all the earth.

cf Roman Missal *Easter Preface* II

O Christ, you have given us a new commandment, that we love one another as you have loved us. You call it new because you strip away the old man and clothe us with the new. In fact it is not just any love that renews man, but the love which you distinguish from the one that is purely human when you add: as I have loved you. This new commandment renews only the one who accepts it and obeys it... Lord, make this love renew us, make us new men, heirs of the New Testament, men who sing the new canticle. Make this love which has renewed all the just of ancient times, the patriarchs and prophets, as later the blessed Apostles—make it continue to renew the nations and gather in the whole human race, no matter how much spread throughout the world, make of all a single new people, the body of your bride.

cf St. Augustine, *In Io* 65:1

182 — MARY'S HUMILITY

O Mary, the Lord has looked upon your lowliness, and has done great things for you *(Lk 1:48-49)*

1. St. Bernard says: "It is not hard to be humble in the hidden life, but to remain so in the midst of honors is a truly rare and beautiful virtue" (*on the "Missus"* 4:9). The Blessed Virgin was certainly the woman whom God honored most highly, whom he raised above all other creatures; yet no creature was so humble and lowly as she. A holy rivalry seemed to exist between Mary and God; the higher God elevated her, the lowlier she became in her humility. The angel called her "full of grace" and Mary "was troubled" (Lk 1:28-29). According to St. Alphonsus' explanation, "Mary was troubled because she was filled with humility, disliked praise, and desired that God only be praised" (Glories of Mary II 1:4). The angel revealed to her the sublime mission which was to be entrusted to her by the Most High, and Mary declared herself "the handmaid of the Lord" (ib. 38). Her thoughts did not linger over the immense honor that would be hers as the woman chosen from all women to be the Mother of the Son of God, but she contemplated in wonder the great mystery of a God who willed to become incarnate in the womb of a poor creature. If God wished to descend so far as to give himself to her as a Son, to what depths should not his little handmaid abase herself? The more she understood the grandeur of the mystery, the immensity of the divine gift, the more she humbled herself, submerging herself in her nothingness. Her attitude was the same when Elizabeth greeted her, "Blessed are you among women" (ib. 42). Those words did not astonish her, for now she was already the Mother of God, and she remained steadfast in her profound humility. She attributed everything to God whose mercies she sang, acknowledging the condescension with which he "had regarded the low estate of his handmaid" (ib. 48). That God had performed great works in her she knew and acknowledged, but instead of boasting about them, she directed everything to his glory. With reason St. Ber-

nardine exclaims: "As no other creature, after the Son of God, has been raised in dignity and grace equal to Mary, so neither has anyone descended so deep into the abyss of humility" (4 Ser feasts B.V.M. 3,3). Behold the effect that graces and divine favors should produce in us: an increase of humility, a greater awareness of our nothingness.

2. "If you cannot equal Mary's absolute purity," says St. Bernard, "at least imitate her humility. The virtue of chastity is admirable, but humility is essential. A simple invitation calls to the first: 'He that can take, let him take it;' for the second, we have an absolute command: 'Unless you become as little children, you shall not enter into the kingdom of heaven.' Chastity, therefore, will be rewarded; humility will be demanded. We can be saved without virginity, but not without humility. Even Mary's virginity would not have been pleasing to God without humility. Mary certainly pleased God by her virginity, but she became his Mother because of her humility" (*On the "Missus"* 1:5).

The greatest qualities and gifts, such as the spirit of penance or of poverty, virginity, the call to the apostolate, a life consecrated to God, even the priesthood, are sterile if they are not accompanied by sincere humility. Furthermore, without humility, they might be a source of danger for the soul. The higher the place we occupy in the Savior's vineyard, the higher the life of perfection we profess, and the more important the mission which God has entrusted to us, the deeper we need to plant the roots of humility. Mary's maternity was the fruit of her humility; she conceived in humility. Even so, the fruitfulness of our interior life, of our apostolate, will depend on our humility and will always be proportioned to it.

Only God can accomplish great things in us and by us, but he will not do so unless he finds us completely humble. Humility alone is the fertile ground in which God's gifts fructify, while it is always humility which draws down upon us divine graces and favors. "There is no queen like humility"—says St. Teresa of Jesus—"for making the King surrender. Humility drew the King from heaven to the womb of the Virgin" (Way 16:2).

What beautiful commingling of virginity with humility! That soul is in no small degree pleasing to God, in whom humility commends virginity, and virginity adorns humility. But how much more worthy of veneration are you, O Mary, in whom fecundity exalts humility, and childbearing consecrates virginity . . . If you, O Mary, had not been humble, the Spirit would not have rested on you. If the Holy Spirit had not rested on you, you would never have become fruitful; for how without him would you have conceived of him? . . . If by your virginity you were acceptable to him, nevertheless, it was by your humility that you conceived him.

Happy were you, O Mary, in whom neither humility nor virginity was wanting. O glorious virginity! which fecundity honored, but did not contaminate. O singular humility! that a fruitful virginity was associated with humility. Which of them is the more wonderful, more incomparable, more unique? In pondering them, we are at a loss to decide which is the more worthy of admiration: the Virgin's fecundity, the Mother's integrity, or the adorable dignity of her off-spring; or again that in such sublime elevation she still preserves her humility.

St. Bernard, *On the 'Missus'* 1:5,9

O Mary, anyone who looks at you is comforted in any anxiety or tribulation or pain, and is victorious over every temptation. Any one who does not know something about God, let him have recourse to you, O Mary. Anyone who does not find mercy in God, let him have recourse to you, O Mary. Anyone whose will is not in conformity, let him have recourse to you, O Mary. Anyone who falters on account of weakness, let him have recourse to you who are all strong and powerful. Anyone in constant struggle, let him have recourse to you who are a tranquil sea... Whoever is tempted... let him have recourse to you, who are the mother of humility, and nothing drives away the devil more than humility. Let them one and all, have recourse to you O Mary!

St. Mary Magdalen de Pazzi, *Colloquies,* Op 3 v.3

183 — MARY'S FAITH

Blessed are you, Mary, because you have believed that what was spoken to you by the Lord would be fulfilled (Lk 1:45)

1. "Blest is she who believed there would be a fulfillment of what was spoken to her from the Lord" (Lk 1:45). Elizabeth's praise of Mary continues to echo through the Church. Great was the faith of the Virgin, who believed without hesitation in the message of the Angel who announced to her wonderful and unheard of things. She believed, she obeyed, and, as the Council confirms in the words of the ancient Fathers, through her faith and obedience she "became the cause of salvation for herself and for the whole human race . . . What the virgin Eve bound through her unbelief, Mary loosened by her faith" (LG 46). On the word of God as announced to her by the Angel, she believed that she would become a mother without losing her virginity; she, who was so humble, believed that she would be truly the Mother of God, and that the fruit of her womb would really be the Son of the Most High. She adhered with entire faith to all that had been revealed to her, accepting, without the least hesitation, a plan that would upset the whole natural order of things: a virgin mother, a creature, the Mother of the Creator. She believed when the Angel spoke to her; she continued to believe even when the Angel left her alone and she found herself in the condition of an ordinary woman who knows that she is about to become a mother. "The Virgin,"—St. Bernard says—"so little in her own eyes, was magnanimous in her faith in God's promise! She, who considered

herself nothing but a poor handmaid, never had the least doubt concerning her vocation to this incomprehensible mystery, to this marvelous exchange, to this inscrutabale sacrament; she firmly believed that she would become the true Mother of the God-Man" (De duod. praerog. BVM 13).

The Blessed Virgin teaches us to believe in our vocation to sanctity, to divine intimacy; and to believe in it not only when God reveals it in the brightness of interior light, but also when the light grows dim and we remain in darkness amid difficulties that try to disturb and discourage us. God never fails us; when he gives a vocation, it is because he wants to finish his work in us, provided we trust ourselves to him with blind confidence.

2. "The Blessed Virgin"—affirms the Council—"also advanced in her pilgrimage of faith . . . a faith never tainted by the least doubt" (LG 58,63), but still always faith. It would be very far from the truth to think that the divine mysteries were so revealed to Mary and that the divinity of Jesus was so evident to her that she had no need of faith. Excepting the Annunciation and the events surrounding the birth of Jesus, we do not find any extraordinary manifestations of the supernatural in her life. Mary lived by pure faith, trusting in God's word even as we must. The divine mysteries which took place in her and around her remained habitually hidden under the veil of faith, assuming an outward appearance common to the various circumstances of ordinary daily life. Hence, they were often concealed under obscure, disconcerting aspects, such as the extreme poverty in which Jesus was born, the necessity of fleeing into exile in order to save him, the King of heaven, from the wrath of an earthly king, the toil undergone to procure for him the strict necessities, and even the lack of these, perhaps. Yet Mary never doubted that this weak, helpless Child, who needed her maternal care and protection just like any other child, was the Son of God. She always believed, even when she did not understand. Witness, for example, the unexpected disappearance of the twelve year old boy who had remained in the temple without his parents' knowledge. St. Luke relates that when Jesus explained his action, giving as the reason that he was carrying out the mission entrusted to him by his heavenly Father, Mary and Joseph "did not understand the words he spoke to them" (cf Lk 2:50). Although Mary knew with certainty that Jesus was the Messiah, she did not know how he was to accomplish his mission, nor how far away from his own he would go to attend to his Father's business. Nevertheless she questioned him no further. She believed that Jesus was her God, and that was enough for her; she was certain, absolutely certain of him.

A faithful soul does not linger to inquire about God's actions; even though not fully understanding them, it believes and, if necessary, follows the manifestations of the divine will blindly. God does not ask us to understand, but only to believe with all our strength.

O incomparable Virgin . . . you are blessed because you believed, as your cousin Elizabeth said; you are blessed because you accepted and sheltered the Savior within your womb; you are much more blessed because you heard his word and kept it; you are likewise blessed because you were so marvelously able to unite within yourself those eight beatitudes which your Son preached on the mountain. You were poor in spirit, and the kingdom of heaven is yours; you were meek, and you possess the land of the living; you began early to weep for the world's ills, and you are comforted; you hungered and thirsted for justice, and now you are filled; you were merciful and so obtained mercy; you were a peacemaker and thus you are pre-eminently a child of God; you were pure of heart, and now you contemplate God clearly; you suffered persecution for justice's sake, and now the kingdom of heaven is yours—you are Queen over all its citizens.

O Queen, I rejoice that you are blessed with so many titles. Oh, if all the nations would be converted to your Son, and with great faith would call you blessed, so that through you they might all succeed in becoming blessed, imitating your life while they are here on earth, so as later to rejoice in your glory in heaven!

L. Da Ponte, *Meditations* II 12:3

O Mary, by believing the Angel when he assured you that, remaining a virgin, you would become the Mother of God, you brought salvation to the world . . . Your faith opened heaven to men . . .

O holy Virgin, you had more faith than all men and angels. You saw your Son in the stable of Bethlehem, and believed him to be the creator of the world. You saw him fly from Herod, and yet believed him the King of kings. You saw him born, and believed him eternal. You saw him poor and in need of food, and believed him the Lord of the universe; you saw him lying on straw, and believed him omnipotent. You observed that he did not speak, and you believed him infinite Wisdom. You heard him cry, and you believed him the joy of paradise. You saw him in death, despised and crucified, and, although the faith of others wavered, you remained firm in believing that he was God . . .

Holy Virgin, by the merit of your faith, obtain for me a lively faith: "O Lady, increase our faith!"

St. Alphonsus, *The Glories of Mary* IV 4:1,2,6

184 — MARY'S HOPE

Hail holy Queen, mother of mercy; our life, our sweetness and our hope!

1. Mary "stands out among the poor and humble of the Lord, who confidently await and receive salvation from him. With her,

the exalted Daughter of Sion, and after a long expectation of the promise, the times were at length fulfilled and the new dispensation established" (LG 55). Thus the Council presents Mary, in whom are summed up all the hopes of Israel; all the yearnings and sighs of the prophets re-echo in her heart and reach a hitherto unknown intensity, which hastens their fulfillment. She more than anyone has hoped for and confidently awaited salvation, and in herself the divine promises are beginning to be realized. In the *Magnificat,* the canticle which burst from Mary's heart when she visited her cousin Elizabeth, we find an expression which specially reveals Mary's interior attitude. "My soul magnifies the Lord, . . . for he has regarded the humility of his handmaid" (Lk 2:46,48). When Mary spoke these words, they revealed the "great things" which God had done in her; but, considered in the framework of her life, they expressed the continual movement of her heart, which, in the full awareness of her nothingness, would always turn to God with the most absolute hope and trust in his aid. No one had a more concrete, practical *knowledge* of her nothingness than Mary; she understood well that her whole being, natural as well as supernatural, would be annihilated if God did not sustain her at every moment. Having become the mother of God, her great mission and the marvelous privileges which she had received from the Most High did not at all diminish the feeling of her lowliness. But far from disconcerting or discouraging her in any way, her humility served as a starting point from which she darted to God with stronger hope. That is why, being really poor in spirit, she did not trust in her own resources, but put all her confidence in God alone. And God, who has "filled the hungry with good things, and the rich . . . has sent empty away" (ib. 53), satisfied her "hunger" and fulfilled her hopes; not only by showering his gifts on her, but by giving himself to her in all his plenitude, he fulfilled in her the hopes of his people.

2. Mary's hope was truly absolute and unshakeable, even in the darkest and most difficult moments. When Joseph, aware of her approaching maternity (of whose origin he knew nothing), "resolved to send her away quietly" (Mt 1:19), Mary, who certainly perceived the anguished state of mind of her pure spouse, and the risk to which she was herself exposed, was unwilling to make known what the angel had revealed to her. Full of confidence in God's help, she preferred to keep silence and to leave her fate in the hands of God. "In quietness and in trust shall be your strength" (Is 30;15), said the Holy Spirit; and so it was with Mary. She was silent without trying to justify herself in Joseph's eyes; she remained serene and tranquil in an extremely difficult and delicate situation, because she was full of confidence in God. Her whole life, besides, was a continuous exercise of heroic hope. In the thirty years spent at Nazareth, when Jesus was a child, a boy, a man like every one else, and there was no outward sign to indicate that he was to be the Savior of the world, Mary never stop-

ped believing and hoping for the fulfillment of the divine promise. When her Son began to be persecuted, when he was captured, tried and crucified, and all seemed finished, Mary's hope was unaltered; rather, it grew with giant strides and gave her the strength to remain steadfast "by the cross of Jesus" (Jn 19:25).

How poor our hope is compared to that of our Blessed Mother! Lacking her complete reliance on God, we always feel the need of resorting to many little personal expedients to obtain some security, some human support. However, everything human is uncertain; we shall always be disturbed and anxious, battered by storms. The darkness frightens us, trials make us irresolute and sometimes, perhaps, even doubt in God's assistance. The Virgin Mary shows us the only way to real security, serenity and interior peace, even in the most difficult circumstances: the way of total confidence in God. "In you, O Lord, is our hope and we shall never hope in vain" (Te Deùm).

O Mary, your hope was so sublime that you could repeat with the holy King David: "I have made the Lord God my refuge" (Ps 73:28)... You were always perfectly detached from earthly affections... in no way relying either on creatures or on your own merits, but leaning only on divine grace, in which you put all your confidence, you were always growing in the love of God...

O Mary, from you we must learn to have confidence in God, most of all in all that regards our eternal salvation... distrusting our own strength and saying: "I can do all things in him who strengthens me" (Phil 4:13). O my most holy Lady, you are the Mother of holy hope... What other hope should I be seeking?

And I have such confidence in you that if my salvation were in my own hands, I should place it in yours, for I rely more on your mercy and protection than on all my own works. My Mother and my hope, do not abandon me... All may forget me, but do you not forget me, O Mother of the all-powerful God. Say to God that I am your child and that you protect me, and I shall be saved...

O Mary, I put my trust in you; in this hope I live and in this hope I long to die, saying over and over: "My only hope is Jesus, and after Jesus, Mary."

St. Alphonsus, the *Glories of Mary* IV:5, I 3:1

O most lovely Mary, my greatest hope after God, speak favorably of me to your beloved Son; let your speech be efficacious for me. Plead my cause faithfully; in your mercy secure for me what I long for, for I put my trust in you, my one and only hope after Christ. Show plainly that you are my gracious mother. Intercede for me that I may be received by the Lord in the holy cloister of his love, in the school of the Holy Spirit, for there is no one more powerful than you to obtain this from your beloved Son.

O faithful Mother, care for your daughter, so that I may become the fruit of ever living love, grow in all holiness, and receive, like dew falling from heaven, the gift of perseverance.

St. Gertrude, *Exercises* 2

185 — MARY'S CHARITY

O Mary, full of grace (Lk 1:28), may your intercession obtain for us an increase in love.

1. "God is love" (1 Jn 4:16), and Mary, who in her position as mother was closer to God and more united to him than any other creature, was also more filled by him than any other. St. Thomas says: "The nearer a thing approaches to its principle, the more it experiences its effect" (St T III 27,5,3). She, whom the Angel greeted as "full of grace" (Lk 1:28) is so much the more full of love. But the fullness of grace and of love in which Mary was constituted from the beginning did not dispense her from the active and assiduous practice of charity nor of all the other virtues. The Council makes this evident in saying: "The Blessed Virgin . . . cooperated in an utterly singular way by her obedience, faith, hope, and burning charity in the Savior's work" (LG 61), and repeatedly points her out as a special model of charity. For her, as for us, life on earth was the "way" where progress in charity was always necessary, where personal correspondence with grace was expected. The excellence of our Lady's merit consisted in her heroic fidelity to the immense gifts she had received. The privileges of her immaculate conception, of the state of sanctity in which she was born, and of her divine maternity were, unquestionably, pure gifts from God; still, far from accepting them passively, as a coffer receives the precious things put into it, she received them freely, as one capable of willingly adhering to the divine favors by means of a complete correspondence with grace. St. Thomas teaches that although Mary could not merit the incarnation of the Word, by the grace she received she did merit that degree of sanctity which made her the worthy Mother of God (cf III^{a}, q. 2, a. 11, ad. 3), and she merited this precisely because of her correspondence with grace. Mary, in the truest sense of the word, is the "faithful virgin," who knew how to increase a hundredfold the talents she received from God. To the fullness of grace bestowed on her through the divine liberality corresponded the fullness of her fidelity.

2. "You shall love the Lord your God with all your heart, and with all your soul, with all your strength and with all your mind" (Lk 10:27). The Lord's commandment is fully realized in Mary, who was perfectly humble and accordingly completely empty of self. Free of all selfishness and of all attachment to creatures, she could focus the full force of her love on God. The Gospel portrays her thus: always completely open to the Lord. Even when the

divine will was obscure and mysterious, she was always ready with an act of full adherence; the "fiat" uttered at the Annunciation was the constant attitude of her heart, entirely consecrated to love (LG 62). The poverty of Bethlehem, the flight into Egypt, the humble laborious life of Nazareth, Jesus' departure for his apostolic work and the solitude in which she remained, the hatred and strife that were unleashed against her Son, the sorrowful way to Calvary were all so many stages of her love, through which she was continually consenting and offering herself, pledging herself ever more intensely to her mission as "the loving mother of the divine Redeemer, an associate of unique nobility and the Lord's humble handmaid" (LG 61). Mary lived her divine motherhood in an act of unceasing dedication to the will of the Father and to the mission of her Son; she knew no hesitation or reservation, asked nothing for herself. One day when she sought to see him and talk to him, she heard him say: "Who is my mother, and who are my brothers? . . . Whoever does the will of my Father in heaven is my brother and sister and mother" (Mt 12:48,50). Mary took these austere words into her heart and with greater love than before continued to live the divine will which demanded such renunciation of her. As she sacrificed the legitimate and holy joy of enjoying her Son, she was doubly united to him because she was as it were fused with him in one single act of oblation to the will of the Father. Thus the Blessed Virgin teaches us that the real love of God and authentic union with him does not consist in spiritual consolation, but in perfect conformity to the divine will.

O Mary, you are full of grace! Far from encountering any obstacle in you to the unfolding of grace, the Holy Spirit always found your heart wonderfully docile to his inspirations, and therefore full of love.

What must have been the joy of the soul of Jesus to feel himself loved to such an extent by his Mother! After the incomprehensible joy that came to him from the beatific vision and from the look of infinite complacency with which his heavenly Father contemplated him, nothing can have rejoiced him so much as your love, O Mary. He found in it a more than abundant compensation for the indifference of those who would not receive him. He found in your virgin heart a fire of undying love that he himself further enkindled by his divine glances and by the inward grace of his Spirit . . . You received from the Father the most perfect of maternal hearts; there was never the least trace of self-exultation there: it was a miracle of love, a treasure house of graces ("full of grace"). Your heart was not fashioned only for Christ . . . it was also fashioned for his mystical Body . . . You enfold in one love Christ and us, his members . . . Souls devoted to you obtain from you a very pure love. Their whole life is a reflection of your life . . . Your desire is to share the love which animates you with those who are yours.

C. Marmion, *Consecration to the most Holy Trinity* 28

O Mary, who are you who were destined for motherhood? How did you merit this?... How will he who created you be formed in you?... You are a virgin, you are holy, you have made a vow: you merited a very great deal, but you received far more... There is made in you him who made you, him through whom you were made, him who made heaven and earth, through whom all things were made. The Word of God is made flesh in you, and becoming man, does not lose his divinity. The Word is united to the flesh... and the wedding chamber of so great a marriage is your womb... (Ser 291:6).

But, O Mary, you were even more blessed for believing in Christ, than for conceiving the flesh of Christ... It would have profited you nothing to be his mother, if you had not borne him more in your heart. More praiseworthy and blessed are you, O Mary, for having done the will of the Father, according to Christ's words: "Whoever does the will of my Father in heaven is my brother and sister and mother" (Mt 12:50)... You who obeyed the will of God are physically only Christ's mother, but spiritually you are his sister and his mother (De virg 2,3,5).

St. Augustine

186 — MARY AND MANKIND

Holy Mary, Mother of God, pray for us sinners.

1. "Mary"—says the Council—"devoted herself totally ... to the person and work of her Son. In subordination to him and along with him ... she served the mystery of redemption" (LG 56). The charity which filled her led her to give herself in one and the same act to Christ, her Son and her God, and to the salvation of men. The same love which bound her to her Son drove her to cooperate with maternal love in the birth and development of those whom he chose as his brothers (cf LG 63). This is the peculiar quality of true love of God; far from narrowing the soul of one who possesses it, it dilates the soul that it may pour out on others the wealth it has accumulated. Such was the characteristic of Mary's charity. Although she was completely filled with the love of God, wholly recollected in loving contemplation of the divine mysteries which were taking place in and around her, her recollection did not hinder her from giving attention to her neighbor; on the contrary, we see her always gracious and attentive to the needs of others. Furthermore her own interior wealth urged her to desire to share with others the great treasures which she possessed. This is the attitude described in the Gospel, when, immediately after the annunciation, she "went in haste" (Lk 1:39) to visit Elizabeth. It would have been very pleasant for her to remain at Nazareth, adoring in solitude and silence the divine Word incarnate in her womb, but the angel had told her of the imminent maternity of her

aged cousin; this was enough for her to feel obliged to go to Elizabeth and offer her humble services. We can say, therefore, that Mary's first act after becoming the Mother of God was an act of charity toward her neighbor. God gave himself to her as a Son, and Mary, who gave herself to him as his "handmaid," wished also to give herself as the "handmaid" of others. The close union which exists between charity toward God and charity toward the neighbor is singularly evident here. Her act of charity toward Elizabeth is in perfect accord with the act of sublime love in which Mary gave herself wholly to God when she pronounced her "fiat."

2. At the birth of Jesus it was the same. Mary, in ecstasy, contemplated him, her divine Son, but this did not prevent her from offering him to the adoration of the shepherds. Here is Mary's supreme charity to men: giving Jesus to them almost as soon as he gives himself to her. She does not wish to be the only one to enjoy him, but would share her joy with all men. And just as she "joyfully showed her first-born Son to the shepherds and Magi" (LG 57) who came to adore him, she would later offer him to the executioners who would crucify him. Jesus was everything to Mary; yet, because of her great charity, she did not hesitate to immolate him for the salvation of men. Can we imagine any charity more exalted, or more generous? Next to God, next to Jesus, surely no one has loved mankind more than Mary.

Another aspect of her charity toward others is evidenced in her tactfulness. When Mary found Jesus in the temple, after three days of anxious searching and keenest suffering at his sudden disappearance, she concealed her own sorrow behind that of Joseph's: "Behold, your father and I have been looking for you anxiously" (Lk 2:48). Tender charity toward her spouse made her profoundly sensitive to his grief and she put it before her own deeper grief. The marriage in Cana gives us another example of Mary's delicacy. While all were occupied with the feast, she alone, although so recollected, noticed the embarrassment of the bridal couple when the wine gave out, and she handled the matter so tactfully that it passed unobserved, even by the chief steward.

Mary teaches us that when our love of God is really perfect, it flows at once into generous love of our neighbor, because as Scripture puts it, we have but one commandment: "He who loves God should love his brother also" (1 Jn 4:21). If, then, we have to recognize that in dealing with our neighbor we are not very charitable, nor very kind to him, nor attentive to his needs, we must conclude that our love for God is still very weak.

O Virgin Mary, you were that pleasant field where the seed of the incarnate Word of the Son of God was sown . . . Into this sweet and blessed field came the Word, grafted onto your flesh, like a seed that is cast into the earth, which germinates in the heat of the sun and bears flower and fruit . . . And so did it come to pass through the heat and fire of the divine love which God felt for the human race, by his casting the seed of his word into your field, O Mary. O blessed, sweet Mary, you have given us the flower, the sweet Jesus. And when did this sweet flower yield its fruit? When he was grafted onto the wood of the most holy cross, for then we received perfect life... The only begotten Son of God, in that he was man, was enveloped in desire for the honor of his Father and for our salvation; and so strong was this immense desire that he ran like one enamored, bearing pain and shame and insult, even to the infamous death of the cross... You had the same desire, O Mary, for you could not desire anything but the honor of God and the salvation of his creatures... So immeasurable was your charity that you would have made a ladder of yourself to put your Son upon the cross, if he had had no other way. And all this is so because the will of the Son dwelt within you.

Obtain for me, O Mary, that it may never leave my heart or my memory or my soul that I have been offered and given over to you. So I beg you to offer me and give me to your dear Son Jesus; and to bring this about as a kind... tender mother of mercy. Let me not fail to be grateful that you have not despised my petition, but have received it so graciously.

St. Catherine of Siena, *Letters* 144

O Mother most admirable, present me to your dear Son as his eternal slave, so that as he has redeemed me by you, by you may he accept me.

O Mother of mercy, I beg you to obtain for me the true Wisdom of God, and for this reason, put me among those you love, teach, direct, nourish and protect as your children and your slaves.

O Virgin most faithful, make me in all things so perfect a disciple, imitator, and slave of the incarnate Wisdom, Jesus Christ your Son, that I may attain through your intercession and example to the fullness of his age on earth and of his glory in heaven.

St. Louis Grignon de Montfort, *True Devotion to the BVM*

187 — MARY'S PRAYER

O Mary, who kept the mysteries of your Son in your heart (Lk 2:19,51), teach me to live in continual prayer.

1. In order to have even a slight understanding of Mary's prayer, we have to try to penetrate the sanctuary of her intimate union with God. No one has ever lived in such intimacy with him—first of all the intimacy of a mother. Who can imagine the closeness of the relationship between Mary and the incarnate Word during the months she carried him in her virginal womb? "Do we think"—writes Sr. Elizabeth of the Trinity—"what must have been in the soul of the Blessed Virgin when, after the Incarnation, she possessed within her the incarnate Word, the gift of

God? In what silence, what recollection she must have buried herself in the depths of her soul in order to embrace that God whose mother she was" (Letter 183). Mary was the sanctuary which concealed the Holy of Holies; the living ciborium of the incarnate Word, she was aflame with love, absorbed in adoration. Carrying within her "the burning furnace of charity," how could Mary not remain all inflamed by it! The more she was inflamed with love, the more she understood the mystery of love which was taking place within her. No one ever penetrated the secrets of Christ's heart as Mary did, or had a greater knowledge of the divinity of Christ and of his infinite grandeur. No one ever felt, as Mary did, the consuming need to give herself to him, to lose herself in him like a little drop in the immensity of the ocean. This was Mary's unceasing prayer: a perpetual adoration of the Word made Flesh within her; a deep union with Christ, continually immersed in him and completely transformed in him by love; continually joining the infinite homage and praise which ascended from the heart of Christ to the Trinity; and ceaselessly offering this praise to the Trinity as the only homage worthy of the divine Majesty. Mary lived in adoration of her Jesus and, in union with him, in adoration of the Trinity.

There is one moment in the day when we, too, can share in this prayer of Mary in a most excellent way: the moment of Eucharistic Communion, when we receive Jesus, real and living, into our heart. How we need Mary to help us profit from this ineffable gift! She teaches us to immerse ourselves with her in her and our Jesus, that we may be transformed in him, and also how to unite ourselves to the adoration which ascends from the heart of Jesus to the Trinity, which she offers with us to the Father to supply for the deficiencies of our adoration.

2. Mary spent thirty years in Bethlehem and Nazareth in sweet family intimacy with Jesus. He was her center of attraction, the object of her affections, her thoughts and solicitude. The life of Mary was centered on him; she took care of him, always seeking new ways of pleasing, serving and loving him with the greatest devotion. Her will vibrated in union with his; her heart beat in perfect harmony with him. She "shared the thoughts of Christ and his secret wishes, in such a way that it can be said that she lived the very life of her Son" (Pius X *Ad diem illum*). Like Mary's life, her prayer was ever Christocentric, and Christ bore it to the Blessed Trinity. It was really the mystery of the Incarnation which brought Mary into the fullness of the Trinitarian life. Her unique relations with the three divine Persons began when the angel told her that she was to be the Mother of the Son of the Most High and would be so by the power of the Holy Spirit. She was, from that moment, the beloved daughter of the Father, the spouse of the Holy Spirit, and the Mother of the Word. These relations were not limited to the time when Mary carried within her the incarnate Word, but were to continue throughout her whole

life, throughout eternity. Thus Mary is the temple of the Trinity. "Nearer than all to Jesus Christ, although at a distance that is infinite," Mary is, "the great 'praise of glory' of the Blessed Trinity" (E. T. 2 Retreat 15).

In Mary we find the most perfect model for souls aspiring to intimacy with God, and at the same time, she is the surest guide for them. She leads us to Jesus and teaches us to concentrate all our affections on him, to give ourselves entirely to him, until we are completely lost and transformed in him. Then, through Jesus, she guides us to the life of union with the Trinity. By reason of sanctifying grace, our soul is also a temple of the Trinity, and Mary teaches us how to abide in this temple as a perpetual adorer of the three divine Persons who dwell therein. "I want to follow this way of life"—wrote Elizabeth of the Trinity—"living here as our Lady did, keeping all these things in my heart, hiding myself, as it were, in the depths of my soul in order to lose myself in the holy Three who dwell there, and to transform myself in Them" (Let 185). May it also be given to us to live, under Mary's direction in this attitude of continual adoration of the Trinity dwelling within our soul.

O Virgin most faithful, you remain night and day in profound silence, in ineffable peace, in a divine prayer that never ceases, your soul ever inundated with heavenly light. Your heart is like a crystal that reflects the divine One, the Guest who dwells in you, the Beauty that knows no setting. O Mary you draw heaven down to you: see, the Father commits his Son to you that you may be his Mother, and the Spirit of love overshadows you. The Blessed Three come to you, and all heaven is opened and abases itself before you . . . I adore the mystery of this God who is made flesh in you, O Virgin Mary.

Mother of the Word, show me your mystery after the incarnation of the Lord; how you lived buried in adoration . . . Keep me ever in a divine embrace. Let me carry upon me the stamp of this God of love.

Elizabeth of the Trinity, *Poetical Compositions* 79, 88

O Mary, you are the soul of interior attention, of perfect silence, of complete and consummate listening. You were poor and humble in the hard work of each day: you lived in the temple, working assiduously; weary and tired in the poverty of Bethlehem; in poverty you traveled earth's road; you were acquainted with the pains and fatigues of daily work; but nothing ever prevented you from being interiorly recollected, from continual inner dialogue, from your silent and ceaseless listening. You were ever a soul of most intense and perfect listening . . .

You heard the word of the great annunciation, and accepted it discreetly and serenely; you heard the songs of the angels over the cradle of your Only-Begotten and welcomed them with glad humility; you heard the word of exile and followed it trustfully and patient-

ly; you heard the word that traced upon you a vast sign of the cross and accepted it with generous courage; you heard from the Lord the hard word which you did not understand, and kept it in your heart, in silence, like a precious gem; you guarded it from all worldly intrusion, protecting it with a veil of grief that was at once afflicted and submissive, into which the inexpressible sorrow of Calvary was already stealing. You did not lose one word... of the Son, nor any one of those spoken interiorly by the Spirit, who had come upon you in the infinite mystery of the Incarnation. You heard and gathered them all: with the devoted ear of a daughter for the great word of the Father, or with the discreet intimacy of a spouse for the inflamed word of the Spirit, or with the loving tenderness of a mother for the sweet words of the Word made flesh in you from your flesh.

G. Canovai, *Suscipe Domine*

188 — SIXTH SUNDAY OF EASTER

YEAR A

Come and see what God has done *(Ps 66:5)*

With the approach of Pentecost, the Liturgy of the Word is centered on the promise of the Holy Spirit and on his action in the Church.

On the evening of the Last Supper Jesus said to his disciples: "If you love me you will keep my commandments. And I will pray the Father, and he will give you another counselor to be with you for ever" (Jn 14:15-16). The observance of the commandments as the evidence of genuine love, which he had recommended many times during his discourse at the Supper, is presented by him as the condition for receiving the Holy Spirit. Only one who lives by love, and therefore in the fulfillment of the divine will, is fit to receive the Holy Spirit who is infinite Love personified. This being so, Jesus, after returning to his Father, will himself send his followers "another Paraclete"—an advocate and defender—who will take his place among the disciples and remain for ever with them and with the whole Church. Since he is "Spirit," his presence and his action will be invisible and entirely spiritual. The world which is immersed in the material and darkened by error will be unable to recognize him or to receive him, because it is in open opposition to the "Spirit of truth." But the disciples, who have been refined and purified by their contact with Jesus, will know him; in fact they know him already, because he is among them (ib. 17), present and operating in Christ. Moreover on Pentecost the Holy Spirit will descend upon the disciples directly; they will be transformed by him to their inmost depths and will find Jesus again in him. "I will not leave you desolate"—the Lord had said—"I will come to you" (ib. 18), referring to his invisible, yet real return through his Spirit, through whom he will continue to assist the Church. Then his words will be realized: "In that day you will know that I am in the Father, and you in me, and I in you" (ib. 20). In fact, it is to the Holy Spirit that the mission of enlightening the faithful in the great mysteries already proclaimed by Jesus is entrusted. Under his influence, the faithful will understand the mystery in which Christ, the eternal Word, God like the Father and the Holy Spirit, is in the Father and the Holy Spirit; they will understand that in the Unity and Trinity of God, the three divine Persons are inseparable: where one is, the other two are also. And they will understand that by living in Christ like the branches on the vine, they themselves enter into communion with the Trinity. These sublime truths are not reserved for a privileged few, but are the patrimony of all the faithful; Jesus promised and sent his Spirit to all, so that they might understand him and live in him.

The Acts (first reading) show clearly how, from the beginning of the Church, the apostles were concerned that the baptized should receive the Holy Spirit. The action of Peter and John was typical: it was the reason for their going to Samaria where the deacon Philip had already preached the gospel and baptized converts. The two Apostles "came down to these people and prayed . . . They laid their hands on them and they received the Holy Spirit" (Acts 8:15,17). Although a Christian has been reborn in the Spirit through baptism, he must still receive the Spirit with greater fullness in the sacrament of confirmation which renews the grace of Pentecost for each of the faithful. Jesus had pointed out how this grace must be corresponded to and lived through love; this is the attitude that God awaits in us before revealing the divine mysteries to us: "He who loves me will be loved by my Father, and I will love him and manifest myself to him" (Jn 14:21).

O Jesus, bestow on us who serve you a sure and immediate consolation, for we are immersed in sadness. Do not stand aloof from our souls, which are in the midst of trials. Do not stand aloof from our hearts whch are surrounded with troubles. But continue to come hastening to us; be near us, yes, be near, you who live everywhere. Just as you used to help your apostles in every circumstance, now bring together in your unity those who love you. Grant that, united in you, we may be able to sing and glorify the Spirit who is the fullness of holiness . . .

We beg you with tears and cry out to you, O God: send us your Spirit, who is the highest good! Let him lead all toward the land that is yours, a level land which you have prepared for those who honor and glorify the Spirit who contains all holiness . . .

To you who are Lord and King of the angels, to you who have power over men and are their creator, to you who with a single nod can command every thing that exists on earth and in the sea, to you your friends and servants cry out: oh! hurry to send us the Spirit who is the fullness of sanctity!

Romano Il Melode, *Hymn of Pentecost*

YEAR B

Lord, that I may abide in your love *(Jn 15:9)*

"Love is of God . . . God is love" (1 Jn 4:7,8). These words of John sum up today's Liturgy.

Love is the Father who "sent his only Son into the world so that we might live through him" (ib. 9; second reading). Love is the Son who gave his life not only "for his friends" (Jn 15:13; Gospel), but also for his enemies. Love is the Holy Spirit who "shows no partiality" (Acts 10:34; first reading), and is impatient to pour himself out on all men (ib. 44). Divine love has anticipated men without any merit on their part: "In this is love: not that we loved God, but that he loved us" (1 Jn 4:10). Without the antecedent love of God which drew us out of nothing and then redeemed us from sin, we would never have been capable of loving. Just as life does not originate from the creature, but from the Creator, so love does not come from us, but from God, its one infinite source.

God's love reaches us through Christ. "As the Father has loved me, so have I loved you" (Jn 15:9). Jesus is the one who pours out his Father's love upon us by loving us with the same love with which he himself is loved by him; he wants us to live in this love: "abide in my love" (ibid). And since Jesus abides in the love of the Father by accomplishing his will, so must we abide in his love through observing his commandments. Here, we see heading the list the one he calls *his* commandment: "Love one another as I have loved you" (ib. 12). Jesus loves his disciples as he is loved by the Father, and they must love each other as they are loved by their Master. By fulfilling this commandment they become his friends: "You are my friends if you do what I command you" (ib. 14). Friendship requires reciprocal love; we reciprocate the love of Christ by loving him with all our heart and by loving our brothers, whom he identifies with himself, considering that anything that is done to the least of them is done to him (Mt 25:40).

In his discourse at the Last Supper, Jesus' insistence in recommending love for each other to his disciples is both touching and striking; his purpose is to form them into a compact community, cemented by his love, where they will all feel like brothers and live for each other. However, this does not mean restricting love to the circle of the faithful; quite the contrary: the more they are merged into the love of Christ, the more capable they will be of carrying this love to all men. How could the faithful be messengers of love in the world if they did not love each other?

They are called to demonstrate through their own conduct that God is love, and that by adhering to him we learn to love, we become love; that the gospel is love, and it was not to no purpose that Christ taught us to love each other; that love based on Christ overcomes differences, annuls distances, eliminates selfishness, rivalries, dissensions. All this does more to convince men and to attract them to the faith than any other means, and is an essential part of that apostolic fecundity that Jesus expects of his followers, to whom he said: "It was I who appointed you, that you should go and bear fruit, and that your fruit should abide" (Jn 15:16). Only those who live in love can bring to the world the precious fruit of love.

Look with love on your people, Lord, and pour out upon them the gifts of your Spirit, that they may constantly grow in the love of truth. May they study and work together for perfect unity among Christians.

Roman Missal *Mass for Christian Unity* 3, Collect

You are love, O God. Your love is revealed to us in this, that you sent your only Begotten Son into the world, that we might live through him. Our Lord himself declared that: greater love can no one have than to give his life for his friends, and Christ's own love is proven in the fact that he died for us. What then, O Father, is the proof of your love for us? That you send your only Son to die for us . . .

It was not we who loved you first; in fact the reason why you loved us was that we might love you . . . If you have loved us in this way, then we must love you in return . . . You are love. What kind of face has love? What shape, what height, what feet or hands? No one can say. Yet it has feet that lead to Church, hands that give to the poor, eyes that can recognize those who are in need . . . These various members are not to be found separately, in various places, but any one who has charity sees them all simultaneously. O Lord, then grant that I may abide in charity so that it may abide in me, that I may remain in it so that it may remain in me.

St. Augustine *In Io* 7:7-9,10

YEAR C

O Jesus, may the Holy Spirit bring to our remembrance all that you have said to us (Jn 14:26)

Today, the Liturgy of the Word shows us the situation of the Church from the Ascension of our Lord until the day when she too will be raised up in his glory.

The physical presence of Jesus is replaced by an interior spiritual presence which is promised to all who love him: "If a man loves me he will keep my word, and my Father will love him; and we will come to him and make our home with him" (Jn 14:23).

Jesus no longer lives among men as a man, but he, who is the Son of God, makes his dwelling place within the faithful, not alone, but with the Father and the Holy Spirit, to whom he is inseparably united. St. Augustine comments: "God, the Trinity, Father and Son and Holy Spirit, come to us when we go to them: they come to us, helping us, we go to them obeying; they come to us enlightening us, we go to them contemplating them; they come filling us with their presence, we go receiving them" (In Io 76:4). The indwelling of the Trinity is the supreme gift which Christ merited for mankind by his death and resurrection, and which he offers to anyone who corresponds with his love by hearing and faithfully putting his words into practice. In order to understand and live so ineffable a mystery we need a particular divine illumination.

This also Jesus promised his disciples: "The Holy Spirit whom the Father will send in my name, will teach you all things, and bring to your remembrance all that I have said to you" (Jn 14:26). He is the interior teacher who introduces us to the living, intimate, and experienced understanding of the truths announced by Jesus, especially the mystery of the Trinity and its indwelling in those who believe, of the call of these to personal communion with Christ and with the Trinity. He gives the true meaning of the Scriptures, the understanding of the divine plan for universal salvation, and guides the Church in accomplishing its mission. This was verified with singular fullness in the life of the early Church when the apostles spoke and acted in total dependence on him. "It has seemed good to the Holy Spirit and to us . . . " (Acts 15:28; first reading), they declared, when resolving the controversy over what burdens to lay upon converts from paganism. It is but human and inevitable that problems and differences should arise in the life of individuals and of the Church, but when the solution is sought and found in full docility to the Holy Spirit, to his interior inspiration and to his directions given through the word of him whose duty it is to interpret the divine will, everything is well and peacefully resolved.

Peace is the precise gift Jesus left to his disciples after having assured them the presence of the Trinity in their hearts and the help of the Holy Spirit. "Peace I leave with you, my peace I give to you; not as the world gives do I give to you" (Jn 14:27). His is a peace that is based on good relations with God, on the observance of his word and on intimate communion with him; it is the peace of those who allow themselves to be guided by the Holy Spirit and who act according to his light. It is a peace which does not dispense us from suffering in this life, but which infuses courage also to face strife fearlessly when this is necessary for being faithful to God. It is a peace which will be absolute, without shadow of disturbance, in the heavenly Jerusalem where Christ, the "Lamb," will be the "lamp" which gives light (Rev 21:23; second reading), and the joy which makes glad the elect for all eternity.

"In that day you will know that I am in my Father and you in me and I in you"... Then at last we shall be able to see what we now believe. Even now you are in us, O Lord, and we are in you, but now we believe it, then we shall have full knowledge of it. Indeed as long as we are in the body as it is now, corruptible and weighing down the soul, we are exiles far from you; we walk in faith and not by vision... You, O Lord, tell us openly that we are in you even now when you say: "I am the vine, you are the branches." On that day when we shall live that life in which death will have been swallowed up, we shall know that you are in the Father, and we in you, and you in us, because then, all that through your work is already begun will arrive at perfection: your home in us and ours in you.

O Lord, at the moment you depart from us you leave us peace; you will give us your peace when you return at the end of time. You leave us peace in this world, you will give us your peace in the life to come. You leave us your peace so that, by remaining in it, we may conquer our enemy; you will give us your peace when we shall reign without fear of enemies. You leave us peace so that, even here, we may love each other; you will give us your peace in heaven, where there can no more be strife.

St. Augustine, *In Io* 75:4; 77;3

189 — MARY'S APOSTOLATE

O Mary, Queen of the apostles, create in me the heart of an apostle.

1. The Council declares: "The perfect example . . . of spiritual and apostolic life is the most Blessed Virgin Mary, Queen of the Apostles. While leading on earth a life common to all men, one filled with family concerns and labors, she was always intimately united with her Son and cooperated in the work of the Savior in a manner altogether special" (AA 4). Mary drew the inspiration and strength of her apostolate from her intense life of prayer and from union with Jesus. Having experienced in intimate contact with God the ineffable reality of his love for men, and being more on fire with it than any other creature, she became more than any other entirely one with the salvific will of God. Indeed she collaborated in a more sublime and efficacious way in the redemptive work of Christ. Hers was an intimate cooperation, for by her blood the Blessed Mother supplied the Son of God with that flesh and human life which made it possible for him, the eternal Word, to become one of us, and to suffer and die for us on the cross. Mary's cooperation was of the highest value since she became the mother of the Savior, willingly and knowingly; in fact, "the Father of mercies willed that the consent of the predestined mother should precede the Incarnation, so that just as a woman contributed to death, so also a woman should contribute to life" (LG 56). Mary

knew from the sacred Scriptures that the Messiah was to be the Man of sorrows, immolated for the redemption of the world. By consenting to become his mother, she thereby consented to link her fate with his and share in all his sufferings. To give a Redeemer to the world, to be willing to see her beloved Son die in torment, was Mary's sublime apostolate, born of her immense love of God.

The greater the love for God, the greater and more effective the apostolate which is derived from it. The reverse is equally true. Every apostolic work which is not animated by charity is *nothing*. "If I give away all I have"—says St. Paul—"if I deliver my body to be burned, but have not love, I gain nothing" (1 Cor 13:3).

2. "Joined by an inseparable bond to the saving work of her Son" (SC 103), Mary accomplished a universal, apostolic mission for the benefit of all mankind. Her apostolate, however, was a quiet one, free from ostentation; it was accomplished in the most humble, hidden and silent way. Mary gave the Redeemer to the world, but in the dark of night, in a poor stable. She shared the whole life of Jesus, but in the obscurity of the little house at Nazareth where she performed the lowly household tasks, amidst the difficulties and sacrifices of a life abounding in unusually toilsome and trying conditions. Even when Jesus, during the three years of his apostolic life, appeared publicly to accomplish the mission entrusted to him by his Father, Mary remained in obscurity, although she followed him and took part in all that happened. She never appeared when her Son was teaching the multitude, nor did she take advantage of her maternal authority to approach him. On one occasion when she sought to speak to him while he was teaching the people in a house, she humbly waited outside (cf Mt 12:46). Mary's apostolate was wholly interior, an apostolate of prayer and, above all, of hidden sacrifice, by means of which she adhered with great love to the will of God. He would ask her to separate herself from her Son after thirty years spent in sweet intimacy with him, to withdraw apart, as if to leave to the apostles and the crowd the place near Jesus which belonged to her as his Mother. Thus in obscurity and silence, Mary shared in the apostolate and sufferings of her Son: Jesus had no sorrow which Mary did not feel and live over again within herself. Her greatest sacrifice consisted in seeing him, her beloved Son, persecuted, hated, condemned to death, and finally crucified on Calvary. Her mother's heart felt the profound bitterness of all this, but at the same time she accepted everything for love, and offered it all for the salvation of souls. It was precisely through her hidden immolation, animated by *pure love,* that Mary reached the uttermost heights of the apostolate. "A little of this pure love"—St. John of the Cross says—"is more precious to God and more beneficial to the Church . . . than all these other works put together" (Sp C 29:2).

Mary shows us how far we are from the truth when, pressed by the urgency of our works, we make our apostolate consist solely in exterior activity, underestimating the interior apostolate of love, prayer, and sacrifice, on which the fruitfulness of our exterior acts depends.

O holy Virgin, form my apostle's heart to the likeness of Jesus' heart; the Father entrusted this Son to you for the whole of his earthly life; it was from you that Jesus learned to love and to offer himself; from you that he learned the joy of sacrifice; this is the real duty of a mother . . . O Mother, stoop down to me and see all that is lacking for me to be an apostle with your Son. You, who received the Spirit a second time in the Cenacle to become the fertile mother of the Mystical Body, O Mother, make an apostle of me.

I ask two special favors of you, and I will not cease begging for them . . . the grace of the spirit of prayer, and the grace of the spirit of humility. That I may be so united to Jesus that all my words may be his words; so convinced of my nothingness, my sinfulness, my uselessness, and of my weakness as never to cultivate the idea of relying on myself, or of being complacent with myself, of wishing to keep even the smallest thing for myself alone. I know that if you help me, if you obtain these two favors for me from Jesus, I will no longer have anything to fear; no longer have to be afraid that my desires for sanctity may be foolish; no longer be afraid of being exalted . . .

I desire to love without measure, to give myself without measure, as I call upon your Son and the Father with the impetuous accents of the Spirit within me, impatient, hungering, distressed—and sure of the salvation of the world, of the return to the Father of all my brothers for whom my priestly heart bleeds until the moment of their return.

P. Lyonnet, *Spiritual Writings*

O immaculate Virgin, O tenderest Mother! . . . you rejoiced that Jesus gave us his life and the infinite treasures of his divinity. How can we not love you and bless you, O Mary, for such great generosity.

You love us as Jesus loves us, and for our sake you are willing to live far from him. To love means to give all, to give one's self, and you wanted to prove that by remaining our support. The Savior knew well the secrets of your mother's heart, the immensity of your tenderness . . . Jesus left us to you, O Refuge of Sinners, when he left the cross to wait for us in heaven.

O Mary, I see you on Calvary's height, standing near the cross like a priest at the altar, offering the sweet Emmanuel, your dear Jesus, to appease the Father's justice. O desolate Mother, a prophet said of you: "There is no sorrow like to your sorrow." O Queen of martyrs, standing there bereft, you pour out all your heart's blood for us.

St. Therese of the Child Jesus, *Poems* 34:21-23

190 — MARY'S MEDIATION

O God, who through the fruitful virginity of blessed Mary bestowed on mankind the rewards of eternal salvation; grant that we may experience her intercession (Roman Missal, Sol. Mother of God)

1. "The Blessed Virgin is invoked by the Church under the titles of Advocate, Auxiliatrix, Adjutrix, and Mediatrix" (LG 62). These titles express her special mission concerning the relations of mankind with her beloved Son. "We have but one Mediator . . . Christ Jesus"—states the Council—"the maternal duty of Mary toward men in no way obscures or diminishes this unique mediation of Christ, but rather shows its power . . . in no way does it impede the immediate union of the faithful with Christ; rather it fosters it" (cf LG 60). How could it ever be thought that Mary, who was so deeply dedicated to the cause of her Son and united with him in one single aim, could be an obstacle in the relationship of the faithful with her Jesus? It is she who has given the world its only Redeemer and Mediator, who in her role as Mother opens to all men the way to her Son and introduces them to his knowledge and love. It is she who, "when she is being preached and venerated . . . summons the faithful to her Son and his service, and to love for the Father" (ib. 65). This all comes about through the positive will of God, who willed to give the world its Redeemer by means of Mary. "When the time had fully come, God sent forth his Son born of a woman"—we read in St. Paul (Gal 4:4). Since she is so closely linked to the Savior, Mary fulfills her function as mediatrix in the highest degree, but always in a way subordinate to him. "All the saving influences of the Blessed Virgin on men"—defines the Council—"flow forth . . . from the superabundance of the merits of Christ, rest on his mediation, depend entirely on it, and draw all their power from it" (LG 60). This in no way prevents Mary's mediation from being real and most precious. We may and should resort to her with full confidence without any fear of confiding too much in her whom Jesus himself gave us as mother. The Liturgy likewise urges us to address ourselves to God through the powerful intercession of Mary: "O God . . . grant that we may be helped in coming to you by the intercession of her whom we believe to be the Mother of God" (RM Mass BVM #4).

2. Mary is Mediatrix between her Son and us for a twofold reason: she *gives* Jesus to us and she *brings us* to him. The Gospel tells us this several times, showing us the typically maternal attitude of Mary as she brought Jesus to mankind. Our Lady offered the Infant Jesus to the adoration of the shepherds and the wisemen; she took him to the temple and presented him to Simeon; by her intercession at Cana, she obtained the first miracle from her Son. On Calvary Mary "united herself with a maternal heart to his sacrifice, and lovingly consented to the immolation of

this victim which she herself had brought forth" (LG 58) and offered it to the Father for the salvation of mankind. In the Cenacle she begged the plenitude of the Holy Spirit for the Apostles and, from that day to the day of her Assumption, she sustained the infant Church by her prayers and maternal encouragement. To find Mary is to find Jesus. This is the whole reason for her existence and her mission: to give Jesus to the world and to souls, and with Jesus, to give his grace and blessings.

Besides, Mary leads men to Jesus: "By her maternal charity"—says the Council—"Mary cares for the brethren of her Son who still journey on earth surrounded by dangers and difficulties, until they are led to their happy fatherland" (LG 62). Mary is the mother, ever solicitous for the eternal salvation of the faithful, begging the grace for them to attain it, and gently calling them back to the right road when they stray; she supplies for their insufficiencies, disposes hearts to open up submissively to grace, and tries to shape them in such a way that they may be pleasing to her Son. As Jesus is the way that leads to the Father, so Mary is the way that leads to Christ. "The Church does not hesitate to profess this role of Mary (as mediatrix). She experiences it continuously, commends it to the hearts of the faithful, so that, encouraged by this maternal help, they may more closely adhere to the Mediator and Redeemer" (ib.).

Draw me after you, O Virgin Mary, that I may run to the fragrance of your perfume.

Draw me after you, for the weight of my sins drags me back . . . Draw me after you, for the malice of wicked enemies deceives me . . . Just as no one comes to your blessed Son unless the Father draw him, so can I also say with certainty that no one comes to your glorious Son unless you draw him by your holy prayers . . . By word and by example you teach true wisdom, since you are the teacher of the wisdom of God; you obtain grace for sinners and promise glory to those who honor you.

You have found grace with God, O sweet Virgin Mary . . . sanctified in the womb of your mother, greeted by the angel, filled with the Holy Spirit, you conceived the Son of God . . . And you received these graces, O humble Virgin, not for yourself alone, but for us also, so that you might assist us in every need.

R. Jourdan, *Contemplationes de B.V.M.*

O Mary, your name has been on my lips and in my heart from my early infancy. When I was a child I learnt to know you as a Mother, turn to you in danger, and trust to your intercession. You see in my heart the desire to know the truth, to practice virtue, to be prudent and just, strong and patient, a brother to all.

O Mary, help me to keep my purpose of living as a faithful disciple of Jesus, for the building up of Christian society and the joy of the holy Catholic Church.

I greet you, Mother, morning and evening; I pray to you as I go upon my way; from you I hope for the inspiration and encouragement that will enable me to fulfill the sacred promises of my earthly vocation, give glory to God, and win eternal salvation.

O Mary! like you in Bethlehem and on Golgotha, I too wish to stay always close to Jesus. He is the eternal King of all ages and all peoples. Amen.

John XXIII, *Prayers and Devotions,* May 2nd

191 — MOTHER OF THE CHURCH

Blessed are you among women, and blessed is the fruit of your womb (Lk 1:42)

1. Vatican Council II stressed the special position of the Blessed Virgin Mary in the history of salvation, and therefore in the history and life of the Church. Mary, the humble daughter of the old Israel, is at the same time the first-born and the mother of the new, somewhat similar to the way in which she is both the child and the mother of God. She is the firstborn daughter of the Church in that she is the first fruit of salvation, "redeemed in an especially sublime manner by reason of the merits of her Son" (LG 53), and therefore the first branch grafted onto Christ, the first member of his mystical Body. But Mary is above all the mother of the Church, for she had been destined from all eternity to be the mother of him who was to give life to the Church itself. The salvation promised by God from the very beginning of the human race came to mankind through this humble Virgin; it took place "when the Son of God took a human nature from her, that he might in the mysteries of his flesh free man from sin" (LG 55). Thus Mary, the first-born of the redeemed became the mother of the redeemed, the mother of the new People of God, so much so that the Fathers "comparing her with Eve, call Mary 'the mother of the living,' and still more often they say 'death through Eve, life through Mary' " (LG 56). The Mother of the Savior is by right the mother of the saved, not only because she begot the Savior unto temporal life, but also because she was intimately associated with his work of salvation. "She conceived, brought forth, and nourished Christ. She presented him to the Father in the temple, and was united with him in suffering as he died on the cross. In an utterly singular way, she cooperated . . . in the Savior's work of restoring supernatural life to souls" (LG 61). Through her union with her Son every act of Mary has salvific value, and the motherly office that she exercises toward him extends to all who believe in him. At the foot of the cross, when Jesus entrusted her to John, and in the Cenacle where she awaited the Holy Spirit amid the disciples, she appears fully in her role of Mother of the Church, which finds support in her maternal heart, and draws strength and apostolic fecundity from her prayer.

2. The Blessed Mother is also "intimately united with the Church" in that she is its model "in the matter of faith, charity, and perfect union with Christ" (LG 63). Mary believed in God and in all his promises without the least shadow of doubt in the most obscure and difficult circumstances, and persevered unshakeably in her faith even when faced with her Son's death at a moment when everything seemed to be collapsing; she is the supreme exemplar of the faith of the Church. Troubles, contradictions and internal defections as well as persecutions and external contests—none of these must diminish faith, and although temptation, doubt and error may threaten, the Church finds support for its faith in Mary. It is precisely because of her faith that the Blessed Mother—as the Liturgy sings—has the power, by herself, to destroy every heresy. (RM 1956, Com Feast BVM).

She is the model of charity. The Virgin of Nazareth who loved God and men more than any other creature ever could, "in her own life lived an example of that maternal love by which all should be fittingly animated who cooperate in the apostolic mission of the Church on behalf of the rebirth of men" (LG 65). The Church—hierarchy and laity—has only to take Mary as its model in order to understand how and in what measure it is to acquit itself of its mission of charity, consecrating itself totally to the service of God and men. But another motive also urges the Church to follow in the steps of the Mother of God and its own mother; like Mary, the Church, too, is mother and virgin through her union with Christ. She is a mother because "by her preaching and by baptism she brings forth to a new and immortal life children who are conceived of the Holy Spirit and born of God. She is a virgin who keeps whole and pure the fidelity she has pledged to her Spouse" (LG 64). The Church achieves all this at an ever higher level by contemplating Mary and endeavoring to imitate her virtues, particularly her perfect adherence to the will of God and her fidelity in welcoming and guarding the divine word. It is the way every member of the Church should follow in order to grow continually in charity and faith, or better—as the Council says—"to keep intact a firm hope and sincere charity" (ibid).

O Mary, you are truly blessed among women, for you changed Eve's curse into a blessing, and through you Adam too . . . was blessed. Truly you are blessed among women, for through you the Father's blessing has been spread over mankind, freeing us from the ancient curse. Truly you are blessed among women, for through you your ancestors found salvation, since you were to give birth to the Savior who would win salvation for them. You are truly blessed, for without seed you have borne as fruit, him who blesses the entire world and redeems it from the curse that made it sprout thorns. You are truly blessed among women, because, though a woman by nature, you will become in reality the mother of God. If he whom you are to bear is truly God made flesh, then rightly do we call you the Mother of God, for you will have given birth to God.

St. Sophronius of Gerus, *In Deiparae Annuntiationem* 2:22

O Virgin Mary, we confide the whole Church to you . . . O "Help of Bishops," protect and assist the Bishops in their apostolic mission, and also all the priests, religious and laity who cooperate in their arduous labors.

You, who were given as Mother to the beloved disciple by your divine Son himself at the moment of his redeeming death, be mindful of the Christian people who put their trust in you. Remember all your children; add weight to their prayers before God, keep their faith strong; strengthen their hope; increase their love. Remember those who are overwhelmed with tribulation and hardship and danger; especially those who are suffering persecution and are in prison for their faith. Obtain strength for them, O Virgin, and hasten the longed-for day of just freedom. Look kindly upon our separated brethren, and deign to unite us, you who brought forth Christ, who is the bridge that unites God and men.

O temple of light, without shadow or stain, intercede with your only-begotten Son, the mediator of our reconciliation with the Father, that he may be merciful toward our shortcomings, and drive all discord from among us, giving our souls the joy of loving.

Paul VI, *Teachings* v.2

192 — THE ASCENSION OF THE LORD

Thursday of the Sixth Week after Easter

God has gone up with a shout of joy; sing praises to God; sing praises to our King, for God is king of all the earth (Ps 47:5-7)

1. The Ascension of the Lord is the crowning of his resurrection. It is his official entry into the glory which was due him after the humiliation of Calvary; the return to the Father which he had foretold on Easter day: "I am ascending to my Father and your Father, to my God and your God" (Jn 20:17) were his words to Magadalen. And to the disciples of Emmaus he had said: "Was it not necessary that the Christ should suffer these things and so enter into his glory?" (Lk 24:26). This shows he was not indicating a future return and glorification, but one that was immediate and already present because it was closely connected with the resurrection. Still, in order to strengthen the disciples in the faith, it was necessary for all to take place in a visible manner, as it did for the forty days after Easter. Those who had seen our Lord die on the cross, amid insults and jeers, must be witnesses to his final exaltation into heaven.

The evangelists treat the facts with considerable moderation, yet their account makes Christ's power and glory stand out: "All authority in heaven and on earth has been given to me" (Mt 28:18), and Mark adds: "The Lord Jesus . . . was taken up into heaven and sat down at the right hand of God" (16:19). On the other hand, Luke records the last great blessing Christ gave his apostles: "While he blessed them, he parted from them and was carried up to heaven" (24:51). Jesus' divine majesty shines through his last talks. He speaks as one who can do everything when he predicts to his disciples that in his name "they will cast out demons, they will speak in new tongues, they will pick up serpents, and if they drink any deadly thing it will not hurt them. They will lay their hands on the sick and they will recover" (Mk 16:17-18). The acts of the Apostles bear their witness to the truth of all this. Then Luke, both in the conclusion of his Gospel and in the Acts, speaks of the great promise of the Holy Spirit who is to confirm the Apostles in their mission and in the powers they have received from Christ: "Behold, I send the promise of my Father upon you" (Lk 24:49); "you shall receive power when the Holy Spirit has come down upon you; and you shall be my witnesses . . . to the end of the earth. And when he had said this, as they were looking on, he was lifted up and a cloud took him out of their sight" (Acts 1:8-9). An exalting spectacle this was that left the apostles astonished, "gazing into heaven," until two angels came to rouse them.

2. A Christian is called to share in the entire mystery of Christ, and hence in his glorification also. He said this himself: "I go to prepare a place for you, and when I go . . . I will come again and will take you to myself, that where I am, you may be also" (Jn 14:2-3). The Ascension is therefore a strong support for hope for us who feel ourselves exiles in our pilgrimage through life, and suffer from being far from God. It is this hope that St. Paul implored for the Ephesians, and desired to see alive in their hearts. "May the God of our Lord Jesus Christ, the Father of glory . . . illumine the eyes of your hearts . . . that you may know what is the hope to which he has called you" (Eph 1:17-18). Upon what did the Apostle base this hope? On the great power of God "which he accomplished in Christ Jesus when he raised him from the dead and made him sit at his right hand in the heavenly places, far above . . . all principality and power [i.e. of the angels] . . . and above every name" (ib. 20-21). The glory of Christ, exalted above every creature, is, in Pauline thought, the proof of what God will do for those, who by adhering to Christ through their faith, and belonging to him as members of a single body of which he is the head, will come to share in his destiny. This authentic Christian teaching allows us to believe and to cherish the firm hope that the faithful today, who share in Christ's death through life's tribulations, will one day also share in his eternal glory.

But the angels who told the Apostles on the mount of the Ascension, "This Jesus who was taken up from you into heaven will come in the same way as you saw him go into heaven"

(Acts 1:11), warned the faithful that they needed to busy themselves with good works while awaiting the final coming of Christ. Christ's earthly mission ends with the Ascension, and that of his disciples begins. The Lord had said to them: "Go therefore, and make disciples of all nations, baptizing them in the name of the Father and of the Son and of the Holy Spirit" (Mt 28:19); it was their duty to make his work of salvation permanent in the world by their preaching, administering the sacraments, and teaching men to live according to the gospel. Moreover Christ wished this to be preceded and prepared for by a period of prayer while they waited for the Holy Spirit who was to confirm and strengthen the Apostles. Thus the life of the Church began, not with action, but with prayer, together "with Mary, the Mother of Jesus" (Acts 1:14).

All-powerful God, look upon your Church which rejoices and gives you thanks in this liturgy of praise, for in the ascension of Christ, our human nature is raised up beside you; grant that we who are members of his body may live the hope that calls us to follow our head into glory (cf Collect, Ascension).

Lord Jesus, the king of glory, the conqueror of sin and death, today you ascended to heaven while the angels sang your praises. Mediator between God and man, judge of the world and Lord of all, you have not abandoned us, but have gone before us into the everlasting dwellings to give us the peaceful confidence that we, your members, will follow where you, the firstborn and the head of the Church, have gone, united with you in the same glory (cf Preface I).

Roman Missal

You have ascended into heaven, O God... you who were enclosed in the womb of a mother, formed by her whom you yourself had formed... you whom the old man Simeon knew as a little one, and honored as great; whom the widow Anna saw suckling and recognized as omnipotent; you, who suffered hunger and thirst for us, who wearied yourself in journeyings for us... you, who were arrested, bound, scourged, crowned with thorns, hung upon the wood of the cross, pierced by a lance; you, dead and buried, ascended into heaven, O God! (Ser 262:4).

Your resurrection, O Lord, is our hope, your ascension our glorification. Grant that we may ascend with you and that our hearts may be raised to you. But grant also that in ascending we may not become proud nor presume on our merits as though they belonged to us; let our hearts be lifted up, but lifted close to you, for to lift them up to anything but you is pride; in raising them to you is security. You who ascend to heaven are made our refuge...

Who is he that ascends? The very one who came down. You came, O Lord, to heal me, you ascended to lift me up. If I raise myself up by myself, I fall; if you raise me up, I remain steady... To you who rise again I say: Lord, you are my hope; to you who ascend into heaven: you are my refuge (Ser 261:1).

St. Augustine

193 — THE HOLY SPIRIT

O Holy Spirit, sent by the Father in the name of Christ to teach us all things, teach us to know you and love you
(Jn 14:26)

1. He charged them: "Do not depart from Jerusalem, but wait for the promise of the Father of which you have heard me speak" (Acts 1:4). In obedience to the instructions they had received, the Apostles joined together in prayer: it was the first Pentecost novena. In harmony with this act of the early Church, it is a beautiful practice during these days for us to turn our minds and hearts to the Holy Spirit in the desire of knowing him better, so as to love him more ardently, and to prepare ourselves for his coming with more intense prayer.

Vatican II says: "God the Father . . . is 'the origin without origin', by whom the Son is begotten, and the Holy Spirit proceeds through the Son" (AG 2). From eternity the Father generates his Word, the perfect, substantial Idea in whom the Father is expressed and to whom he communicates all his goodness, lovableness, divine nature and essence. The Father and the Word, mutually beholding their infinite goodness and beauty, love each other from all eternity, and the expression of this unitive love is a third Person, the Holy Spirit. As the Word is generated by the Father by way of knowledge, so the Holy Spirit proceeds from the Father and the Son by way of love. The Holy Spirit is, therefore, the terminus, and the effusion of the reciprocal love of the Father and the Son, an effusion so substantial and perfect that it is a Person, the third Person of the most holy Trinity, to whom the Father and the Son, by the sublime fruitfulness of their love, communicate their very own nature and essence, without losing any of it themselves. Because the Holy Spirit is the effusion of divine love, he is called "Spirit", according to the Latin sense of the word which means air, respiration, the vital breath. In us, respiration is a sign of life; in God, the Holy Spirit is the expression, the effusion of the life and love of the Father and the Son, but a substantial personal effusion, which is a Person. It is in this sense that the third Person of the Blessed Trinity is called the "Spirit of the Father and the Son", and also "the Spirit of love in God", that is, the breath of divine love. It was in this sense that the Fathers of the Church called the Holy Spirit "the kiss of the Father and the Son", a "sweet, but secret kiss" according to the tender expression of St. Bernard.

Let us invoke the Holy Spirit, the Spirit of love, with the Church, so that he may come to enkindle in our hearts the flame of charity.

2. Although in a veiled manner, the Holy Spirit is already spoken of in the Old Testament, and was even then working in the world. But the explicit revelation of the Holy Spirit and his out-

pouring upon all the people of God were reserved for the New Testament, the fruit and supreme gift of the redemption wrought by Christ. Jesus himself announced that: "When the Paraclete comes, . . . the Spirit of truth who proceeds from the Father . . . will bear witness to me" (Jn 15:26). Jesus shows us the Holy Spirit as a divine Person who "proceeds from the Father", and whom he himself, together with the Father, "will send", precisely because the Holy Spirit also proceeds from him, since he is the Word. This divine Spirit, "the Spirit of truth", will come to continue the work of the Redeemer, and will bear "witness" to him. In fact it will be the Holy Spirit who will interiorly enlighten the Apostles and all who believe in Christ's mystery on the truth of his message and the reality of his divine Person.

He is the Spirit of love in that he proceeds from the mutual love of the Father and the Son, he is the Spirit of truth in that he gives understanding of the divine mysteries and completes Christ's teaching; the special mission of the Holy Spirit is to sanctify the faithful in love and truth. "God's love has been poured into our hearts through the Holy Spirit", says St. Paul (Rom 5:5); and Jesus declared to the Apostles: "The Spirit of truth . . . will guide you into all truth" (Jn 16:13). It is under this aspect that the Church invites us to invoke the Holy Spirit: "Come, O Creator Spirit, visit the minds of your faithful; fill with heavenly grace the souls that you have created" (Veni Creator). He, who with the Father and the Son is one God, the creator of the universe, is thus urged to sanctify his creatures, to illuminate their minds with grace and love. May he who is the "best Gift of God above, the living source, the living fire, sweet unction and true love" come to purify us, to inflame us with his burning love, to comfort us with his sweetness. May he who is "the finger of God's right hand" come to show us the way to holiness, and to be our teacher and our guide.

Holy Spirit, who unite the Father and the Son in one unending beatitude, teach me to live at every moment and in every circumstance, in intimacy with my God, always more perfected in the unity of the Trinity. Above all grant that your Spirit of love may animate the least actions of my life with your holiness, so that for the redemption of souls and the glory of the Father, I may truly be in the Church a host of love in praise of the Trinity.

I beg for a soul of crystal-clear purity, worthy of being a living temple of the Trinity. Holy God, keep my soul whole for Jesus, with all its power to love, unceasingly eager to communicate your infinite purity. Let my soul pass through this corrupt world, holy and spotless in love, alone in your presence, under your gaze alone, without the least blemish or baseness ever darkening the splendor of your beauty in it.

M.M. Philipon, Consecration to the Most Blessed Trinity

O divine fire coming from above, when you begin to inflame man's heart, his passions quickly diminish and lose their strength; however heavy their weight, they become lighter; and in the measure that ardor grows, the human heart may come to feel itself so light as to fly up like a dove . . . (Ps 54:7)

O blessed fire that enlightens without being consumed, and if it does consume, destroys only evil inclinations, so that life may not be extinguished! Who will cause me to be enveloped by this fire? It is a fire that purifies me with the light of true wisdom, which expels from my spirit the darkness of ignorance and the blindness of an erroneous conscience; a fire that transforms the coldness of laziness, selfishness, and negligence into the heat of love. It is a fire that will not let my heart grow hardened, whose warmth makes it always flexible, obedient, and devoted; that frees me from the heavy yoke of earthly cares and worldly desires, and lifts my heart so high on the wings of the holy contemplation that nourishes and increases charity that I can but repeat with the prophet: "Gladden the soul of your servant, for to you, O Lord, do I lift up my soul" (Ps 86:4).

St. Robert Bellarmine, *The Ascent of the Mind to God VI:6*

194 — THE SPIRIT OF CHRIST

O Holy Spirit, who consecrated Christ with your anointing, and guided him throughout his life, deign to direct my footsteps (Lk 4:18,1)

1. In Sacred Scripture, the Holy Spirit is repeatedly called "the Spirit of Christ" (Rom 8:9), "the Spirit of Jesus" (Acts 16:7). Christ is the incarnate Word, made man, but still always remains the Word, the Son of God, from whom, as from the Father, the Holy Spirit proceeds. Therefore we must say that the Holy Spirit is the Spirit of Christ, for the very reason that the Person of Christ is none other than the Word. When we speak of Christ, we mean the Messiah, the Word incarnate, and in this case also, we may say that the Holy Spirit is his Spirit. The Savior's entire life unfolded under the influence of the divine Paraclete. His conception took place through the Holy Spirit who descended upon Mary and overshadowed her; when the Virgin Mother met Elizabeth, she too was invested with the Spirit and, "filled with the Holy Spirit" (Lk 1:41), she greeted in Mary the Mother of God. In a similar way, when Jesus was presented at the temple, Simeon, "inspired by the Spirit" (Lk 2:27), went to meet him and recognized in him the Savior. From the very first moment of his earthly existence, Christ was filled with the Holy Spirit and radiated him. When Jesus went to the Jordan to be baptized, the Baptist bore witness to him, saying: "I saw the Spirit descend as a dove from heaven and it remained on him" (Jn 1:32); this was the external manifestation of the unfathomable fullness of the Holy Spirit which filled

the soul of Christ to overflowing. Jesus possessed the Holy Spirit with a fullness which cannot be measured, not only because as the Word he is one and same with the Father and the Holy Spirit, but also because as man, by virtue of the hypostatic union, his most holy soul is invaded by the divine Spirit. "He whom God has sent"—says St. John—"utters the words of God; for it is not by measure that he gives the Spirit" (Jn 3:34). Jesus, who possessed "the whole fullness of deity" (Col 2:9), also possessed the whole fullness of the Holy Spirit, who is preeminently *his* Spirit.

2. Luke is particularly careful to emphasize how upright all of Jesus' behavior was, and how guided by the Holy Spirit: "Jesus, full of the Holy Spirit, returned from the Jordan, and was led by the Spirit . . . into the wilderness" (4:1); concerning the end of this period the evangelist remarks: "Jesus returned in the power of the Spirit into Galilee" (4:14). The Holy Spirit acted unceasingly in Christ, inspiring all his actions, his preaching, his miracles, and his very prayer, as Luke states very clearly: "Jesus rejoiced in the Holy Spirit and said: 'I praise you, Father, Lord of heaven and earth, that you have hidden these things from the wise and understanding and have revealed them to babes' " (Lk 10:21). Thus the Savior's entire life proceeded under the prompting of the Holy Spirit, and it was under this same impulse that his supreme sacrifice was accomplished according to St. Paul's teaching: "Christ . . . offered himself without blemish to God, . . . through the eternal Spirit" (Heb 9:14).

The divine Spirit was continuously acting in Jesus' soul, which was ever most docile to his promptings. The Holy Spirit met this sublime piece of creation, the soul of Christ, and invaded it, directed it, guided it in the accomplishment of its mission, stimulating it to total adherence to the divine will, and bringing it into God with unparalleled transports, because it was completely under his sway. Just as the Father is well pleased with Christ, his beloved Son, so also the Holy Spirit "finds his delight in the soul of the Redeemer as in his favorite temple" (Myst. Corp.).

By his passion and death, Jesus has merited his Spirit for all mankind and wishes to diffuse it more and more within our hearts, so that the Spirit may direct us throughout our lives and lead us to holiness.

O Holy Spirit, Spirit of the Father and of the Son, who proceeds from them in unity of origin and unites them both in unity of love and of spirit! Spirit of eternal Love, you who subsist personally in the Godhead, and divinely complete the eternal processions! I adore you and give you thanks for that holy and wonderful work with which you accomplished the sacred mystery of the Incarnation! In eternity you are the divine term of the divine procession and you are also, in the fullness of time, the principle of a new state, of the state of hypostatic union which is the source and origin of all the holy operations, of all the emanations of grace which a reverent heaven and earth admire. In the most Blessed Trinity, you are the sacred bond between the divine Persons, and in the Incarnation you unite a divine Person to a human nature . . . You give to the Word, in the bosom of his Mother, a new nature, clothing him with our human nature!

O Holy Spirit! You are the Spirit of Love, and you accomplish on earth that work of love, that divine union, that incomparable alliance that joins earth to heaven, created being to uncreated Being, and God to man, in so close a union that the result is for ever a God-man and Man-God.

P. de Berulle, *Les Grandeurs de Jesus* 2:2

Only you are holy, O Jesus. Only you are holy, because through your incarnation you are true Son of God; only holy because only you possess sanctifying grace in its fullness so as to distribute it to us; only holy because your soul was infinitely docile to the promptings of the Holy Spirit who inspired and regulated all your movements, all your acts, and made them pleasing to your Father.

C. Marmion, Christ, *The Life of the Soul* 1:2

195 — SEVENTH SUNDAY OF EASTER
YEAR A

Father . . . give glory to your Son (Jn 17:1)

Today the Liturgy brings to our minds the priestly prayer of Jesus, and the prayer of the Apostles in the company of Mary while awaiting the Holy Spirit; a fitting theme for preparing our souls for the approach of Pentecost.

Jesus uttered his priestly prayer aloud in the Cenacle, surrounded by his disciples, with his passion close at hand: "Father, the hour has come! Glorify your Son that the Son may glorify you, since you have given him power over all flesh to give eternal life to all whom you have given him" (Jn 17:1-2). Jesus' thought is turned toward his "hour", the hour of his death, through which he will enter into the glory of the resurrection, and at the same time into that glory which, as the Son of God, he had had with the Father before the world was made (ib. 5). When he came into the world, he emptied himself of this glory to take "the form of a servant" (Phil 2:7), but now that he is about to leave the world through death, he asks to be brought into it again. In fact, his mission cannot be completed with death—a dead man neither gives glory to God nor life to men; death is the first indispensable act, but it necessarily demands a second: resurrection in glory. Precisely because he will rise again in glory after voluntarily accepting death, Christ will glorify the Father and will save mankind, having the power to give us eternal life. This is why, in asking for his own glorification, Jesus is but asking for the glory of the Father and the salvation of us all.

After praying for himself, Jesus prays for his Apostles. they belong to the Father not only because they are his creatures, but also because they were chosen by him for his apostolate, and the Father gave them to the Son on account of that choice: "Yours they were and you gave them to me" (Jn 17:6). Jesus has loved them and cared for them with a self-abnegation that was more than paternal, that was divine. He has shared with them his mystery of being the Son of God and transmitted to them the words of the Father to which they had corresponded: "I have given them the words which you gave me, and they welcomed them" (ib. 8). Now that Jesus is about to leave them, he is anxious about them; he seems reluctant to leave them in the world, exposed to danger and strife, and he confides them to the Father with touching tenderness: "I am praying for them . . . for those whom you have given me, for they are yours . . . I am no more in the world, but they are in the world, and I am coming to you" (ib. 9,11). The Apostles must remain to continue his mission, but the Father will watch over them: "Holy Father, keep them in your name" (ib. 11).

Some fifty days later when Jesus had passed through death and had already entered into his glory, the Apostles were again together in the Cenacle. The Master is no longer there to pray among them and for them, but Mary is there to uphold them with her presence. They have not forgotten the prayer of Jesus, which they will one day hand down to us in written form—and we can well imagine that they made it their own; they ask as he did for the glory of the Father and for salvation for men, and implore for themselves the help they need to be faithful witnesses to Christ. In this manner they await the coming of the Holy Spirit, persevering "with one accord . . . in prayer together . . . with Mary, the Mother of Jesus" (Acts 1:14). Thus should the faithful of every age prepare themselves for Pentecost: glorifying God with prayer and with good works, disposing their hearts to receive the Holy Spirit, praying for the Church and its shepherds, and for the salvation of all men. Mary is always there in the midst of the faithful to inspire and strengthen their prayer.

O Father, glorify your Son! Establish his reign in the hearts of all who love him; bring under his scepter the souls that have turned away from him; draw to him those, who sitting in darkness, do not yet know him! Father, glorify your Son, so that in his turn, he may glorify you in manifesting to us your divine being, your perfection, your will!

O Jesus, most powerful High-Priest, now that you are seated at the right hand of the Father and enjoy your victory and power in all its fullness, ask your Father, as you promised, to send us another comforter. Through the sufferings of your humanity you merited this grace for us; the Father will hear you because he loves you.

C. Marmion, *Christ in His Mysteries* 17, p. 337

O Lord, you promised the Father: "I shall make known your name to my brothers; in the midst of the assembly, I shall sing your praises".

Sing, O Word, the praises of the Father, and make your Father known to me! Your words will save me and your song will teach me. Up until now I have erred in my search for God. But now that you enlighten me, Lord, you help me to find him who is my God and your Father, and I welcome him through you. I become an heir with you from the moment that you are not ashamed of your brother.

Clement of Alexandria, *Protrepticus,* 11

YEAR B

O holy Father, keep us in your name, consecrate us in the truth (Jn 17:11,17)

There emerges from today's readings the portrait of an apostle, the disciple of Christ, outlined in the Gospel in the priestly prayer of our Lord and completed by the other two readings.

Before parting from his Apostles to go to his passion, Jesus gave them into his Father's care, to watch over them in his place. He knew he was leaving them exposed to the dangers and hostility of that "world" for which he said he was not praying (Jn 17:9). We are not speaking here of the world as the creation of God, which is always good in itself, but of the world of sin, ruled by the devil. The Apostles do not belong to him—"they are not of the world"—and for this very reason "the world has hated them" (ib. 14); nevertheless they would have to live in it to accomplish their mission. Therefore Jesus said to his Father: "I do not pray that you should take them out of the world, but that you should keep them from the evil one" (ib. 15). This prayer indicates the guidelines of behavior for every apostle: to live in the world to make it Christian, without allowing himself to be swept away by its snares, nor fearing its hatred, which is assured him since he does not belong to it. Of all the snares of the world, the one most to be feared is error, which by distorting conscience drags us into every kind of ruin. This was the reason Jesus asked his Father: "Sanctify them in the truth; your word is truth" (ib. 17). It is the truth which comes from God—his word—which must characterize the apostles and immunize them from the world's errors; they must therefore be "sanctified" in this truth and completely dedicated to its service. By separating them from the unsanctified world, this consecration consecrates them to truth even to the sacrifice of self, after the example of the Master who "consecrated himself" for their sake even to sacrifice on the cross. Such is the meaning of his words: "For their sake, I consecrate myself, that they also may be consecrated in truth" (ib. 19).

Jesus' prayer is deeply overshadowed by the thought of the traitor: "I guarded them"—he says to the Father—"and none of them is lost, but the son of perdition, that the Scriptures might be fulfilled" (ib. 12). This loss which so pained him and had been foreseen, but not caused, by the prophecies, is proof that only one who deliberately resists God's love is lost. At this point the Acts of the Apostles (1st reading) relate the election of Matthias to fill the place left vacant by Judas. The criterion for the choice is interesting: the man to be chosen must have followed Jesus from the beginning of his public life until his death, because—as St. Peter says—he "must become with us a witness to his resurrection" (Acts 1:22). The apostle of every time is called to give witness to the resurrection of our Lord, for it is the irrefutable proof of his divinity and of his power as Savior. But how does one bear witness today to a fact which took place many centuries ago? Scripture gives the documentation, yet many refuse to accept it. But there is a still more convincing argument, the behavior of the apostles, particularly their love for each other, which as Jesus asked, must make them "one" (Jn 17:11). This is the theme developed by the second reading: "If we love one another God abides in us" (1 Jn 4:12). And he dwells in us not only for the life and joy of those who believe in him, but also because through their love they make him present to their brothers and help them to believe. Through their love they testify that "the Father has sent his Son as the savior of the world" (ib. 14), that the Jesus whom they preach as having died and risen again for the redemption of mankind is not a myth, but that he redeemed them in such a way that they are made capable of overcoming all selfishness even to their all becoming as "one".

O Lord God, our one and highest good, by this holy exchange of gifts you share your divine life with us; grant that our lives may bear witness to the truth with which you enlighten us.

Roman Missal, *Offertory,* 6th Wed. of Easter

"I have given your word to them". That word that drew your followers from the world, oh! may it still produce this effect! Every time we hear or read your word, O Jesus, may this word of yours which came out from God, lead us back whence it began. This is the word that does not let us find delight in the world, because it makes us savor the truth that the world neither knows nor wants to know, because the truth judges it. The world is false in everything, a deceiver in everything, and your word, O Jesus, opens our eyes to see this illusion, this deceitfulness of the world. Your word forms the pure delight of souls who are disillusioned and disgusted with the world.

Grant, O Lord that I may savor your word, so that the world may not surprise me with its deceits . . . May I penetrate and probe this word to its depths, put it in my heart, and never tire of proclaiming it . . . Let it be my comfort in exile, my counsel, my light, my love, my hope. Grant that when I listen to it, I may understand it,

and recognize that that understanding is also your gift, O Lord.
cf J.B. Bossuet, *Meditations on the Gospels* II. 52:2

YEAR C

Heavenly Father, I pray that we may all be one, that the world may believe (Jn 17:21)

The Liturgy of the last Sunday of Easter could be defined as a summary of the wonderful fruits of the Paschal mystery: the descent of the Holy Spirit, the testimony of the disciples, the union of the faithful, and the final return of Christ.

The first reading (Acts 7:55-60) shows us Stephen, "full of the Holy Spirit", who, after his courageous speech to the Sanhedrin, is going to be permitted to gaze into the sanctuary of the divinity: "Behold I see the heavens opened and the Son of Man standing at the right hand of God" (ib. 56). This last statement opens the way to his martyrdom: he is the first disciple to follow the Master unto death. But whereas Jesus suffered in the darkness of agony, Stephen contemplates in rapture the heavens opened, precisely because he is enjoying the fruits of his Lord's horrible death, who, by his death on the cross, had earned strength for all the martyrs, and when ascended into heaven, had sent his Spirit to all the faithful. The promise of Jesus is fulfilled in Stephen in a wonderful way: "You shall receive power when the Holy Spirit has come upon you, and you shall be my witnesses" (Acts 1:8). These infallible words are to be the strong support of every persecuted Christian.

But there is another testimony the faithful must give to Christ: their fraternal union. This is the concern of the last passage of Jesus' prayer that is offered for our meditation today. Having prayed for his Apostles, our Lord prays for all those who through the centuries will believe in him, and asks that: "they all may be one; even as you, Father, are in me and I in you, that they also may be one in us" (Jn 17:21). The union he asked for us who believe was above all union with the Father and with the Son, the sole source of our mutual union. We are mature as Christians when we achieve a personal encounter with God, which then overflows into our personal encounter with our brothers; the first encounter is the base, the foundation for the second, while the second is the visible and real test of the authenticity of the first. Jesus wants our union with God and among ourselves to be something so perfect that it reflects the union that exists between himself and the Father: "that they may be one, even as we are one" (ib. 22); to be a motive of credibility for the world: "that the world may believe that you have sent me" (ib. 21). He insists on this point in a quite impressive way: "I in them, and you in me—that they may become perfectly one—so that the world may know that you have sent me and have loved them even as you have loved me" (ib. 23). We could say that Jesus confides the faith of the world to our ability to demonstrate by means of our fraternal union, the love with which God loves and saves mankind. It is a tremendous responsibility and one to which we give all too little thought; may not the weakness of the faith of modern society be perhaps attributed to weakness of unity among us believers? The one way to remedy this deficiency is to make room for Jesus so that he may live fully in his faithful—"I in them . . .", he says, that he may love in us all and unite us all in his love.

Nevertheless, absolutely perfect union exists only in heaven; on earth it is impossible for it not to feel the limitations of the creature. Still, it is a goal toward which we need to strive without ever tiring, by continually calling for divine help. "Come, Lord Jesus" (Rev 22:20; 2nd reading) is the last cry of Scripture and the unceasing sigh of the Church, as it awaits the final return of the Lord, calling upon him continually to come to sustain and strengthen the unity of her children.

Lord, pour out upon us the fullness of your mercy, and by the power of your Spirit remove divisions among Christians. Let your Church be more clearly revealed as a sign for all the nations, that the world may be filled with the light of your Spirit and believe in Jesus Christ whom you have sent.

Roman Missal, *Mass of Christian Unity C, Collect*

God and Lord of the universe, in your goodness make us worthy of this hour, in spite of our wretchedness; make us united to each other without insincerity or pretense, by the bond of peace and charity: make our union strong through the sanctifying action of your divine knowledge, with the help of your only Son, our Lord God and Savior, Jesus Christ. Be blessed and glorified with him and with the most Holy Spirit, the Spirit of goodness who gives life . . . You are the God of peace, of mercy, of charity, of pardon and of goodness, with your only Son and the most Holy Spirit.

Lord, may your peace and your serenity, your charity and your grace, and the loving mercy of your Godhead be with us and among us all the days of our life.

Early Christian Prayers 301; 308

196 — SWEET GUEST OF THE SOUL

O Holy Spirit, who dwell within us, make us a temple of your glory (R M Tues. 7th week of Easter)

1. The Acts of the Apostles relate the case of the Christians of Ephesus who, though baptized with John's baptism, had not only not received the Holy Spirit, but did not even know of his existence. Paul therefore instructed them and baptized them "in the name of the Lord Jesus" and when he "had laid his hands upon them, the Holy Spirit came on them" (Acts 19:5-6). John's bap-

tism was but a preparation, as he had said himself: "I baptize you with water, but he who is mightier than I is coming . . . He will baptize you with the Holy Spirit and with fire" (Lk 3:16). It was of this latter baptism that Jesus spoke to Nicodemus: "Truly I say to you, unless one is born of water and the Holy Spirit, he cannot enter the kingdom of God" (Jn 3:5); this is the baptism through which Christ shares his Spirit with the Church and with all the faithful, that they may live his very life. "In order that . . . we may be unceasingly renewed in him"—teaches Vatican Council II—(Christ) "has shared with us his Spirit, who existing as one and the same being in the head and in the members, gies life, unity and movement to the whole body. This he does in such a way that his work could be compared by the holy Fathers with the function which the soul fulfills in the human body, whose principle of life the soul is" (LG 7). By virtue of Christ's baptism, the Holy Spirit—the third Person of the most Holy Trinity, equal in all things to the Father and to the Son, the Spirit of love proceeding from the Father and the Son, the life-giving Spirit that rules the life of the Savior—descends upon the Church and upon each of the faithful, giving life to the Church as a whole and to each individual member. "One and the same" in Christ, in the Church and in the faithful, the Holy Spirit is the vital and sanctifying principle of the Church; through him the Church and each of the faithful live in Christ and of Christ. Whoever belongs to Christ has the Spirit of Christ, says St. Paul (Rom 8:9).

2. "If you love me, you will keep my commandments, and I will pray the Father and he will give you another Counselor to be with you forever, even the Spirit of truth" (Jn 14:15-17). When Jesus promises the Holy Spirit to his disciples, he makes only one condition: genuine love, which is proved by deeds, through a generous compliance with the divine will. The Holy Spirit, the Spirit of love, cannot be given to any one who does not live in love. But the Holy Spirit is assured to any one who lives in love and therefore in grace, by the infallible promise and all-powerful prayer of Jesus. It is not a question of a passing gift restricted to the moment in which the sacraments are received, or perhaps limited to a particular time, but of a stable, permanent gift: the Holy Spirit is sent in order to "abide" with us forever. The divine Paraclete "abides" in the faithful in the state of grace: "in whose hearts the Holy Spirit dwells as in his temple" states the Council (LG 9). He is "the sweet guest of the soul" (Seq.) and the more the soul grows in grace and love, the more the Holy Spirit is pleased to dwell in it, and act within it to bring about its sanctification.

The Holy Spirit abides in us in order to form us into Christ's image, to urge us to fulfill God's will, to support us in our struggle against evil and in attaining good. "The Spirit helps us in our weakness" (Rom 8:26), and by making our cause his own, "he himself intercedes for us" (ib.) with the Father. If the baptized have so powerful an advocate, and so vigorous a support, why do we so rarely reach sanctity? This is the awful mystery of our freedom, and at the same time of our responsibility. God created us free, he does not sanctify us against our will. If we Christians do not attain holiness it is simply because we do not give full liberty to the action of the Holy Spirit within us, but hinder him by our sins, and our lack of docility and generosity. If we would use our freedom to open ourselves completely to the invasion of the divine Paraclete and submit to his promptings in everything he would take us under his guidance and make us saints. So we need to pray with the Church: "Come, Holy Spirit, wash the stains of guilt away, on our dryness pour your dew . . . bend the stubborn heart and will, melt the frozen, warm the chill . . ." (Seq.).

O holy Spirit, Paraclete, perfect in us the work begun by Jesus: enable us to continue to pray fervently in the name of the whole world; hasten in every one of us the growth of a profound interior life; give vigor to our apostolate so that it may reach all men and all peoples, all redeemed by the blood of Christ, and all belonging to him. Mortify in us our natural pride, and raise us to the realms of holy humility, of true fear of God, and of generous courage. Let no earthly bond prevent us from honoring our vocation, no cowardly consideration disturb the claims of justice, no meanness confine the immensity of charity within the narrow bounds of petty selfishness. Let everything in us be on a grand scale: the search for truth and our devotion to it, and readiness for self-sacrifice, even to the cross and death; and may everything finally be according to the last prayer of the Son to his heavenly Father and according to your Spirit, O Spirit of love, which the Father and the Son desired to be poured out over the Church and her institutions, over the souls of men and over nations.

John XXIII, *Prayers and Devotions,* Nov. 13

O powerful Spirit, send the dew of your sweetness, and grant that, with my senses under control, my soul and my spirit may enjoy the fullness of the graces of your great mercy. Cultivate the impressionable ground of my hardened heart of flesh so that it may be able to receive your spiritual seed and make it bear fruit.

We confess that only through your great wisdom do the gifts blossom and grow in us. It is you who ordain the apostles, inspire the prophets, instruct the doctors, give speech to the dumb and open the ears of the deaf . . .

Be very near to protect me, and strengthen me with the grace of your compassion; dispel the dismal fog of negligence from my spirit and with it scatter the darkness of sin that I may be able to rise with penetrating understanding from earthly life to the eternal heights.

St. Gregory of Narek, *Book of Prayers*

197 — THE SPIRIT OF THE CHILDREN OF GOD

O Holy Spirit who bear witness that we are the children of God, make me a true child of God *(Rom 8:16)*

1. In baptism, the faithful soul is mysteriously associated with Christ's death and resurrection, and receives his Spirit, who justifies it by regenerating it in a new life. "He saved us"—says St. Paul—"by the baptism of regeneration and renewal in the Holy Spirit (Tit 3:5). With baptism the Holy Spirit begins his work of sanctification in us, which is especially one of "purification," that is, a purification from sin and a "regeneration" through grace. In this way, man, "redeemed by Christ and made a new creature in the Holy Spirit" (GS 37), receives from him a new spirit, the spirit of adoption as a child of God. "God has sent forth the spirit of his Son into our hearts, crying 'Abba' (Father!)" (Gal 4:6), declares the Apostle. We attribute the grace and the spirit of adoption in a special way to the Holy Spirit, who is the Spirit of the Son. It is the Holy Spirit who infuses into us at baptism the sense of being God's child, who urges us to turn to God with filial trust, calling him "Father," and in addition makes us certain of his adoption. "The Spirit himself bears witness with our spirit that we are children of God" (Rom 8;16).

The sacrament of confirmation marks a second stage of the action of the Holy Spirit within us. St. Luke relates that Peter and John "laid their hands on them [the Samaritans] and they received the Holy Spirit; they had only been baptized in the name of the Lord Jesus" (Acts 8:16-17). This is what takes place in each of us as a result of the sacrament of confirmation: the Holy Spirit renews his outpouring in us, and confirms us in the spirit of a child of God in our faith and in our practice of Christian life.

Besides, the Holy Spirit does not act only through baptism and confirmation, but in each of the other sacraments also; the Liturgy of these days especially recalls his action in regard to penance, affirming that "he is our forgiveness" (RM Sat. before Pent.). Since the action of Christ is present in all the sacraments, the action of the Holy Spirit cannot be lacking. All Christian life, beginning at birth, is enveloped in the secret and mysterious action of the Holy Spirit; in him every one who believes is made alive and sanctified and made through him a son in the Son.

2. Speaking of the Holy Spirit, the Council says: "He is the Spirit of life, a fountain of water, springing up to life eternal. Through him the Father gives life to men" (LG 4). Although the grace that gives us spiritual life is the gift of the whole Trinity, still we attribute its creation particularly to the Father, and that it was merited for us by the Son through his passion and death, and is diffused in our souls by the Holy Spirit; in fact it is to him, the Spirit of love, that the work of our sanctification is attributed in a special way. This work is not limited to the sacraments; the Holy

Spirit is always active in the hearts of the baptized; he is the interior teacher who "sanctifies and leads the People of God and enriches it with virtues" (LG 12). Above all the Holy Spirit arouses and sustains in believers "their sense of faith" (ib.), giving them a deep understanding of Christ and of his gospel, according to what our Lord himself said: "the Paraclete, the Holy Spirit whom the Father will send in my name, will instruct you in everything" (Jn 14:26). The Holy Spirit accomplishes this duty not only by enlightening us interiorly, but also through external means, and especially by the Sacred Scriptures and the teachings of the Church.

"Holy Scripture is the word of God inasmuch as it is consigned to writing under the inspiration of the Spirit of God;" it makes "the voice of the Holy Spirit resound in the words of the prophets and apostles" (DV 9,21). This is the reason why meditating on the sacred books is something like "going to the school" of the divine Paraclete, who, while helping the mind to penetrate the meaning of God's word, moves the will to put it into practice. Also, through the magisterium of the Church, the Holy Spirit instructs, enlightens and calls upon us, for he was given to the Church to guide her "into all the truth" (Jn 16:13), preserving her from error and deviation.

When we are docile to the light and to the internal and external promptings of the Holy Spirit, and are resolved to act in accordance with these impulses, the Spirit himself accompanies us and assists us with actual grace so that we can bring our virtuous undertakings to completion. In this way the Holy Spirit is continually assisting God's children, guiding and sustaining them in their search for truth, and in their practice of evangelical perfection.

My God . . . the living Love wherewith the Father and the Son love each other, you are the author of supernatural love in our hearts—the living spring, fire, charity . . . I acknowledge you as the giver of that great gift, by which alone we are saved, supernatural love. Man is by nature blind and hard-hearted in all spiritual matters; how is he to reach heaven? It is by the flame of your grace, which consumes him in order to new-make him, and so to fit him to enjoy what without you he would have no taste for.

It is you, O almighty Paraclete, who have been and are the strength, the vigor and endurance of the martyr in the midst of his torments. You are the stay of the confessor in his long, tedious, and humiliating toils. You are the fire, by which the preacher wins souls, without thought of himself, in his missionary labors.

By you we wake up from the death of sin, to exchange the idolatry of the creature for the pure love of the Creator. By you we make acts of faith, hope, charity, and contrition. By you we live in the atmosphere of earth, proof against its infection. By you we are able to consecrate ourselves to the sacred ministry, and fulfill our awful engagements to it. By the fire which you kindled within us, we pray, and meditate, and do penance. As well could our bodies live, if the sun were extinguished, as our souls, if you are away.

My most holy Lord and Sanctifier, whatever there is of good in me is yours. Without you, I should but get worse and worse as years went on. Increase in me this grace of love, in spite of all my unworthiness. It is more precious than anything else in the world. I accept it in place of all the world can give me. O give it to me! It is my life.

J.H. Newman, *Meditations on Christian Doctrine,* XIV, 4

O Lord, we beg you to grant us keener understanding . . . and to open our senses more fully to the truth, so that by reflecting in the Holy Spirit on what was written by the Holy Spirit, and by expressing the realities of the Spirit in a spiritual way, we may be able to explain the Scriptures according to God and the Holy Spirit who has inspired them.

Origen, *Early Christian Prayers* 58

198 — THE SPIRIT OF THE CHURCH

O Holy Spirit, grant that the Church, united in your love, "be of one heart and soul" (Acts 4:32)

1. The Church which was founded by Christ to prolong his work of salvation through the centuries, is animated by his same Spirit; in fact, on the very day of Pentecost, strengthened by the divine Paraclete, she began her mission to the world by proclaiming the gospel. "It was from Pentecost"—teaches the Council—"that the 'Acts of the Apostles' took their origin. In a similar way, Christ was conceived when the Holy Spirit came upon the Virgin Mary. Thus too Christ was impelled to the work of his ministry when the same Holy Spirit descended upon him at prayer" (AG 4).

The Church lives, grows and operates in the world under the influence and guidance of the Holy Spirit, whom Christ sent "from the Father . . . to carry out his saving work inwardly, and to impel the Church toward her proper expansion" (ibid). All that the Church has accomplished in two millenia of Christianity has been done by virtue of this divine Spirit who has never ceased helping her and infusing into her the necessary vigor for accomplishing her mission. Nevertheless the Holy Spirit does not guide the Church by an easy path, free from trouble or contest, but rather supports her so she can proceed through all these difficulties in peace and constancy, happy to suffer for Christ. The first apostles, who were full of joy "that they were counted worthy to suffer dishonor for the name" (Acts 5:41), are a typical example. In like manner, when Paul was leaving the Church of Asia in accordance with divine inspiration that urged him to go elsewhere, he declared "And now, behold, I am going to Jerusalem, bound in the spirit, not knowing what shall befall me there, except that the Holy Spirit testifies to me in every city that imprisonment and afflictions await me" (Acts 20:22-23). He was aware that he was risking his life, but this did not make him recoil from "testifying to the gospel of the grace of God" (ib. 24).

Just as it was for the newborn Church, so is it for the Church today: her abiding strength lies in allowing herself to be guided by the Holy Spirit, as it were "bound" by him; and through faith in this "bond" that unites her intimately to the Spirit, she obtains courage to bear witness to Christ and to spread the gospel in spite of opposition and persecution. Here again the words of Jesus are fulfilled: "When the Paraclete comes . . . whom I shall send to you from the Father, he will bear witness to me and you also will be witnesses (Jn 15:26).

2. The witness that Jesus asks of his Church is at the same time a testimony of faith and of love. In his prayer to the Father, he had asked for his followers: "Sanctify them in the truth" (Jn 17:17), that is, let them be so dedicated and consecrated to the truth of the gospel as to be ready to spend their lives, and even to sacrifice them, for its diffusion. In the same prayer he had added: "May they become perfectly one. so that the world may know that you have sent me" (ib. 23). The mutual love of the disciples and the perfect union that results from it must give testimony to the world that the Son of God was made man and came to bring divine love to men; it must bear witness to the veracity and worth of Christianity.

While the Holy Spirit, who is the Spirit of truth and love, is making the Church capable of bearing witness to the faith and of spreading it abroad, he continues to strengthen her and unite her internally, in order to make her perfect in unity, "so that the world may believe" (ib. 21). "The Holy Spirit"—says the Council—"is the principle of union for the whole Church and for each and every one of those who believe" (LG 13). Where the Spirit acts, and men do not block his action, he always promotes union of hearts and minds, awakens a true sense of brotherhood, and continually "produces and urges love among the believers" (ib. 7).

In order to work together for unity in the Church, the first and most important step is to further the growth in ourselves of the love which the Holy Spirit pours into each baptized person, so that it may produce the fruits of charity, harmony, and peace. To pray for unity and universal peace, and at the same time allow the seed of selfishness, intolerance, and antipathy for others, which all breed discord, to ferment in our hearts, would indeed be contradictory. This is why St. Paul wrote to the early Christians: "I therefore, a prisoner for the Lord, beg you to live a life worthy of the calling to which you have been called, with all lowliness and meekness, with patience, forbearing one another in love, eager to maintain the unity of the Spirit in the bond of peace" (Eph 4:1-3).

All this is not easy for human weakness, but the Holy Spirit dwells in each of us to support our efforts, to remind us of all Jesus' teachings on the commandment of love, and to help us translate these into life.

O Holy Spirit, you are in the Church what the soul is to the body; the Spirit that animates her and quickens her, the Spirit that safeguards unity even while your action is producing manifold and diverse effects; you bring her all her vigor and beauty . . .

O Holy Spirit, promised and sent by the Father and by Jesus, you gave this plenitude and intensity of supernatural life to the first Christians; dissimilar as they were, they had, however, on account of the love that the Holy Spirit poured forth in them, "but one heart and one soul."

But also today you abide in the Church in a permanent, indefectible manner, therein exercising an unceasing action of life and sanctification . . . You render her infallible in the truth. By your action a wonderful supernatural fruitfulness springs up in the Church; you plant and unfold in virgins, martyrs, and confessors those heroic virtues which are among the marks of holiness . . . You are the Spirit who by your inspiration works in souls, rendering the Church . . . holy and without blemish, worthy of being presented by Christ to his Father on the day of final triumph.

C. Marmion, *Christ in His Mysteries,* 17 (pp 335-336)

O Holy Spirit, when you give testimony to our spirit that we are children of God, this testimony gives consolation. But you are also given to increase our fervor, when, by breathing with greater strength on our hearts, you light the mighty flame of charity, that we may glory not only in our hope as children of God, but also in tribulations, esteeming insult a glory, disgrace a joy, and scorn an honor . . . O Holy Spirit, fulfill the days of Pentecost in us, days of forgiveness and of rejoicing. (In festo Pentecostes 3:8).

O Spirit of love, arouse in us the yearning to walk with our God; only you can do this, you who look into the hidden depths of our hearts, who know our thoughts and intentions, who will not countenance the least imperfection in the heart that you possess, but quickly destroy it with the fire of your tender attention.

O sweet and gentle Spirit who bend our wills, direct them ever more and more toward your own, so that we may know it clearly, love it dearly, and follow it effectively. (In festo Pentecostes 2:8).

cf St. Bernard

199 — GUIDED BY THE SPIRIT

Come Holy Spirit... Come, Father of the poor; come, giver of God's gifts; come, light of men's hearts (Seq).

1. "May your Spirit, O Lord, come upon us to fill us with your gifts and make our hearts pleasing to you" (RM, 7 Thurs East., Collect). This prayer invites us to reflect again upon the interior action of the Holy Spirit in the faithful. Sanctifying grace and the theological and moral virtues infused in baptism place the Christian on the supernatural plane, and put him in a position to act supernaturally toward God and toward holiness. But our manner of acting always remains human, and hence limited and imperfect. Even when human intelligence is illuminated by faith, it is always inadequate before God, and incapable of knowing him as he is; as long as we live on this earth, we know God "as in a mirror, dimly;" only in heaven shall we see him "face to face" (1 Cor 13:12). Since we know God imperfectly, we are not capable of a perfect orientation toward him, nor of loving him effectively with all our heart and with all our soul and with all our mind (cf Mat 22:37). The way that leads to God, and hence the demands of sanctity, are known to us only up to a certain point; often we cannot discern the will of God as it applies to us, nor distinguish what is more perfect and more pleasing to the Lord. If this is so, must we renounce holiness? Not at all, God who wants us to be holy has also provided us with the means to become so. "The Holy Spirit . . . will teach you all things" (Jn 14;26); Jesus' promise is infallible. The Spirit, who "searches everything, even the depths of God" (1 Cor 2:10), who has a perfect knowledge of God's nature and mysteries, and at the same time knows all the demands of holiness, as well as our limits and our weaknesses, comes to meet us as father and teacher in order to lead us to sanctity. He is an interior teacher who, while enlightening us in the divine mysteries, molds our heart so as to be pleasing to God. "Creator Spirit, come, visit the minds of your faithful, and fill with heavenly grace the hearts you have made" (Veni Creator).

2. "All who are led by the Spirit are sons of God" (Rom 8:14). Sons should resemble their father, and have the same spirit. God has given his Spirit to all the baptized, but not all of us allow ourselves to be guided by him, and so do not attain our status as sons. Only those who surrender docilely to the action of the Holy Spirit fully live the grace of adoption, and as true sons reach the goal of union with God in love. As long as we advance on our own initiative, our orientation toward God will always remain incomplete, because it will be in *a human manner;* but when we let ourselves be guided by the Holy Spirit who acts in *a divine manner,* he will direct us completely toward God. By his gifts, the Holy Spirit acts directly on our will: he urges, inflames, and attracts it to himself, and enlightens our mind through love. This is the

genesis of that inexpressible "sense" of God and of divine things which gives us a taste of God and directs us toward him more than any reasoning on our part could ever do. Then we perceive by intuition that God is the only One, infinitely above all his creatures; we sense that he is worthy of all our love, that in the face of his infinite lovableness, all that we are able to do for him is nothing. Then we are led to make a total gift of ourselves. This is the way that, under the influence of the Holy Spirit, the baptized go to God as his children, wholly drawn by love for the Father and the desire to do his will. It is the one true way that leads to holiness.

The action of the Holy Spirit is powerful and effective; yet he is always the Spirit of love and does no violence to our liberty as men, but waits for us to cooperate lovingly with his promptings and to yield ourselves to his will out of love. If he meets with resistence he withdraws his favors and leaves us in our mediocrity. This is why St. Paul exhorts us not to live "according to the flesh," that is, according to those inclinations that cause us to assert ourselves and our own will more or less independently of God; rather, we should live "according to the Spirit" (Rom 8:4). "To set the mind on the flesh is death, but to set the mind on the spirit is life and peace" (ib. 6). This is the life and peace of God's children: "to be guided by the Spirit"; it is the reasoning behind our desire to live our baptism: "If we live by the Spirit, let us also walk by the Spirit" (Gal 5:25).

You know that what man stands most in need of is not an outward guide . . . but most of all and in first place, an inward, intimate, invisible aid. You intended to heal him thoroughly, not slightly; not merely to reform the surface, but to remove and destroy the heart and root of all his ills. You then purposed to visit his soul and you departed in body that you might come again to him in spirit. You did not stay with your Apostles therefore, as in the days of your flesh, but you came to them and abode with them for ever with a much more immediate and true communion in the power of the Paraclete.

J.H. Newman, *Meditations on Christian Doctrine* XII, 4

O Holy Spirit, enkindle in me the fire of your love and the flame of eternal charity. Multiply in me the holy transports of love which will bring me rapidly to transforming union. Make not only my will, but all my senses and faculties, completely submissive to your divine will, so that I shall no longer be ruled by my pride, but solely by your divine impulse. Then everything in me will be ruled by love, in love, in such a way that when I work, I shall work through love; and when I suffer, I shall bear everything through love. Grant that the supernatural may become the "natural" atmosphere in which my soul moves. Grant me constantly . . . your loving assistance, the awareness of God, and the delightful knowledge of your divine presence within me. Make me docile, tractable, and prompt to follow your inspirations. Grant that I may never neglect even one of these and that I may always be your faithful little spouse! Make me ever... more recollected, more silent, more submissive to your divine action, more alert to receive your delicate touches. Draw me into the inmost depths of my heart where you reside, O sweet divine Guest, and teach me to watch constantly in prayer.

Sr. Carmela of the Holy Spirit, *unpublished writings*

200 — TRANSFORMED INTO CHRIST'S IMAGE

O Holy Spirit let the glory of the Lord Jesus be mirrored in us so that we may be changed into his likeness (2 Cor 3:18)

1. Vatican Council II observes that "the holiness of the Church is unceasingly manifested... through those fruits of grace that the Spirit produces in the faithful" (LG 39). The most perfect of these fruits, to which all the others are ordered, is conformity with Christ. The Encyclical "Mystici Corporis" says expressly: the Holy Spirit "is communicated to the Church... so that she and each of her members may become daily more and more like to our Savior." Those whom God foreknew "he... predestined to be conformed to the image of his Son" (Rom 8:29); every Christian is holy and pleasing to God to the extent that he has become like Christ. And it is the Holy Spirit who is the artisan who will fashion the traits of the divine resemblance in us, making us "daily more and more like to our Savior." If we would cooperate fully with his action, each day would witness some progress in our becoming more like Christ. Struck by this thought, Sr. Elizabeth of the Trinity prayed: "Spirit of love, descend within me and reproduce in me as it were, an incarnation of the Word, that I may be to him another humanity wherein he renews his mystery" (Elevation). If Christ is the model to which all the baptized should conform, there is no presumption in aspiring to become so like him that he can renew "his mystery" in us, or rather, prolong in us his work of glorifying the Father and of redeeming men. Indeed this is exactly Jesus' desire in sending us his Spirit.

In order to make us like Christ, the Holy Spirit initially communicates to us Christ's sanctity by pouring grace into us; this grace is identical in its nature with the grace that sanctifies the Soul of Christ. He possesses it without limit, we in an infinitely lesser degree; nevertheless it is the same principle, the same seed of sanctity. This is why the full development of grace can bring us to identification with Christ, to being transformed into his very image by "the Lord who is the Spirit" (2 Cor 3:18).

2. "And we all, with unveiled faces, beholding the glory of the Lord, are being changed into his likeness from one degree of glory to another... (by) the Lord who is the Spirit" (2 Cor 3:18).

Because they are children of God the baptized reflect in themselves the "glory" of Christ, that is, the grace of his "sonship." This can be so completely accomplished—"with unveiled faces," that is without any screen—that we are changed "into the very likeness" of the Lord through the action of his Spirit, who dwells in his faithful. The ideal of perfect conformity with Christ is something so sublime that it utterly surpasses our capacity, and it would be folly to think of attaining to it by our own strength, yet it is attainable through the power of the Holy Spirit "who has been given to us" (Rom 5:5) and always remains with us to sustain our weakness. The Holy Spirit arouses within us the desire to imitate Christ, to assimilate his sentiments and his way of life; he infuses supernatural energies, sustains our good will and our potential for good by his divine strength. He who guided Jesus to the perfect fulfillment of the Father's will guides us along the same path. He enlightens us in regard to the divine will, makes us appreciate it as our greatest treasure, and love it as our greatest good, because only in the will of God will we find our sanctification and be able to become like Christ. As for Jesus, so also for us, the divine will must become food and drink for our souls to the point where there "will be nothing in us that is contrary to God's will, and in all and through all we shall be motivated by the will of God" (cf Asc I, 11:2).

The Holy Spirit desires to achieve all this in every baptized person, on condition that he is docilely open to his action.

In expectation of Pentecost, the Liturgy calls upon the Holy Spirit to come and purify the hearts of the faithful (RM, Offertory). Only the Holy Spirit can remove all the obstacles—the attachment to our own will, the selfishness and the fickleness—which impede the grace of adoption from permeating our entire life, so that the completely purified spirit can welcome within it, "without veils," the bright radiance of Christ's glory and be transformed into his image.

My beloved Jesus, I wish to follow with you the rule of love, by which I can renew and spend my whole life in you. Place it in the care of your Holy Spirit so that at all times I shall be most prompt in keeping your commandments. Conform my conduct unto yours; and strengthen me in your love and in your peace . . . Engulf my spirit in your Spirit so powerfully and so deeply that I may in truth be entirely buried in you; and abandoning myself in union with you, may forget myself, and no one may hear of me any more, but only of your love.

My God, life of my soul, what am I? How far I am from you? I am like a grain of dust that the wind lifts up and blows away. Come in the might of your charity, deign to bring forth in its power the burning wind of your omnipotent love, and to cast me into the impetuous whirlwind of your Spirit, and receive me into your bosom with loving solicitude. Then I shall truly begin to die to myself and live only in you, my sweet love.

Let me be lost in you, and surrender myself so entirely in you that no trace of myself may remain in me, just as a grain of dust is blown away and leaves no trace of its going. Transport me thus entirely into your love's affection that in you there may be an end to all my imperfection and I may no longer have any life outside of you. Grant that I may so lose myself in you that for all eternity I may never find myself except in you.

My Love, my Love, open unto me the innermost depths of your goodness; let all the waterfalls of your kindly fatherhood run down upon me; let all the fountains of the great abyss of your infinite mercy burst open over my head. Let the depths of your charity engulf me, and let me be submerged in the depths of your most indulgent pity. Let me be lost in the flood of your living love, as a drop of the sea is lost in its immensity . . . as a burning spark dies in the rushing current of the river.

St. Gertrude, *Exercises* 4:4-6

O Jesus, infuse in me a great desire of being guided, led and moved in everything by your Spirit. You did nothing as man except at the impulse of the Holy Spirit and at his command . . . Help me surrender without reserve or resistence to this Spirit, the Father of the poor and the Giver of gifts, and I shall surely be led along your same pathway and in the manner that you desire. The Holy Spirit draws me to turn to the Father as you did: Abba, Father!

C. Marmion, *A Master of the Spiritual Life* 16

201 — THE WAY OF THE CROSS

Vigil of Pentecost

"Come, Holy Spirit, best of consolers . . . ; rest in toil; shelter in heat; comfort in tears" *(Sequence)*

1. "We ourselves who have the first fruits of the Spirit groan inwardly as we wait for . . . the redemption of our bodies. For in this hope we were saved" (Rom 8:23-24). Although we have been redeemed by Christ, as long as we are living on earth, we have not yet attained a complete and definitive redemption; as the apostle says, we are saved in hope. Besides, our body has not yet been glorified as Christ's was, and—with the limitations inherent in matter, and the defects of a nature injured by sin—constitutes the reason for so much struggle and sorrow. From this comes the state of suffering that accompanies our entire life on earth; it is the pain of our regeneration, beginning at baptism, which goes on being accomplished day by day under the guidance of the Holy Spirit, whose "first fruits" we have received. Therefore, even in suffering, a Christian cannot be a pessimist: hope is not in vain, tribulations are not useless, but when accepted for the love of God are the great means for total regeneration, for full conformity to Christ.

The Holy Spirit cannot work in us to assimilate us to Christ, nor lead us to sanctity, except by the way of the cross. Vatican Council II states: "One and the same holiness is cultivated by all who are moved by the Spirit of God, and who obey the voice of the Father . . . follow the poor Christ, the humble and cross-bearing Christ, in order to be made worthy of being partakers in his glory" (LG 41). For the Christian there is no other form of the holiness that can make us share in Christ's glory than that which makes us share in his cross. We are "moved" toward this holiness by the Holy Spirit, who lighting the love of Christ in our hearts, makes us understand the value of the suffering which assimilates us to him. We shall never enter deeply into the spiritual life and the imitation of Jesus, unless we live the mystery of his cross in our own flesh. St.Teresa of Jesus teaches that even the highest contemplative graces, where the action of the Holy Spirit is dominant, have as their purpose making souls more generous in carrying the cross. "God could not grant us a greater favor than to give us a life that would be an imitation of the life his beloved Son lived. Thus I hold for certain that these graces are meant to fortify our weakness that we may be able to imitate him in his great suffering" (IC VII 4:4).

2. "Come, Holy Spirit . . . where you are not, man has nothing" (Seq). One of the situations in which we become the more conscious of our lack of ability, our nothingness, is that of profound suffering. The Holy Spirit must infuse fortitude to make us capable of bearing with serenity certain crosses from which, from a human viewpoint, there is no hope of relief. "The Spirit helps us in our weakness"—says St. Paul—and "the Spirit himself intercedes for us with sighs too deep for words" (Rom 8:26). He becomes our prayer, prays with us and for us, involving himself in the mystery of a petition which the Father cannot resist. When, under the weight of suffering, we find it impossible to pray, we still have one resort: to unite ourselves to the secret "groaning" which the Spirit raises up from the bottom of our heart to the Father, so that in him and through him, we may repeat Christ's prayer: "Abba, Father! . . . not what I will, but what you will" (Mk 14:36).

On the other hand, there are sufferings along the road of the spiritual life which are caused by the action of the Holy Spirit himself, who purifies our souls in order to prepare them for greater intimacy and union with God. No matter how we may try to renounce our own wills in order to conform them to God's, and to rid ourselves of our old selves and all our evil tendencies in order to clothe ourselves with Christ, we shall never succeed by ourselves in attaining to total detachment and total renunciation. The Holy Spirit then meets our good will and subjects us to external and internal trials. "The Holy Spirit"—says St. John of the Cross—"wounds the soul by destroying and consuming the imperfections of its bad habits. This is the work of the Holy Spirit in which he disposes it for divine union and transformation in God through love" (Fl 1:39). It is impossible for this to take place without suffering, even intense suffering, but it is most beneficial because, accepted with generosity, it completes our purification, and makes us fit for the full invasion of grace. All we need do is to let ourselves be led, and to surrender ourselves with confidence to the action of the Spirit who tests us and afflicts us, not to torment, but to lead us at last "into the glorious liberty of the children of God" (Rom 8:21); the "liberty" to adhere to God, to enter into union with him so as to make "one spirit with him" (1 Cor 6:17).

O Spirit of truth, make me know your Word; teach me to remember all he has said; enlighten me, guide me, make me conformable to Jesus as "another Christ" (alter Christus), by giving me his virtues, especially his patience, humility, and obedience; let me take part in his redemptive work by making me understand and love the cross.

O consuming Fire, divine Love in person, inflame me, burn me, consume me, destroy all self-love in me, transform me entirely in love, bring me to the nothing that I may possess the All; bring me to the summit of the "mountain" where dwells only the honor and glory of God, where all is peace and joy in you, O Holy Spirit! Grant that here below—through suffering and loving contemplation—I may arrive at the most intimate union with the Blessed Three, until I go to contemplate them in the face to face vision of heaven, in the peace, joy and security of the perpetual banquet.

Sr. Carmela of the Holy Spirit, *Unpublished writings*

Where shall I go, my God, and to whom shall I turn if I turn away from your Spirit? If I receive rest amid toil, comfort amid tears, and am tended by the best of consolers in every tribulation and distress—is not all this your Spirit, Lord? . . . O Holy Spirit, you have said that for those who love God, all things work to good. Oh! revive my faith and make me truly believe this consoling promise, from which springs . . . hope. I do not ask you to free me from tribulation, but to change this tribulation into an exercise of true virtue for me, and into an increase of holy love . . . O sweet Guest of my soul, make me feel your blessed presence, for you promised to be with your faithful servant when he suffers: "I will be with him in trouble" (Ps 91:15) . . . I beg you for sweet and tranquil patience with the courage that is necessary to suffer without fault, without lamenting, without despondency of spirit, indeed with serene peace and with . . . merit. As I confidently wait for the consoling effects of your infinite goodness, I rest in peace beneath your wings, and commit my spirit, my body, and all that I have into your hands, so that your will may always be done in me.

Bl Elena Guerra, *Invocations and Prayers to the Holy Spirit*

202 — PENTECOST

Send forth your Spirit, O Lord, and renew the face of the earth (Ps 104:30)

1. "The Spirit of the Lord has filled the whole world, and he who holds all things together knows what is said, alleluia" (RM). This truth, first spoken in the book of Wisdom, is fully verified on the day of Pentecost, when the apostles and their companions "were all filled with the Holy Spirit, and began to speak in other tongues as the Spirit gave them utteance" (Acts 2:4).

Pentecost is the realization of Jesus' promise: "If I go, I will send him to you" (Jn 16:7); it is the baptism he announced before ascending into heaven: "You shall be baptized with the Holy Spirit" (Acts 1:5); it is also the fulfillment of his words: "If any one thirsts, let him come to me and drink . . . Out of his heart shall flow rivers of living water" (Jn 7:37-38). Commenting on this final episode, the evangelist notes: "He said this about the Spirit, which those who believed in him were to receive; for as yet the Spirit had not been given, because Jesus was not yet glorified" (ib. 39). The Spirit was not yet present in his fullness, but we cannot think that he was absent from the just. The Gospel witnesses to his presence with Elizabeth, with Simeon, and others besides. Jesus told his apostles on the eve of his death: "You know him for he dwells with you" (Jn 14:17); even more, when he appeared to the Eleven who were together in the Cenacle on Easter evening, "he breathed on them and said to them: 'Receive the Holy Spirit' " (Jn 20:22). The Holy Spirit is the "gift" par excellence, infinite as God is infinite; and although any one who believes in Christ possesses him, he can always be received and possessed more fully. His descent upon the Apostles on the evening of the Resurrection testifies that this ineffable gift is closely linked to the Easter mystery; he is the supreme gift of Christ, which he has the right and power to confer on us, since he died and rose for our redemption. The descent of the Holy Spirit on the day of Pentecost renews and strengthens this gift; it no longer takes place in an intimate, private form as on Easter evening, but solemnly, with external public manifestations to show that the gift of the Spirit is not reserved for a priviledged few, but is intended for every one, just as Christ died, rose and ascended into heaven for every one. The Easter mystery thus culminates not just in the Resurrection and Ascension, but also in Pentecost, which is its final act.

2. When men, driven by pride, and, as it were, in defiance of God, purposed to build the famous tower of Babel, they were no longer able to understand each other (Gen 11:1-9; 1st reading of vigil Mass). When the Holy Spirit descended, the opposite took place: no longer was there confusion of languages, but rather the "gift" of languages which permitted men "from every nation"

(Acts 2:5) to understand each other; no longer was there separation, but rather a fusion of people who came from different countries. To bring about unity is a fundamental work of the Holy Spirit—out of diverse nations and races, to make but one people, the people of God joined together by the love that the Paraclete comes to pour out in men's hearts.

St. Paul recalled this thought when writing to the Corinthians: "For by one spirit we were all baptized into one body—Jews or Greeks, slaves or free—and all were made to drink of one Spirit" (1 Cor 12:13). The divine Paraclete, the Spirit of love, is the spirit and bond of union among believers, from which he forms a single body, the Mystical Body of Christ, the Church. This work begun at Pentecost, was directed toward renewing the face of the earth, just as he had once renewed the hearts of the Apostles, shattering their way of thinking that was still tied to Judaism, and launching them upon the conquest of the whole world, without distinction of race or religion. This was facilitated in a concrete way by the gift of tongues, which allowed the early Church to spread with greater rapidity. Although that gift ceased with time, it was, and still is, substituted for by another, no less powerful for attracting men to the gospel and for uniting them: the gift of love. The language of love is understood by everyone: the learned and the ignorant, fellow-countrymen and foreigners, believers and non-believers. It is especially for this reason that the Church, as a whole and in each individual believer, always needs Pentecost to be renewed. Even though the Holy Spirit is already present, we always need to pray: "Come, Holy Spirit, fill the hearts of your faithful, and enkindle in them the fire of your love" (Gosp Alleluia). Pentecost took place fifty days after Easter, but it must not be considered a closed episode; rather, it is a reality which is always in action in the Church. The Holy Spirit, who is already present in believers, (in fact, precisely because of this presence) makes them desire to receive him more fully; and he himself expands their hearts in order that they may be capable of receiving more and more of his outpouring.

Come, Holy Spirit, Come! and from your heavenly home, shed a ray of light divine! Come, Father of the poor! Come, the source of all our store! You, of comforters the best; you, the soul's most welcome guest; sweet refreshment here below; in our labor, rest most sweet; grateful coolness in the heat; solace in the midst of woe. O most blessed Light divine, shine within these hearts of yours, and our inmost being fill! Where you are not, man has naught, nothing good in deed or thought, nothing free from taint of ill. Heal our wounds, our strength renew; on our dryness, pour your dew; wash the stains of guilt away: bend the stubborn heart and will; melt the frozen, warm the chill; guide the steps that go astray. On the faithful, who adore and confess you evermore in your sevenfold gift descend; give them virtue's sure reward; give them your salvation, Lord; give them joys that never end. Amen. Alleluia.

Lectionary, *Pentecost Sequence*

O Holy Spirit, substantial Love of the Father and the Son, uncreated Love dwelling in the souls of the just, come down upon me like a new Pentecost and bring me an abundance of your gifts, of your fruits, and of your grace; unite yourself to me as the most sweet Spouse of my soul.

I consecrate myself entirely to you; invade me, take me, possess me wholly. Be the penetrating light which illumines my intellect, the gentle motion which attracts and directs my will, the supernatural energy which gives energy to my body. Complete in me your work of sanctification and love. Make me pure, transparent, simple, true, free, peaceful, gentle, calm, serene even in suffering, and burning with charity toward God and my neighbor . . .

Come, O life-giving Spirit, to this poor world, and renew the face of the earth; preside over new organizations and give us your peace, that peace which the world cannot give. Help your Church, give her holy priests and fervent apostles. Fill with holy inspirations the souls of the good; give calm compunction to sinful souls, consoling refreshment to the suffering, strength and help to those who are tempted and light to those in darkness and in the shadow of death.

Sr. Carmela of the Holy Spirit, *unpublished writings*

O Holy Spirit, who have transformed cold and fearful hearts into warm loving hearts, filled with courage . . . accomplish in me what you did on Pentecost: enlighten, inflame and strengthen my soul, and prepare it to render God love for love. Make this love consist of holy works, constant self-denial, sincere humility, fervent devotion, and generous sacrifice; a love like that with which you inflamed the new believers in the Cenacle.

Bl. Elena Guerra, *Invocations and Prayers to the Holy Spirit*

SOLEMNITIES — FEASTS

203 — SAINT JOSEPH

March 19

Behold the good and faithful servant whom the Lord has placed in charge of his household *(Entrance)*

1. Today's Liturgy in honor of St. Joseph brings out the chief characteristics of this humble, silent man who occupied a place of first importance in the entrance of the Son of God into human history. A descendant of David—"son of David" as the Gospel says (Mt 1:20)—he is the link that joins Christ to that line of descent from which Israel awaited the Messiah. Thus the pro-

phecy made to David is verified through the humble carpenter of Nazareth: "Your house and your kingdom shall be made sure for ever before me; your throne shall be established for ever" (2 Sam 7:16; 1st reading). Joseph is not the natural father of Jesus for he did not give him life, but he is the virginal father who, by the divine command, fulfills a legal function in his regard: he gives him a name, establishes him in a household, acts as his guardian, provides for his sustenance. This very intimate relationship with Jesus comes to him through his marriage with Mary.

Joseph is the "just man" (Mt 1:19) to whom was entrusted the mission of being the virginal spouse of the most exalted of God's creatures, and the virginal father of the Son of the Most High. He is "just" in the full sense of the word, which signifies perfect virtue and holiness. He possesses a justice which pervades his whole being, through a total purity of heart and life, a total adherence to God and to his will. All this takes place in a pattern of life that is as humble and hidden as possible, and yet is resplendent with faith and love. "The just man lives by faith" (Rom 1:17); and Joseph, the pre-eminently "just man" lives this virtue to its maximum.

The second reading very fittingly (Rom 4:13,16-18,22) speaks of Abraham's faith, presenting it as a type or symbol of St. Joseph's. Abraham believed "against hope" (ib. 18) that he would become the father of a great family, and he continued to believe it even when, in obedience to the divine command, he was about to sacrifice his only son. Faced with the confusing mystery of Mary's motherhood, Joseph believed the angel's words: "That which is conceived in her is of the Holy Spirit" (Mt 1:20), and, cutting short all hesitation, obeyed his command: "Do not fear to take Mary, your wife" (ib.). Even more than Abraham, he had to believe what was humanly unthinkable: the motherhood of a virgin, the incarnation of the Son of God. Because of his faith and obedience, he merited to have these great mysteries accomplished under his roof.

2. The entire life of St. Joseph was one prolonged act of faith and obedience in the most obscure and humanly difficult circumstances. Shortly after the birth of Jesus he heard the words: "Rise, take the child and his mother, and flee to Egypt" (Mt 2:13); and later, the angel of the Lord commanded: "Go into the land of Israel" (ib. 20). Immediately—by night—Joseph obeyed. He did not delay, did not ask for explanations, did not offer objections. He is literally "the wise and faithful steward, whom his master will set over his household" (Lk 14:42), entirely at God's service, always ready at his signal, on the alert to serve him. A dedication such as this reveals a perfect love; Joseph loved God with all his heart, with all his mind, with all his strength.

His position as head of the Holy Family, caused him to enter into a special intimacy with God whose place he held; he carried out his orders, and interpreted his will in regard to Mary whose husband he was and in regard to the Son of God made man, whom he saw grow under his very eyes, whom he sustained by his labor. Ever since the angel had revealed to him the secret of Mary's motherhood, Joseph lived in the orbit of the mystery of the incarnation; he was its spectator, its guardian, its adorer and its servant. His existence was to be consumed in these duties, in a climate of communion with Jesus and Mary, and of silent and adoring prayer. He neither had nor sought anything for himself; Jesus called him father, but Joseph knew well that he was not his son, and Jesus himself would confirm this: "Did you not know that I must be in my Father's house?" (Lk 2:49). Mary was his wife, but Joseph knew that she belonged exclusively to God, and he watched over her for him, assisting her in her mission as mother of the Son of God. Then when his work was no longer needed, he disappeared in silence. St. Joseph still occupies a most important place in the Church, continuing, for the entire family of believers, the work of silent and provident guardianship begun for the little family of Nazareth. Thus the Church venerates him, and invokes him as its protector, and thus too the faithful regard him while they study to imitate his virtues. For all of us, in the dark moments of life, St. Joseph's example is an encouragement to unshakable faith, to unreserved adherence to the will of God, to unstinting service.

O Joseph, proclaim . . . the wonders that your eyes have contemplated: you saw the Infant resting in the arms of the Virgin; you adored him with the Wise Men; you gave glory to God with the shepherds according to the angels' words: pray to Christ, God, that our souls may be saved . . .

Your soul was ever obedient to the divine command; and filled with a purity without equal, O blessed Joseph, you deserved to receive as bride her who is pure and immaculate among women; you were the guardian of this Virgin, when she merited to become the tabernacle of the Creator . . .

You led the pure Virgin from the city of David into Egypt, that holy Virgin who was like a mysterious cloud that keeps the Sun of justice hidden in its breast . . . O Joseph, priest of the incomprehensible mystery!

With what wisdom, O Joseph, you assisted God who became a child in the flesh; you served him like one of his angels; he enlightened you directly; you welcomed within you his spiritual rays. O blessed one! You seemed all resplendent with light in your heart and in your soul. He who with one word has shaped heaven, earth and the sea was called the workman's son, your son, O wonderful Joseph! You were constituted father of him who is without beginning, and who glorified you as the minister of a mystery that surpasses all understanding.

How precious was your death in the eyes of the Lord, O blessed Joseph! Consecrated to the Lord from infancy, you were the holy guardian of the Blessed Virgin, and you sang with her the canticle:

"Let every creature bless the Lord, exalt and praise him for ever and ever. Amen."
Hymn of the Greek Church, from *Les plus beaux textes sur St. Joseph*

O Joseph, man of wisdom, rich in goodness . . . you were made holy by holding Christ in your arms. Now sanctify those who celebrate your memory, O just one, Joseph most holy, husband of the all holy Mother of God . . . O happy one, never cease asking the Word to free from temptation those who venerate you. You watched over the Immaculate one, who was ever a virgin, within whom the Word was made flesh. You watched over her after the mysterious birth. O Joseph, who bore God in your arms, remember us with her.
Giuseppe l'Innografo, from *Les plus beaux textes sur St. Joseph*

204 — THE ANNUNCIATION OF THE LORD

March 25

Here I am, O God, I come to do your will *(Resp Ps)*

1. The dominant motif in the Liturgy of this solemnity is that of offering, of a total donation to God. It is sung in the entrance antiphon, repeated in the response of the responsorial psalm, proclaimed in the second reading: "I have come to do your will, O God!" (Heb 10:5-7). It expresses the attitude of Christ and of his mother, so intimately united in an identical action of offering and accepting.

St. Paul took these words from the psalter (Ps 40:8-9) and considered them as though uttered by the Son of God in the act of his incarnation: "When Christ came into the world, he said: 'Sacrifices and offerings you have not desired, but a body you have prepared for me; in burnt offerings and sin offerings you have taken no pleasure.' Then I said: 'Lo, I have come to do your will, O God' " (Heb 10:5-7). But before the Son of God spoke his offering in time, before he assumed the body which his Father had determined to prepare for him in the virginal womb of a humble woman, it was necessary for the same offering to be made by her who was to be his mother. Indeed, God, infinitely respectful of his creature's freedom, "willed that the consent of the predestined mother should precede the incarnation" (LG 56). Mary spoke this offering at the time of the angel's annunciation: "Behold, I am the handmaid of the Lord; let it be done to me according to your word" (Lk 1:38). The difference in terminology in no way affects the identity of meaning and of disposition. The "Behold the handmaid of the Lord" is the perfect echo in time of the eternal "Behold" of the Word, and makes possible its accomplishment. Her offering is based upon that of Christ, and forms one single sacrifice, which Mother and Son will live, inseparably united up to its consummation upon Calvary, for the glory of the Father and the redemption of men. So today, guided by the Liturgy, we celebrate the most exalted offering that was ever made to God, from which our salvation springs. While we thank Christ and his Mother for this immense gift, we beg them to make us able to offer ourselves unreservedly to God, so that his will may be done in each of us. "Behold, I come, O God to do your will."

2. Jesus appears to us on the Solemnity of the Annunciation more joined to Mary than ever, not only in the Gospel account, but in Isaiah's prophecy as well which is read in the first reading (7:10-14). At a critical moment in Israel's history, the prophet informed King Ahaz that God would send an extraordinary savior, who would be born of a virgin. "Behold, a virgin shall conceive and bear a son, and shall call his name Emmanuel" (ib. 14). Although this prophecy was spoken in the historical context of that particular period it is too explicit for us not to recognize in it the mysterious announcement of the incarnation of the Son of God in the womb of the Virgin of Nazareth. Thus does Matthew interpret it, quoting it verbatim at the end of his account of the birth of Jesus: "All this took place to fulfill what the Lord had spoken by the prophet: 'Behold, a virgin shall conceive and bear a son, and his name shall be called Emmanuel (which means, God with us)' " (1:22-23). Only Jesus was born of a virgin; only he is truly "God with us."

In today's Gospel Luke refers to the historical fact of the annunciation of the birth of Jesus (1:26-38). His account is distinctly Marian, whether we consider that only Mary could have related it to him, or because she herself is the protagonist. Everything in it is in relation to him who is to come: Jesus. He is pointed out as the "Son of the Most High," to whom will be given "the throne of David . . . and of his kingdom there will be no end" (ib. 32-33). His conception in Mary's womb will take place through a special divine intervention, not through man's: "The Holy Spirit will come upon you, and the power of the Most High will overshadow you" (ib. 35). Before the unheard of greatness of such an announcement, Mary disappears into the shadows in an act of faith and humility without parallel. Precisely because she is humble, she believes things that are humanly impossible; first of all the human race, she believes in Christ the Son of God who, through an inexplicable mystery, is about to become true man within her. Believing this, she accepts it, but her humility does not permit her to offer herself to God except in the role of his handmaid, as his servant; and God responds immediately, making her the unsullied mother of his Only Son. It is a mystery of infinite mercy on the part of the Most High; an act of utter humility and faith on Mary's part. "The Virgin hears, believes and conceives," says St. Augustine (Ser 196:1,1).

Humility and faith are the fertile soil in which God accomplishes the miracles of his omnipotent love.

O Word, you leap toward your creature, your image, and for love of the flesh clothe yourself in the flesh; for love of my soul, you condescend to join to your divine person an intelligent soul... O incredible union! O paradoxical interpenetration! You, who are he who is, come in time; uncreated, you make yourself a created object. You, who cannot be contained in any space, enter into time and space, and a spiritual soul becomes the intermediary between divinity and the heaviness of flesh. You who enrich, become poor, and undergo the poverty of my flesh, in order that I may be enriched by your divinity. You who are fullness, empty yourself, despoil yourself for a little while of your glory so that I may share in your fullness.

What a wealth of goodness! What an immense mystery envelops you! I was made a sharer of your image, my God, but I did not know how to preserve it; now it is you who become a sharer of my flesh to save the image that you had given me, and to make my flesh immortal.

St. Gregory Nazianzen, *Prayer* 45:9

O Mary, vessel of humility, in whom there resides and burns the light of true knowledge by which you were raised above yourself! For this reason you were pleasing to the eternal Father and, loving you with singular love, he captivated you and drew you to himself. By this light and fire of your charity, by the unction of your humility, you attracted and inclined the divinity to come to you, even though he had been first drawn to come to us by the ardent fire of his own unfathomable charity...

O Mary, my sweet love, in you is written the Word from whom we receive our knowledge of life... I see that this Word, as soon as he was written in you, was not without the cross of holy desire; that as soon as he was conceived in you there was grafted upon and added to him the desire to die for the welfare of man, on whose account he took flesh...

O Mary, today your soil has brought forth a Savior for us... O Mary, blessed are you among all women... because today you have given us of your flour. Today the Godhead is joined and kneaded so thoroughly into our humanity that this union can never be broken, neither by death nor by our ingratitude.

St. Catherine of Siena, *Prayers and Elevations.*

205 — VISITATION OF THE BLESSED VIRGIN MARY

May 31

Blessed are you, O Virgin Mary, because you have believed (Lk 1:45)

1. "Rejoice and exult with all your heart, O daughter of Jerusalem! . . . The Lord, your God, is in your midst; a warrior who gives victory" (Zeph 3:14,17). Today the Liturgy applies the

prophetic words of Zephaniah to the Blessed Mother. Mary is the daughter of Jerusalem who is called to rejoice because God has made himself present within her in a singular manner, taking human flesh in her virginal womb. The ark of the Covenant, the meeting tent, and the temple of Jerusalem where the most high God used to manifest his presence to his people, pale by comparison with this humble virgin who has become the ark and the living temple of him who created her. Through her means the Son of God is the powerful Savior who comes to visit and redeem us, his people, to give us light and to guide our feet into the way of peace (Lk 1:68,79). Jesus' first visit to men was in fact carried out through Mary, who immediately after the Annunciation went "in haste into the hill country" (Lk 1:39) to visit her aged cousin, whose extraordinary pregnancy had been revealed to her by the angel. The Blessed Mother thus began her mission of carrying Christ to the world, and she began it in haste, without delay, urged on by the interior impulse which set her on the road toward mankind, which was awaiting, and in such need of, a Savior. The inconveniences of a journey into hilly country did not trouble her, her dignity as Mother of God did not hold her back, but rather urged her on because she realized that the privilege of her divine motherhood was ordained for the salvation of the world.

One day, Jesus will himself go in person to find the Baptist on the banks of the Jordan; and he, who is the Son of God, will ask to be baptized by his forerunner, his own creature. Mary anticipated this attitude of humility on the part of her Son, and she, who was the Mother of God, went to visit the mother of the Baptist, who was a great man, but only a man. She went to visit her, not to be served on account of her own dignity, but rather to serve Elizabeth, taking toward her as toward God, the attitude of a humble handmaid. Jesus, living in Mary and borne by her, guided her along the way of humility and service that he himself would travel, and would point out to men.

2. "The Lord, your God . . . will rejoice over you with gladness, he will renew you in his love" (Zeph 3:17). God took pleasure in Mary, who by her faith and love "received the Word of God in her heart and in her body" (LG 53), and carried him with tender care along the roads of Judea. God renews his covenant of love with men in the Virgin; in her the Word joyfully celebrated his marriage with mankind, and, though hidden in her maternal womb, revealed his presence. "And when Elizabeth heard the greeting of Mary, the babe leaped in her womb" (Lk 1:41). At that joyful leap, Elizabeth, enlightened interiorly by the Holy Spirit, recognized in her young cousin the Mother of the Savior and broke forth in a song of praise: "Blessed are you among women, and blessed is the fruit of your womb! And why is this granted to me, that the Mother of my Lord should come to me? . . . And blessed is she who believed that there would be a fulfillment of what was spoken to her from the Lord" (ib. 42-43,45). Mary made no protest before this torrent of praise; she knew very well it did not belong

to her, but solely to God, and immediately referred the praise to him. "You, Elizabeth, glorify the mother of the Savior"—says the Virgin—"But 'my soul magnifies the Lord.' You say that at the sound of my voice the child in your womb leaped for joy, but 'my spirit rejoices in God my Savior' . . . You proclaim me blessed for having believed, but the reason for my faith and happiness is the look which divine goodness has turned upon me. So, 'henceforth all generations will call me blessed, because God has regarded the humility and littleness of his handmaid' " (St. Bernard, De duod. praerog. 12). The Magnificat is simply Mary's response to Elizabeth's praise, a response which causes all the praise received to redound to God. Mary disappears in her canticle; God alone is exalted and magnified, while she remains in her humble position of handmaid. As in her praise, so also in her entire life: in the three months in which she lived with her cousin, and throughout her entire existence, Mary remained, always and only, the handmaid who served in humility, hidden in the background. She served the cause of her Son and then disappeared into the shadows.

"Outdo one another in showing honor . . . Contribute to the needs of the saints . . . Do not be haughty, but associate with the lowly" (Rom 12:10,13,16). These exhortations of the Apostle vividly portray Mary's attitude and encourage us to follow in her footsteps.

Let your Church praise you, O Lord, for the great things you have done for those who, like Mary, have believed in your Word; and like John, have felt the hidden presence of Christ your Son, so also may the people joyfully recognize the living presence of their Lord in the Eucharistic mystery.

Post Communion

O Mary, you "went with haste into the hill country" to greet Elizabeth, and there you stayed to help her for three months . . . O holy Virgin, how fervent is your charity in its search for grace, how luminous the virginity of your flesh, how great the humility which makes you hasten to serve others! If it is true that those who humble themselves will be exalted, what is more sublime than your humility, O Mary? When Elizabeth caught sight of you she was astonished, and exclaimed: "Why is this granted me, that the Mother of my Savior should come to me?" But she was to be still more astonished to see that you, like your Son, came not to be served, but to serve.

St. Bernard, *De aquaeductu* 9

In praising your Son, O Mother of God, we all honor you as a living temple. The Lord dwelt in your womb; he who received the universe into his hand made you holy and rich in glory; he taught us all to sing:

"Hail, abode of God and of the Word; hail, holy one, holier than all the saints; hail, ark clothed in gold by the Holy Spirit; hail, inexhaustible treasure of life . . . hail, for you trophies are raised on high; hail, by you enemies fall; hail, health of my body; hail, salvation of my soul."

O Mother, worthy of every praise, Mother of the Word, most holy above all the saints, accept this offering now: free us all from every misfortune, and ransom from future suffering all those who together proclaim: Alleluia!

Romano Il Melode, "*Inno acatisto*" 23:4

INDEXES OF ABBREVIATIONS

SACRED SCRIPTURE

The abbreviations used for the various books of the Bible are those given at the beginning of the RSV version. Unless otherwise noted, all scriptural quotations are taken from the RSV Common Bible.

THE DOCUMENTS OF VATICAN COUNCIL II

AA	Laity	LG	Dogmatic Constitution of the Church
AG	Missions	NAE	Non-Christians
CD	Bishops	OE	Eastern Churches
DH	Religious Freedom	OT	Priestly Formation
DV	Revelation	PC	Religious Life
GE	Christian Education	PO	Priests
GS	Church in the Modern World	SC	Liturgy
IM	Social Communication	UR	Ecumenism

The text used is The Documents of Vatican II edited by Walter M. Abbott, S.J.

AUTHORS AND WORKS FREQUENTLY CITED

T.J.	ST TERESA OF JESUS, *Works*	J.C.	ST JOHN OF THE CROSS *Works*
F	Foundations	Asc	Ascent of Mt. Carmel
IC	Interior Castle	Cs	Counsels to a religious
Life	Life	Ct	Cautions
Med	Meditation on the Song of Songs	DN	Dark Night
		Fl	Living Flame
Sol	Soliloquies (Exclamations)	Let	Letters
Sp Test	Spiritual Testimonies (Relations)	Say	Sayings of Light and Love
Way	Way of Perfection	Sp C	Spiritual Canticle

Note: Fl and SpC are generally cited from redaction B; where A is used, it is indicated by Sp C-A and LF-A.

T.C.J.	ST THERESE OF THE CHILD JESUS *Writings*	E.T.	SR. ELIZABETH OF THE TRINITY *Writings*
Auto	Autobiography, Autobiographical Mss.	1 R	First Retreat
NV	Last Conversations (Novissima Verba)	2 R	Second Retreat
		Let	Letters (French edition)

For the works of St. Teresa of Jesus, St. John of the Cross and St. Therese of the Child Jesus, the ICS texts have been used throughout (except for the Foundations, not yet published) except in rare cases which are noted in their proper places. An English version of the works of Sr. Elizabeth of the Trinity is under preparation.

MISCELLANEOUS

RB	Roman Breviary	cf	compare
RM	Roman Missal	Let	Letter
RRo	Roman Ritual—old	p.	page
Lect	Lectionary	v.	volume

ENGLISH REFERENCES

Anselm, St. — Proslogion, Wisdom of Catholicism, ed. by A. Pegis, New York, Random House, Inc., 1949

Augustine, St. — The Confessions of, New York, Sheed and Ward, 1943

On the Psalms, Vol. 1, Ancient Christian Writers, Vol. 29, Westminster, Md., Newman Press, 1960

Bellarmine, St. Robert — The Ascent of the Mind to God, London, Burns, Oates and Washbourne, Ltd., 1928

Bernard, St. — Sermons on the Canticle of Canticles, Vol. 1, Dublin, Browne & Nolan, 1920

Sermons on Advent and Christmas, New York, Benziger Bros., 1909

Blosius, Ludivicus — Paradise of the Faithful Soul, New York, Benziger Bros., 1926

Bonaventure, St. — The Souls Journey into God, The Tree of Life, The Life of St. Francis, New York, Paulist Press, 1978

Catherine of Siena, St. — The Dialogue of, New York, Benziger Bros., 1925

Early Christian Prayers	A. Hamman, Chicago, Regnery, 1961
Eudes, St. John	Meditations on Various Subjects, New York, Kenedy, 1947
de Foucauld, Charles	Meditations of a Hermit, Burns & Oates, London, Orbis Books, New York, 1981
Gertrude, St.	The Exercises of, Westminster, Md., Newman Press, 1956
John XXIII, Pope	Prayers and Devotions, New York, Doubleday Image Books, 1969
	Journal of a Soul, McGraw-Hill, New York, 1965
Kempis, Thomas	Following a Christ, New York, Catholic Publications Press, 1924
Lawrence of the Resurrection, Br.	The Practise of the Presence of God, Phil., Griffith and Rowland Press
Leo the Great, St.	The Sunday Sermons of the Great Fathers, Vol. 2, Chicago, Regnery, 1964
Liguori, St. Alphonsus	The Glories of Mary, New York, Redemptorist Fathers, 1931
Marmion, O.S.B., Abbot	Christ the Life of the Soul, St. Louis, Herder, 1925
Marmion, O.S.B., Abbot	Christ the Ideal of the Monk, St. Louis, Herder, 1926
	Christ in His Mysteries, St. Louis, Herder, 1924
	The Trinity in our Spiritual Life, Westminster, Md., Newman Press, 1953
de Montfort, St. Louis Mary	True Devotion to the Blessed Virgin Mary, Bay Shore, New York, Montfort Fathers, 1949
Newman, J.H.	Meditatioans and Devotions, Longman's, Green and Co., New York, 1907
Paulinus of Nola, St.	The Poems of Paulinus of Nola, Ancient Christian Writers, Vol. 40, Westminster, Md., Newman Press, 1975
de Pazzi, St. Mary Magdalen	The Complete Works of, Vols. I, II, III, IV Carmelite Fathers, Aylesford, Westmont, Illinois, 1974
Philipon, O.P., M.M.	The Spiritual Doctrine of Sr. Elizabeth of the Trinity, Westminster, Md., Newman Press, 1962
Sezze, St. Charles of	Autobiography, trans. by L. Perotti, Chicago, 1963
Suso, Bl. Henry	The Exemplar, Life and Writings of Bl. Henry Suso, 2 Vols., Dubuque, Iowa, Priory Press, 1962
Thibaut, Dom Raymund	Abbot Columba Marmion, A Master of the Spiritual Life, St. Louis, Herder, 1942
Thomas Aquinas, St.	Summa Theologica, Complete Edition, 3 Vols. New York, Benziger Bros. Inc., 1947, 1948

FOREIGN REFERENCES

St. Alphonsus	Practica d'amar Gesu Christo, Ed. Paoline, Alba
St. Ambrose	Commento al Vangelo Luca 2 voll., Citta Nuova, Roma 1966
Bl. Angela of Foligno	Il libro della B. Angela da Foligno, A. Signorelli, Roma, 1950
St. Augustine	Commento al Vangelo e alla prima Epistola di S. Giovanni, Citta Nuova, Roma, 1968 Esposizione sui Salmi, v. 1 (1967); vols. 2 (1971) Citta Nuova, Roma
P. de Berulle	Le grandezze di Gesu, Vita e Pensiero, Milano, 2 ed., 1967
J.B. Bossuet	Meditazioni sul Vangelo, v.1, (1930); v. 11, (1931). V. Gatti, Brescia
St. Brigid of Sweden	Le celeste rivelazioni, Ed. Paoline, 1960
G. Canovai da Madrone	Suscipe Domine, La Civilita Cattolica, Roma, 1949
St. Catherine of Siena	Preghiere ed Elevazioni, a cura di I. Taurisano, Ferrari, Roma, 1920 Epistolario, 6 voll., a cura di Misciatelli, Giuntini-Bentivoglio, Siena
Sr. Elizabeth of the Trinity	J'ai Trouve Dieu, Oeuvres Completes, Tome Ib, II Paris, Les Editions du Cerf, 1979, 1980
Charles de Foucauld	Opere spirituali (Antologia), Ed. Paoline, Milano 2 ed., 1964
R. Giordano	Contemplazione sull'amore divino, L. E. Fiorentina, Firenze, 1954
Bl. E. Guerra	Allo Spiritu Santo (ossequie preghiere), Institute S. Zita, Lucca, 1955
Pope St. Leo the Great	Il sistero pasquale, Ed. Paoline, Roma, 1965
St. Leo IX	Quelques Prieres composees par les Papes, Convento del Cenacolo, Piazza Priscilla, Roma
Liturgia — CAL	Revista del Centro di Azione Liturgica, Roma
Lyonnet, P.	Scritti spirituali, Borla, Torino, 1963
Pope Paul VI	Insegnamenti, 9 voll., Pliglotta Vaticana, 1963-71
E. Poppe	Intimita spirituali, Ed. Paoline, Pescara, 4 ed., 1961
L. Da Ponte	Meditazioni, 2 voll., Marietti, Torino, 1852
Ruysbroeck	Oeuvres de Ruysbroeck l'Admirable, 3 voll. Vromant, Bruxelles, 1922
C. B. Da Varano	Le opere spirituali, Ed. Franscane, Jesi 1958